A YEAR WITH THE NEW TESTAMENT

VOLUME 1

DR. DAVE DORST

Published by White Blackbird Books, an imprint of Storied Publishing

Permission requests and other questions may be directed to the Contact page at www.storied.pub.

Unless otherwise indicated, Scripture quotations are from the NIV Bible.

THE HOLY BIBLE, NEW INTERNATIONAL VERSION® NIV® Copyright © 1973, 1978, 1984 by International Bible Society® Used by permission. All rights reserved worldwide.

ISBN: 978-1-951991-08-1

Cover design by Sean Benesh

Edited by Jonathan Dorst, Claire Berger, Emily Dahlquist, Julie Serven, and Doug Serven

PRAISE FOR A YEAR WITH THE NEW TESTAMENT

A Year With the New Testament fills a much-needed void in the devotional landscape. Each entry progresses through the New Testament with context and depth in ways that set it apart. The brief observations engage the head and the heart, which make this devotional a tool for one's growth in loving God with "heart, soul, mind, and strength." Dr. Dorst has given Christians a wonderful resource that will surely become a beautifully blended book alongside one's Bible.
Jeremy Fair
Pastor, Christ Presbyterian Church

Imagine a pastor who has preached, taught, loved, and shepherded people across half the USA for nearly a half-century. Now imagine asking him what daily practice best produces joyful, Bible-loving Christians, and he tells you, "Prayer-soaked time with the New Testament." Dave Dorst is such a pastor and his *A Year With the New Testament* is his gift to you. In this marvelous devotional, Dorst leads readers through the Scriptures into a living friendship with God in Christ. Here are detailed but accessible, verse-by-verse daily guides for studying, loving, praying, and practicing God's Word. May this book be your faithful companion this year!
R. Carlton Wynne
Assistant Pastor, Westminster Presbyterian Church

Dr. Dorst's year-long devotional was an incredible journey for me. The lessons deepened my understanding of Scripture and my need for a Savior. I am so grateful for his wisdom and insight into Scripture.
Chris Tidland
Former PGA golfer
Deacon, Grace Presbyterian Church

I have always had a love/hate relationship with daily devotionals. They are either far too simple and stripped down—nothing more than an inspirational quote or two—or they read more like a dense commentary that offers very little personal encouragement. Dave Dorst's book is such a gift. Not only does it help the reader connect with God and his Word on a daily basis, but its biblical insight and thought-provoking questions will challenge you to truly stop, reflect, pray about, and ACT on what you just read.
Thomas Fitzpatrick
Author, *Driven by Desire*

This rich New Testament devotional delivers a daily satisfying meal for the Christian believer. With Dr. Dorst's insights peppered with commentary notes, historical theology, hymn references, and more, this practical guide to absorbing the Bible is not too light or heavy. It's exactly right. The consistent format helps like coming to a familiar friend each time, yet surprises still fill the pages with unique questions and prompts for each passage. The prescribed prayer ahead of each reading was always a needful reminder that I need the Holy Spirit to apply God's Word to my heart. The guided prayer encouraged me to approach the Bible less like a terrified child, and more like a dependent, yet expectant one. Thank you!

Izzy Beisiegel
Former LPGA golfer
Author, *Adele's Adventures* series

A Year with the New Testament is a year of growth. Our LifeGroup enjoyed this as its curriculum with daily connection through scripture and weekly meeting to share. This will also be our daily devotional plan for the coming year, and I have already started it again. Hallelujah! Thank you, Dave Dorst!

Harry T. Jones
Presbyterian elder
Christian business leader and mentor

A Year with the New Testament was transformative for my husband and me. We have now gone through the study three times, twice together and once in a small group. The daily study guide enhances the reading of Scripture, bringing new life to familiar passages. The thoughtful questions and Scripture memory challenge the reader to go deeper into the passage, creating "muscle memory" of important Bible truths. Our notebook copy is well-worn and on our bookshelf as a resource to return to again and again.

Elizabeth Mitchum
Director of Children's Ministries, First Presbyterian Church

In *A Year With the New Testament*, Dave Dorst has given followers of Jesus a gift that defies classification. It's neither a devotional that feels like sugar-coated cereal nor a Bible study that feels like homework. It isn't a dry commentary with little real-world application. With brief yet remarkably profound insights, my friend and fellow traveler engages our head, heart, and hands, helping us walk each day with Jesus.

Scott Seaton
Pastor, Emmanuel Presbyterian Church

The Bible is the most read book of all time, but it also may be the least understood. Today people regard it as an inkblot, seeing in it what they want to see. Dr. Dorst pulls us back from this swirl with daily readings that are both relevant to us and faithful to the text. Part devotional and part commentary, this guide allows questions that emerge when reading Scripture to surface a desire to know its author better.

Timothy H. Filston
Pastor, First Presbyterian Church

CONTENTS

Introduction   vii

January   1

February   87

March   161

April   247

May   335

June   411

Works Cited   493

About White Blackbird Books   497
Also by White Blackbird Books   499

INTRODUCTION

Why bother with another devotional study guide? Christian bookstores are full of devotionals.

But in my survey of the available studies, I haven't found one that focuses only on the New Testament and explains its message from a consistently Reformed perspective. Most devotionals use the Bible as a point of departure to tell inspirational stories or use a verse or two to provide "principles for living."

The goals of this study are to look closely at what the New Testament itself says and to faithfully apply it to our lives. There is no attempt—either explicit or implicit—to disparage the Word of God in the Old Testament. However, the many studies of the Bible in one year are by necessity overviews or surveys. There is just too much material in the entire Bible to enable an in-depth study, unless one has several hours a day to devote to the task. This devotional is written for busy people, but busy people willing to devote twenty to thirty minutes a day to serious Bible study.

This study will not be exhaustive. One pastor in New England spent his entire forty-year ministry preaching on the first chapter of Romans! However, this study will provide:

1. An acquaintance with the major and minor themes of the New Testament
2. An understanding of the writers and how their works fit together (by God's Spirit)
3. An encouragement to form a lifelong discipline of daily devotions
4. Most importantly, an opportunity to know God better and apply his will to your life

A Year With the New Testament is intended for middle schoolers through adults. Though middle schoolers may have to stretch to understand all that is written, my thirteen years of ministering with them taught me never to underestimate their ability to grow. My prayer is that some families might agree to do this study together and that each person would share what God is teaching them. This is an excellent study for small groups to do individually and then discuss all together. It also is meant for seekers, those willing to investigate what the New Testament teaches about the person and work of Jesus Christ. For anyone willing to consider the claims of Christ, there is no more dangerous book to read than the New Testament. Reading this book transformed my life as well as the lives of countless others. If one person finds Christ in a deeper way through this study, it will have been worthwhile (Luke 15:7).

Materials necessary for this study are:

1. An accurate translation of the New Testament. I'll primarily quote from the New International Version, a generally accurate and readable translation that many evangelical Christians own. There are many other modern translations that are very good (especially the New American Bible and English Standard Version). For good paraphrases, read J. B. Phillips' *The New Testament in Modern English* or Eugene Peterson's *The Message* as companions to your translation. A paraphrase isn't a translation and shouldn't be used for serious study, but it can sometimes help to clarify difficult passages.

2. A notebook and pen. My prayer is that you will refer back to the notes that you take in this study over and over again. Before you read the notes I've provided, jot down your own observations and questions. I adapted the P.R.O.A.M.P.T. (Pray, Read, Observe, Apply, Memorize, Pray, Tell) format from Chuck Miller's Discipleship Ministry Seminar. The A.C.T.S. (Adoration, Confession, Thanksgiving, Supplication) method of prayer is well-known, though I have been unable to discover who originated it. Take notes not only on the passage, but keep a record of your prayers and God's answers.

To quote a major author of the New Testament, my prayer is that *"your love may abound more and more in knowledge and depth of insight, so that you may be able to discern what is best and be pure and blameless until the day of Christ"* (Phil. 1:9–10).

This study is dedicated to my incredible family—Ann who has loved me with the grace of Jesus Christ for more than fifty years of marriage; my godly sons Dave, Jonathan, and Josh; awesome daughters-in-law Kath and Rachel; and my six precious grandchildren: Madeleine, Miles, Wesley, Eliza, Alayna, and Natalie.

I also thank God for the churches I've served over the past forty-five-plus years as an ordained minister: the "First Presbyterians" of Pittsburgh, Bethlehem, Houston, and Thomasville; Beverly Heights U.P. in Mt. Lebanon, Pennsylvania; Christ E.P.C. in Houston; Bethany/Rio Vista in Ft. Lauderdale; Northwest Presbyterian in Dublin, Ohio; and Grace Evangelical Presbyterian in Leesburg, Florida.

Rev. Jonathan Dorst volunteered to tackle the books of Jude and Revelation. Most of December's studies are his fine work.

Soli deo gloria

JANUARY

JANUARY 1

JESUS' "ROOTS"

PRAY

Open my eyes that I may see wonderful things in your law.

—Psalm 119:118

READ

Matthew 1:1–17; Luke 3:23–38

OBSERVE

The importance of the Gospel of Matthew is obvious from its position as the first book of the New Testament. It was the most influential gospel in the early church, as evidenced by quotes from the early church fathers. The symbol associated with Matthew is the lion; Jesus is the Lion of Judah. The gospel is strongly Hebraic in character—written by a Jew for Jewish readers, revealing Jesus as the fulfillment of Old Testament history and prophecy. Matthew is appropriately located as the bridge between the Old and New Testaments.

The author is Matthew, also known as Levi (Matt. 9:9, Mark 2:14), a former tax collector. He must have become a teacher in the early church because his gospel is organized according to the way a teacher would transmit the lessons of the Great Teacher. Much of Matthew is arranged in groups of threes, fives, and sevens for greater ease in teaching and remembering. He organizes the teaching sections according to five themes—Sermon on the Mount (chapters 5–7), Missionary Instructions to the Twelve (chapter 10), Parables of the Kingdom (chapter 13), Greatness and Forgiveness in the Church (chapter 18), and Last Things (chapters 24–25).

This study will use Matthew as the focus of the Synoptic Gospels ("synoptic" means "see together" and includes Mark, which many believe was the first gospel, and Luke). Parallel passages from Mark and Luke will be explored at the same time as we study Matthew. Then we will examine the unique material in Mark and Luke. John will be occasionally included with the other gospels, but it is not a Synoptic Gospel because John's point of view is very different from the other three Evangelists.

Now let's turn our attention to the genealogy of Jesus Christ:

Matt. 1:1–17, Luke 3:23–31—Even a casual examination of the two genealogies reveals great differences, especially the closer one gets to the birth of Jesus. The usual explanation is that Matthew, a Jew, would be careful to trace Jesus' ancestors through his legal (though not his natural) father, Joseph. Luke, a Greek, was not as influenced by Jewish patriarchal thought and follows Christ's ancestors through Mary's family. Mary was a major source of Luke's gospel, and the Beloved Physician gives special prominence to women. If this is true, Jesus' grandfathers were named Jacob (Joseph's father) and Heli (Mary's father). The family tree was critical to the Jews and important to the Greeks. Until Alex Haley's bestseller *Roots*, Westerners (other than Mormons, whose theology depends on genealogy) have typically had little interest in genealogies. But most civilizations throughout history have considered them crucial. Bible translators report that when tribes first read the Gospel of Matthew in their own language, this genealogy has a tremendous impact. It establishes for them that Jesus was a real person and not just a story, like so many of their religious traditions.

Though we don't have the time or space to do a thorough review of all the Old Testament characters mentioned by Matthew and Luke, we can make a few key observations:

1. Matthew introduces the list as "the book of the genealogy of Jesus Christ." It means literally "the book of the genesis." Matthew may have been trying to parallel Genesis 5:1ff. "Jesus" was his common earthly name (we'll see its meaning in tomorrow's study). "Christ" wasn't Jesus' last name. It is the Greek word for the Hebrew "Messiah," which means "the anointed one," God's special emissary. It would be more accurate to call him, "Jesus *the* Christ." Matthew divides his genealogy into three groups of fourteen. To the Jews, seven was the number of perfection, and fourteen was perfection doubled. Matthew's heritage causes him to highlight Abraham, the father of the Jewish nation (Gen. 12:2). The next division begins with David, the greatest king, whose reign was the Golden Age of Israel. The next epochal event in Israel's history was the destruction and fall of the Davidic kingdom and the deportation to Babylon. The genealogy then points to a Greater King. Luke, whose gospel is written primarily for Gentiles, goes back to the universal father, Adam (Luke 3:38).
2. Interestingly, Matthew (and not Luke) mentions four women in the genealogy of Jesus. Each of these women represent something irregular in the line of the Messiah. It may have been Matthew's attempt to answer questions about Jesus' birth by showing that God has always worked in

history through unusual means. Tamar (v. 3) had twins from an incestuous union with her disobedient father-in-law, Judah (Gen. 38). Rahab (v. 5) was the Canaanite prostitute who helped save the life of the Hebrew spies who came to Jericho (Josh. 2). Ruth (v. 5) was a Moabite foreigner (Ruth 1–4), though certainly the most noble of the four women mentioned! "The wife of Uriah" (v. 6) was Bathsheba, David takes Bathsheba and then murders her husband (1 Sam. 12).

APPLY

Matt. 1:3, 5–6—Do you ever judge people because of their reputation or occupation? Try to imagine how God can use even the most sinful person. After all, he transformed you and me!

MEMORIZE

Try to remember the four key women in the history of the Messiah.

PRAY

Adoration: Praise God for the way he acts in history.

Confession: Admit the times you've judged and condemned people like these four women.

Thanksgiving: Be grateful that God redeems even sinful acts to fulfill his plan.

Supplication: Intercede for hurting or lost people in your family tree.

TELL

Share with someone how God uses weak and sinful people (like us!) to accomplish his purposes!

JANUARY 2

THE BIRTH OF JESUS CHRIST

PRAY

For understanding of the importance of the Virgin Birth and to apply its truth to your life.

READ

Matthew 1:18–25; Luke 1:26–38

OBSERVE

The accounts in Matthew and Luke, though in agreement on the basic points, stress different details. They both tell us that Mary and Joseph were betrothed. Both accounts emphasize that Mary was a virgin before the birth of Jesus. Let's examine the differences, which enable us to get a fuller picture.

Matt. 1:18–21—Matthew tells the story from Joseph's point of view. Though Matthew stresses that the child was produced by the Holy Spirit (v. 18), it's clear that Joseph didn't know that initially. Jewish betrothal was significantly more binding than modern engagements. Unfaithfulness during the betrothal period was considered adultery under Jewish law (punishable by stoning), and a betrothal could only be dissolved by a certificate of divorce. The man and woman were considered "husband" (v. 19) and "wife" (v. 20), though there had not been a marriage ceremony.

Because Joseph was a righteous man (v. 19), he needed to do the proper thing legally and divorce Mary. Because he was a merciful man, he wanted to do it quietly. In verses 20–21, dreams play a big part in Matthew's account of the Nativity (as we will see in tomorrow's study). The message from the angel of the

Lord in Joseph's dream stresses two important concepts to the Jews: 1) The Messiah would be the Son of David, the fulfillment of numerous Old Testament prophecies. 2) Names are significant. "Jesus" is the Greek form of the Hebrew "Joshua," which means "the Lord saves." The Jews expected the Messiah to forgive sins, but not in the way Jesus would fulfill that prophetic promise.

vv. 22–25—In verse 23, Matthew introduces his first Old Testament quote, taken from Isaiah 7:14. Though the Hebrew could be translated either "young woman" or "virgin," Matthew makes it emphatic that the proper interpretation of Isaiah 7:14 is that God was foretelling a virgin birth. The Isaiah prophecy also gives a second name to the Messiah—Emmanuel, "with us, God."

Jesus is God's clearest evidence that he is always with us. The Virgin Birth is crucial theologically. It proves Christ to be holy from the beginning, a unique conception for the unique God/man. Verse 25 clearly implies that Joseph and Mary had normal sexual relations after Jesus was born. This rejects the idea of Mary's perpetual virginity (not to mention Matt. 12:46, where Jesus' brothers and sisters are mentioned).

Luke 1:26–34—Luke's account is told from Mary's point of view. Here the angel (archangel Gabriel) is in physical form, not in a dream. He comes during the sixth month of Mary's kinswoman Elizabeth's pregnancy. Luke locates the events in Nazareth, Jesus' hometown. "Greetings" in Latin is *Ave* in Latin, from which the song "Ave Maria" gets its name. The fact that God chose her is what made Mary highly favored. In verses 29–34, Mary's reaction to the angelic announcement seems very normal. She exhibits the same fear that almost all biblical characters have when encountering an angel. She then wonders how she will have this special son when she has not yet married Joseph nor had sex. She was obviously a girl committed to purity (most commentators believe that Mary was a young teenager when this happened).

vv. 35–38—Gabriel's answer is both awesome and reassuring. It will be a miracle brought by the Holy Spirit. He already did something special for Elizabeth who was old and barren (1:7). Gabriel's conclusion applies to us: *"Nothing is impossible with God."* Mary accepts his words with great faith.

APPLY

Matt. 1:19—Even though Joseph had the legal right to condemn Mary, he chose to be gentle. How about you? Do you choose mercy rather than judgment?

vv. 22–25—The Virgin Birth is tremendously important. Since Jesus was not born by human means, he did not inherit "sin passed from Adam." His supernatural birth points to the unique activity of God.

MEMORIZE

Luke 1:37

PRAY

A: Praise God's awesome power.

C: Confess your lack of faith.

T: Thank God for the remarkable things he's done in your life.

S: Ask for Mary and Joseph's faith to believe God for big things.

TELL

Share with a fellow Christian why you think the Virgin Birth is important.

JANUARY 3

JESUS GOES INTERNATIONAL

PRAY

Ask God to show you the importance of listening for his voice just as Joseph did.

READ

Matthew 2:1–23

OBSERVE

vv. 1–8—Matthew doesn't tell us any of the events prior to Christ's birth. We'll see those later in Luke. He begins with the birth in Bethlehem in Judea. This birth was a fulfillment of prophecy—Micah 5:2. Herod the Great was king from 37 BC to 4 BC. The dating of Jesus' birth wasn't done until centuries later, and it was erroneous. He was probably born between 6 and 4 BC.

The Magi were astrologers (not philosophers or "wise men") from Persia or Southern Arabia. The Jews considered them idolaters. It's most likely that they were Zoroastrians, not followers of God. There is no indication from the text that there were only three of them. When Matthew indicates that Herod was troubled "and all Jerusalem with him," he is probably understating the case. Herod was a megalomaniac who killed his sons because he thought they wanted to usurp his throne. One contemporary of Herod wrote, "I would rather be Herod's pig [he wouldn't kill a pig because he was a Jew] than his son."

vv. 9–12—The fact that the star "stopped over the place where the child was" seems to rule out the naturalistic explanation that it was the conjunction of Jupiter and Saturn, which occurred in 6 BC. Notice that Jesus was in a house by the time the Magi arrived. It was possibly weeks, months, even two years (v. 16) after Jesus was born when they arrived, contrary to the Christmas pageants which have them arriving on the heels of the shepherds. Gold was a typical gift to present to a king, but incense and myrrh were unusual, more connected to death than birth. Did the Holy Spirit lead them to a gift whose significance would only be clear thirty years later? The Spirit certainly communicated with them through a dream, even though they were not believers.

vv. 13–15—The third "dream sequence" in Matthew warns Joseph to flee to Egypt. Hosea 11:1 is cited to show the Messiah as the fulfillment of the promise to Israel. His "exodus" to Egypt recapitulates the history of God's people—going to Egypt then returning to the Promised Land.

vv. 16–18—True to his nature, Herod orders the "Slaughter of the Innocents." Though it is a fulfillment of Scripture (Jer. 31:15), that makes Herod no less guilty. Innocent people are always hurt by sin. In a small village like Bethlehem, the number of boys two and under would be few, but that doesn't diminish the act's brutality.

vv. 19–23—Dreams give Joseph additional information about Herod's death and warn him to avoid the reign of his tyrannical son, Archelaus (4 BC to 6 AD). Nazareth is an obscure town in Galilee that isn't mentioned in the Old Testament. It's difficult to tell which prophecies Matthew refers to in verse 23. It may be a combination of several passages, particularly Isaiah 11:1, in which "branch" is the Hebrew *neser*.

APPLY

vv. 12–13, 19—It took faith for Joseph and the Magi to respond to God's message given through dreams. Are you open to the Holy Spirit's "inner voice" to you?

MEMORIZE

A key prophecy of the birth of Christ is Micah 5:2 (Matt. 2:6).

PRAY

A: God is the Lord of all the earth and even uses unbelievers to accomplish his will.

C: Confess a time recently when your sin hurt someone else.

T: Thank God for revealing himself in so many different ways.

S: Ask God to reveal his will to you through his Word and through circumstances like he did to Joseph and the Magi through their dreams.

TELL

Someone about an experience in which God communicated with you in an unusual way.

JANUARY 4

JOHN THE BAPTIST

PRAY

Ask God to give you the boldness, courage, and integrity of John the Baptist.

READ

Matthew 3:1–12; Mark 1:1–8; Luke 3:1–20

OBSERVE

v. 1—John was most likely Jesus' second cousin. His title in Greek is literally, "John, the one who baptizes." John the Baptizer is more accurate than John the Baptist. The desert of Judea was a rough place to live.

v. 2—The word "repent" (*metanoeo*) means "a change of mind" which results in a change of behavior. The reason for John's hearers to repent was because a new reality had come, the Kingdom of Heaven in the person of Jesus of Nazareth. Matthew is the only gospel writer to use the expression "the Kingdom of Heaven." He uses it thirty-three times. The other gospel writers use, "the kingdom of God," which Matthew only uses four times. Pious Jews were very reluctant to say or write the name of God for fear of violating the Third Commandment (Exod. 20:7).

v. 3—The prophecy of John's ministry is found in Isaiah 40:3. Luke adds Isaiah 40:4–5. All Israel expected a forerunner to the Messiah (whom Malachi 4 calls "Elijah"). The gospel writers are saying, "Here he is!" in John.

vv. 4–6—John the Baptist is a link between the Old and New Testaments. He followed the tradition of Elijah (2 Kings 1:8) and the other desert prophets with his simple lifestyle. Luke emphasizes his call to reject materialism (Luke 3:10–14).

Some commentators believe that the "locusts" mentioned here were not the insects (though locusts were "clean" insects and edible—Lev. 11:2–22) but a plant grown in that region. The Jordan River is the principal river in Palestine, beginning in the snows of Mt. Hermon in the north and ending in the Dead Sea. Its closest point to Jerusalem is about twenty miles east, and it is pretty small—more of a stream than a river in most places.

vv. 7–10—The Pharisees were a legalistic and separatistic group who kept the law of Moses strictly but often hypocritically. John and Jesus reserved their strongest criticisms for them. The Sadducees were theological and political liberals who denied key elements of the faith (the resurrection, angels, and spirits) and tried to ally themselves with the Romans, whom the Pharisees hated. John calls both groups to repentance (they probably didn't appreciate being called a "brood of vipers") and warns them against thinking that they have any standing with God because of their heritage (v .9). John would get in the face of anyone who says, "God is love, and he would never condemn anyone to Hell." In verse 10, we see that the law's function is to convict and convert sinners.

vv. 11–13—John continues his "Fire Sermon" by pointing to the One who will baptize with the Holy Spirit and with fire, Jesus Christ. Fire is an Old Testament symbol for purification (cf. Mal. 3:2–3; 4:1). John recognizes his relationship to Jesus (v. 11), which we'll focus on when we study John's gospel.

APPLY

vv. 2, 8—Repentance is necessary for cleansing and restoration. Are there any sins you're holding on to?

vv. 11–12—What is your view of Jesus and yourself? Do you see him as your Lord and Master whose sandals you are not fit to carry?

MEMORIZE

Matthew 3:3

This gives us John's place in redemptive history.

PRAY

A: Praise God's justice and righteous judgment.

C: Confess your sin and need of repentance.

T: Thank God people have cared enough to tell you the truth, like John.

S: Ask Jesus to purify you for his ministry.

TELL

Describe to someone your view of the relationship between God's law and his grace.

JANUARY 5

THE BAPTISM OF JESUS

PRAY

Ask God to help you understand the significance of Jesus' baptism.

READ

Matthew 3:13–17; Mark 1:9–1; Luke 3:21–22

OBSERVE

Although the three gospel accounts are substantially alike, Matthew gives the most detail.

v. 13—Jesus came a long way (as far as one hundred miles) to be baptized by John. This is his first appearance as an adult in the Gospel of Matthew. There is an abrupt transition from his infancy to the beginning of his ministry. Luke will tell us what little we know about the intervening years.

v. 14—John is surprised when Jesus appears for baptism. The baptizer had just predicted that Jesus would be the super-baptizer, with the Holy Spirit and with fire. It seems inappropriate to John that Jesus should be appearing as a recipient for baptism. Dale Bruner comments:

> The first surprise in Jesus' adult ministry, then, is in fact the first deed of his ministry; his seeking baptism at all. I like to consider this Jesus' first miracle: the miracle of his humility. The first thing Jesus does for us is *go down with us*. His whole life will be like this. It is well known that Jesus ended his career on a cross between thieves; it deserves to be as well known that he began his ministry in a river among penitent

sinners. From his baptism to his execution Jesus stays low, at our level, identifying with us at every point, becoming as completely one with us in our humanity in history, as, in the church's teaching, he was completely one with God in eternity. Jesus "at-one-ment" with the human race, visible already at baptism, is as impressive and as important for human salvation as Jesus' at-one-ment with the heavenly Father, most visible at the Transfiguration and most potent at the cross. (Bruner, *Matthew: The Christbook*, 83)

v. 15—Why was Jesus baptized since he never sinned? Jesus tells us that it was "to fulfill all righteousness," that is, every ordinance of God for his people. Luther saw in Christ's baptism a clear prefiguring of the cross. To Luther, Jesus was saying, in effect, "Although I am not myself a sinner, yet nevertheless I now bring with me the sin of the whole world." As it is the outward symbol of inward faith in Christ, adult Christian baptism marks the beginning of ministry, as it was for Jesus.

vv. 16–17—This is one of the great Trinitarian passages of the New Testament. Though the word "trinity" is never used in the Bible, it is impossible to deny that Scripture clearly teaches that God is one essence in three persons. All three persons of the Godhead are unmistakably present at Jesus' baptism: God the Holy Spirit takes the form of a dove and descends upon Jesus; God the Father affirms and commissions Christ with his words from heaven; and God the Son is obedient to the Father. Alan Cole writes:

> As in the book of Genesis, God created by his Word and "through his Spirit," so it was fitting that, at the very commencement of God's work of re-creation in the hearts of men, there should be the same operation of the whole Godhead. Here, on Jordan's banks, God speaks his Word again, and again the Spirit is brooding over the waters. (Cole, *The Gospel According to Mark*, 58)

APPLY

v. 15—Baptism is a seal that you are the Lord's servant. How are you serving him?

MEMORIZE

Matthew 3:17

God's words to his Son are his stamp of approval and commission to ministry.

PRAY

A: Praise the Triune God, whose fellowship is a model for all human relationships.

C: Admit that your pride has kept you from acts of humility.

T: Thank you, Jesus, for identifying with us in your baptism.

S: Ask for God's help to be humble and obedient like Jesus and John.

TELL

Share with a Christian friend why you believe Jesus chose to be baptized.

JANUARY 6

JESUS IS TEMPTED AND TESTED

PRAY

Ask God to help you to see how Christ's temptations apply to your life.

READ

Matthew 4:1–11; Mark 1:12–13; Luke 4:1–13

OBSERVE

All three accounts of Jesus' temptation are very similar, but there are subtle nuances in each account that add to the overall picture.

v. 1—Mark's brief account emphasizes that the Spirit *drove* Jesus into the wilderness. Matthew and Luke use the gentler term, "led." In any case, it was clearly God's will for Jesus to be tempted or tested (the same Greek word, *pierazo*, can mean either tempt or test) as he begins his ministry.

vv. 2–4—The forty days of fasting and testing in the desert correspond to the forty years of Israel's testing in the desert. Experts in fasting indicate that after an initial period of hunger, the body adjusts to a fast until around the fortieth day, when intense hunger returns. So Jesus was most vulnerable to the temptation of food. The significance of Jesus' temptations is best understood in terms of testing what sort of Messiah he would be. The first temptation lures him to use his supernatural power to meet his own needs. He quotes Deuteronomy 8:3 to assert the priority of God's Word (our spiritual need) over bread (our physical need).

vv. 5–7—The second temptation proposes that Jesus capture a large following by performing flashy miracles. The devil's tactics haven't changed a lot since the first temptation. He approached Eve with a skeptical question, "Did God really say, 'You must not eat from any tree in the garden'?" He then promises that she will be like God. His cynical challenge to Jesus begins, "If you are the Son of God…" and continues with a promise taken from Psalm 91:11–12. The devil (*diabolos*, the accuser) is an accomplished theologian who quotes Scripture for his own purposes. Knowledge of God's Word is never enough (James 2:19). Jesus answers by applying God's Word correctly (Deut. 6:16).

vv. 8–11—The third temptation is more sweeping. The devil, the ruler of this world (John 12:31), offers to make Jesus COO of all the earth, chief assistant to CEO Satan. All that's required is a simple act of worship. Jesus rebukes the evil one and calls him "Satan" which means "adversary." Jesus' third quote from Scripture is taken from Deuteronomy 6:13. It's important for us to memorize God's Word because it is our primary defensive and offensive weapon against the attacks of the devil and his angels. Luke's conclusion to the temptation narrative is ominous, "The devil… left him until an opportune time" (Luke 4:13). This would by no means be the end of the temptations Jesus would face. Matthew concludes with the grace note, "angels came and attended him."

APPLY

vv. 3–10—What are some temptations Satan is using against you? How are you dealing with them?

MEMORIZE

See if you can memorize the three Scriptures Jesus used against the devil—verses 4, 7, and 10.

PRAY

A: Praise God the Son, who was tempted in every way as we are, yet without sin (Heb. 4:15).

C: Confess your own weakness when faced with temptation.

T: Thank God for his Word, our strong defense against the flaming darts of the evil one.

S: Ask for strength as you face temptation today.

TELL

Share with a close friend a victory God has enabled you to win over a particular temptation.

JANUARY 7

JESUS BEGINS HIS MINISTRY: PREACHING, TEACHING, AND HEALING

PRAY

Ask God to show you the ministry he has for you to do today and in the future.

READ

Matthew 4:12–25; Mark 1:14–20; Luke 4:14–15, 5:1–11

OBSERVE

Luke adds "flavor" to Matthew and Mark's basic story of the beginning of Christ's ministry.

v. 12—With the arrest of John, Jesus may have realized that Judea was not a safe place for prophets, so he returned to Galilee because it was not yet time to risk ending his life.

vv. 13–16—The new center for Christ's ministry would be Capernaum, which was on the northern rim of the Sea of Galilee. As usual, Matthew sees this as a fulfillment of prophetic Scripture (Isa. 9:1–2).

v. 17—Jesus' initial message was identical to John's (compare with 3:2).

vv. 18–22—Luke 5:1–11 provides details to the calling of Simon Peter and Andrew. It's a lot more evident from Luke's account why they were willing to leave their nets and follow Jesus. This could be considered Jesus' first miracle over nature in the Synoptics, and it had a profound effect on Simon Peter. He begins to recognize that this is not an ordinary teacher, and his response is reverential awe: *"Go away from me, Lord. I am a sinful man!"* (v. 8). Luke also tells us that the sons of Zebedee, James and John, were involved in this miracle. The conclusion of both accounts is the same. Jesus calls them to follow him, and he tells them that he will make them fishers of men. The first command Jesus gives to his disciples is to share their faith and bring others into the kingdom (we will see later that it's also his last!).

vv. 23–25—Matthew identifies Jesus' threefold ministry as teaching, preaching, and healing. He taught in the synagogues on the Sabbath, preached to large crowds in the open air during the week, and healed all the time. The Church should continue Christ's ministry in the power of the Spirit in these three areas.

APPLY

v. 19—Do you take seriously Jesus' command to catch people for his kingdom?

v. 20—Are you willing to follow Christ even when you're not sure of the destination?

v. 23—How does God want to use you in the ministry of preaching, teaching, and healing?

MEMORIZE

Matthew 5:19

This is Jesus' first command to his disciples (and us).

PRAY

A: Praise the Sovereign over nature.

C: Confess your reluctance to be a fisher of men.

T: Thank God for healing you physically and emotionally.

S: Ask God to use you as a "fisherman" today!

TELL

Share the Gospel with someone as the Spirit gives you opportunity.

JANUARY 8

THE BEAUTIFUL ATTITUDES

That you might understand and live the Beatitudes today.

READ

Matthew 5:1–12

OBSERVE

vv. 1–2—The construction and verb tenses in these two verses suggest that Jesus taught on mountainsides repeatedly, and that the Beatitudes may be a distillation of that teaching. Some see an echo of Moses going up on the mountain. Unquestionably, Jesus is assuming the role of a rabbi, who always sat to teach. It's unclear exactly who his audience was—the disciples are singled out in this beginning of the Sermon on the Mount, but the conclusion (7:28–29) mentions "the crowds." The word "beatitude" comes from the Latin *beatus*, "blessed."

v. 3—The first Beatitude sets the stage for the rest. There are two Greek words for poor: *penes*, which describes the working man who struggles with too much month and not enough income, and *ptochos*, the person who is without resources altogether, totally bankrupt. Jesus uses the latter. The person who realizes that he or she is spiritually bankrupt, absolutely unable to please God on his own efforts, and in total need of divine grace, is the person who will experience the kingdom of heaven. God hates spiritual pride. The humble will be blessed.

v. 4—Some commentators spiritualize mourning and suggest it means sorrow over sin. That's possible, but the more obvious meaning is that God comforts those who genuinely grieve. "Jesus beatifies mourning, not moping (cf, especially 6:16–

18). He does not counsel the long face. He does, however, bless real sadness, a state that can as easily coexist with an outwardly happy life as can all the other normal contradictions of living" (Bruner, *Matthew: The Christbook*, 139). Scripture commends godly grief, which looks in hope to Christ (1 Thess. 4:13) versus worldly grief, which only laments one's loss. God will comfort (the word used for the Holy Spirit) those who grieve.

v. 5—Meekness is not weakness. Biblical commentator William Barclay points out that the Greek word describes the golden mean between excessive anger and absence of anger. It was used of a wild animal that had been domesticated. Meekness, then, is having your anger under the control of God and being obedient to his voice. It is deciding to be gentle. God declares that those who choose the path of gentleness are the hope of his earth and will inherit it.

v. 6—The fourth Beatitude commends those whose greatest desire is to please God. The Bible consistently teaches that those who seek God will be found by him, and he will richly bless them. "Righteousness" describes both a right relationship with God and doing what is right.

v. 7—The first four Beatitudes invert the world's value system and assert that those who acknowledge that they are needy are truly blessed. The second four focus on the bliss of those who act in love. The structure is similar to the Ten Commandments. Mercy is highly exalted in Matthew's gospel. Twice Jesus quotes Hosea 6:6: "*I desire mercy, not sacrifice*" (9:13 and 12:7). Matthew's gospel alone includes the parable of the unmerciful servant (18:21–35). As in that parable, God shows mercy to the merciful. Only those who truly know God's mercy can be merciful.

v. 8—This is the favorite Beatitude of mystical Christians throughout the ages, those who want to see God face-to-face. Augustine taught that this purity was "faith which works by love" (Gal. 5:6). Luther stressed that a pure heart came from replacing one's own ideas with what God says in his Word.

v. 9—Despite their history of conflict, peace was always highly prized by the Jews. Even today, Jews in Israel greet one another with "Shalom." Shalom (*eirene* in Greek) describes a right relationship with God, which results in a right relationship with others, and harmony within oneself. Those who promote peace are God's sons (his children) because they're doing his work. Christ came to make peace through his work on the cross (Eph. 2:14). John Stott writes, "The incentive to peacemaking is love, but it degenerates into appeasement whenever justice is ignored. All authentic Christian peace-making exhibits the love and justice—and so the pain—of the cross" (Stott, *The Cross of Christ*, 296–297).

vv. 10–12—We are not to be masochists who seek out persecution. But if we are faithful to Christ in an evil and often hate-filled world, we will be rejected (2 Tim. 3:12). We are blessed when we are persecuted because we are following in the footsteps of the prophets and of Christ himself. The promises come full circle, for the promise of the kingdom is the same as the one given to the poor in spirit.

APPLY

vv. 3–6—Do you acknowledge that you are truly needy and totally dependent on God for everything of lasting value in your life?

vv. 7–9—How can you act more lovingly toward those around you today?

MEMORIZE

Try to memorize at least one of the Beatitudes. The first would certainly be valuable.

PRAY

A: Praise the God of all blessing, who gives us far more than we deserve.

C: Confess any areas in which the Spirit convicted you as you were doing this study.

T: Thank God for the persecution you have experienced for the sake of Christ.

S: Ask God to help you be more faithful in the areas you confessed.

TELL

Share something new and important you learned from this study with someone else.

JANUARY 9

SALT, LIGHT, AND THE LAW

PRAY

Your word is a lamp to my feet and a light for my path.

—Psalm 119:105

READ

Matthew 5:13–20; Luke 14:34–35

OBSERVE

This section acts as a transition between the Beatitudes and Christ's new teaching on the law.

v. 13—In the time of Christ, salt functioned primarily as a preservative. In the days before refrigerators, it was rubbed into meat to keep it from spoiling. To the Jews, it also represented wisdom (Col. 4:6). Furthermore, it adds flavor and causes thirst. Believers are to be interesting and wise, preserving and presenting God's truth so as to create a thirst for it in those around them. Salt only works well if it is spread around yet remains distinctive.

vv. 14–16—Light is the dominant symbol in the Bible—from creation (Gen. 1:3) to glorification (Rev. 22:5). It represents goodness, guidance, life, and love. The meaning here is primarily the former: "let your light shine ... that they may see your good deeds and praise your Father in heaven." Light must not be hidden.

vv. 17–20—"The law and the prophets" was the Jewish term for the Old Testament, which Christ endorses without qualification. "The smallest letter" is the Greek *iota* ("It doesn't make one iota of difference"). "The least stroke of a pen" described the flourish at the bottom of some Hebrew letters. Christ declares that all Scripture is authoritative and to be obeyed. In the next section of chapter 5, however, he will correct the misinterpretations of the Scribes and Pharisees, which led the people astray. In context, "righteousness" involves a right relationship with God through faith that results in right living.

APPLY

v. 13—How are you increasing the world's thirst for Jesus? Do you have any unbelieving friends with whom you are developing a relationship that can lead to sharing your faith?

vv. 14–16—What good works are people seeing you do which they can attribute to God's work in you?

vv. 17–20—Are you taking God's Word seriously and applying it to your life faithfully?

MEMORIZE

Matthew 5:17

This is a crucial statement of Christ's relationship to the Old Testament.

PRAY

A: Praise God, who faithfully fulfills his Word.

C: Confess those times you have failed to be salt and light.

T: Thank God for his inspired, inerrant Word.

S: Ask God to lead you to a good work that can "shine" today.

TELL

Share with someone why you believe that the Bible is the Word of God.

JANUARY 10

YOU HAVE HEARD THAT IT WAS SAID, BUT I TELL YOU

PRAY

Ask God to give you a deeper understanding of how his commandments apply to your life.

READ

Matthew 5:21–48; Luke 6:27–36, 12:57–59

OBSERVE

As Jesus said in the previous verses, he didn't come to abolish the law, but to fulfill it—to give it a fuller meaning, to deepen our understanding and application. He gets to the heart of each commandment because they deal with the heart and not just the outward behavior.

vv. 21–27—Jesus recognizes that the root of the sixth commandment, *"You shall not murder,"* is anger. *Raca* was an obscure Aramaic term of abuse that may mean "Empty headed!" or "You are nothing!" "You fool" was more a moral than an intellectual judgment. Fools in Scripture are those who refuse to heed God's wisdom (Ps. 14:1). Jesus first warns his disciples not to express inappropriate anger toward others. He then instructs them on what they should do if they realize that a brother is angry with them. In verses 23–24, Jesus teaches that relationships are more important than religious observances. Reconciliation is not only obedient, it is wise (vv. 25–26, cf. Luke 12:57–59).

vv. 27–32—Lust is at the heart of the seventh commandment, *"You shall not commit adultery."* Looking at a woman lustfully is more than just a glance; it is a gaze that plots a seduction. As Luther said, "The birds will fly over your head; don't make a nest for them." Verses 29 and 30 are hyperbole—exaggeration for effect—one of Jesus' favorite teaching devices. He was stressing the seriousness of sin. He was not encouraging mutilation which at least one church father (Origen) practiced.

Jesus quotes Deuteronomy 24:1, in which Moses gives implicit permission for Israelites to issue a certificate of divorce. Jesus will expand on this passage in chapter 19, which we will study later. In this brief section, Jesus makes it clear that God intends marriage to be a lifetime commitment, and divorce is only permissible when one party has severed the marriage bond through adultery.

vv. 33–37—The ninth commandment, *"You shall not bear false witness,"* is behind Jesus' teaching here, though he quotes Numbers 6:21 and Deuteronomy 23:21. In his wonderful book *The Cost of Discipleship*, Dietrich Bonhoeffer points out that disciples of Jesus Christ should have such a reputation for telling the truth that they don't need to buttress their statements with oaths. In Jesus' day, swearing by oaths had become an art form that permitted technical dishonesty. It hasn't changed much today. When someone uses an oath to validate his promise ("Let me be honest with you")—beware! Most Christians don't believe that this prohibition precludes lawful oaths in court. Others, like the Quakers, extend it to any and all oaths. Taken in isolation, this passage sides with the Quakers, but the "Analogy of Faith" (Scripture is its own best commentary) allows for oaths (see Matt. 26: 63–64).

vv. 38–48—This section addresses our response to enemies. *"An eye for an eye and a tooth for a tooth"* (Exod. 21:24) may be a valid legal standard, but it doesn't work for personal relationships. Gandhi, who practiced Jesus' ethics, said that the *lex taliones* (law of the claw), when applied consistently, results in a lot of blind and toothless people. Jesus and Paul (Rom. 12:19–21) prohibited retaliation or revenge but taught love in action as a way of transforming enemies. God is kind and merciful, actively loving even his enemies, the unjust (v. 45). Though all of the major versions are unanimous in translating the Greek *telios* as "perfect," Jesus could not mean that men are to be morally perfect in the same way God is. *Telios* comes from *telos* which means "end," "goal," "mature," or "complete." In context, the quality of maturity that marks a believer is unselfish love and mercy for others, even those who deserve no mercy. The attitude of "perfection" Christ calls for isn't sinlessness but a basic intention of kindness and love.

APPLY

v. 23—Is there a brother or sister who has something against you? What will you do to be reconciled?

v. 28—Is your commitment to sexual purity firmly in place? How can you avoid temptation?

v. 44—What loving thing can you do for an enemy today?

MEMORIZE

Matthew 5:27

This is the key to avoiding sexual sin. It begins in the heart.

PRAY

A: Praise God that he is loving and kind toward sinners.

C: Confess your anger, lust, false witness, and lack of love for enemies.

T: Thank God that he is quick to forgive and restore us when we repent.

S: Ask God for his Spirit's help to control anger, lust, and lying and to actively love the unlovely.

TELL

Confess your struggle in one of these areas and ask a righteous friend to pray for you (James 5:16).

JANUARY 11

PIETY IS LIKE SOAP

PRAY

Ask God to help you see the times you've tried to impress others with your religious observances.

READ

Matthew 6:1–18; Luke 11:1–4

OBSERVE

The Lord's Prayer is given in the context of how to practice our faith appropriately.

v. 1—The topic sentence for this section begins, *"Beware of practicing your piety before men in order to be seen by them."* Jesus doesn't appreciate show-offs of any kind but particularly not religious show-offs. He gives three examples of what to avoid when practicing your faith.

vv. 2–4—Jesus paints a humorous picture of hypocrites (literally "play actors") giving offerings. A trumpet heralds their generous gift. If you give to impress people and they are impressed, you've received your reward. Jesus doesn't reject the reward motive, he urges us to aim for a higher reward from the Father.

vv. 5–8—Christ isn't prohibiting public prayer (Matt. 18:19–20), just showy prayers. Contemporary Christians should take verse 7 seriously in our prayer groups. Do we ever heap up empty phrases ("I just really want to thank you, Father, for just being a really great Father, Father…")? Do we think that God hears us better when we use many, flowery words? The Lord's Prayer (it really should be called The Disciples' Prayer) is a model of a simple but powerful prayer. Luke quotes the disciples asking Jesus to teach them how to pray (11:1). This is the only time they are recorded as asking him to teach them anything specific. They must have recognized that prayer was the source of Jesus' spiritual power.

vv. 9–10—Biblical prayer begins with praise, acknowledging who God is—the Father in heaven—and praising his holiness—may your name be kept holy. Prayer that is pleasing to God seeks first the advancement of his kingdom, not our own. We are to pray according to God's will (1 John 5:14) and to seek to bring our wills into conformity to his so that God's will is done on earth as it is in heaven.

v. 11—People sometimes say, "I never pray for myself or my needs," as if that were a superior attitude in prayer. God wants us to ask him to meet our legitimate needs (James 4: 2–3) and for us to acknowledge that he is the one who meets our needs.

vv. 12, 14–15—The only petition that Jesus emphasizes by repetition is the need to confess our sins and forgive the sins of others. Though many commentators try to work their way around the clear message of these verses, it is inescapable. If we are not willing to forgive others, we will not experience God's forgiveness. We must take this seriously. It's the message of the Parable of the Unforgiving Servant (18:23–35), a parable unique to Matthew.

v. 13—Remember that the same Greek word can be translated "temptation" or "testing." James 1:13 tells us that God does not tempt anyone with evil, so "Do not lead us into testing" would be the preferred translation here. The second phrase could be translated "Deliver us from the evil one" as well as "evil." That phrase isn't included in Luke's version of the prayer. "The sixth petition keeps us from thinking of ourselves as spiritual heroes. We do not pray, 'Bring on temptation!' We do not go looking for tests of strength. More modestly we pray for protection and guidance" (Bruner, *Matthew: The Christbook*, 255). Neither gospel includes the words that Protestants add to the prayer, "For thine is the kingdom and the power and the glory, for ever. Amen." They are absent from the most reliable manuscripts.

vv. 16–18—The third spiritual show to avoid is fasting to impress others. Notice Jesus says, *"When* you fast," not, *"If* you fast." As the word suggests, fasting is "moving more quickly" toward a spiritual goal. We refrain from food to spend the time in prayer and meditation. Jesus practiced it and commended it. The command to wash your face could apply symbolically to all of these religious acts. When we wash our faces, we use soap to get them clean. But we don't leave traces of soap on our face to impress others with how clean we are. Piety is like soap.

APPLY

vv. 5–7—Do you need to simplify your prayers particularly when you're praying with others?

v. 12—Whom do you need to forgive? Make a decision to do that, and formulate an action plan.

v. 16—Be open to a time when God is calling you to fast.

MEMORIZE

Matthew 6:14–15

This is the part of the prayer which Jesus emphasizes.

PRAY

Pray the Disciples' Prayer thoughtfully, phrase by phrase, today. Apply it to your life.

TELL

Go to someone who has hurt you, and tell that person that you forgive him or her.

JANUARY 12

CHRIST AND CONSUMERISM

PRAY

Ask God to show you the attitude he wants you to have about material possessions.

READ

Matthew 6:19–34; Luke 11:33–36, 12:22–34

OBSERVE

Jesus taught more about money and material things than any other single subject. He showed that money can be an immense obstacle to following him and that money could be a force for good. It is powerful.

vv. 19–21—The Jews considered treasure in heaven to be that which was generously given to others. Earthly possessions will all rot and decay. Heavenly treasure is preserved by God. This passage is very personal to me. It was the text of the first sermon I ever preached. The day before I was to deliver it, thieves broke into my parents' house and set it on fire to cover their tracks. Almost all of our possessions were destroyed. I could preach this message with conviction, because I lost nothing that really mattered.

vv. 22–23—These verses don't seem initially to fit their context. However, if the word "generous" is substituted for "good" and "grudging" for "bad" (both are legitimate senses of the Greek words), then the messages are complementary. Jesus wants us to look at the world with generous eyes that admit God's light.

v. 24—The NIV translates the Aramaic word *mammon* as "money." It could just as easily be translated "possessions" or "property" or "things." Translating the word, however, causes us to lose the fact that Mammon was a Canaanite god, the god of prosperity. The key issue here is whom we *serve*. Luther points out, "It is no sin to *have* money and property…. But you must not let it be your master. You must make it serve you, and you must be its master" (Luther, *Sermon on the Mount,* 189). The New Testament doesn't see wealth as intrinsically wrong (1 Tim. 6:17–19). It is materialism and uncaring wealth that are condemned. Jesus doesn't say that we *should* not serve two masters but that we *cannot* serve two masters. In this materialistic society, we need to take a long, hard look at ourselves to see whether Christ or money is more important to us.

vv. 25–34—This much-loved passage is really about worry and anxiety. Jesus tells us not to worry five times here. He argues from the lesser to the greater—God takes care of birds and wildflowers, so won't he take care of us? God knows that we need food and drink and clothing, and he will provide them. Notice that Jesus doesn't preclude us being concerned that *others* have food, drink, and clothing (cf. Matt. 25:31–46). He forbids selfish anxiety. If we Westerners aren't concerned about food, drink, and clothes, he certainly includes us in verse 34 when he tells us not to be anxious about the future. The key is priorities—keeping the main thing the main thing. The main thing to Jesus is God's kingdom and righteousness. If God is first, we can be sure he will take care of secondary things.

APPLY

vv. 19–24—Are you laying up treasure in heaven, or are you hoarding your treasure on earth?

v. 25—Are you worried about anything? Give it to God, and leave it with him.

MEMORIZE

Matthew 6:33

PRAY

A: Pray to the God who provides.

C: Confess your anxiety about money and the future.

T: List some of the things God has so graciously provided for you.

S: Ask God to remove your worry and replace it with concern for his kingdom.

TELL

Discuss with a friend your views on the place of material things in your lives.

JANUARY 13

ON JUDGING AND PRAYING

PRAY

Ask God to give you his perspective on judging and praying.

READ

Matthew 7:1–12; Luke 6:37–42, 11:5–13

OBSERVE

Luke enriches Matthew's more basic account with two parables.

vv. 1–6—Jesus' predominant emphasis when it comes to judging is to be slow to judge. And if you do judge, beware of hypocritical judging. The standards you use in judging others will be applied to you. The New Testament doesn't forbid judging. There are three Greek words translated "judge" in most translations. They are all variations on the Greek word *krino*.

1. Jesus uses the basic word, "to sit in judgment" in verse 1. Some people—judges and juries in a courtroom, elders in a church, employers, etc.—have the responsibility of judging others. They must not be overly critical (vv. 3–5) and condemn in others what they do themselves. Luke adds the parable of the blind leading the blind (6:39–40) to suggest the absurdity of someone judging another for what they don't see in themselves.
2. Romans 2:1–3 uses the word *katakrino* "to judge down" or to condemn. Christians are never to condemn anyone. Only God has that right.
3. 1 Corinthians 2:15 says, "The spiritual man makes judgments (*anakrino*)

about all things, but he himself is not subject to any man's judgment (*krino*)." *Anakrino* means "to judge up" or "to judge for the purpose of improvement." Believers are continually urged to do that for one another (cf. Gal. 6:1). However, verse 6 teaches that we are not to "judge up" unbelievers because they lack the spiritual maturity to receive constructive criticism and will reject it and attack us. Paul echoes that truth in 1 Corinthians 5:12.

vv. 7–11—Each of the verbs in verse 7 suggests repeated and continual action: "Keep on asking, keep on seeking, keep on knocking." Luke reinforces the importance of persevering in prayer with his Parable of the Insistent Friend in Luke 11:5–8. God is not deaf to our requests. He will answer in his time. Both Matthew and Luke compare God to an earthly father. If we, who are evil (a clear indication of Christ's belief in the doctrine of original sin!), still give good gifts to our children, how much more will God give us his good gifts? Luke specifies that the good gift is the Holy Spirit, the best gift of all! Christ's teaching here should free us from our fear that God is just waiting for us to surrender to him in prayer so that he can send us to a terrible place or force us to do whatever is most distasteful to us. That is not the Father we have. Our good Father gives us the best—not always what we want, but what we need.

v. 12—At first glance, the Golden Rule doesn't seem to fit with the rest of this section (somewhat like the discussion of dogs and pigs). But there is an obvious connection because Jesus begins with "So...." The connecting thought is generosity (we saw this in 6:22). God is extravagant with us in response to our prayers. We should also be generous to provide to others what is the best for them. The way to gauge that is to put yourself in their shoes and ask, "What would I most want in the same situation?" Though there are different versions of the Golden Rule in other religions, most of them are stated in a negative form ("Don't do what you would not want done to you"). Jesus states it positively. It's in keeping with his love ethic, in which *agape* love is caring for another's highest good.

APPLY

v. 4—Are you careful not to judge others hypocritically?

v. 7—About what concern does God want you to persist in prayer?

v. 12—Put the Golden Rule to practice in some specific way today.

MEMORIZE

Either Matthew 7:7 or 7:12 would be great verses to memorize.

PRAY

A: Praise the God who answers prayer and gives good gifts to his children.

C: Confess the times you have judged others harshly and hypocritically.

T: Thank God for good gifts he has given you recently.

S: Be persistent in asking God for the power of the Holy Spirit, the best gift of all.

TELL

Look for a chance to gently share with a fellow believer a "judgment for improvement" that might help his walk and witness.

JANUARY 14

LEARN TO DISCERN

PRAY

Direct me in the paths of your commands, for there I find delight.

—Psalm 119:35

READ

Matthew 7:13–29; Luke 6:43–49, 13:22–30

OBSERVE

Once again, Luke separates the teaching that Matthew puts together.

vv. 13–14—This passage is the clearest argument possible against universalism, the idea that everyone will eventually get to heaven, only by different routes. The road to eternal life is narrow, and only a few find it. That truth should be both sobering (when we think of lost friends) and thrilling (God has chosen us to be one of the few).

vv. 15–20—Jesus has just said in verses 1–6 that we shouldn't sit in judgment, but here he emphasizes the importance of spiritual discernment. Fruit signifies the results of a person's life. Christians are not judges but "fruit inspectors." If you watch false prophets long enough, you will see that the results of their ministries are not in keeping with Scripture. There may be spectacular results for a short while ("hot house fruit"), but over the long haul their true colors will show. The discerning Christian learns to recognize that it's not a matter of outward appearance (v. 15).

vv. 21–23—This is a difficult passage to understand. Verse 21 seems to suggest that the way to enter the kingdom of heaven is by good deeds—doing the will of the Father. But verse 22 rejects that thesis outright. The false believers had an entire catalogue of good deeds they did which all seem compatible with the Father's will. Apparently it's possible to do impressive things spiritually and still not have a saving relationship with Christ. Verse 23 clarifies the situation. The key to entering heaven is to know Christ and to be known by him. In keeping with the rest of Scripture and to make sense of this entire passage, doing the will of the Father is ultimately to have a personal relationship with the Father through the Son (John 17:3). This passage is even more sobering than verses 13–14 because it suggests that even leaders in the Church (prophets, exorcists, miracle workers) will not find eternal life. Luke's parable (13:24–30) makes it clear that some who see themselves leading the heavenly parade (the "first") won't go there, while some whom the leaders consider cast out (the "last") will be saved.

vv. 24–29—This is the conclusion to the entire Sermon on the Mount. The well-known parable makes it clear that God's Word is a solid foundation for life. Notice that the foolish man is not uninformed. He has heard Christ's words, but "does not put them into practice." Those who are hearers only (James 1:22) build their lives on sand. Jesus' hearers were amazed at the authority of his teaching. The rabbis were fond of "stringing pearls," quoting several rabbis to establish authority for their teaching. Jesus didn't need to quote anyone because he had the Father's authority. We'll see this more clearly when we study John's gospel.

APPLY

v. 20—Where do you see God's fruit in your life?

v. 23—Are you sure that you know Christ and are known by him? If not, invite him into your heart by faith now.

MEMORIZE

Matthew 7:13–14

These are key verses in this age that sees all religions as equally valid.

PRAY

A: Praise the God who knows you through and through and still loves you.

C: Confess the times that you have been foolish and haven't obeyed God's Word.

T: Thank God for his Word, which is a strong foundation.

S: Pray for discernment to see which of the messages you will hear today are truth.

TELL

Share with a Christian friend or your small group your understanding of this passage.

JANUARY 15

THE GENTLE HEALER CAME INTO OUR TOWN TODAY

Ask God to show you how Christ's healing ministry applies to your life today.

Matthew 8:1–17; Mark 1:29–34, 40–45; Luke 4:38–41, 5:12–16, 7:1–10

These healings are grouped together in Matthew, but they are separated in Mark and Luke.

vv. 1–4—Leprosy was the dreaded disease of Jesus' day. The leper had to dwell outside the city, banished from the fellowship of all but other lepers. He had to tear his clothes, bare his head, wear a covering on his upper lip, and shout, "Unclean! Unclean!" any time he was close to healthy people. It didn't contribute to a positive self-image! In the middle ages, whenever a person was discovered with leprosy, the priest preceded the leper into church and read the burial service.

In Jesus' day, they were called "the living dead." Touching a leper was unthinkable for a Jew, but Jesus didn't hesitate when the leper approached him. The reason Jesus sends him to the priest and commands him to tell no one are the same— Christ wanted to do nothing to offend the people he came to reach first, the Jews. Mark tells us that the leper did tell others, and this kept Jesus from being able to enter towns freely. Disobedience to Christ, regardless of the motive, always ends up hampering the work of the kingdom.

vv. 5–13—Centurions commanded one hundred troops. They were the backbone of the Roman army. This is the first of six centurions in the New Testament, and all of them are spoken of positively. The Roman attitude toward slaves was even worse than the attitude of early Americans. Commentator William Barclay quotes Aristotle: "A slave is a living tool, just as a tool is an inanimate slave" (Barclay, *The Gospel of Matthew*, 307). It's obvious, however, that this centurion loved his slave and grieved for his suffering. Centurions knew the importance and power of authority. This soldier knew Jesus had the authority to heal his servant. Christ recognizes the faith implicit in the centurion's statement. The soldier's humility is also impressive.

Augustine wrote, "By owning himself unworthy for Christ to enter his house, he became worthy for Christ to enter his heart" (Augustine, *Sermons*, 1262:1:298). Jesus had just healed a leper who was forced to live outside the covenant community. Here he praises the faith of a Gentile who was totally outside the covenant community, and he contrasts that faith with many "subjects of the kingdom" (Jews) who will be rejected from heaven. It's faith, not church membership, that matters to Christ.

vv. 14–17—Jesus didn't need a big audience to perform his miracles. His touch brings instant healing, and Peter's mother-in-law's gratitude is expressed in glad service. Note that Simon Peter was married, but under the extraordinary circumstances of Christ's call, he left his wife for three years (Matt. 19:27–29). She joined Peter for his further ministry (1 Cor. 9:5). Since the Roman Catholic Church claims that Peter was the first pope, his marriage should call into question whether mandatory celibacy for clergy is biblical. After healing Peter's mother-in-law, Jesus spends an evening healing all who were sick or demon possessed. Matthew again sees it as a fulfillment of prophecy, specifically Isaiah 53:4. All diseases which are healed are done so by our Sovereign God. But does he heal all our diseases, and can we claim that healing, as many do today? We only need to look at the example of Paul, a great man of faith, to see that not all diseases are healed (2 Cor. 12:8–10). But God wants us to pray for healing, and to pray in faith (James 5:15). God's power is still available to heal whenever he wills.

APPLY

vv. 1–3—Do you ever treat people like the Jews treated lepers? How can you be more like Christ?

vv. 11–12—Do you think there will be surprises in heaven? Don't ever count anyone out.

MEMORIZE

Matthew 8:10

This is a reminder that faith is the key to a right relationship with Christ.

PRAY

A: Praise God for his authority over illness.

C: Confess your failure to pray faithfully for others' healing.

T: Thank God for the times you've been healed.

S: Ask for physical and emotional healing for some people who need it.

TELL

Share with someone your theology of healing.

JANUARY 16

THE COST OF DISCIPLESHIP

PRAY

Ask God to show you the cost of following Christ and that he would make you willing to pay the price.

READ

Matthew 8:18–22; Luke 9:57–62

OBSERVE

Matthew emphasizes that Jesus is more than a healer. He's the Lord who calls us to costly obedience.

vv. 18–20—Jesus often sought to escape the crowds, an interesting strategy when we consider the numbers obsession of the contemporary church. He frequently crossed the Sea of Galilee which apparently was a restful journey for him. Matthew identifies Luke's "man" as a "teacher of the law." The scribe sees in Jesus a teacher worth following, but Jesus isn't flattered by the offer from this intellectual. Perhaps he senses that the scribe only views him as another rabbi (Jerome commented that Jesus' response may have been different if the teacher had addressed him as "Lord"). Christ makes it clear that the "wherever" includes a life of homelessness with no promise of a prestigious academy setting. The implication is that the would-be follower decides not to follow. How many contemporary "believers" would follow Jesus if they recognized that the cost of discipleship included deprivation and lack of creature comforts?

vv. 21–22—At first glance, Jesus' response to the second man (who already appears to be a disciple) is hard hearted. Isn't Jesus violating the fifth commandment by prohibiting the man from attending his father's funeral? The answer requires an understanding of first-century idioms. The expression "bury my father" didn't mean that the man's dad had recently died. If he had, the son wouldn't be with Jesus. He would be with the other mourners. The expression meant that the son was expected to fulfill his filial duties until his father's death. The man may have been putting off Christ's call for years. "For Jesus, discipleship is rough going and the world is a place of the walking dead. The world is in mortal need of disciples who will follow Jesus into rough engagement with it. The world is death; discipleship is life" (Bruner, *Matthew: The Christbook*, 317). The third example Luke gives us is a little more difficult, a man who wants to say goodbye to his family (9:61–62). Jesus ruthlessly lays out the demands of discipleship. Perhaps he senses the same sort of equivocation as the second would-be disciple. Jesus teaches that his kingdom comes first, a consistent theme we'll encounter forcefully when we study Matthew 10:34–39.

APPLY

vv. 18–22—Do you have any excuses as to why you can't follow Jesus whole-heartedly?

MEMORIZE

Luke 9:62

This is a statement of radical discipleship

PRAY

A: Praise God that he is uncompromising, demanding our all.

C: Confess specific areas where you have held back from giving him your all.

T: Thank God for the spiritual life you have been given as you follow Christ.

S: Pray for someone you know who has shrunk back from the cost of discipleship. Christ calls them again and again.

TELL

When you share your faith, don't stress how easy it is to be a Christian. The New Testament emphasizes the opposite. Honesty and integrity requires that we present the cost of discipleship.

JANUARY 17

JESUS CALMS THE STORM

PRAY

For the ability to recognize the storms in your life and for the faith to trust Jesus to calm them.

READ

Matthew 8:23–27; Mark 4:35–41; Luke 8:22–25

OBSERVE

Matthew and Luke's accounts are almost identical. Mark gives the most concrete detail to the story.

v. 23—Matthew suggests, and Mark and Luke make it very clear, that it was Jesus who suggested this boat ride. That's significant in light of the events that follow.

v. 24—The Sea of Galilee (which is really a lake) is like a half-filled cup of tea, surrounded by tall hills. It is very easy for winds and storms to come whipping off those hills and create an instant squall. Mark tells us Jesus was asleep on a cushion in the stern. This was the place for a distinguished guest. A carpet was placed on the floor of the boat and a cushion upon the carpet.

vv. 25—Keep in mind that at least four of the disciples were fishermen. Why would they ask a carpenter to help them? Mark indicates that the disciples' exclamation was full of anger as well as fear. They weren't just afraid that they were going to drown, they were upset that Jesus didn't seem concerned. Psalm 127:2b gives an idea of how Jesus was able to sleep in the midst of a storm. He even rested in faith!

v. 26—Fear and faith are mutually exclusive in the Bible. The most frequent command in Scripture is, "Praise the Lord!" The second most frequent is, "Fear not!" (It appears 365 times!) Fear is incompatible with trust in God (2 Tim. 1:7) and love for God (1 John 4:18). Jesus answers their SOS, as he also does for us. Matthew and Luke tell us that he rebuked the wind and the waves. Mark gives his actual words, "Quiet! Be still!" Some claim that this miracle was a coincidence. Storms on the Sea of Galilee often stop as quickly as they start. Why is that explanation unsatisfying?

v. 27—Matthew says that the disciples were amazed. Mark indicates that they were terrified and Luke combines the two. Why is it that this incident makes a deeper impression on the disciples than anything they've seen thus far? Who is it that controls the wind and waves (see Exod. 14:21)? The disciples' fear and their question both indicate that they have a way to go in their understanding of just who Jesus is.

APPLY

v. 26—What are your current fears? How can trusting Christ's sovereignty remove their power and enable you to walk in faith?

MEMORIZE

Mark 4:40

This helps us remember the relationship between fear and faith.

PRAY

A: Praise the God who controls nature.

C: Confess your fear and lack of faith when storms have come in your life.

T: Thank God for peace in turmoil.

S: Pray for someone whose life is full of storms.

TELL

If you're doing this study with others, discuss why this was a miracle and not a coincidence.

JANUARY 18

MY NAME IS LEGION

PRAY

Can the story of demon possession teach you anything? Absolutely! Ask God to show you specific applications.

READ

Mark 5:1–20; Matthew 8:28–34; Luke 8:26–39

OBSERVE

This story presents one of the difficulties in interpreting the Synoptic Gospels. How do you harmonize very similar accounts that include different details? All three gospels place the exorcism directly after the stilling of the storm, so they appear to be describing the same event. But Matthew has two demon-possessed men. Mark and Luke only have one. There are three possible explanations:

1. Matthew is recounting another situation in which Jesus encountered not one but two men. Given the setting that we've already noted, that is highly unlikely, as is the thought that Jesus sacrificed more than one herd of pigs!
2. There may have been two men, but only one became known in the Christian community. Therefore, Mark and Luke ignored him.
3. It's possible that one of the two demon possessed men was more prominent and acted as the spokesman.

I'm inclined to consider a combination of explanations 2 and 3, though no one can say for sure. Let's use Mark's detailed account as our main source.

Mark 5:1—Some manuscripts read, "the region of the Gerasenes," others "Gadarenes," still others "Gergesenes." The only city archeologists know as Gerasa was thirty six miles southeast of the Sea of Galilee. Gadara was only six miles inland and more likely the location of this event. It is a town full of limestone caves, which served as tombs. This is the first time Jesus enters into Gentile territory, a significant factor in the rest of the story.

vv. 2–5—The setting is like a horror movie, complete with a frightening monster. Would you have been afraid to confront someone who lived in a graveyard, screamed constantly, was so insane that he "mangled himself with sharp stones" (the actual Greek), and was so strong that he tore chains apart and broke iron cuffs to smithereens? The fact that Jesus approached the demoniac shows his raw courage, borne of the confidence of One filled with the Spirit. It's interesting that the demoniac is self-destructive. One of the ways Satan always works is to cause people to "mangle (themselves) with sharp stones." Satan hates life and health and is the father of destruction (John 10:10a).

vv. 6–8—The first act of the demoniac is to fall on his knees in front of Jesus, in keeping with James 2:19. His words are both typical and atypical. Like other demon-possessed people, he recognizes exactly who Jesus is, "Son of the Most High God." But unlike others, he tries to reason with Jesus. The expression "What do you want with me?" is a figure of speech which means "Let me alone." Jesus, of course, rebukes the demon in no uncertain terms.

v. 9—Jesus doesn't reason with him. He asks his name. To the Jews, a person's name described his nature (Exod. 3:13–14), and made it possible to interact with and influence him. Jesus was asking the man to confess the kind of evil power which enslaved him. A legion was a Roman regiment of six thousand troops.

vv. 10–13—Although many people have written in recent years about demon possession (Scott Peck's *People of the Lie* is excellent), we still know so little in this area that we can only ask questions and suggest possible answers. Why did the demons ask to be sent into the pigs? Luke 11:24–26 states that a demon wanders endlessly until it finds a body to inhabit. Why did Jesus agree to the demons' request? It may have been an outward sign to the crowd and to the man himself that the demons had, in fact, been expelled. Some suggest that if the owners of the pigs were Jews who sold this forbidden and unclean meat to the Gentiles, this was a way of punishing them as well. Whatever the reason, Christ showed his power to be far greater than a huge assembly of evil forces. The Christian who is walking in the power of the Holy Spirit (like Jesus did) has nothing to fear from "Satan's angels." "The one who is in you (the Holy Spirit) is greater than the one who is in the world (Satan)" (1 John 4:4).

vv. 14–17—The reaction of the herdsmen and townspeople is interesting. Instead of praising God for the miraculous healing of this man who had caused them such grief, they ask Jesus to get out of the city. Their fear of Jesus is understandable (the disciples' reaction is the same when he stills the storm), but their action is not. Perhaps they feared that Jesus would expose their evil like he did with the demoniac. Mark includes a key phrase in verse 16 that Matthew and Luke omit, "and told about the pigs as well." Maybe they valued pigs (and the *denarii* they represented) more than they valued people. Whatever their reason, the sad thing for the Gedarenes is that Jesus answered their request. There is no record of him returning to this region. Don't ask God for something you're not prepared to receive. He may answer your prayer for patience by putting some difficult situations before you!

vv. 18–20—Note the difference in the response of the healed man. Why doesn't Jesus answer his "prayer" positively? Most likely, it was because of the region where he lived. Though Jesus has told Jews he healed to keep quiet about it (Matt. 8:4, Mark 1:44), he tells this Gentile to witness freely. The Decapolis was made up of ten Roman cities. The new man must have had a tremendous ministry.

APPLY

v. 5—Are there any self-destructive patterns in your life like overeating, substance abuse, reckless driving, inability to forgive yourself, thoughts of suicide, etc? With Christ's help, how can you overcome these harmful behaviors?

MEMORIZE

Mark 5:19

Especially concentrate on the part in quotation marks.

PRAY

A: Praise God for his awesome power over evil.

C: Confess any self-destructive patterns.

T: Thank God for the ways he has healed you and others you know.

S: Ask for courage to witness boldly and change harmful patterns.

TELL

"Tell them how much the Lord has done for you, and how he has had mercy on you."

JANUARY 19

THE ROOFTOP CAPER

Ask God to show you how unusual circumstances can be an opportunity for Christian witness.

READ

Mark 2:1–12; Matthew 9:1–8; Luke 5:17–26

OBSERVE

Once again, Matthew is the odd man out, omitting the rooftop caper. Mark and Luke agree that the paralytic's friends had to lower him through the roof in order to get him to Jesus. We'll again follow Mark's fuller account.

Mark 2:1—Jesus' "own town" (Matt. 9:1) was now Capernaum and the house possibly Peter and Andrew's (Mark 1:29).

v. 2—The poem "One Solitary Life" and other verbal portraits of Jesus have pictured him as a lonely mystic who primarily related to individuals. That's not the picture we see in the gospels. Jesus was frequently surrounded by standing-room only crowds, especially in his early ministry. It's ironic that he is nearly deserted at the end of his life. Notice that the primary event was the preaching of the Word, not healing.

vv. 3–4—Barclay writes:

> The roof of a Palestinian house was flat. It was regularly used as a place of rest and quiet, and so usually there was an outside staircase which ascended to it. The

construction of the roof lent itself to what the ingenious four proposed to do. The roof consisted of flat beams laid across from wall to wall, three feet apart. The space in between the beams was filled with brushwood packed tightly with earth. It was the easiest thing in the world to dig out the filling between two of the beams; it did not even damage the house very much, and it was easy to repair the breach again. (Barclay, *The Gospel of Mark*, 39–40)

v. 5—Jesus was always impressed by the kind of faith that refused to be stopped by obstacles. The four men were determined to bring their friend into the presence of Jesus. They were convinced that healing was there. Notice that Jesus saw their faith, not the faith of the crippled man, and responded to it. Our faith can be a real blessing to someone else. Witnessing is not "converting people." It is bringing them before the power and presence of Christ and encouraging them to respond to his love. How interesting that Jesus' first words to the paralytic are "Son, your sins are forgiven." The man came for physical healing and received the more important spiritual healing first. We need to remember that priority when we're praying for healing today. Sometimes, it takes more faith to accept a situation than to be healed. Joni Eareckson Tada wrote, "I was healed of the need to be healed."

vv. 6–7—The dictionary definition of blasphemy is "irreverent use of God's name." The scribes were right to accuse Jesus of blasphemy for claiming to forgive the man's sins if Jesus were only a human teacher, prophet and healer. Only God can forgive sins. If Jesus was not God, he was not good. Rather than being a good teacher, which many humanists accept, Jesus was a blasphemer and a liar. It's impossible to be neutral about Jesus. He doesn't allow it. He demands that we accept him as God-in-the-flesh Savior and Lord or reject him completely (Rev. 3:15–16).

vv. 8–11—Jesus knew exactly what they were thinking. His question was full of irony. The scribes thought it was easy for Jesus to say, *"Your sins are forgiven."* But, in fact, it was easier for him to heal the man. Many people can heal bodies, only One can heal souls. The major function of Christ's miracles was to support his claim to deity.

v. 12—The crowd's reaction is also intriguing. With whom do they connect the healing? Do you think they made the connection between Jesus and God the Father?

APPLY

v. 5—How determined are you to bring your friend(s) face-to-face with Jesus?

MEMORIZE

Mark 2:5

PRAY

A: Praise the healer of bodies and souls.

C: Confess your fear and unwillingness to bring your friends to Jesus.

T: Thank God for the person or persons who faithfully brought you to Christ.

S: Ask God to give you the opportunity to share your faith in Christ with at least one person this week.

TELL

Share how Christ has healed you spiritually with that one person.

JANUARY 20

DR. JESUS, THE BRIDEGROOM

PRAY

Only God can help us to see that we are "more sinful than we ever imagined, yet more loved than we could ever hope!"

—Tim Keller

READ

Matthew 9:9–17; Mark 2:13–22; Luke 5:27–39

OBSERVE

The Synoptic Gospel accounts are practically identical except for Luke's addition that old wine is better.

vv. 9–13—Mark and Luke identify the tax collector as Levi, the son of Alphaeus. Matthew calls himself by his Christian name, which is a variation of the word "disciple." It was the name bestowed on him by Jesus. Matthew had likely seen Jesus previously and even known him in order to respond immediately to his command, "Follow me." He walked away from a lucrative job. Tax collectors (called "publicans" by the Romans) were agents of the imperial government. They paid what amounts to a licensing fee to Rome and then they were permitted to extort as much money as they could from the populace, using Roman soldiers as enforcers. As Jewish turncoats and rip-off artists, they were universally despised.

Christ's call of Matthew shows that he was not willing to "give the people what they want" in his effort to reach them. If he were totally "seeker friendly," he would never have chosen Matthew as a disciple. The seekers who did come to him on this occasion were other tax collectors and notorious sinners. It says a lot about Jesus' warmth and acceptance that sinful people felt comfortable around him. He uses the dinner at Matthew's house as a teaching opportunity. The separatistic Pharisees were the logical people to question Christ's fellowship with tax collectors and other sinners.

Jesus quotes a popular proverb, "It is not the healthy that need a doctor but the sick." We need to remember that today, for the Church is called to be a hospital for sinners, not a museum for saints. Jesus quotes Hosea 6:6, which was one of his favorite passages. The word "righteous" should probably be in quotes, for Jesus surely spoke that last phrase with profound irony. It's those who think they are righteous in themselves who are sick. Only those who recognize and admit that they are sick sinners can be healed.

vv. 14–15—The Pharisees made weekly fasting part of their addition to the law of Moses. The only fast specified in the Old Testament law was on the Day of Atonement. John the Baptist's disciples, several of whom had joined Jesus' band, kept the ceremonial law carefully. Their fasting, in keeping with their leader's teaching (Matt. 3:8), was probably for purification as an indication of their repentance. Fasting is usually a sign of sorrow in the Bible. When the Israelites lost a battle, national fasting was in order. Here, Jesus uses a mini-parable that everyone can understand.

Who is happier than a bridegroom on his wedding day? At a time of joy, why fast? The image of Christ as the bridegroom and the Church as his bride is a rich New Testament analogy. After discussing the joy that the bridegroom brings, Jesus immediately adds a somber note. There will be plenty of time for fasting when he is gone. Even at this early stage of his ministry, Jesus was aware of his impending death. There is still a controversy today between whether joy or sorrow should be the characteristic attitude of a Christian.

One group—represented by people like Ron Sider, author of *Rich Christians in an Age of Hunger*—would stress the second half of verse 15. Until the Second Coming, Christians should be suffering servants identifying with the poor and disenfranchised and sharing their struggle.

The other group—the Norman Vincent Peale/Robert Schuller school—would emphasize the first half of the verse. Christians should be positive and happy at all times since the bridegroom is still with us through the power of the Holy Spirit.

Both are extremes. Christians should be led by the Spirit so that our spirits fit the situation. Paul says, *"Rejoice with those who rejoice, mourn with those who mourn"* (Rom. 12:15). We are to be joyful at all times (Phil. 4:4), but that joy is a deep-seated assurance of God's grace, not always a surface smile.

vv. 16–17—Christ's coming to earth instituted the New Covenant (Testament) with God. The first thing he said publicly was, *"Repent, for the kingdom of heaven is near"* (Matt. 4:17). At other times, he declared that the kingdom was "at hand" and "in your midst." Christ is the great dividing point of history (BC, before Christ and AD, *anno Domini*, in the year of our Lord). He fulfilled the law in himself (Matt. 5:17). The ceremonial law no longer reigns. He does. He couldn't be just another rabbi or prophet. He is the New Thing (see Isa. 43:18–19). Jesus couldn't be just a patch on the blue jeans of Judaism—the patch would be stronger than the cloth and tear it apart.

In the time of Martin Luther, it was impossible to patch up the abuses of the Roman Catholic Church. The time for Reformation had come. Some are asking the same question today. God is bringing revival to his world, but can the wineskins of the Church contain the new wine? When wineskins grow old, they become hard and unyielding. New wine bubbles and releases pressure, and that can burst old skins. The old wineskin of Judaism could not contain the new wine of Christianity. *The Problem of Wineskins* is a a thought-provoking book by Howard Snyder. It addresses this question. Luke's addition about the quality of old wine (Luke 5:39) warns us not to be too hasty to throw out quality institutions. It's possible, however, that Luke's statement is ironic, that Jesus is trying to explain why the Pharisees won't try his new way.

APPLY

v. 11—Do you have any non-Christian friends whom you eat meals with? Ask God to lead you to those relationships or, if you already have them, to bless them.

v. 17—Can you think of any old wineskins that the Church should discard in order to receive the new wine of the Spirit?

MEMORIZE

Matthew 9:12

This is a reason to reach out to "sinners."

PRAY

A: Praise the Great Physician, who is our bridegroom, perfecting his bride.

C: Confess that you, as the bride of Christ, need to have your dress cleaned.

T: Thank him for his mercy, joy, and the new wine of the Spirit.

S: Pray for someone you know who is self-righteous. Ask God to show him or her that they are a sinner in need of grace. Is that someone you?

TELL

When you get the opportunity, share that message sensitively with your self-righteous friend.

JANUARY 21

A SICK WOMAN AND A DEAD GIRL

PRAY

Ask that the Miracle Worker would do wondrous things in and through you.

READ

Matthew 9:18–26; Mark 5:21–43; Luke 8:40–56

OBSERVE

A pattern is emerging. Mark and Luke tend to report miraculous healings in more depth and detail than Matthew. It's likely that Jesus' healing ministry was not as important to Matthew in establishing his claim to being the Messiah. We will again follow Mark's account which provides the most information.

Mark 5:21–25—As we noted previously, large crowds seemed to wait for Jesus. In the crowd on the side of the lake near Capernaum was a man named Jairus. The ruler of a synagogue was one of the most respected men in the Jewish community. He was the president of the board of elders who were responsible for the good conduct of worship services. Jairus must have heard a lot of criticism of Jesus from the other elders. But in his great moment of need, he saw beyond their petty jealousy and humbled himself at the Lord's feet. We can imagine his friends observing the scene and shaking their heads. Nowhere in the gospels does Jesus deny a request made in faith.

vv. 25–26—Mark interrupts the story of Jairus' daughter to insert a beautiful story within the story. This woman would have been ceremonially unclean for twelve years and forbidden ordinary social contacts, including worship in the temple.

Mark makes it plain that earthly physicians could do nothing to heal her. Notice that Luke, a medical doctor, softens Mark's language (Luke 8:43).

vv. 27–29—Hearing about Jesus isn't enough. Like the woman, we must act upon what we've heard. Her faith is great because she believed that Jesus could heal her with so little contact. The only one with greater faith in Christ's healing power was the centurion (Day 15) who tells Jesus, *"But just say the word and my servant will be healed."* Like the centurion, her faith is rewarded with an instant healing.

v. 30—This verse is revealing because it shows that Jesus was conscious of the flow of healing power from himself to the sick. Healing was not easy for Christ. It took something out of him. Perhaps this is why Jesus always retreated for times of prayer and recuperation after times of healing.

vv. 31–32—The disciples still had not figured Jesus out. They think his question is unreasonable. They are insensitive to the situation, and Jesus ignores them.

vv. 33–34—Jesus' question was compelling to the one who was healed. It was not enough for her to believe in her heart. She had to confess with her mouth (Rom. 10:9). In addition to her ceremonial uncleanness, another reason she comes in fear and trembling is that it was not considered proper for a woman to speak in public. It would have been especially risky to approach a crowd in that culture. Jesus affirms her and confirms the healing and adds a key benediction: *"Go in peace."* As we've seen, this rich word conveys physical, mental, emotional, and spiritual wholeness. She needed healing in all four areas.

vv. 35–36—Imagine being Jairus in this situation. Knowing how sick his daughter was, he must have felt impatience at the delay and then anger when the report comes that his daughter is dead. As we saw previously, Jesus contrasts fear and faith.

v. 37—This was the first appearance of Jesus' inner circle of Peter, James, and John. Jesus called them to his side at key times in his ministry. Two of the gospels come from these key witnesses. Peter is generally acknowledged as the source for the Gospel of Mark. The third was an early martyr (Acts 12:2).

vv. 38–40—The louder the weeping and wailing, the more important the dead person. It was customary even to hire mourners. Jesus' statement to the mourners is profound. A Near Eastern figure of speech was to say that a dead person had "fallen asleep" (see John 11:11). But in this case, it was like sleeping since Jesus knew that he was going to resuscitate the dead girl. The mourners' laughter may be ridicule, or it may be insincerity. In either case, their unbelief excluded them from seeing an amazing thing—the Lord of nature shows himself to be the Lord of life and death.

vv. 41–43—*"Talitha koum"* is a command in the Aramaic language; *talitha* is a term of endearment for a little girl, much like *abba* (daddy) for a father. Twelve was a special age to Jewish girls as well as boys. At this age, a girl became a woman and was able to marry. Jesus is back in Jewish territory, thus the warning against spreading the news. Perhaps he was concerned for the girl also. People might treat her as a freak if they knew she had been raised from the dead. Luke 8:55, "Her spirit returned," reinforces the crowd's impression that she was really dead, not in a coma. Eating food was an indication of health and life (see Luke 24:41–43).

APPLY

v. 28—Is there something in your life or the life of someone you know that needs Jesus' touch? Bring them to him.

MEMORIZE

Mark 5:36

Notice especially the last part of the verse.

PRAY

A: Praise the God who is sovereign over life and death.

C: Confess the times when you have embraced fear rather than faith.

T: Thank God for his tender love toward old ladies, children, and you.

S: Ask God for the same life-changing power that flowed through Jesus (Rom. 8:11).

TELL

Share with someone an area in your life in which you are experiencing God's peace.

JANUARY 22

THE HARVEST IS PLENTIFUL, BUT THE WORKERS ARE FEW

PRAY

Ask God to show you the harvest field he has for you.

READ

Matthew 9:27–38

OBSERVE

There are similarities between the healing of these two blind men and the healing of Bartimaeus (Mark 10:46–52), but significant enough differences in Jesus' words to them that they are probably separate accounts. The rest of the passage is unique to Matthew.

vv. 27–31—The two blind men knew that Jesus was a Son of David, which was a primary requirement for the Messiah. The most intriguing aspect of Jesus' healing ministry was that he treated each person differently. Here, he meets the blind men indoors, apart from the crowds. Those who called Jesus "Son of David," typically knew him only from a distance. It was a popular title for the crowds (Matt. 15:22, 20:30–31; Mark 10:47, 12:35–37). Jesus seems to be testing the sincerity of their faith in a face-to-face encounter. Sooner or later, each of us must come face to face with Jesus and encounter him alone. Jesus again ties healing to faith and repeats the warning to keep the incident quiet, which the formerly blind men ignore (as did others).

vv. 32–34—This is the first mention of someone who was mute and demon-possessed. Previously, the demonized people had all recognized Jesus and spoke out in fear. After Jesus heals the formerly mute man, the interesting speakers are the crowd and the Pharisees. The crowd recognizes that Jesus was a unique healer just as they had previously praised him as a unique teacher (Matt. 7:28–29). The Pharisees make their first accusation that Jesus cast out demons by the power of the demonic. Christ will answer that slander in chapter 12 (Day 28).

vv. 35–38—Christ's preaching, teaching, and healing ministry is summarized in verse 35. In verse 36, we see his heart of compassion. Jesus saw the crowds as lost without a leader, as sheep without a shepherd. What he says in 37–38 is just as true today. Opportunities for ministry are abundant. There are profound needs all over the world. Most of all, billions of people have never heard the Gospel presented in a clear way in their language.

APPLY

v. 38—Where is your harvest field, and are you willing to be a worker? There are people you know who have never heard an intelligent presentation of the claims of Christ.

MEMORIZE

Matthew 9:37–38

PRAY

A: Praise God that he is working all over the world.

C: Confess your fear and reluctance to share your faith.

T: Thank God for those who shared the Gospel with you.

S: Ask the Lord of the harvest to send workers to the field.

TELL

Are you praying for those around you who don't know Christ? Look for an opportunity today to tell one of them about what Christ has done for you.

JANUARY 23

THE DISCIPLES BECOME APOSTLES

PRAY

Ask that God would make you both a disciple and an apostle today.

READ

Matthew 10:1–23; Mark 3:13–19, 6:7–3; Luke 6:12–16, 9:1–6, 10:1–11

OBSERVE

Matthew consolidates all of the passages dealing with the first ministry journey of the twelve. Mark and Luke separate the listing of the disciples with the ministry. Luke includes the sending out of seventy-two people who were part of the larger group of people who accompanied Jesus from time to time. Their experience was very similar to that of the twelve.

v. 1—All of a disciple's authority and power are a gift from Jesus.

vv. 2–4—This is one of those list-of-names passages which the casual reader might pass over quickly. But there are rich insights to be found by examining the twelve men Jesus chose.

Brothers Peter and Andrew were fishermen, as were James and John, the "Sons of Thunder." Peter figures prominently in the gospels as the dominant disciple. His brother Andrew is featured in John's gospel as the one who brings Peter to Jesus (John 1:40–42). James and John, along with Peter, formed Jesus' inner circle. At least one stormy argument revolved around their mother's ambition for these brothers to be top dogs in Christ's kingdom (Matt. 20:20–28). As we noted earlier,

James was the first disciple to be a martyr (Acts 12:2). John is also known as "the disciple whom Jesus loved" in his gospel.

Philip appears infrequently by himself in the gospels, most significantly when he asks Jesus a key question in John 14:8. Bartholomew, "Son of Talmai," has traditionally been identified by his other name, Nathaniel, the first person to call Jesus Son of God (John 1:49).

Thomas was a twin (sometimes he was known as "Didymus," the Greek word for twin). His real first name was Judas, a very common Jewish name. Thomas has gone down in history as a doubter, but once he was convinced, he would say, "My Lord and my God!" (John 20:28) and follow Jesus to his death.

Matthew (Levi) has already been identified (Day 20). His name means, "gift," and just as his new life was a gift, he must have been a gift to the disciple band as well.

James, the son of Alphaeus, is also called "James the younger" in Mark 15:40. He has also been identified as Cleopas, one of the disciples surprised on the Emmaus road (Luke 24:18) by the risen Lord.

Thaddeus ("big chest") is also called Lebbeus ("big hearted") in some of the manuscripts of Mark. He must have been a brave and affectionate man.

Simon the Zealot was part of a revolutionary party whose express aim was to overthrow the Romans.

Judas Iscariot, who betrayed Jesus, was also most likely a revolutionary. Some think that Iscariot means, "man of Kerioth," a town south of Galilee. But the prefix *ish* ("man" in Hebrew) was not typically used at the time of Christ. Another explanation is that Iscariot comes from *sikariotes* which meant "dagger bearer." Judas could have been one of the Sikariotes who held a knife under his cloak waiting to plunge it between the third and fourth rib of a Roman soldier. Betrayal would have been nothing new to him. Some suggest that Judas joined up with Jesus to start a revolution and became disillusioned when Jesus chose the path of peace. His betrayal might have been an attempt to force Jesus' hand.

The disciples were a fascinating collection. At least one revolutionary lived side-by-side with a former Roman employee. Impulsive men like "Rocky" (Peter) and the Sons of Thunder walked the same paths as unemotional and quiet men. A big-hearted disciple sought to understand a thief who resented an act of mercy (John 12:5–6). Christ's closest followers represent a supreme example of unity in diversity, the model for the New Testament church. They were twelve common men, no theologians, yet they turned the world upside down for Christ. Verse 2 is the first time they are called "apostles," which means, "those who are sent out." The word "disciple" means "learner."

vv. 5–8—It's clear that the focus of Jesus' ministry at the beginning were his kinsmen, the Jews. They were also the disciples' first evangelistic targets. Their message was to be the same one Jesus announced originally (Mat. 4:17). Jesus also gave them the authority and power to heal. Their ministry was to be free of charge. The job of the Church is to continue the earthly ministry of Jesus Christ.

vv. 9–10—The disciples were to travel light and depend on the generosity of others for their needs.

vv. 11–15—They were also to depend on the hospitality of others for their lodging. The blessing of peace from the disciples would be significant, given the spiritual authority Jesus committed to them. However, Christ warns them to expect rejection. This is an important corrective to our success-obsessed churches. God will judge those who reject his message. Sodom and Gomorrah were destroyed for rejecting God's law, but it will be even worse for those who reject the Gospel.

vv. 16–20—Christ's apostles should expect active opposition as well as rejection. Sheep cannot be careless in the presence of wolves. Believers are to be innocent where doing evil is concerned but wise in understanding it. Christ already blessed persecution for his sake in the Beatitudes (Matt. 5:10–12). Here he promises his followers that they'll be given the right thing to say when they are brought before the authorities. Verse 20 is the first mention of the Holy Spirit in Matthew since Christ's baptism.

vv. 21–23—These verses are difficult to understand. It seems to many commentators that Jesus moves beyond this initial missionary assignment of the apostles to talk about the end times. The language of verses 21–22 is similar to the Olivet Discourse in Matthew 24. Verse 23 is particularly difficult to interpret. Calvin thought that Jesus was referring to his coming to the apostles' aid when they were in desperate circumstances (Calvin, *A Harmony of the Gospels*, vol. I, 302). Others suggest that Jesus was emphasizing that the mission to the Jews should continue until he returns to the earth. In any case, Jesus was encouraging his missionaries not to be foolish and remain in a place where they are to be persecuted. It's acceptable to him to care for our safety.

APPLY

v. 16—What does this command mean to your current situation?

vv. 19–20—Don't be afraid to share your faith. The Holy Spirit will give you the right words, even when you feel uncomfortable!

MEMORIZE

Matthew 10:16

This is Christ's wise advice.

PRAY

A: Praise the God who calls, sends, and judges.

C: Confess that you have been reluctant to leave your comfort zone for the cause of Christ.

T: Thank God for the promise that the Holy Spirit will speak through you when you get into tough situations.

S: Ask God for courage to stand up to persecution, which will come if you are faithful.

TELL

Discuss with a Christian friend or group what kind of persecution you are likely to experience today for the sake of Christ.

JANUARY 24

RADICAL DISCIPLESHIP

PRAY

Ask God to give you understanding on how to apply these "hard sayings" to your life.

READ

Matthew 10:24–11:1; Luke 12:1–12, Luke 14:25–27

OBSERVE

Luke's account is a shortened version of Matthew's with some minor differences.

vv. 24–25—Christ's message here is one he repeats often. His servants should expect persecution just as he was persecuted. Beelzebub, "Lord of the Flies," was a Canaanite deity, part of the Baal cult.

vv. 26–31—Jesus addresses our fear of persecution by reminding us that this life isn't what ultimately matters. In the judgment, everything will be disclosed, including evil words and deeds. If we have an eternal perspective, we should fear God, who controls our eternal destiny, rather than people who can only affect our body. When facing persecution, we must remember that God will never abandon us. Nothing occurs apart from his will, and he is in control of even the smallest details of our lives. Complaining about our circumstances or fearing other people both reveal a lack of faith.

vv. 32–33—These verses need to be understood in context. Jesus is not teaching salvation by witnessing. He's already told us that many who prophesied in his name will be lost (Matt. 7:22–23). Instead, he is stressing the seriousness of being steadfast. The person who caves in during persecution and denies Jesus is a person whose faith is suspect. The early church generally followed this distinction and usually refused to readmit people who had denied Christ in order to save their skin.

vv. 34–39—This is one of the most difficult passages in all of Scripture to interpret. We've got to be careful to understand it in light of all that the Scriptures teach but not to dismiss its strong message. Jesus elsewhere says that he did come to bring peace to those who trust in him (John 14:27). But the emphasis in this passage is that faith in Christ can divide people, even families. In that sense, Jesus brought a sword.

In a Bible study, a woman once commented on verse 37: "There's a passage that will never be preached on Mother's Day." I took up her challenge and stressed in the sermon that anything or anyone whom we place ahead of Christ is an idol. God hates idol worship; it violates the First Commandment. Furthermore, loving our parents or children more than Christ lays upon them a burden that they cannot bear. They were never meant to meet our needs the way Jesus can. Luke 14:26 sounds even harsher to our Western ears. We are commanded by Jesus to *hate* our parents. The Greek word can be translated "love less." It helps to know that we are also to hate our own lives, in comparison to the love we have for Jesus Christ. Jesus says that those who love family more than they love him are not worthy of him. Again, we need to understand that statement in the context of all of Scripture. None of us is worthy of Christ. We are lost in sin. We don't make ourselves worthy by loving our parents less or even by taking up the cross. Jesus alone makes us worthy.

Luther wrote, "It is not because I am worthy that Christ died for me, but because Christ died for me, I am worthy." In this passage, being worthy is being faithful to Christ, consistent with our profession of him as Lord.

John Adams, the second President of the United States, defines "worthy" in this sense in a letter he wrote to his grandchildren:

> Have you considered the meaning of the word "worthy"? Weigh it well…. I had rather you should be worthy possessors of one thousand pounds honestly acquired by your own labor and industry, than of ten millions by banks and tricks. I should rather you be worthy shoemakers than secretaries of states or treasure acquired by libels in newspapers. I had rather you should be worthy makers of brooms and baskets than unworthy presidents of the United States procured by intrigue, factious slander and corruption. (McCullough, *John Adams*, 608–609)

The cross represents suffering, and Christians must not avoid it. We are not to pursue suffering for its own sake—this is masochism—but the reality is that suffering will always come to us. Verse 39 expresses the wonderful paradox of the Christian life. Whoever tries to protect his life and control it will discover that he is not in control and will, in fact, be lost. Those who surrender their lives to Christ and follow him will find abundant life.

vv. 40–42—Another consistent principle in the gospels is Christ's profound identification with his followers: *"Whatever you did for one of the least of these brothers of mine,
you did for me"* (Matt. 25:40). The way people treat Christ's representatives reveals
their attitude toward him. Jesus promises to reward those hospitable and generous
people. Even the smallest act of kindness (a cup of cold water) will be noticed. The
New Testament doesn't ignore or devalue the rewards for following Christ.
Instead, the promise of eternal reward is frequently presented to motivate us to
faithfulness.

Matt. 11:1—It's clear that these "hard sayings" were meant for Jesus' disciples.
The crowds were not ready then, and they certainly aren't ready now, to hear and
understand this radical teaching—at least not without much interpretation.

APPLY

vv. 26–27—Remember that everything will be disclosed in the final judgment. Are
there some things that you should be disclosing (through confession) to the Lord
right now?

vv. 29–30—Never forget that Jesus cares about you individually and intimately.

vv. 30–31—God knows everything about you and still loves you completely.
Rejoice!

v. 39—How can you lose your life for Christ's sake today?

MEMORIZE

Matthew 10:39

This is a great verse to guide the direction of your life.

PRAY

A: Praise God for his sovereign care.

C: Confess that you have often put people and things before Christ.

T: Thank God for his mercy and new beginnings.

S: Pray that missionaries you know would be received graciously.

TELL

Discuss with a Christian friend or small group the radical message of Matthew
10:32–39.

JANUARY 25

JOHN THE BAPTIST'S LAST QUESTION AND JESUS' ANSWER

PRAY

Pray that God would reassure you in your doubts, just as Jesus reassured John.

READ

Matthew 11:2–19; Luke 7:18–35, 16:16

OBSERVE

The accounts in Matthew and Luke are almost identical.

vv. 2–3—John had been imprisoned at the beginning of Jesus' ministry (Matt. 4:12). Apparently, he languished there for quite some time and must have been discouraged and even depressed. No doubt, the Accuser was working overtime in John's mind, causing him to question whether the cause he promoted was worth the imprisonment and death he faced. We shouldn't judge John too harshly. His question may have been more of an expression of his need for reassurance than of his doubts about Jesus. "The one who was to come" was another way of saying "the Messiah." John wanted to be sure that Jesus was the real deal, the true Messiah promised to Israel. Then his life and death would have been worthwhile.

vv. 4–6—Jesus gives a succinct summary to John's disciples as a way of encouraging John the Baptist. Faith comes from seeing Christ's works (chapters 8, 9) and hearing his words (chapters 5–7, 10). These are the same things people need to encounter today. Christ's personal message in verse 6 is touching. He's saying in effect, "Hang in there, John; keep believing in me, and you will be blessed."

vv. 7–19—After preaching a mini-sermon to John, Jesus preaches a sermon about him. It's a model of effective preaching. Jesus introduces his message by beginning with the people's experience. They all knew John and had gone out to the desert to see him. Jesus introduces Scripture, telling the people that they had gone to see a prophet, in fact *the* prophet spoken of in Malachi 3:1, the one who prepares the way for the Messiah. Jesus explains that Scripture in verses 11–15. John was the greatest prophet. He fulfilled the role that the Jews expected—"the Elijah who was to come." They believed that an Elijah-like prophet (if not the first great prophet himself) would precede the coming of the Messiah. Jesus makes a radical, key distinction. John was the greatest of those "born of women," but he who is least in the kingdom of heaven is greater than John. Those in the kingdom are those who are not just born of women, but those who have been born again (John 3:5–6).

Verse 12 is a difficult verse to understand. Everyone agrees about the first part of the verse. Jesus is setting the context, "From the days of John the Baptist until now...." It's the rest of the verse that is the problem. The NIV translates the middle of the verse as "the kingdom of heaven has been forcefully advancing." The verb translated "forcefully advancing" (in the middle voice) can also be rendered in the passive voice, "suffers violence." Likewise, the last part of the verse can be translated, "and forceful men lay hold of it" or "violent men are trying to wipe it out." The Greek equally allows either interpretation.

This is a time when the first rule of biblical interpretation—the analogy of faith—is very important. The analogy of faith teaches that Scripture is best interpreted by other Scripture. When there is an unclear verse or passage, let a more obvious verse or passage make its meaning clear. Luke 16:16 is much clearer than Matthew 11:12. Luke's verse makes it clear that Jesus is saying that people must hold onto the Gospel forcefully. The world is evil and will do everything it can to snatch us away from the Lord. Christians must be warriors who hold fast to the faith once delivered to the saints. John was that kind of warrior. The last part of Jesus' sermon applies the Scripture to his listeners. He compares his generation to a group of negative couch potatoes, who won't become involved but love to criticize. They condemned John for being an ascetic and condemned Jesus for being a guy who loved parties and people. The last phrase, *"But wisdom is proved right by her actions"* is very similar to Jesus' earlier teaching, *"by their fruit you will recognize them"* (Matt. 7:20).

APPLY

vv. 4–6—What works and words can you offer the Lord in order for you to continue his earthly ministry?

v. 16—Are you too much of a spectator? Get moving!

MEMORIZE

Matthew 11:4–6

This is an ambitious task, but Jesus' reply to John is worth memorizing.

PRAY

A: Praise Jesus that he is kind and patient.

C: Confess that you, like John, have sometimes allowed your doubts to have too much influence in your thinking.

T: Thank the Lord that he lived an abundant life and wants you to as well.

S: Pray for someone who is on the sideline judging Christianity rather than wrestling with Christ's claims.

TELL

The interpretation provided for verse 12 is by no means the only one possible. If you are doing this study with a small group, discuss other possible interpretations of this difficult verse.

JANUARY 26

A CONDEMNATION AND AN INVITATION

PRAY

Ask God to show you complementary aspects of his nature today—that he is both loving and just.

READ

Matthew 11:20–30; Luke 10:12–15, 21–22

OBSERVE

The account in Matthew is nearly identical to the verses in Luke.

vv. 20–24—Capernaum sits on the northwest shore of the Sea of Galilee, and it was the center of Jesus' ministry. Bethsaida, "house of nets," was the name given to two towns in Galilee. One was on the western side of the lake, the other on the eastern. The western town was also known as "Bethsaida of Galilee" and was the hometown of Peter, Andrew, and Philip (John 1:44). Bethsaida on the east was the place where Jesus healed a blind man with his "second touch" (Mark 8:22), and it was also where Jesus fed the 5,000 (Luke 9:10). Korazin (also spelled Chorazin in some translations) was about two miles from Capernaum. The gospels don't mention any specific miracles that were performed there. Perhaps those are some of the many stories about Jesus that didn't get written down (John 21:25). The word Jesus uses for miracles here is *dunameis*, from which we get "dynamite." His works were full of power and meant to turn people's attention and hearts toward God in repentance. Tyre and Sidon were pagan cities that were once beautiful but now lie in ruin. The major prophets spoke against these coastal cities (Isa. 23, Jer. 25:22, Ezek. 26–28) for their wickedness and cruel treatment of Israel.

Ezekiel's prophecy is the most amazing. He said that the great city of Tyre, which shone in splendor (28:7) would be scraped down to bare rock (26:4) and never be rebuilt (26:19–21). If you were to go to the ancient city of Tyre today, you would find it a place where fishermen spread their nets on barren rock (26:5), an amazing fulfillment of prophecy.

Sodom (usually linked with her sister city Gomorrah) was a place of immorality and evil. Angels blinded the men of Sodom who wanted to have sex with them (while they were guests of Lot), and then God destroyed Sodom and Gomorrah by raining down burning sulfur from heaven. Lot and his family were spared, though Mrs. Lot didn't learn a lot from the experience (Gen. 19:26).

Christ's point is that even these wicked cities would have repented if they had seen what the people of Bethsaida, Korazin, and Capernaum witnessed through Jesus' miracles. There is no evidence that these cities persecuted or rejected Christ. They simply didn't respond. William Barclay comments:

> The sin of Chorazin, of Bethsaida, and of Capernaum was the sin of doing nothing. Many a man's defence is: "But I never did anything." That defence may be in fact his condemnation. (Barclay, *The Gospel of Matthew, Vol. II*, 13)

Billy Graham once commented that if God does not judge sinful America, he will have to apologize to Sodom and Gomorrah!

vv. 25–30—Immediately after considering those who have not responded, Jesus addresses those who have. It was not the proud intellectuals who embraced Jesus but those with child-like faith and little children themselves. This was according to the Father's pleasure. It's hard to avoid the strong message of election in verses 26–27—that God (Christ) chooses those who are to be saved. Verses 28–30 are some of the most familiar words of Jesus. Even though Jesus decides to whom the Father will be revealed, the invitation is still issued to all, and those who are called must respond. The essential call to discipleship is, "Come to me." Apart from Jesus, we are burdened and weary with the grind of life. With him, there is rest and refreshment. For oxen to work properly in a yoke, the driver of the plow must match up animals of similar strength. The picture here is that the immeasurably strong Jesus Christ adapts to our weakness and pulls with us at a speed we can handle. He is gentle (Greek *praus*, "meek," Matt. 5:5), and his strength is under control.

APPLY

vv. 21–24—It's important to recognize that we are responsible for the truth that we have been given.

v. 28—What burdens are you carrying? Give them to the Lord, and receive his rest.

MEMORIZE

Learn as much of Matthew 11:28–30 as you can. Even one of these verses will encourage you.

PRAY

A: Praise the Son, who judges, chooses, and gives rest.

C: Confess the burdens that you haven't surrendered to the Lord.

T: Thank God for revealing his truth.

S: Ask God for rest for your soul in a troubled area.

TELL

Share with someone why you believe that God must be both just and merciful.

JANUARY 27

THE LORD OF THE SABBATH

Ask God to show you clearly how he wants you to observe the Sabbath.

READ

Matthew 12:1–21; Mark 2:23–3:12; Luke 6:1–11

OBSERVE

The accounts in the three gospels are very similar, but each gives a little different emphasis depending on the purposes of the gospel writer.

vv. 1–8—The conflict evident in these verses is the clash between law and grace, legalism and mercy. The Pharisees were the masters of rigid application of the Old Testament law, forgetting both the spirit of the law and its deeper spiritual purpose. The Fourth Commandment prohibits work on the Sabbath, but the Mishnah (rabbinical commentary on the law) went well beyond Scripture to detail what constitutes work. The Pharisees, who put the Mishnah on par with Scripture, added so many man-made laws to the Fourth Commandment that it was stifling. A person couldn't even spit on the Sabbath because they considered that "digging a furrow."

Jesus proves to them from Scripture that God did not intend the Fourth Commandment to be a millstone around the neck of his people. In 1 Samuel 21:1–6, David and his companions went into the temple and ate the shewbread when they were hungry. The great priest Samuel does not criticize David or the priest who gave him the bread.

Jesus also states that the temple priests are considered exempt from the Sabbath legislation as they carry out their duties. And Jesus is far greater than any priest or even the temple itself, a bold claim to make before the Jews who revered the temple. Jesus quotes once again his favorite Old Testament text, Hosea 6:6, *"I desire mercy, not sacrifice."* That was precisely the problem of the Pharisees (and other legalists). They desired sacrifice rather than mercy, as the next story will make abundantly clear.

Verse 8 establishes the overarching principle—the Son of God is the one who gives the correct interpretation of the Old Testament law. Jesus is Lord of the Sabbath as he is Lord of all of life. Though the Sabbath is to be a day of rest, it is not to overrule mercy to the hungry or needy.

Throughout history, Christians have understood Jesus' words to mean that works of necessity and mercy are permissible on the Sabbath. Where contemporary Christians disagree is over the meaning of rest. Does keeping the Sabbath preclude any form of recreation? This issue is certainly not clear from Scripture.

vv. 9–13—As so often happens in the gospels, a visual illustration of the principle Jesus has just articulated is presented. The Pharisees are already angry that Jesus has superseded their interpretation of the Sabbath, so they look for a test case with which to accuse him. Jesus zeroes in on their double standard in verses 11–12. The Pharisees were wealthy businessmen who loved money (Luke 16:14). They would go into a pit to rescue a sheep that represented a monetary investment, yet they resented Jesus healing a man. How hypocritical!

Jesus shows his mercy by healing the man, and the Pharisees show their coldheartedness by using that mercy as a nail in Jesus' coffin. This is the first indication in Matthew that they were plotting to kill him. Mark 3:5–6 adds that Jesus was angry and deeply distressed at their stubborn hearts. This is a perfect example of righteous anger. It's also instructive that Mark, who most presents Christ's humanity, records his anger. Mark also tells us that the Pharisees teamed up with the Herodians—their sworn enemies politically—to get rid of Jesus.

vv. 15–21—As we might expect, given Matthew's purpose of establishing Jesus as the Messiah promised in the Old Testament, Christ's healing ministry and mercy are shown to be a fulfillment of Isaiah 42:1–4, which the Jews recognized as a Messianic prophesy. What a beautiful description of the Messiah! He proclaims justice to the nations, justice that can only be found in a right relationship with him. His justice will eventually triumph, even though it sometimes looks like evil is getting the upper hand. He is gentle and will not break the bruised person or snuff out his faltering faith. He alone is the hope of all nations!

APPLY

v. 8—How does Jesus want you to celebrate his day of rest?

MEMORIZE

Matthew 12:8

Apply this to your life.

PRAY

A: Praise God that he is merciful and gentle.

C: Most contemporary Christians aren't guilty of legalism regarding the Sabbath, but failure to rest—how about you?

T: Thank God for the hope you have in Christ.

S: Pray for a "bruised reed" or "smoldering wick" whom you know.

TELL

Discuss with a Christian friend or small group what your practice of the Sabbath should be.

JANUARY 28

JESUS AND THE KINGDOM OF EVIL

PRAY

Ask God to give you a balanced, biblical perspective on evil.

READ

Matthew 12:22–45; Mark 3:20–30; Luke 11:14–32

OBSERVE

Matthew's account is the most complete. Mark includes Jesus' family among those who were saying that he was not in his right mind. Luke adds a woman who exclaims that Jesus' mother was blessed.

vv. 22–23—The common people draw the correct conclusion from Jesus' wonder-working ministry: *"Could this be the Son of David?"* (the Messiah). Jesus was not opposed to people believing in him as a result of his miracles (John 14:11). He only said that it was *more* blessed to believe without visual evidence (John 20:29).

v. 24—It's the religious professionals who attribute the wrong source and the wrong motives to Jesus. Beelzebub, the Lord of the flies and the prince of demons, was the evil equivalent of Michael, the archangel.

vv. 25–29—Jesus answers their slander with impeccable logic. If the prince of demons is driving out other demons, there is a civil war going on in hell that makes no sense at all. Jesus may have been sarcastic in verse 27, but it's possible that some of the Pharisees did exorcisms. If so, he is using their own experience to augment his argument. Their own experience would prove that demonic power doesn't drive out demons. Verse 28 argues in favor of the ironic interpretation of verse 27. Jesus' ministry of exorcism proves that the kingdom of God has come with him (this is one of the few times Matthew uses the name of God). The "mini-parable" in verse 29 continues the argument. Satan is indeed a strong man. He must be subdued by a greater power (God's) before what belongs to him can be removed (demons).

v. 30—Compare this verse with Luke 9:50. At first glance, they seem contradictory. This is a good illustration, however, that Scripture needs to be understood in context and examined carefully. The context of Matthew 12:30 is people who are attacking Jesus personally—"He *who is not with* me *is against* me." Opposition to Jesus or even neutrality is unacceptable. The person who is not involved with Jesus in evangelism ("gathers with me") is not a follower, in fact he is part of the problem—he scatters. In Luke 9:50, the context is a person who is driving out demons in the name of Jesus who is not part of the disciple band. *"Do not stop him,"* Jesus said, *"for whoever is not against* you *is for* you." Here Jesus is rebuking an exclusivistic attitude among his disciples. They were not the only true believers (nor is any one Christian church or denomination), and they should welcome others who claim the name of Christ and bear fruit for his kingdom.

vv. 31–32—These verses have also been greatly misunderstood. Christians with tender consciences have often worried that they have committed the unforgivable sin and blasphemed the Holy Spirit. If you are worried about having done it, stop worrying. You haven't! In the context of this passage, the ones who blaspheme the Spirit are those who don't care and who persistently attribute to evil what is clearly from God. The dominant interpretation throughout history of the "blasphemy of the Holy Spirit" is the person who persistently and consistently rejects the work of the Holy Spirit though they have ample evidence that he is real. Notice two important things: 1) Every other sin and blasphemy will be forgiven. Though taking God's name in vain is a serious sin, it is not unforgivable. 2) The Holy Spirit is a person who can be personally offended.

vv. 33–37—We've already seen the principle that *"by their fruit you will recognize them"* (Matt. 7:20). Jesus emphasizes that the outward expressions—our words—are a direct reflection of the inner disposition—our hearts. There is no stronger statement in Scripture than verses 36–37 concerning the importance of watching our tongues. Jesus is not teaching justification by words here, which would just be a variation of justification by works. He's already made the point that our words reveal what is in our hearts, and that is where our faith, or lack of faith, will be found.

vv. 38–42—People today still seek proof that God is real and that Christ is God. But Jesus would not then and will not now perform miracles on command. He tells the skeptics that a sign will be given—the sign of Jonah—which is a prophecy of his death and resurrection. The same is true of skeptics today. If they doubt the reality of Christ, look at the evidence for the resurrection, God's ultimate sign (Rom. 1:4). Jesus also claims to be greater than Jonah and Solomon, who impressed the Queen of Sheba (1 Kings 10:1–13). If Christ was not God in the flesh, he should be rejected as an egomaniac (see also Matt. 12:6)!

vv. 43–45—Jesus returns to the subject of unclean or evil spirits. It was a further warning to his generation who largely rejected him. Christ came into the towns of Israel and symbolically swept them clean of demonic oppression. But unless the Holy Spirit takes up residence in the cleansed person, he is an empty shell with no defenses. Even more evil will enter. Dale Bruner comments:

> Jesus summons us to "fill the house," to join the Church and take her worship services seriously, to appropriate and be filled with the Holy Spirit given to us in baptism, and to become Jesus' disciples in the world of our work. For our empty, swept, tidy house *will* be filled, sooner or later, by *something*, because houses are meant to be lived in. The question is not, "Will I become all involved or not?" It is, "With what shall I become all involved"? (Bruner, *Matthew: The Christbook*, 470)

APPLY

v. 36—Ask God to reveal your "careless words" today before you can say them.

MEMORIZE

Matthew 12:36

This will help you control your tongue.

PRAY

A: Praise him who is far greater than the "strong man."

C: Confess your careless words yesterday or even today.

T: Thank God for forgiving every sin that you confess and even those you can't remember.

S: Pray for someone you know who wants "proof" of God's existence. Ask God to reveal himself to that person and to use you in the process.

TELL

Can you give a reasonable defense of your belief in the deity of Christ? If not, read a book like *Evidence That Demands a Verdict* by Josh McDowell or *Know Why You Believe* by Paul Little.

JANUARY 29

JESUS' TRUE FAMILY

PRAY

For God's help to enable you to believe your beliefs and doubt your doubts.

READ

Matthew 12:46–50; Mark 3:31–35; Luke 8:19–21

OBSERVE

The three synoptic accounts are almost identical. Luke edits Jesus' words somewhat. There is a lot of important truth to apply in this little vignette about Jesus' family.

vv. 46–47—It's significant that Jesus' mother and brothers stood *outside* while Jesus was talking to the crowd. They did not want to be identified as his disciples because his brothers did not believe in him (John 7:5), and even his mother questioned his sanity (Mark 3:21). The actions of Christ's family are symbolic of the whole nation of Israel (John 1:11). The Jews "stood outside" the circle of God's redeeming love in Christ, yet called for God and expected him to come running. They presumed on a physical relationship—*"We are descendants of Abraham"* (John 8:31)—instead of cultivating a faith relationship. Mary, the mother of Jesus, is particularly interesting. She had believed the angel who told her that her son would be the Son of the Most High (Luke 1:45). She knew the amazing signs surrounding Christ's birth and pondered them in her heart (Luke 2:19). Yet, at this point, she didn't understand her son.

vv. 48–50—Christ declares that his true kindred is his family of faith, those who do the will of his Father in heaven. Notice that Jesus requires more than just *knowing* God's will. Friedrich Nietsche, the German philosopher who began the "God is dead" movement, had an amazing mind and memorized the entire New Testament. He was like Satan, a person who knew the truth (James 2:19), but opposed God's truth with all his being. While we may not be opposed to the truth, the failure to do God's will is the same result as unbelief. It is the *doers* of God's will who are blessed (James 1:22). Any time we begin to feel smug or that we have "arrived" spiritually, we would do well to remind ourselves of this truth.

APPLY

v. 50—Think of a particular expression of God's will (revealed in Scripture) that you can do today.

MEMORIZE

Matthew 12:50

PRAY

A: Praise God, whose will is perfect.

C: Confess the times you have been a hearer and not a doer of the Word.

T: Thank God for the opportunity to be faithful today.

S: Pray for specific areas in which you might do God's will.

TELL

If you're doing this study with a small group or with someone else, discuss this question: Is God's will a destination or a way of traveling? Try to support your opinion with Scripture.

JANUARY 30

THE PARABLE OF THE SOWER

PRAY

Ask God to make you fruitful as you study this key parable.

READ

Matthew 13:1–23; Mark 4:1–20; Luke 8:4–15

OBSERVE

The accounts are almost identical. Matthew adds a blessing to the disciples. Luke describes the good soil as "those with a noble and good heart."

vv. 1–3a—One of Jesus' favorite teaching settings was beside the lake (Sea of Galilee). When the crowds got too big, he could always go out into a boat and teach from there. He must have had a powerful voice! The word "parable" is from the Greek *paraballo*, which literally means, "to throw beside." A parable, therefore, is basically a comparison story. Although the rabbis sometimes used parables, Jesus was the master parable teller. Why did he use them?

1. Stories always interested the crowds. Jesus was far from the synagogue audience who wanted to hear biblical exposition. The common people responded to simple tales of the earth, vineyards, and livestock.
2. The Jews were accustomed to parables and believed them to be effective in communicating truth. One of the most famous Old Testament stories was the prophet Nathan's bold parable of the lamb, which he told to King David (2 Sam. 12:1–7).
3. Parables made people think for themselves. This is at least part of the

explanation of verses 13–15 (taken from Isa. 6:9–10). Those who want to remain spiritually blind and deaf can easily miss the point of parables, but those who quest after truth will find the application in their own lives.

vv. 3b–23—We need to understand the parable as a whole, as well as the individual details. One of the mistakes made in interpreting parables is to try to find a spiritual meaning in every single detail, some of which is meant only to be background or setting. Saint Augustine made allegories of the parables, assigning some spiritual meaning to all of the details. For example, in the Parable of the Good Samaritan, Augustine saw Damascus representing heaven, the robber representing sin, and each one of us as the victim. He missed the point of the story, which is clearly meant to answer the question, "What is love?" In the Parable of the Sower, Jesus graciously supplies the interpretation, and it is somewhat more allegorical than many other parables. Let's attempt some generalizations and applications:

1. There are three significant elements in this parable: the sower, the seed, and the soil.
2. The sower is the same in each case. Jesus was presenting himself as the sower, but it applies to anyone who preaches the Word. Notice that no blame is attached to the sower for the poor nature of the harvest. Too often, church people point to the pastor as the reason for the church's failure. If a church is obeying Christ, it should bear fruit regardless of how "flashy" the pastor is, as long as he is presenting the Word faithfully.
3. The seed is the Word (Luke adds, "of God" (Luke 8:11)). Again, it is the same seed that is scattered among the different types of soil. It is only the Word of God that produces growth. The time that the minister or other teacher is guilty is when he substitutes his own theories for the Word.
4. The only variable in the parable is the soil. It represents four kinds of people who hear the good news: 1) "hard" people who reject the Gospel immediately; 2) "shallow" people who *seem* to accept the word but fall away when it becomes tough to be a Christian; 3) "worldly" people whose growth is stifled by love for material things and a preoccupation with earthly problems; and 4) "reproducers"—people who accept and understand the Word and reproduce their faith in others. The Greek word translated "hear" in verse 9 also could be translated "obey." It's only the obedient who really hear the Word of God. It seems pretty clear that only the last group of people are genuinely saved.
5. This parable teaches a truth we already observed in Matthew 7:14: *"Small is the gate and narrow the road that leads to life, and only a few find it."* Jesus says it another way in Matthew 22:14: *"For many are invited, but few are chosen."* Just because someone prays a prayer at an evangelistic meeting or knows the right answer to theological questions doesn't make him a Christian. It's the same message we saw yesterday—it's only those who do the will of the Father who belong to his family.

APPLY

vv. 18–23—Which type of soil are you? If you say "good soil," where is your fruit?

MEMORIZE

Matthew 13:23

This is another way of defining a genuine Christian.

PRAY

A: Praise God that he is the ultimate Sower who gives growth.

C: Confess any of the "worries of the world" or "deceitfulness of wealth" that stand between you and following Christ wholeheartedly.

T: Thank God for the seed, the Word of God.

S: Pray that you would be fruitful for the kingdom today.

TELL

Discuss with another Christian or a small group two questions that this parable raises—1) Does this parable teach that a person can lose his salvation (see John 10:27–28 and John 17:12)? 2) Can a person be a Christian and not bear fruit (compare Matt. 7:17–20 and 1 Cor. 3:1–4)?

JANUARY 31

THE "SEPARATION" PARABLES

PRAY

Ask God to show you how these parables apply to your life.

READ

Matthew 13:24–30, 36–43, 47–50

OBSERVE

These two parables are unique to Matthew.

vv. 24–30, 36–43—The early church, like the Church today, was a "mixed multitude"—composed of genuine believers and spiritual counterfeits. Even Jesus' hand-picked band of disciples contained a "son of perdition [hell]" (John 17:12). How can this be when the sower is faithful and has planted good seed in God's field? Jesus continues the metaphor begun in the Parable of the Sower. The explanation is not just that the soils (hearers) are different.

There is another, very different sower. The enemy who sows weeds is none other than the devil, who produces his own followers, the sons of evil. Jesus warns the servants of the owner, the Church, not to be too hasty about removing false believers because some true believers might be uprooted in the process. Efforts to purify the Church throughout history have almost always resulted in judgmentalism and spiritual elitism. We don't see clearly enough to remove the weeds perfectly. Michael Green writes:

> You will never get a pure Church, for it is made up of impure people like you and me.
> Therefore you have to live and work in a church which is as mixed and ambiguous as

your own motives on a bad day! There will be a bewildering array of failure, betrayal, sin, pride and folly in every church, and the answer, says Jesus, is not to try to pluck up the weeds and get rid of them. That only disturbs the wheat. Let both grow together. At harvest time, at the end of the day, God will know how to separate the false from the real, the churchman from Christ's man, the weeds from the wheat. The one who determines the separation is not us, but God. (Green, *Matthew for Today*, 137)

This does not mean, of course, that the Church should never practice discipline or remove those who are guilty of gross sin and are unwilling to repent (see 1 Cor. 5 and Matt. 18:17). The harvest time is "the end of the age," either the time of our death or the Second Coming of Christ, when all humanity will be judged. Jesus taught that hell is a literal place of great suffering (v. 42). Yes, the fiery furnace is a metaphor, but it's a metaphor meant to denote something far more terrible than we can imagine.

You cannot be true to Christ's teaching and deny the reality of hell. In stark contrast, heaven is portrayed as incredibly beautiful, where the "righteous will shine like the sun in the kingdom of their Father." Have you ever been in a beautiful setting on a bright sunny day and thought, "This is pretty close to heaven!"? Isn't it amazing to consider that you will be like the sun in heaven, a radiant reflector of the beauty of the Son?

vv. 47–52—The Parable of the Net has a similar message to the Parable of the Weeds. The difference here is that the separating is done right away, rather than after a longer period of growth. It could be that Jesus is warning that there will be some immediate judgment in this life. After all, the Church has to decide who should be admitted based on whether or not they have a credible profession of faith. Or Jesus could be describing what happens at the end of the age, with the angels functioning as the fishermen. That seems to be the more likely explanation, given the earlier parable and the beginning of verse 49. We don't have the benefit of the explanation he provides for the two previous parables we've examined, so our conclusions must be more tentative.

APPLY

v. 30—Don't be too eager to have a "perfect church." If there were such a group, you and I would ruin it!

MEMORIZE

Matthew 13:43

This will increase your joyful expectation of heaven.

PRAY

A: Praise God that he is a righteous judge.

C: Confess your tendency to be too judgmental.

T: Thank God that he is patient with you.

S: Intercede for someone who has difficulty accepting the reality of hell.

TELL

Share with that person why you believe hell to be a biblical and moral necessity.

FEBRUARY

FEBRUARY 1

KINGDOM GROWTH PARABLES

Ask Jesus to open your eyes to the growth of his kingdom.

READ

Matthew 13:31–35; Mark 4:30–34; Luke 13:18–21

OBSERVE

The accounts in the Synoptics are practically identical, though Mark doesn't include the Parable of the Yeast.

vv. 31–32—Except for the Parable of the Sower, all of the parables in Matthew 13 begin, "The kingdom of heaven is like…" In interpreting these parables, it's essential to remember that the comparison to the kingdom of heaven is the central point. Some have suggested that the Parable of the Mustard Seed teaches that the kingdom must always exist in the midst of evil, for the birds of the air coming to roost is often a picture of evil in the Old Testament (Dan. 4:12, 20–27; Ezek. 17:19–24, 31:2–14). But that interpretation fails to appreciate Christ's thesis and emphasis. The point Jesus makes is that the kingdom starts small, a mustard seed is really tiny, but grows to a great size—some mustard bushes grow to twelve feet in height. The birds of the air may refer to the Gentiles, as in the Old Testament, but it is not a negative reference in this context. Jesus taught this parable to disciples who could be discouraged because their numbers were so small. His optimistic message was, "Don't get discouraged, we've only just begun." The Church today, which numbers more than one billion adherents from that mustard seed in

Palestine, must not get discouraged either. The kingdom of heaven continues to grow. South Korea was the mustard seed in the twentieth century. Africa and China are becoming a tree in the twenty-first century.

v. 33—Leaven ("yeast" in the NIV) is also a frequent metaphor for evil. When the Jews fled in the Exodus from Egypt, they didn't have time to use leaven in their bread to make it rise. Unleavened bread, then, was associated with the Exodus and the Passover and seen as holy. All leaven had to be carefully removed from Jewish homes before the family was ready to celebrate the Passover. Jesus gives leaven a negative connotation when he says, *"Be on your guard against the yeast (leaven) of the Pharisees and Sadducees"* (Matt. 16:6). Christ is referring to the influence the scribes and Pharisees had through their teaching. But in this parable, leaven is used in the sense of positive influence. As Paul writes in 1 Corinthians 5:6, *"a little yeast works through the whole batch of dough."* The kingdom of heaven, represented by the Church of Jesus Christ, may seem small in comparison to all of society, but it has a powerful influence. One writer notes:

> Despite its appalling failures and sins, it is beyond question that the Church has had down the ages an amazing record in medical care, social work, education, liberation of women and slaves, the defence of prisoners, the aged, the helpless, and those whom society neglects. (Green, *Matthew for Today*, 138–139)

Jesus may have intended to shock his listeners by using the image of leaven. To the respectable people, his followers must have seemed distasteful. The Gentiles who would become Christians would be more so. But God uses those things despised by the world to usher in his kingdom (1 Cor. 1:26–29).

vv. 34–35—We've already explored some of the reasons Jesus used parables. Another reason is that they reveal things that were previously hidden, as Psalm 78:2 teaches. The sincere student will find profound truth in the parables.

APPLY

vv. 31–32—Can you think of something God has done in your life that began small but has grown much larger? Is there a small opportunity in your church or community that he might be calling you to undertake?

vv. 33–34—Is there a minor change you could make in your life that would result in a major change for the better? How about the way you spend your time?

MEMORIZE

Memorize Matthew 13:32 to remind yourself that God's kingdom continues to grow and expand.

PRAY

A: Praise God that he changes people and nations in a quiet way.

C: Confess the times that you have been pessimistic about the influence of Christianity.

T: Thank God for the growth you see in your life and in your church.

S: Pray that you might plant a small seed today.

TELL

Is there someone you've been praying for who might be fertile soil for that tiny seed?

FEBRUARY 2

THE VALUE OF HIDDEN THINGS

PRAY

"Lord, open my eyes that I might see the value of those things right around me that I often ignore."

READ

Matthew 13:44–46, 51–58; Mark 6:1–6

OBSERVE

The Parables of the Hidden Treasure and the Pearl are unique to Matthew. Mark's account of Jesus' rejection in his hometown includes the statement that Jesus was amazed at their lack of faith.

vv. 44–46—These two parables are almost identical in their message. Something of great value is found. The finder sells all that he has and then uses the proceeds to buy the valuable item. The obvious application is that the kingdom of heaven is of such supreme worth that when we finally grasp its infinite value, "we will joyfully let go of all competing claims on our lives and make it our one great possession" (Mounce, *Matthew*, 135).

vv. 51–52—To understand Christ's teaching is to stand under its authority. Verse 52 suggests that when we come to Christ, he doesn't ask us to forget all that we've known before we met him or deny our previous gifts and talents. He wants to use the best of our talents and experience, the old treasures, but we are to use them in light of the new treasures we have found in him. A person like Paul was a brilliant teacher and writer before he came to Christ. Jesus heightened Paul's gifts and redirected them in a godly way. Paul was a tremendous blend of the old and the new. It's the same with any new Christian. Jesus wants to use one's background and experience to serve his kingdom.

vv. 53–54—Jesus returns to Nazareth for the second time in his ministry. He goes to his hometown synagogue to teach. Prior to his return to Nazareth, his ministry had primarily been outside the church, at the seaside or in the villages. This will be the last time Jesus enters the synagogue until the last week of his life. The initial response of the people of Nazareth was the same as everywhere else; they were amazed. Nobody denied his wisdom or the power of his miracles.

vv. 55–56—The problem with the Nazarenes was that they sought to explain Jesus away rather than accept his authority. They were unwilling to believe that a new revelation could come from someone who had grown up in their village. In a real sense, Jesus was the hidden treasure and they wouldn't "buy" him. The word used here for carpenter is not the common word for a woodworker. It is the word for a craftsman. We can be sure that Jesus never made a cheap table or chair!

vv. 57–58—This had to have been one of the low points in Jesus' ministry. He quotes a proverb full of historic significance. The great Old Testament prophets were all rejected by the Jews. Later, Jesus will teach a profound parable tying his rejection to that of the prophets, the Parable of the Tenants of the Vineyard (Matt. 21:33–46). The gospels teach that lack of faith can limit what God will do. Mark tells us that just as his neighbors initially were amazed at Jesus' teaching, he was amazed at their unbelief (Mark 6:6). It is the only time when Jesus is said to be amazed at anything.

APPLY

v. 46—Do you view your relationship with Christ as the greatest treasure in your life, the pearl of great price? Are you willing to joyfully surrender everything else for the surpassing worth of knowing him and being known and loved by him?

v. 55—Jesus was a craftsman who honored God with his work. Is your work honoring the Lord who gave you gifts and abilities to serve him in your vocation?

v. 58—Is your lack of faith limiting what Christ can do in and through you?

MEMORIZE

Matthew 13:58

This helps us remember the importance of faith as the corrective lens that enables us to see God's hand in our lives.

PRAY

A: Praise God, whose kingdom is of infinite value.

C: Confess the times you have devalued the familiar.

T: Thank God for opening your eyes to see his treasure.

S: Ask God to show you the old treasures as well as the new that he wants to use in your life.

TELL

Share with a Christian friend why you believe that God's kingdom is so valuable.

FEBRUARY 3

JOHN LOSES HIS HEAD

PRAY

Ask God to teach you something from the example of both John and Herod.

READ

Matthew 14:1–12; Mark 6:14–29; Luke 9:7–9

OBSERVE

Luke really gives the Reader's Digest account, and Matthew's account is fuller, but Mark's gospel gives the complete account of the death of John the Baptizer. We'll follow Mark's account.

Mark 6:14–16—Jesus' fame reaches the court of Herod Antipas, the ruler of Galilee. This Herod was the son of Herod the Great, the king of Judea when Jesus was born. We'll explore the popular idea that Jesus was Elijah or one of the prophets when we study Peter's great confession (Matt. 16:13–20). Let's concentrate here on those who were saying that Jesus was the reincarnation of John. Jesus and John had some similarities: they both lived a simple lifestyle, emphasized repentance, and proclaimed the truth courageously. But they were very different. John camped out and preached in the wilderness near the Jordan River. Jesus was always on the move. John was a Nazirite (Num. 6:1–12) who didn't shave, cut his hair, drink wine, or go near a dead body. Jesus drank wine and went to parties and touched dead bodies to bring them back to life. John was the herald, but Jesus was the King. It was probably Herod's guilty conscience that caused him to think that Jesus was John, risen from the dead.

vv. 17–29—This flashback tells us how John came to be in prison, from which he had previously sent messengers to Jesus (Matt. 11:2-19, January 25). Let's contrast John's character with that of Herod.

Herod was:

1. Lustful and unconcerned with God's law, placing himself above it (v. 17).
2. Spiritually curious, but unable to understand the truth because of his hard heart (v. 20).
3. Foolish and full of pride. Herod makes a ridiculous, drunken offer to the daughter of Herodias and then feels compelled to keep his word, even though the result is murder.

In contrast, John was:

1. Righteous. He was determined to follow God's law personally and to courageously confront the king (v. 18). The verb tense indicates that John told Herod repeatedly that his relationship with his brother's wife was wrong.
2. Uncompromising. He could have probably saved his skin if he had backed down, but he continued to tell Herod the truth even when he was in prison (v. 20).
3. A witness even in death. Matthew tells us that after the burial, John's disciples "went and told Jesus" (Matt. 14:12). It's evident from several passages that follow in the gospels that John's death had a major impact on Jesus. It was one of the signs that pointed to the inevitability of Jesus' own martyrdom.

No doubt many of John's disciples joined with Jesus, just as others of John's followers already had. John's purpose is summed up in John 3:30: *"He must become greater. I must become less."* John was truly a fulfillment of the words in Psalm 116:15: *"Precious in the sight of the Lord is the death of his saints."* Two other characters in the story deserve a brief mention and condemnation. Herodias tries to cover her sin of adultery with murder. She forgets that though she will no longer have to deal with John, she will have to deal with a much more potent Judge after death. Herodias' daughter (whom legend has named Salome) proves that even obeying one's parents can be sinful if the parent's command is in direct conflict with the law of God.

APPLY

v. 9—Do you ever over-promise? Be careful not to promise others (especially if you are a parent) anything that you shouldn't or that will be too difficult to deliver.

v. 18—Do you have as high a regard for the truth as John did? Where do you compromise the truth when it is uncomfortable?

MEMORIZE

Mark 6:18

This shows us the courage of God's messenger to confront evil.

PRAY

A: Praise God that his truth endures beyond the grave.

C: Confess the times that you have compromised the truth to avoid unpleasant consequences.

T: Thank God for examples like John.

S: Ask God for courage to stand boldly for Christ.

TELL

Lovingly point out to someone you know well when they disobey the law of God (Gal. 6:1). Be sure that it's not an area where you are also guilty (Matt. 7:3) and humbly admit your own sin (Matt. 7:5).

FEBRUARY 4

JESUS FEEDS THE FIVE THOUSAND

PRAY

Pray that you may appreciate Jesus as the one who meets your needs and trust him more.

READ

Matthew 14:13–21; Mark 6:30–44; Luke 9:10–17; John 6:1–14

OBSERVE

This is one of very few incidents prior to Holy Week that are recorded in all four gospels. It was an important event in the life and ministry of Jesus Christ. Matthew will be our basic text, but we can learn a lot by looking at the parallel accounts as well.

v. 13—Jesus was human just as we are. When he experienced a devastating emotional blow through John's death, he wanted to be alone to reflect and pray. As usual, the crowds wouldn't let him. Mark 6:33 adds the significant detail that the crowds ran around the perimeter of the lake in order to beat Jesus and the disciples to their destination. This explains why the crowds brought no food; they were in a hurry.

v. 14—The word translated "compassion" describes the ability to empathize with surpassing tenderness, like a mother with her newborn baby. Mark 6:34 adds that Jesus saw the crowd like sheep without a shepherd. They needed someone to give them direction and tend to their needs.

v. 15—The disciples were not as compassionate as Jesus. Their objections are all reasonable—it was late, they were far from town and food for this mob would cost two-thirds of the average working man's yearly salary (Mark 6:37; John 6:7). Alan Cole comments:

> All their calculations were correct, but they had forgotten Christ, the incalculable factor. At the "unreasonableness" of Christ their suppressed irritation grows, for God's way is ever folly to the natural man (1 Cor. 1:18). This miracle is therefore an illustration of the central stumbling block of Christianity: we all stand condemned with the disciples. (Cole, *The Gospel According to Mark*, 113–114)

vv. 16–17—Jesus was always trying to expand the disciples' faith, as he does with us. Again, the disciples' response is full of human logic. John 6 adds a wonderful note to the story. It was a young boy who was wise enough to bring the five loaves and two fish. John tells us that they were barley loaves (John 6:9), the food of the poorest of the poor; more the size of a dinner roll than a loaf of bread. The small salt-fish were the size of sardines. This wasn't much to work with for five thousand men plus women and children! Jesus, however, takes our meager offerings and expands and perfects them so that they are great and powerful tools of his kingdom.

vv. 18–19—The shepherd organizes the sheep. Mark uses two vivid word pictures that make the scene even more vivid. The word translated "groups" in the NIV (Mark 6:39–40) is the usual Greek word used to describe rows of vegetables in a garden. The other little detail Mark adds is that the grass was green. By that word, we can pinpoint the time of this miracle to mid-April, the only time in Palestine when the grass is green. Can you picture this unique human vegetable garden "planted" on the green grass by the Sower of the Word?

vv. 20–21—When Jesus provides, we have all that we need and then some. David wrote, *"The Lord is my shepherd, I shall not be in want"* (Ps. 23:1). The number twelve is extremely significant: to the Jews it was the number of completion (represented by the twelve tribes of Israel). It also meant that each of the disciples had a basket full of leftovers. It would be hard for them to forget what Jesus did on this hillside. The feeding of the five thousand was more accurately the feeding of the eight thousand or even ten thousand when you add women and children.

APPLY

v. 14—What situations cause you to feel compassion? It could be that God wants you to become involved in ministering to those needs.

v. 19—Christ can do great things even with our little offerings.

MEMORIZE

Matthew 14:18

If we bring what little we have to Jesus, he will use it!

PRAY

A: Praise the God who multiples our offerings.

C: Confess that you, like the disciples, often try to limit what God will do by your human logic.

T: Thank God for the abundance he has poured out upon you.

S: Ask the Shepherd for what you need. Direction? Compassion? Spiritual food? He will satisfy you.

TELL

Pray for a person who is like a sheep without a shepherd. Tell that person in some way, verbally or nonverbally, that you and Jesus care about him or her.

FEBRUARY 5

JESUS WALKS ON THE WATER

PRAY

Ask God for the boldness of Peter and greater faith!

READ

Matthew 14:22–36; Mark 6:45–56; John 6:15–21

OBSERVE

Matthew's is the only account that includes Peter's wet walk. It's very unusual for John to include a story and not Luke.

vv. 22–23—John 6:15 tells us a significant additional detail that further explains why Jesus sent his disciples away in the boat, and he went to the mountainside. The people wanted to force Jesus to become a king after he had fed them miraculously. If he hadn't sent his disciples across the lake, which ones might have jumped on the revolutionary bandwagon? Verse 23 gives an intimate portrait of what was Jesus' common practice. Both before (Mark 1:35) and after ministering to others, Jesus spent significant amounts of uninterrupted time talking with his Father. A study of pastors in Minnesota discovered that the average pastor spends three minutes a day in prayer. Maybe that's why there are so many average pastors! If God the Son needed to pray continually, how much more do we weak and sinful humans require the power that comes only from communion with God!

vv. 24–27—One commentator remarks:

This episode is a good illustration of the life of discipleship seen as a constant experience of testing and deliverance; for it was not through stubborn self-will, but through direct obedience to the Lord's command that the disciples found themselves in this plight. Thus the storm in no way showed that they had deviated from the path of God's will: God's path for them lay through that storm, to the other shore of the lake. (Cole, *The Gospel According to Mark*, 115–116)

The Romans divided the night (6 p.m. to 6 a.m.) into four watches. Jesus came to his disciples around 3 o'clock in the morning. We might judge the disciples as superstitious with their fear of a ghost, but keep in mind that this is the first time human beings ever saw anyone walk on water. In our familiarity with that expression, we can lose the awesome wonder of the moment. Jesus, no doubt realizing the unusual nature of his walk, doesn't rebuke them for their fear but comforts them.

vv. 28–31—Don't you love Peter? He didn't have his whole act together, but he gets high marks for courage. His experience on the water can be a kind of parable for us. If we concentrate on our circumstances (the wind, waves, etc.) we can feel overwhelmed and go under, but if we keep our eyes fixed on Jesus and his power, we can triumph over adversity. St. Augustine wrote, "He came treading the waves; and so he puts all the swelling tumults of life under his feet. Christian—why afraid?" Jesus' rebuke to Peter could be said to us, *"You of little faith, why do you doubt?"* Jesus could do anything that was in God's will, and so can we (Phil. 4:13)!

vv. 32–33—This little footnote to the story is tremendously significant. For the first time, the disciples as a group clearly see who Jesus is, the Son of God. Keep this in mind when we study Matthew 16:13-20 (February 10). Previously, when Jesus had calmed the storm, the disciples had asked, *"What kind of man is this?"* (Matt. 8:27). Now they had their answer.

vv. 34–36—As soon as he touches dry land, Jesus is in demand. In all of the accounts of Christ's healings, nobody ever came to give to him, only to get from him. He receives all that he needs from the Father.

APPLY

v. 24—Can you think of a time when following God's will was like rowing against the wind? Do you feel that the Christian life is easy or hard? How do you reconcile passages like Matthew 11:29 and Luke 9:23–24?

vv. 28–31—Are you willing to take a risk for Christ even if you look foolish? Trust that he will redeem the situation.

MEMORIZE

Matthew 14:33

If you believe that Jesus is the Son of God, you must worship him.

PRAY

A: Praise the Lord of nature.

C: Confess your lack of faith as it's expressed in nagging doubts.

T: Thank God for his gentle kindness when you are afraid.

S: Intercede for someone who needs Jesus' healing touch.

TELL

Encourage someone with the parable of Peter on the water.

FEBRUARY 6

IT'S WHAT COMES OUT THAT COUNTS

PRAY

Search me, O God, and know my heart; test me and know my anxious thoughts. See if there is any offensive way in me, and lead me in the way everlasting.

—Psalm 139:23–24

READ

Matthew 15:1–20; Mark 7:1–23

OBSERVE

Mark's account is a little easier to understand, so we will use it as our text.

Mark 7:1–5—The fault-finding commission from Jerusalem (whom we last saw in Matthew 12) returns. It's a fact of life that when people are looking for something to criticize, they will find it. The target is Jesus' oversight of the disciples. The Pharisees and teachers of the law (scribes) didn't view Jesus and his disciples as guilty of bad manners, or dirty in the hygienic sense, but as unclean in the sight of God. The commission's standard wasn't the Old Testament. It was the scribal commentary on the law known as the Halakah. They equated their traditions with the Word of God. The tradition concerning hand-washing was as rigid and rigorous as their Sabbath laws. Barclay describes the ritual like this:

> First, the hands were held with the fingertips pointing upwards; the water was poured over them and must run at least down to the wrist; the minimum amount of water was one quarter of a log, which is equal to one and a half egg-shells full of water. While the hands were still wet, each hand had to be cleansed with the fist of the other.

At this stage, the hands were wet with water that was unclean because it touched unclean hands. So, second, the hands had to be held with fingertips pointing downward and the water had to be poured over them in such a way that it began at the wrists and ran off at the fingertips. After all that had been done, the hands were clean. (Barclay, Commentaries, 167)

In Jesus' day, one rabbi forgot the ceremony at one meal and was removed from his synagogue. Another rabbi who was jailed by the Romans used his drinking water for handwashing and nearly died of thirst.

vv. 6–8—Jesus doesn't apologize for his disciples. Instead, he gets to the heart of the problem with the religious leaders: 1) They were hypocrites. The Greek word means "actors." The scribes and Pharisees put on one religious performance after another, all designed to impress people. 2) Their deeper theological problem was that they put human traditions before the Word of God. The fellowship that puts the traditions of men alongside the Word of God forfeits the blessing of the Holy Spirit. The Spirit honors the Word he inspired, not our additions to it.

vv. 9–13—Jesus chooses an outstanding example of "nullifying the Word of God by (their) tradition," though there were many. The practice of Corban grew out of the greed of the trustees of the temple. Not only did it deprive parents of the help their children should provide (ignoring the Fifth Commandment), it was a means of selfishness for the children since they didn't have to turn over their land or money until they themselves died. Jesus strongly upheld the biblical teaching about family life and the obligations of family members to one another. He only forbids those ties becoming more important than commitment to him.

vv. 14–20—Jesus had repudiated the practice of the Pharisees, but he hadn't tackled the validity of the ritual law itself. If the ritual law were binding, then the disciples stood condemned for eating with unwashed hands. In the mini-parable of verse 15, Jesus dismisses the ritual addition to the law by stressing that true religion doesn't consist in externals (what a person eats, wears, prays, etc.) but with what is inside a person. This doesn't mean that we can use illegal drugs or drink to drunkenness. That would indicate a bad attitude within us, which Jesus describes at the end of the passage. There is an amazing statement in the parenthesis of verse 19: *"In saying this, Jesus declared all foods 'clean.'"* This was a radical teaching for Jews who had been raised on the holiness code of Leviticus. Jesus fulfilled the ceremonial law. It is no longer binding on Christians. We don't have to worry about whether foods are kosher or not. They are all clean.

vv. 21–23—The heart of the matter is what comes from our hearts. The things that come from the heart and make us unclean are:

1. Evil thoughts—every outward act of sin is preceded by an inward act of choice.
2. Sexual immorality—fornication would be a better translation, referring to sex outside of marriage.
3. Theft—there are two words for a thief in Greek: a bold pirate who steals for a cause and someone like Judas, a deceitful, sneaky thief.
4. Murder

5. Adultery—remember that both of these sins spring from a sinful attitude (Matt. 5:21–32, January 10).
6. Greed—the desire to always have more, especially that which belongs to someone else.
7. Malice—delighting in wrongdoing (see Rom. 1:32).
8. Deceit—it comes from the Greek word for "bait" and describes a trickster.
9. Lewdness—a disposition that resists all discipline.
10. Envy—literally "the evil eye," someone who would destroy the happiness of others.
11. Slander—the Greek word is *blasphemia*; when applied to God it's blasphemy, to men it's tearing down another's reputation (James 3:6–12).
12. Arrogance—a person who appears humble can be inwardly arrogant if he believes that he is better than others.
13. Folly—not stupidity, but a person who thinks that sin is a joke.

Notice that Jesus makes no distinction between sins of thought and sins of action.

APPLY

v. 6—Are you an actor? Do you sometimes do things for show rather than conviction?

v. 8—Have you ever taken someone's opinion (a teacher perhaps) as more convincing than God's Word? Please don't do that with this study! Test what is written to see whether it is consistent with what God says.

vv. 21–22—Is there anything in this list that describes something that you need to confess and repent of?

MEMORIZE

Mark 7:15

This is the New Testament holiness code.

PRAY

A: Praise the Holy Spirit who makes us clean.

C: Confess any violations of the thirteen attitudes Jesus mentions.

T: Thank God for your parents.

S: Pray that you might honor them well.

TELL

If you have an accountability or prayer partner, share about a particularly difficult sin for you to overcome. Ask for prayer (James 5:16).

FEBRUARY 7

WHEN JESUS WASN'T VERY "CHRISTIAN"

PRAY

Ask for God's help to understand this difficult story.

READ

Matthew 15:21–28; Mark 7:24–30

OBSERVE

Matthew's account is more complete than Mark's.

v. 21—Tyre and Sidon were Gentile cities of Phoenicia, the great maritime province of Syria. These cities were forty and sixty miles northwest of Capernaum, Christ's farthest entrance into Gentile territory by a long shot. Why does Jesus go there? There are several possible reasons.

It could be that Jesus had been trying unsuccessfully for some time to withdraw from the crowds for some rest and recovery. Traveling this far into Gentile territory would probably provide a quiet retreat for Jesus and the disciples.

However, this section immediately follows the teaching on clean vs. unclean practices. Could Jesus be attempting to destroy, for his disciples, the Jewish distinction between clean and unclean people? The inclusion of the Gentiles becomes a major theme and controversy in the rest of the New Testament.

Barclay suggests another possibility:

> Ideally these Phoenician cities were part of the realm of Israel. When, under Joshua, the land was being partitioned out, the tribe of Asher was allocated "as far as Sidon

the Great ... reaching to the fortified city of Tyre" (Josh. 19:28–29). They had never been able to subdue their territory and they had never entered into it. Again is it not symbolic? Where the might of arms was helpless, the conquering love of Jesus was victorious. The earthly Israel failed to gather in Phoenicia; now the true Israel had come upon them. (Barclay, *Commentaries*, 181)

v. 22—Mark describes the Canaanite woman as a "Greek" (which referred to her religion) and a "Syrophonecian" (which described her nationality). Apparently Jesus' reputation as a healer had traveled this far; she also had accurate information about his qualifications as the Son of David.

vv. 23–24—It's difficult to understand Jesus' silence in the face of the woman's cries. Perhaps he was waiting for her to approach him again to show her sincerity. In any case, he gives her his initial mission statement, that he was sent only to the lost sheep of Israel.

v. 25—The word "knelt" has the sense of worship. It's the word for deep respect as well as grief.

vv. 26–28—George Bernard Shaw, the famous British novelist and atheist, commented on verse 26 by writing, "This is one time that Jesus was not a Christian." Shaw failed to understand the subtlety and irony in Jesus' statement. It's true that "dog" was a Jewish term of abuse for a Gentile. The Jews compared Gentiles to the vicious, wild dogs that roamed the countryside in attacking bands. However, there was another word for domesticated dogs, what we would call lap dogs. This is the word Jesus uses. He further makes it a diminutive—"little dogs" or "puppies." Since trash collection was not practiced at that time, the family dog acted as the garbage can. People wiped their hands (they didn't use utensils or napkins either) on a piece of bread and gave it to the dog. That is what the clever woman references when she responds to Jesus' honest, but not unkind, statement. Jesus is impressed by her great faith and grants instant healing.

APPLY

v. 28—Jesus is always impressed by persistent faith. What concern do you need to continue to bring before him? Is there someone you know who needs healing—spiritual or physical?

MEMORIZE

Matthew 15:28

This verse helps us to remember the importance of faith.

PRAY

A: Praise the Son of David who has compassion on all sons and daughters.

C: Confess the times that you have lacked the faith to persist in prayer.

T: Thank God that he has a plan for all the peoples of the earth.

S: Intercede for missionaries in the area of Syria, a very difficult field.

TELL

When you have the opportunity, share the importance of not making judgments based on one verse of Scripture.

FEBRUARY 8

JESUS FEEDS THE FOUR THOUSAND

PRAY

Pray for the ability to learn spiritual lessons the first time.

READ

Matthew 15:29–39; Mark 8:1–10

OBSERVE

The two accounts are very similar.

vv. 29–31—It's significant that Matthew tells us that Jesus "went up on a mountainside and sat down." It would be similar in our culture for a writer to say, "He went up on a mountainside and took the pulpit." When a rabbi sat down, he began to teach. Jesus usually blended teaching and healing. Imagine yourself in this scene. It would be like a massive, moving hospital ward. People were carried up the mountain by their friends and came running down praising the Lord!

v. 32—We noted Jesus' compassion when we studied the feeding of the five thousand. In this case, the people had been with him for a longer time, three days. They were fasting in the biblical sense, going without food in order to make rapid spiritual progress.

v. 33—The disciples complaint is almost the same one they voiced at the feeding of the five thousand (Matt. 14:15). The gospels don't always give us a lot of chronological clues. It may have been many months between these two situations, but it still seems that the disciples should have remembered what happened before. But before we're too harsh with them, can you think of a time when God showed you something, yet you doubted him when the situation recurred?

vv. 34–39—The word for "basket" here is different than the one in Matthew 14. In the feeding of the five thousand, the disciples used a *kophinos,* the basket carried by Jews, which was shaped like a water pot. The word here is *sphuris,* a larger basket shaped like a hamper (see Acts 9:25), which the Gentiles used. The difference in baskets points up a reason for including both stories. Christ is the Bread of Life, and he is meant for all people.

APPLY

v. 33—Think of something that Christ has done for you more than once that you still have difficulty accepting (for example, bringing good out of bad circumstances). Learn to discern that you can trust him.

MEMORIZE

Matthew 15:31

This is the proper response to the work of Christ.

PRAY

A: Praise the God of compassion.

C: Confess the times you've been a slow learner.

T: Thank God for his patience.

S: Ask God for compassion for everyone, not just those close to you.

TELL

Remind someone you love that Jesus is able to provide for all that they need.

FEBRUARY 9

BE WARY OF "RELIGIOUS" PEOPLE

Ask God for discernment to see Pharisaism in yourself and others.

Matthew 16:1–12; Mark 8:11–21

The discussions in Matthew and Mark are similar, but Matthew's is more complete.

vv. 1–4—This passage is full of irony. Here was a man who had fed more than nine thousand people with twelve small loaves and a few fish. He was a man who had raised the dead, cleansed lepers, walked on water, healed every imaginable disease, cast out demons, and taught with the authority and wisdom of God. And they ask for a sign! The other ironic thing is that the Pharisees thought that if Jesus would produce a sign on the spot, it would prove that he was from God. It would have proven the exact opposite! Producing a spectacular sign to impress others was one of Satan's temptations (Matt. 4:5–7). The Pharisees, who were so self-righteous and religious, were actually the instruments of Satan. Jesus tells them that they can interpret the weather accurately by looking at the sky, but they cannot interpret what God is doing right in front of their eyes. He refuses to provide a sign on demand and tells them that the only sign they will be given was the sign of Jonah. This was a repetition of the prophecy of Christ's death and resurrection that Jesus had stated in Matthew 12:39–40.

vv. 5–6—We commented on this passage earlier when we discussed the Parable of the Leaven (Matt. 13:33, February 1). Here, Jesus uses leaven (or yeast) in a negative way. It was a symbol of evil, an unseen yet pervasive influence. Teachers always have a lingering influence on students, either for good or ill.

vv. 7–12—The disciples must have had a guilty conscience for forgetting to bring bread because they thought about it as soon as Jesus mentioned yeast. In this section, the disciples are shown to be very slow learners. In case we should feel superior to them, remember that this story was told by a disciple. They may have been slow, but they were honest and didn't try to paint themselves in a noble light. Even though Jesus had provided bread in spectacular fashion twice, the disciples still don't get it. The number of basketfuls left over from the feeding of the five thousand was twelve, the complete number. The leftovers from the feeding of the four thousand were seven basketfuls, the perfect number. What Jesus is saying is this: "I am complete and perfect. I can take care of all of your needs." Amen and Amen!

APPLY

v. 1—Do you ever seek a sign from God rather than proceeding in faith? What are more reliable ways to discover God's will than signs?

vv. 9–10—Is Jesus able to give you everything you need? If you believe that, why are you anxious?

vv. 11–12—Do you see any leaven (yeast) in our society? How can you avoid it, or diminish its influence over you?

MEMORIZE

Matthew 16:6

God wants us to be very careful about those we allow to influence us.

PRAY

A: Praise him who provides (Gen. 22:14).

C: Confess those times you've sought signs rather than Christ.

T: Thank God for giving you discernment.

S: Pray for someone you know who is seduced by false teaching.

TELL

Discuss with a Christian friend or small group the yeast in today's society and what can be done about it.

FEBRUARY 10

PETER'S CONFESSION AND RENUNCIATION

PRAY

Ask for Peter's boldness to confidently declare that Jesus is the Messiah and Son of God.

READ

Matthew 16:13–28; Mark 8:27–9:1; Luke 9:18–27

OBSERVE

Luke doesn't include Peter's rebuke of Jesus' prophecy of his death. Matthew and Mark are very similar, but we will concentrate on Matthew's more complete account.

v. 13—As they came to the great city north of Galilee, Caesarea Philippi (named after Herod Phillip, ruler of that region), Jesus arrived at a crisis point in his ministry. He was about to "resolutely set out for Jerusalem" (Luke 9:51), where death awaited, and he had to know whether his closest followers really knew who he was. The answer to that question mattered to the very future of Christianity. And so it was perhaps with some trepidation that Jesus asks the first question, *"Who do people say the Son of Man is?"*

v. 14—Jesus already knew the answer to that question (see Mark 6:14–15). What are some of the answers of people today? Some would echo the words of Tim Rice and Andrew Lloyd Webber, the writers of *Jesus Christ, Superstar*: "We don't see Jesus as God, but as a good man and a great teacher who came along at the right time." C. S. Lewis answered that idea years ago when he wrote that a person who talked about himself like Jesus did would be neither a good man nor a good teacher, but an egomaniac and a lunatic—if he were not God.

vv. 15–16—It's easy to answer in the third person and give the views of others, but inevitably Jesus asks each one of us, "Who do you say I am?" Impulsive Peter receives a divine flash of light and speaks the words that have echoed down through the centuries. This was the first time that anyone, including the demon possessed, had called Jesus "the Christ," the Greek word for the Hebrew *messiah*, God's anointed one.

vv. 17–20—It's very interesting that Matthew contains Jesus' rich benediction pronounced to Peter, but Mark does not. If Mark is The Gospel According to Peter, as most New Testament scholars believe, why doesn't Mark include the blessing? There are two good possibilities: 1) humility—Much of Mark's material came from Peter's sermons and to quote the Lord's high praise would have seemed conceited. 2) memory—It could be that the thing Peter remembered most vividly was what happened next.

In any case, we can be thankful that Matthew included the blessing. Verse 17 shows that spiritual insight, especially about the person of Christ, is not something we figure out, but something that God reveals to us. Verses 18 and 19 are not bestowing special authority on Peter, as the Pope or anything else. Jesus is using a play on words in verse 18. Peter (*petros* in Greek) means "rock." The rock on which the Church will be built is not the person of Peter but his confession. Though evil is strong, it will never overcome the church. Though verse 18 is addressed to Peter (you, singular), two chapters later (18:18), Christ says the identical words about binding and loosing, to the disciples as a whole (you, plural). The loosing and binding refers to the church's authority to pronounce forgiveness in the name of Christ.

v. 21—Now that the disciples knew the truth of Christ's identity, he revealed his destiny to them more fully. They needed to know that the Messiah would fulfill the role of the Suffering Servant (Isa. 53:4–9). He makes six predictions of his death in the gospels. The cross did not take him by surprise (John 10:18).

vv. 22–23—One moment Peter is blessed as an instrument of God. The next moment, he's an instrument of Satan! Peter's sin was to think he knew better than Christ. He let his emotional feelings for Jesus stand in the way of God's plan. He had recognized that Jesus was the Messiah but failed to recognize the implications of what the Messiah must be and do. The popular view among the Jews of the Messiah was that he would be a conquering warlord who would set up God's kingdom on earth by destroying Israel's enemies. That concept died hard even among the disciples (Acts 1:6). There was no room in the popular conception for a Messiah who would die a sacrificial, atoning death as described in Isaiah 53.

v. 24—Christ makes it clear that authentic discipleship involves putting aside our egos and agendas (literally "say no to self"). We don't have to go looking for a cross. It will be there whenever we follow Jesus Christ. Christianity involves playing Follow the Leader in the power of the Holy Spirit.

vv. 25–26—Christianity is not primarily a matter of right and wrong (though it certainly has an ethical dimension) but life and death. The paradox Jesus presents is that those who think they can preserve their lives (by healthy living, or accumulating comforts, or any other means) are deluded. Even the wealthiest person cannot cheat death. But whoever gives his or her life to the cause of Christ will find meaning and purpose in this life. *And* life everlasting.

v. 27—The reference here is to the final judgment. The reward will be primarily based on what each person has done with Christ, but there will also be a judgment of works for believers (Matt. 10:41–42; 1 Cor. 3:10–15).

v. 28—It's difficult to be certain about what Jesus is saying here. Some interpreters believe that Jesus was promising his listeners that his second coming would occur before all of the disciples died, and Jesus was wrong. That is a serious accusation to level against Jesus and the Bible. Another interpretation is that Jesus was prophesying an event that would occur very soon, his Transfiguration. In both Matthew and Mark, this statement immediately precedes the story of the Transfiguration. Others believe it refers to the resurrection of Christ. Still others believe that the Son of Man came into his kingdom in 70 AD when the temple fell and the Jewish nation was judged. We will explore these problems more fully when we examine Matthew 24.

APPLY

v. 14—What are some other current views of Jesus that you've heard or read about? How would you answer them?

v. 24—Notice that the emphasis isn't on denying yourself things but denying yourself. What does that mean in your life?

MEMORIZE

Matthew 16:24

This is a powerful statement of what it means to be a disciple of Christ.

PRAY

A: Praise the Son of Man, who willingly suffered for you.

C: Confess your unwillingness to take up the cross of suffering.

T: Thank God for revealing himself to Peter and to you.

S: Ask for the Spirit's help to lose your life for Christ and others today.

TELL

Share with someone what it means to you to deny yourself.

FEBRUARY 11

THE TRANSFIGURATION

Ask God to translate this mountaintop study into the valleys you enter today.

Matthew 17:1–20; Mark 9:2–29; Luke 9:28–43

Luke's is the briefest account, Matthew's is in the middle, and Mark's is the fullest version of the story. We'll follow Mark.

Mark 9:2–3—The traditional location for the Transfiguration has been Mt. Tabor in the south of Galilee. But at 1,000 feet, it hardly qualifies as a "high mountain," and there was a fortress at the top of the mountain at the time of Christ. The more likely location is beautiful Mt. Hermon near Caesarea Philippi, a peak of 9,200 feet that overlooks the Sea of Galilee. Luke 9:28 tells us that Jesus took his inner circle with him to pray. The word for "transfigured" describes highly polished gold, or the glare of the noonday sun. The experience is very similar to what happened to Moses on Mt. Sinai (Exod. 34:29–35).

v. 4—Moses represents the law and Elijah the Prophets, two major divisions of the Old Testament (the third being "the Writings" of poetry, wisdom literature, etc.). Matthew and Mark don't tell us the subject of their conversation with Jesus, but Luke 9:31 indicates that they discussed Jesus' upcoming death in Jerusalem. The word Luke uses for death is a very unusual Greek word, *exodus*, which means "departure." The first Exodus led God's people out of captivity. That's exactly what Christ's death did for us—he led us out of captivity to sin and gave us freedom.

vv. 5–6—The majesty of this great event blew Peter's mind. He refers to it many years later (2 Pet. 1:16–18) as proof of the truth of the Gospel. But at this time, Peter has what we might call an "edifice complex." He wants to make the mountaintop experience last by building some booths.

vv. 7–8—A cloud is a biblical symbol for the presence of God (Exod. 16:10, 19:9, 24:16). God's voice speaks for the second time (Christ's baptism is the first). The voice comes at two crucial times for Jesus: when he is beginning his ministry and when his ministry is ending. As at the baptism, the Father stresses that Jesus is God the Son and that he is loved by the Father. Whereas the voice of God was more directed to Jesus at his baptism, stressing the Father's pleasure in the Son, the voice here is more directed to the disciples, stressing that they should listen to the Son. When Moses and Elijah vanish, they see Jesus only. The disciples (and we) are given graphic evidence that the Old Testament was fulfilled in Christ (Matt. 5:17).

vv. 9–10—The full meaning of the Transfiguration would dawn on the disciples only after the resurrection. They were forbidden to tell others about it until then. It's important in understanding the disciples' reactions on Easter morning that they never understood that Christ would literally rise from the dead.

vv. 11–13—We've already discussed the fact that Jesus viewed John the Baptist as the fulfillment of the Elijah prophecy.

vv. 14–19—Jesus rejected Peter's suggestion to build booths because he knew that there was a need that he must meet in the valley. As always in the gospels, times of prayer and fellowship prepare Christ for times of service. In this case, it's interesting to notice the attitude of the scribes. They were probably debating whether the boy's possession was the result of his sin or his parents'. The hypocrites stand around and debate morality and law while the disciples try to do something about human pain.

vv. 20–29—Matthew 17:15 tells us that the boy was an epileptic, and he exhibits all those symptoms. But before we impose our superior scientific knowledge and say that the ignorant people confused epilepsy and demon possession, look at verse 25. Jesus rebuked the demon. Those who dismiss demon possession say that either Jesus was wrong and captive to the error of his culture, or he accommodated his listeners by putting on a show of casting out a demon. The former explanation convicts Jesus of ignorance, the latter of hypocrisy; neither are acceptable in God the Son. The only satisfactory explanation is that the boy had a demon in addition to epilepsy or a demon who caused epilepsy. Having said that, don't equate epilepsy with demon possession!

Three other things worth noting in this passage are:

1. Jesus turns around the father's statement (v. 22) in verse 23. When Jesus says, *"Everything is possible for him who believes,"* the rest of Scripture (1 John 5:14) requires us to understand his meaning as, "Everything in God's will is possible…"
2. Jesus doesn't rebuke the father for his honest statement in verse 24.

Sometimes that's exactly what we need to say to Jesus: "I do believe; help me overcome my unbelief!"

3. The father's failure was due to lack of faith. The failure of the nine disciples was due to lack of prayer (vv. 28–29). In essence they were the same thing.

APPLY

v. 4—What kind of captivity has Christ delivered you from?

v. 5—Do you ever make a god out of Christian community?

v. 7—What is the beloved Son calling you to do today?

MEMORIZE

Mark 9:24

This is to help you in those times you lack faith.

PRAY

A: Praise the majesty of the Transfigured One.

C: Confess the times you preferred to remain in the holy huddle like Peter rather than reaching out to human need.

T: Thank God for delivering you from your captivity to sin and sickness.

S: Ask God what ministry he has for you in the valley today.

TELL

Ask a fellow believer to join you in a bold request that you are praying.

FEBRUARY 12

THE TEMPLE TAX AND DEATH PREDICTIONS

PRAY

PRAY

Ask God to help you to respect authority even when leaders are misguided.

READ

Matthew 17:22–27, 20:17–19; Mark 9:30–32, 10:32–34; Luke 9:43–45, 18:31–34

OBSERVE

Matthew is the only one to tell the story of the fishy temple tax. The death prediction passages are very similar in the three gospels.

vv. 22–23—This is Jesus' second prediction of his death and resurrection. The major difference from the first announcement, just after Peter's confession, is that the reaction of all of the disciples is noted: they were "filled with grief." Perhaps the message of his death was so overwhelming that the good news of his resurrection didn't register with Christ's followers. They didn't seem surprised by the crucifixion. The resurrection took them completely off guard.

vv. 24–27—The story of the temple tax is unique to Matthew. The question posed by the tax collectors is different from the one Jesus is asked later: *"Is it right to pay taxes to Caesar or not?"* (Matt. 22:17). The temple tax wasn't paid to the Romans but to the Jews. It was a rare instance when Rome allowed a conquered kingdom to levy a tax. In this case, it was to maintain the temple. The two drachmas represented two days' wages for the average working man, so it wasn't a small sum.

Jesus' question to Peter illustrates the fundamental issue—Christ is the king who ushers in a new kingdom. He and his disciples are technically exempt from the requirements of the old kingdom (represented by the temple), but Jesus follows the principle of not offending the "weaker brothers" (see 1 Cor. 8 and Rom. 14). Some object to this miracle as violating Christ's commitment to do no selfish miracles (Matt. 4:3–4). Barclay proposes that what Jesus was really telling Peter was that the disciple should go fishing and earn the money necessary to pay the tax for Jesus and himself (Barclay, *The Gospel of Matthew*, 171–172). That is a terrible attempt to "demythologize" this miracle. It is the one time in the gospels that we are not shown the completion of the miracle, but it's obvious that Matthew does not intend this to be a folk tale or that Jesus was speaking metaphorically. The clear implication is that Peter went fishing and found a *stater*, a four-drachma coin, in the mouth of the first fish he caught. Michael Green points out that the species of fish most common in the Sea of Galilee has a large mouth which has no problem holding a larger coin than the *stater* (168).

20:17–19—Jesus' third and final prediction of his death and resurrection (other than the brief expression at the Passover—26:2) occurs with no comment from the disciples. They can't say that they weren't warned! We may criticize their blindness, but we also are slow learners who often don't respond to God's warnings.

APPLY

v. 27—We are citizens of heaven and sojourners on the earth. But Christ calls us to be subject to the legitimate laws of the state and to be careful not to offend the ruling authorities. Are there any laws that are particularly annoying to you (e.g., speed limits, income taxes)? In obeying them you are obeying Christ.

MEMORIZE

Matthew 20:18–19

Remember the fact that Jesus gave three eloquent warnings to his disciples of his impending death and resurrection. We are all the more accountable because we have the totality of Scripture!

PRAY

A: Praise the Son of Man who knew he was going to die a horrible death, but went to Jerusalem anyway.

C: Confess the times that you have been a slow learner.

T: Thank God for his provision for you to pay your taxes.

S: Ask God for the faith to obey his word—the first time!

TELL

Discuss with a Christian friend why you think Jesus prepared his disciples three times.

FEBRUARY 13

THE GREATEST IN THE KINGDOM

PRAY

Ask God for the faith of a child and ask him to protect you from harming one of his little ones.

READ

Matthew 18:1–9, 19:13–15; Mark 9:33–50, 10:13–16; Luke 9:46–50, 17:1–3, 18:15–17

OBSERVE

v. 1—The setup for Christ's teaching is a little different in each of the gospels. Mark states that an argument had begun among the disciples concerning who was the greatest, and Luke adds that Jesus knew what they were thinking. Matthew doesn't reference the argument but picks up the story at the point of the disciples' question, which Mark and Luke indicate was prompted by their internal squabble. Mark and Luke add that Jesus' teaching was in contrast to the disciples' sectarianism. In Mark, they objected to someone who was not part of their group driving out demons. In Luke, they wanted to call down fire from heaven to consume the Samaritans.

vv. 2–4—In all three gospels, Jesus uses a child as a visual object lesson of true greatness. Jesus commends childlike faith not childish faith. Children trust implicitly and believe that their parents are able to do anything. We're to have that same attitude toward God. However, Scripture does not affirm a faith that is naïve or uninformed, a Christian who doesn't grow and mature spiritually (Heb. 5:11–14).

vv. 5–6—In light of the crisis of sexual abuse of children in the church, these verses should be highlighted. We're never to cause another Christian to stumble in faith (Rom. 14:13). But God is especially concerned about children, who must be protected and nurtured.

vv. 7–9—Jesus addresses the larger problem of temptation. His teaching in these verses is hyperbole—exaggeration for effect, which was not only a popular form of teaching in his day, but considered very clever. Jesus uses exaggeration to empha-size that our eternal destiny is infinitely more important than anything else, including our bodies (which are very precious to most people—Eph. 5:29).

APPLY

v. 6—Is there anything in your behavior that could cause a child to stumble? What do you need to do to change it?

MEMORIZE

Matthew 18:3

This helps us remember the importance of a childlike faith.

PRAY

A: Praise God for his holy hatred of sin.

C: Confess the times you've been a bad influence on others.

T: Thank the Holy Spirit for power to resist temptation.

S: Pray for someone who is facing heavy testing.

TELL

If you're a parent, discuss with a fellow parent some ways you both could protect your children from the world's temptations. If you're a child, discuss with a friend some of the temptations to avoid.

FEBRUARY 14

FORGIVENESS IN ACTION

Ask God to reveal to you where you need to forgive and be forgiven.

Matthew 18:15–35 (we will study Matthew 18:10–14 when we look at Luke 15)

This section is unique to Matthew, but a tremendously important teaching section.

v. 15—Previously, Jesus had addressed the situation in which we recognize that we have sinned against a brother (Matt. 5:23–24). This is the opposite scenario, but his command is the same—the Christian is to take the initiative to be reconciled. The first crucial step is to keep the matter private: "just between the two of you." This does not mean that it's okay to discuss it with a friend for advice on how to best approach the person who has hurt you, nor does it permit sharing it with a prayer partner (or group) to intercede for you. It is to be private. If people would follow this biblical injunction, most of the Christian gossip in the Church would be squelched.

v. 16—The one or two witnesses shouldn't be handpicked cronies you have already influenced against your brother but objective parties who can act as mediators, perhaps church elders.

v. 17—In keeping with other passages that discuss church discipline (like 1 Cor. 5) and as a logical application of Christ's words, who should be informed is initially the leadership of the Church who can provide additional objective discernment of the situation. If the church leadership determines that the sinner is guilty and unrepentant, their verdict should be communicated to the larger church, and the unrepentant sinner should be excommunicated. That's the meaning of "treat him as you would a pagan or a tax collector." Keep in mind that Jesus was not consigning the unrepentant sinner to hell. Jesus himself had a powerful evangelistic ministry with pagans and tax collectors. Jesus is saying that the person who will not repent when confronted three times with unmistakable evidence is probably not a Christian. We should approach the person as though he or she needs to receive the Gospel.

v. 18—The meaning of "binding" and "loosing" has to do with forgiveness. In the name of Christ, and with his delegated authority, the leadership of the church has the authority to pronounce that a sin is forgiven (loosed) or not forgiven (bound) according to whether the biblical requirements of confession and repentance have been met.

vv. 19–20—The power of the Church in prayer is extended by Jesus. Not only does the Church have the power to pronounce forgiveness, but when we agree together in prayer, those prayers have great power and effectiveness. This is a tremendous argument for the value of corporate prayer. The understanding of the rest of Scripture, of course, is that we agree on that which is in God's will (1 John 5:14). Christ promises his presence to the Church in a special way when we gather. We don't have to invoke his presence or plead for it (the term "invocation" is flawed)—where two or three gather in his name, he is there!

vv. 21–22—The rabbis taught that we were required to forgive someone who sinned against us three times. Peter, in an attempt to be magnanimous, extends it to seven times. Peter thinks Jesus will be impressed with his gracious generosity. Jesus isn't impressed. The Greek words can be translated either "seventy-seven times" or "seventy times seven." Regardless of the number chosen, Christ's message is that we are required to forgive over and over again. There is no limit.

vv. 23–35—The Parable of the Unforgiving Servant is a powerful short story that illustrates the importance of forgiving one another "from the heart" (v. 35). Once again, Jesus uses hyperbole to compare the debt we have to God (the master) versus the debt that other people (fellow servants) have to us. The unforgiving servant owed his master the equivalent of more than a billion dollars. The Greek word translated "ten thousand" is *myrion*, from which we get the English word "myriad." It could also be translated "beyond number." Jesus wanted his hearers to think of an amount of money beyond which they could even imagine. A hundred *denarii*, the amount the fellow servant owed, would be about $10,000 today. There were six thousand *denarii* to a single talent, so the ungrateful servant had been forgiven of a debt at least six hundred thousand greater than his fellow servant owed him. That is the difference between the extent of our sin toward God as compared to the sins of others toward us.

Why did the master rescind his forgiveness and toss the ungrateful servant into jail? In essence, why would God choose not to forgive us? It's not that we earn his forgiveness by forgiving others. But if we fail to forgive others their relatively small offenses, it is proof positive that we have not really appreciated or fully accepted the Master's grace. That's when we are lost and imprisoned in a selfish cell of our own making.

APPLY

vv. 15–17—Do you consistently apply this process when you have a difference with a fellow Christian? If the Church really lived these verses, most of the divisions in the body of Christ could be healed.

vv. 19–20—Recognize the tremendous power Jesus grants to group prayer. Take seriously the privilege of agreeing in prayer with other believers.

v. 35—Whom do you need to forgive from the heart today?

MEMORIZE

Matthew 18:15

If you follow this one principle, your relationships will improve greatly.

PRAY

A: Praise God for his amazing grace.

C: Confess your unwillingness to forgive a particular individual who has hurt you.

T: Thank God for forgiving the serious sin you recently confessed.

S: Pray for that individual who has hurt you and ask God to richly bless him or her.

TELL

Tell someone who has sinned against you that you forgive and ask to be reconciled.

FEBRUARY 15

JESUS AND DIVORCE

PRAY

Pray for God's perspective on divorce to influence you instead of society's.

READ

Matthew 19:1–12; Mark 10:1–12; Luke 16:18

OBSERVE

Although the dialogue is a little different in Matthew and Mark, the content of Jesus' message is similar. Luke simply includes Jesus' bottom line in a collection of teachings.

vv. 1–2—Chapter 19 begins a pair of new developments in Christ's ministry. The previous 18 chapters were located mainly in Galilee. Chapters 19–28 take place in Judea, the capital area of Palestine. It would be like a local hero going to Washington, DC, to state his case. Also, rather than initiating action as he has thus far in the gospels, Jesus primarily reacts to the questions and statements of others, especially his opponents, in the rest of Matthew.

v. 3—The Pharisees' question was a trap for Jesus. If he said that divorce was lawful, they would accuse him of relaxing the law. If he said that it was not lawful, they would accuse him of placing himself above Moses.

vv. 4–6—Christ articulates the eternal principle from creation—God's intention is that marriage, the one flesh relationship, should be for a lifetime.

v. 7—In predictable fashion, the Pharisees play their Moses card. Moses had allowed for divorce in Deuteronomy 24:1–4. Men were permitted to issue a certificate of divorce, but women were not.

v. 8—Jesus interprets Moses' position as being a concession to sin, part of God's permissive will, but certainly not his directive will for his people.

v. 9—This is one of the hard sayings of Jesus, which many in our society and even in the Church have relaxed. It is a tragedy that the divorce rate among professing Christians in America is little better than the rate of unbelievers. Jesus permits one exception to his no divorce policy—marital unfaithfulness. The Jewish school that followed Rabbi Shimmai defined marital unfaithfulness broadly—failure to perform domestic duties could constitute unfaithfulness. Rabbi Gamaliel defined it narrowly as adultery. Jesus clearly sides with Gamaliel in the stricter interpretation. If a marriage partner has broken the one flesh covenant by having sexual intercourse with someone else, the offended party is permitted to divorce, but they are not commanded to do so.

The only other biblical rationale for divorce is given by Paul in 1 Corinthians 7:12–16. There, Paul deals with a situation in which one member of the marriage has become a Christian and the other has not. (Marriage between a professing Christian and an unbeliever should never happen—2 Cor. 6:14). The Christian must not divorce the unbeliever. The believer should make every effort to win his or her partner to the Lord and, failing that, attempt to live at peace. But if the unbelieving partner desires to separate, the Christian should let him or her go. Some interpreters believe that remarriage after divorce is not permitted by the Bible. A logical interpretation of verse 9 is that remarriage is anticipated. It's adultery if the divorce is not for biblical grounds, but if the innocent spouse was a victim of adultery by the guilty spouse, the remarriage is not adulterous.

In 1 Corinthians 7, Paul says that the believer who is deserted by an unbelieving spouse is not "bound" in such circumstances (v. 15). It's clear in context (v. 39) that the meaning "of not being bound" is the freedom to remarry, as long as it is to a fellow Christian. Though the Bible provides two exceptions, the thrust of Christ's teaching is to condemn the practice of easy divorce. At the beginning of the twenty-first century, the statistics in America were frightening—the majority of children will live in a home situation without two parents some time during their growing years. Incompatibility or "growing apart" are not valid reasons for Christians to divorce. The Holy Spirit can heal hurts and restore relationships. The Church needs to fight for marriages and against divorce.

vv. 10–12—The disciples' reaction is predictable in a culture that permitted divorce as casually as ours does. Jesus' reply isn't saying that it's better not to marry. He has already said that God's general intent was for men and women to marry (vv. 4–6). He is addressing those few people who genuinely have the gift of celibacy. Those who can accept that situation should. Paul expands on this in 1 Corinthians 7:32–38. Some believe, however, that he wrote what he did because of impending persecution (vv. 29–31).

APPLY

vv. 3–9—What is your position on divorce? Does it square with what Jesus says?

MEMORIZE

Matthew 19:9

This is Jesus' position on divorce.

PRAY

A: Praise God for creating marriage.

C: Confess if you've taken marriage too casually.

T: Thank God that he loves marriage.

S: Pray for a marriage that you know is in trouble.

TELL

When you have the opportunity, share with a spouse or a friend about how God heals hurts.

FEBRUARY 16

THE RICH YOUNG RULER

PRAY

Ask God to give you his perspective on wealth and his kingdom.

READ

Matthew 19:16–30; Mark 10:17–31; Luke 18:18–30

OBSERVE

This story made a big impression on the disciples, and all three of the Synoptic Gospels record it in depth. The descriptions are substantially alike, but Mark's account gives us some additional detail, so we'll follow his version.

Mark 10:17–18—The first detail Mark gives us is that the man ran to Jesus and threw himself at Jesus' feet in the middle of the highway, a real act of humility. (see Luke 18:18 for why he is called the rich young ruler). Many people misinterpret Jesus' answer to the "good teacher" question. Barclay, for example, says that Jesus was attempting to take the young man's focus away from him and place it on God the Father. Jesus is doing exactly the opposite. In his own clever way, Jesus was saying, "I am God. If you want eternal life, follow me."

vv. 19–20—Jesus always deals with a person on his or her own level first. This man was works-oriented, as we can see by his own words, "What must I do…." So Jesus answers him by rehearsing the law. Interestingly, Jesus only quotes the so-called Second Table of the Ten Commandments, those laws dealing with our duty toward our neighbor. Like Paul (Phil. 3:4–6), this man could honestly say that he had observed the law flawlessly. But he must have realized that outward observance was not enough; he still needed something or he wouldn't have come to Jesus.

vv. 21–22—Mark is the only one of the gospel writers to include the fact that *"Jesus looked at him and loved him."* What was it that Jesus saw in the young man? Maybe it was his sincerity, or perhaps Jesus saw great potential in the rich young ruler. Whatever it was, Jesus wouldn't lower the standards of discipleship in order to make an easy convert, even if he loved the person in a special way. Jesus gets to the heart of the matter when he tells the rich man to sell all that he has and give it to the poor. The young man's problem was with the Tenth Commandment as well as the First. He loved riches more than righteousness, possessions more than Christ. Verse 22 is one of the most tragic statements in the Bible. The rich young ruler is the only person in the New Testament who is said to have gone away sad from the presence of Christ.

vv. 23–27—Jesus directed some of his heaviest teaching and strongest words to the question of wealth. The disciples' initial reaction was shock. They may have assumed, as did most of their contemporaries, that rich people have made it, even in the kingdom of God. Jesus dispels that notion with a humorous comparison— ever try threading a needle with a camel? The camel was the largest animal around Palestine at the time of Christ. Christ prefaces the camel comment with an important truth: *"How hard it is to enter the kingdom of God!"* This includes both rich and poor; in fact, all of us. Jesus makes it clear in verse 27 that salvation is impossible for men to achieve—it is only possible with God (Eph. 2:8–9).

vv. 28–31—When faced with the example of a man who was unwilling to leave his riches behind, Peter attempts to justify himself and his fellow disciples by pointing out their sacrifices (though their often-torn nets and little boats were no big deal). We might expect Jesus to rebuke Peter, but he doesn't. The Lord doesn't judge our sacrifice as great or small by what we give away, but by what we keep. This is the lesson of the widow's penny (Mark 12:41–44) and the story of Ananias and Sapphira (Acts 5:1–11). Jesus further reassures the disciples by saying that they will be repaid. Notice that this is not a pie in the sky reward. Jesus emphasizes, "in this present age." Since the disciples did not become wealthy landowners, what did Jesus mean? He could only be referring to one thing, the Christian community. The Christian disciple is surrounded by the love and provision of countless brothers and sisters in Christ's family. But Christ is also realistic and doesn't promise us a rosy existence. With the blessing of Christian fellowship also comes the promise of persecution. Eternal life is the greatest promise of all, the Christian's eager expectation (1 Cor. 15:19). Verse 31 is an example of how Jesus turns the world's values upside down. The rich young man was a ruler in this world, but it is the lowly disciple who will ultimately rule.

APPLY

v. 19—How are you doing with respect to the Second Table of the law? Remember that Jesus emphasizes our attitudes as well as our actions—e.g., hatred equals murder and lust equals adultery.

v. 21—How about covetousness? Are you content with what you have or do you covet things?

v. 28—What have you left behind to follow Christ?

MEMORIZE

Mark 10:27

Remember how big God is.

PRAY

A: Praise God, who makes the impossible possible.

C: Confess your reliance on riches.

T: Thank God for showing you the danger of covetousness.

S: Pray for a rich young ruler you know.

TELL

Share with your family why material things aren't most important to you.

FEBRUARY 17

THE PARABLE OF THE WORKERS IN THE VINEYARD

PRAY

Ask God to show you the crucial truth in this parable.

READ

Matthew 20:1–16 (this parable is unique to Matthew)

OBSERVE

vv. 1–2—Most of the parables in Matthew begin, "For the kingdom of heaven is like…." Jesus wants us to understand the conditions for entering and prospering in the kingdom in which his Father reigns. The setup here would be very familiar to his listeners. The typical village square in Jesus' day had an area where the men of the village who were day laborers formed a labor pool. Landowners who needed labor would come and select some of them to work for the day. The daily wage was one *denarius,* which was subsistence pay.

vv. 3–7—The Jewish day began at sunrise (6 a.m.) and concluded at 6 p.m. This landowner hired additional workers at 9 a.m., noon, 3 p.m., and 5 p.m. The expression "the eleventh hour" has come into the English language to signify the last possible opportunity. It's a sign of the workers' desperation that they remained at the labor pool until 5 p.m. Unlike slaves, who could count on being fed regularly, or children of landowners who were well provided for, the day laborer's existence was precarious. Notice that the owner makes no financial arrangement with the later workers other than to pay them "whatever is right."

vv. 8–16—The conclusion of the parable gives one of the most glorious descriptions of the generosity of God. Jesus' listeners, and all those who operate on a works mentality, would be shocked and even offended that those who worked only one hour would receive the same as those who worked twelve. They would join the latter workers in their complaint of verse 12. But the owner, who obviously represents God, makes the case for grace. He has the freedom and the right to be generous. In context, Jesus might have told this parable as a warning to his disciples who wanted extra credit (Matt. 19:27–30) for their sacrifices. Every believer, no matter when they come to Christ or how much or how little they sacrifice, is equally precious to God. In the wider sense, the rest of the New Testament communicates that truth to Jewish Christians. They are not the most favored nation in God's eyes; Gentiles are equally valuable and important. An application for the Church today applies to the "charter member syndrome." Often, long-time members of a church feel that they have a vested interest in controlling the direction of the church. They resent new members who bring new ideas. This parable speaks powerfully against the "we've always done it this way" mentality. Those who have truly experienced the grace of the Master count it a privilege to work for him for a lifetime and welcome gladly those who come into the kingdom after them.

APPLY

v. 15—Do you ever find yourself resenting younger believers who are being recognized by the church? Ask God to give you his generosity of spirit.

MEMORIZE

Matthew 20:16

Notice that Jesus qualifies this statement in Matthew 19:30.

PRAY

A: Praise the God of grace.

C: Confess the times that you have resented new believers.

T: Thank God that everyone comes into his kingdom equally.

S: Pray for someone who is trying to work his way in.

TELL

Share with a friend or a small group why you think this parable is important.

FEBRUARY 18

THE GREATNESS OF SERVANTHOOD

PRAY

"I am a servant, listening for my Master's call."

—a contemporary Christian song

READ

Matthew 20:20–28; Mark 10:35–45

OBSERVE

Mark has the request coming from James and John. Matthew includes their mother. The two gospel writers may be recording separate incidents, or Mark may have excluded Mrs. Zebedee for his own reasons. Perhaps he wanted to focus on the ambition of the brothers. In Matthew's account, she fades from the picture quickly.

vv. 20–21—This is a good example of how a parent's desire for her children can be sinful even though it sounds pious. James and John's mother was still thinking of Jesus as an earthly messiah who would usher in his kingdom in this world.

vv. 22–23—Jesus quickly turns the focus to the Sons of Thunder. The cup was an Old Testament symbol for suffering (Ps. 75:8; Isa. 51:17; Ezek. 23:32–34). The response from James and John is foolish and proud (neither one of them followed him to the cross, although John was there). Jesus doesn't rebuke them. He instead underlines the fact that they will indeed suffer for his sake. Verse 23 stresses the Son's voluntary subordination to the Father (1 Cor. 11:3).

v. 24—The ten react strongly because they were also guilty of the same sin as James and John (Mark 9:34). We often most dislike in others what is present in ourselves.

vv. 25–28—The expression "lord it over them" is a good translation, but it is full of irony for the Christian. For us, "Lord" is the title for Christ, the one who condescended to our level. To "lord it over" someone is a contradiction in terms. Interestingly, Jesus changes the word from "servant" (*diakonos*), a waiter or waitress, to "slave" (*doulos*), a person who had no rights whatsoever. Paul referred to himself as the *doulos* of Christ. The concept of slavery to Christ is critical in the New Testament (1 Cor. 9:19; 2 Cor. 4:5; Gal. 5:13). The reason for our service is the supreme statement of verse 28. If the Lord of the Universe came to serve us, we should serve others. The last phrase is also full of meaning. A ransom is the price paid to buy back a slave. It was typically thirty pieces of silver. The Old Testament is full of the ransom concept. God ransomed Israel when they were slaves in Egypt. The psalmist makes it clear that no human can truly ransom another (Ps. 49:7–9). Christ's death ransomed us from our bondage to Satan and set us free to serve the Lord gratefully (Rom. 6:20–22; Gal. 5:1).

APPLY

v. 26—Think of a specific way that Christ wants you to serve others today.

MEMORIZE

Matthew 20:26-28

It's a long section, but tremendously important to remember.

PRAY

A: Praise Jesus that he is our Servant.

C: Confess the times that you've "lorded it over" others.

T: Thank God for opportunities to serve.

S: Pray for a chance to serve someone today.

TELL

Discuss with a friend or your small group how Jesus turns the world's standards upside down.

FEBRUARY 19

JESUS HEALS THE BLIND

PRAY

Ask the Lord to open your eyes to what he wants to do for you today.

READ

Matthew 20:29–34; Mark 10:46–52; Luke 18:35–43

OBSERVE

The three gospel writers may be writing about separate events, but the basics of each account is very similar. They are near Jericho, and a blind man or men call him "Son of David." Jesus asks what he (they) wants him to do for him (them), and then he heals him (them). Mark's and Luke's accounts are easy to harmonize —Mark learned the blind man's name (Bartimaeus, which may mean "Son of filth" in Aramaic) but Luke did not. It's the second blind man in Matthew that is different. Once again, it may be that Bartimaeus was more prominent in the early church, and so the second man was forgotten.

vv. 29–31—Jericho, the ancient city first captured by Joshua (Josh. 6), is five miles west of the Jordan River and fifteen miles northeast of Jerusalem. The scene as Jesus leaves Jericho is that of a renowned rabbi surrounded by his students and making a pilgrimage to the Holy City for the Passover. It was customary for every male Jew who lived within fifteen miles of Jerusalem to attend the Passover there. Those who were unable to go would line the streets of a town like Jericho to see the illustrious Passover pilgrims and wish them well. The blind men were part of that large crowd.

Blind people had a very difficult time in the ancient world. There was no United Way to provide for them and, unless they had loyal friends or family, they were relegated to the status of beggars. It didn't help that many Jews considered their problem to be the result of sin (John 9:1–2). Sometimes, the young men of the village would mock beggars even to the point of pelting them with manure. But these blind men were not to be deterred. They knew enough about Jesus to know that he was of the tribe of Judah, a son of David. It's very possible that they recognized that this was a Messianic title, for the Messiah would come from the household of David (Jer. 33:14–17; Luke 1:32–33). Couple that with the fact that they addressed him as "Lord," the faith of the two blind men is impressive.

vv. 32–33—In the midst of possibly thousands of people, Jesus hears the cry of two outcasts in need. Christ was obviously aware of their problem, but he asks the needy person to confess their specific need. He does the same with us in prayer. Notice that he says much the same thing to the blind men that he said to James and John (Matt. 20:21), but the request and the response are very different. If Jesus were to ask you right now "What do you want me to do for you?" what would you ask? In Mark's account, Bartimaeus calls Jesus *Rabboni*, which is Aramaic for "my master." It was the highest title of honor in the Jewish schools. The only other person to use it in the New Testament is Mary Magdalene (John 20:16).

v. 34—The blind men are among the very few people Jesus healed who immediately followed the Great Healer. Barclay comments, "[They] began with need, went on to gratitude, and finished with loyalty—and that is a perfect summary of the stages of discipleship" (Barclay, *Gospel of Mark*, 272).

APPLY

v. 32—How would you answer Jesus' question?

MEMORIZE

Matthew 20:32

This is an important offer from Jesus that we should regularly remember.

PRAY

A: Praise the God of compassion and healing.

C: Confess the times you've ignored hurting people like the blind men.

T: Thank God for your sight.

S: Pray for someone who is spiritually blind.

TELL

Share with a Christian friend Jesus' offer in Matthew 20:32.

FEBRUARY 20

PALM SUNDAY

PRAY

Pray for the words and attitude to properly praise the Prince of Peace.

READ

Matthew 21:1–11; Mark 11:1–11; Luke 19:28–44; John 12:12–19

OBSERVE

As we move into Holy Week, we begin to see the events of Jesus' life recorded in all four gospels, though not always identically and not always from the same point of view. Matthew and Mark give the basic Palm Sunday account. Since Luke adds the most detail, we will follow his Palm Sunday narrative. John adds the fact that the crowds were enthusiastic because they had heard that Jesus raised Lazarus from the dead.

Luke 19:28—The Jews always referred to "going up to Jerusalem" because it was a city set on a hill and higher in elevation than the surrounding countryside (Ps. 48:1–2).

Palm Sunday

—Palm Sunday begins in the twin cities of Bethpage, "House of Figs," and Bethany, "House of Dates." They were less than a Sabbath day's journey (one mile) from Jerusalem. The Mount of Olives overlooks the Holy City and is only several hundred yards from the East (Golden) Gate.

vv. 30–35—Although this is the first recorded visit of Jesus to Jerusalem in the Synoptics, John's gospel makes it clear that Jesus and the disciples went to the capital city several times for the great feasts. Maybe Jesus had arranged with a friend in Bethany or Bethpage beforehand, or maybe it was a supernatural revelation that Jesus related to the two disciples. Whichever it was, the colt's owners were certainly sympathetic to the cause for they knew Jesus as "the Lord." That title is rarely used in the gospels.

vv. 36–38—The drama that unfolds is no accident. Matthew and John both quote Zechariah 9:9: *"Say to the daughter of Zion, 'See your king comes to you, gentle and riding on a donkey, on a colt, the foal of a donkey'."* Most Jews would be familiar with that prophecy. In the Ancient Near East, if a conquering king entered a city riding on a horse, it symbolized that he was still at war. If he rode a donkey, he came in peace. The dramatic entry symbolized two things: 1) Jesus identified himself publicly as the King of the Jews, the Messiah, and 2) He is the Prince of Peace, not the warlord that the people wanted.

The actions of the people suggest that they were ready to crown Jesus king, but not in the spiritual sense. When they spread their garments before him, they did exactly as the crowd had done for the warrior Jehu when he was anointed king (2 Kings 9:13). Matthew, Mark, and John record the crowd shouting, "Hosanna!" which means, "Save us, we pray!" "Blessed is he who comes in the name of the Lord" was the regular greeting given to the pilgrim when he reached the temple, but it meant much more when the people called Jesus "the king" and added, "Peace in heaven and glory in the highest!" "He who is coming" was the title the Jews often used for Messiah. Between the lines of these exclamations is the hope that Jesus would be the one who would pull off a supreme miracle by defeating the hated Romans.

vv. 39–40—The Pharisees' reaction is typical. They hated Jesus and rejected anything and anyone who praised him. Christ's famous response to them indicates that, though he was humble, Jesus did not deny who he was nor the appropriate nature of praising him.

vv. 41–44—There is a beautiful chapel on the Mount of Olives called *Dominus Flavit*, "Our Lord Weeps." It commemorates Jesus' lament over Jerusalem. He weeps over the blindness of the people whom he already knows will not recognize him for who he really is. Verses 43–44 are a prophecy of the destruction of Jerusalem, which would occur in 70 AD. Christ ties that destruction to their rejection of him.

APPLY

v. 31—If Jesus' disciples (the church) came to you today and said, "The Lord needs it," what would they be referring to that you have?

vv. 37–40—Keep in mind that the Lord loves to hear his people's praise.

v. 41—Is there something in your city that Christ weeps over? What might he want you to do about it?

MEMORIZE

Luke 19:40

This proclaims the truth that all creation praises the Son of God.

PRAY

A: Praise the humble King of Kings.

C: Confess the times you have been unwilling to part with something the Lord needs for his ministry.

T: Spend a significant time in praise and thanksgiving today in keeping with the Palm Sunday passage.

S: Intercede for someone who is spiritually blind and facing destruction.

Tell

The next time you have the opportunity to worship, "Praise God in a loud voice" for all the miracles you have seen.

FEBRUARY 21

JESUS CLEANSES THE TEMPLE

PRAY

Ask God to show you the value of righteous anger and the danger of unrighteous anger.

READ

Matthew 21:12–17; Mark 11:15–19; Luke 19:45–48; John 2:13–24

OBSERVE

John's account of Jesus cleansing the temple appears to be early in his ministry, but the Synoptics all have the cleansing during his last week of life. The traditional explanation is that Christ cleansed the temple twice, but another possibility is that John's gospel is not a chronological account, and that most of the gospel focuses on the last week of Christ's life. In any case, the temple cleansings are sufficiently similar that we can study them together.

vv. 12–13—Matthew's language is very matter of fact. Mark indicates that Jesus saw the temple situation on Sunday but went to Bethany for the evening (Mark 11:11). His expression of anger on Monday, then, was not spontaneous rage but a considered response. The money-changers and animal-sellers were part of an elaborate system of rip-offs that the priests blessed. Animal vendors sold acceptable sacrifices (the only ones judged so by the priests) at exorbitant prices. Money changers replaced the foreign currency of pilgrims with the local money needed to pay the temple tax. The usual charge was half a day's wage. Mark 11:16 indicates that these con men were using the outer court (The Court of the Gentiles) as a thoroughfare for their goods. It was supposed to be a place of prayer for the

Gentiles and a place of spiritual preparation for the Jews before they entered the inner courts. Does the violence of Christ's actions surprise you? John 2:15 tells us that he made a whip of cords from the temple drapes and lashed the thieves. The Church often portrays Jesus as "gentle Jesus, meek and mild" and the one who teaches us to be good little boys and girls and not upset the status quo. This is an entirely different person—a man of action who provoked reactions! He would not allow sin to go unchallenged.

vv. 14–17—In contrast to the Lord, the chief priests and teachers of the law expressed sinful anger. They resented Jesus for attracting attention to himself (and away from them) by his miraculous healings. They also resented the fact that the children were praising him. "Hosanna to the Son of David" was definitely a Messianic praise. As he often does, Jesus answers them with Scripture, a quote from Psalm 8:2. He probably spent the evening in the home of Lazarus, Martha, and Mary.

APPLY

vv. 12–13—Is there anything in your church or society that should prompt you to righteous anger? How would the Lord have you express it?

v. 14—The same Lord who afflicted the comfortable also comforted the afflicted.

MEMORIZE

Matthew 21:13

This helps you remember proper reverence for the house of God.

PRAY

A: Praise God for his righteous wrath.

C: Confess any time that you have failed to respect God's house.

T: Thank God for the Church, his house of prayer.

S: Pray for the children in your church that they might praise the Lord in a way that is pleasing to him.

TELL

Share with someone the difference between righteous and sinful anger.

FEBRUARY 22

JESUS CURSES THE FIG TREE

PRAY

Ask God to teach you about prayer through the story of the fig tree.

READ

Matthew 21:18–22; Mark 11:12–14, 20–25

OBSERVE

Matthew and Mark are the only ones who record this little story. Mark's account covers two days. Matthew has only one day.

vv. 18–20—Mark points out that the reason the fig tree had no fruit was that spring is not the season for fig trees to bear fruit. Jesus wasn't ignorant of that fact. Why, then, did he curse the fig tree? The best explanation is that the story of the barren fig tree is an acted-out parable. The fig tree was a well-known symbol for the nation of Israel (Jer. 24:10). Jesus was saying that God's Son came to Jerusalem looking for the fruit of faith, and he found none. It is fitting that this passage is connected to the cleansing of the temple, for the message is very similar.

vv. 21–22—Jesus uses the withered fig tree as an illustration of the power of prayer. The key words are faith and belief—trusting God to accomplish what he wills. Peter Marshall gives the illustration of a child who gives a toy to his father to fix. The child is so anxious that he keeps bugging his dad, making it difficult for the father to do his work. Finally, the child grabs the toy back and says, "You weren't going to fix it anyway!" A lot of our prayer is like that. We lack trust and we demand that God do it our way. Mark 11:25 also adds the importance of forgiveness if we want our prayers to be answered.

APPLY

v. 22—One way to pray in faith believing that God will answer is to pray God's Word. He is always faithful to his Word, and his Word communicates his will. Revolutionize your prayer life by praying the words of Scripture.

MEMORIZE

Matthew 21:22

This is a promise. 1 John 5:14 is the condition.

PRAY

A: Praise God who answers prayer.

C: Confess your lack of faith.

T: Thank God for miraculous things you've seen him do.

S: Intercede for a really difficult situation that you know about.

TELL

Share with someone else that prayer request and ask him or her to join you in praying about it.

FEBRUARY 23

JESUS QUESTIONS THOSE WHO QUESTION HIS AUTHORITY

PRAY

Ask God to help you to understand (stand under) his Word today.

READ

Matthew 21:23–32; Mark 11:27–33; Luke 20:1–8

OBSERVE

The three accounts are practically identical in recounting the dialogue between Jesus and the religious authorities. Matthew is the only one who adds the Parable of the Two Sons.

vv. 23–24—It was now Tuesday of Holy Week. The rumblings of the coming storm grow louder and louder. Jesus strolls among the huge marble columns of the temple in rabbinical fashion and teaches his followers. The religious mafia comes and angrily demands to see Christ's credentials. They are particularly incensed over his cleansing of the temple, which affected their pocketbooks. The chief priests and elders formed the Sanhedrin, the council of seventy men who ruled over the religious affairs of the Jews.

v. 24–27—Jesus is so clever and wise! Once more, he turns the tables on them. His question is much more than a clever trick. It is a moral probe that gets to the heart of his opponents' problem. They were spiritually blind, more concerned with something being safe or unsafe than it being right or wrong. If they had confessed their misjudging of John, they could have been forgiven. They could have even seen that John pointed to Jesus as the Messiah. They didn't have the guts to say what they thought—that John was a rabble-rouser—because they were afraid that the common people might reject them. Ironically, the accusers walk away weakly, condemned by their own contradictions and lack of courage.

vv. 28–32—The Parable of the Two Sons would certainly qualify as one of the lesser known of Jesus' parables. But it has a very important message, both for his time and for now. In the context of Jesus' time and teaching, the first son represents the obvious sinners. They did not respond to the initial call to work in the vineyard (Israel, the kingdom of God), but they changed their mind when Jesus came. The other son is like the older brother in the Parable of the Prodigal Son. He claimed to be dutiful, but didn't respond to the call that Jesus proclaimed. The religious leaders should have been touched when they saw tax collectors and prostitutes entering the kingdom. Instead, they condemned them and the Messenger of the Kingdom. In today's Church there are many who say that they are followers of Jesus Christ. They know the Bible and they know theology, but when it comes to taking action for the kingdom, they are too busy. The Lord then bypasses the pillars of the Church and uses new believers who may lack the biblical and theological knowledge but who have a heart for the Lord. What pleases God most is when people both know their faith and live their faith (Ja. 1:22).

APPLY

vv. 28–32—Which of the sons in this parable do you identify with? God doesn't want you to be like either one! He wants us to respond positively to him and then follow through.

MEMORIZE

Matthew 21:31

"I tell you the truth, the tax collectors and the prostitutes are entering the kingdom of God ahead of you." This verse will help us remember that it's not knowledge, but a loving response to Christ that matters (1 Cor. 8:1).

PRAY

A: Praise God for his wisdom.

C: Confess the times that you've been like the first brother.

T: Thank God for his mercy in saving sinners (like you and me).

S: Intercede for someone caught up in empty religion.

TELL

With a friend or your small group, discuss how the Parable of the Two Sons applies to you.

FEBRUARY 24

THE PARABLE OF THE TENANTS OF THE VINEYARD

PRAY

Pray that you might understand and be able to communicate the powerful truth of this parable.

READ

Matthew 21:33–46; Mark 12:1–12; Luke 20:9–18

OBSERVE

Mark gives the basic parable, Luke adds some explanation, but Matthew gives the fullest portrayal of both the parable and Jesus' application.

v. 33—The vineyard, like the fig tree, is a symbol for Israel. The basic structure for this parable is taken from Isaiah 5:1–7. It wouldn't have taken long for the authorities to see that this was another statement of judgment against them.

vv. 34–36—Christ's parable departs from Isaiah 5 at this point. While in both passages the owner of the vineyard is God the Father and the tenants of the well-equipped vineyard are the people of Israel, Isaiah's point is that wild grapes (representing disobedience) are growing. Christ's parable goes much deeper. The owner sends servants, who represent the prophets, to call the tenants back to their responsibility to the owner. The Jewish leaders were willing to admit that their forefathers had killed the prophets (see Matt. 23:29–39), but they were unwilling to admit that they were about to do the same thing.

vv. 37–39—This is a profound statement of Christ's self-understanding. Those who claim that Jesus didn't understand himself to be the Son of God are ignoring passages like this. Jesus sees himself as part of the prophetic line, but he realizes that he is much more. He is the Son. There is great feeling in the words, "They will respect my son." Notice that the tenants recognized who the son was, but they also realized that to respect him meant to give up the ownership that they were claiming. Isn't that true of people today?

vv. 40–41—The idea that the owner would punish the tenants and turn the vineyard over to other tenants (the Gentiles) would have shocked the Jewish leaders. Luke 20:16 says that their response was, "May this never be!" This phrase is translated as "God forbid!" in the RSV and "Surely not!" in the ESV.

vv. 42–44—Jesus quotes Psalm 118:22–23, the same psalm the people proclaimed on Palm Sunday: *"Hosanna! Blessed is he who comes in the name of the Lord!"* The stone-the-builders-rejected passage prophecies that though evil may have the upper hand for a brief time, the Son of God will rule as the cornerstone of the New Kingdom, his Church. The Gentiles, not the Jews, become the people of God since they will bear God's fruit. Many of the manuscripts of Matthew don't include verse 44, which is a further statement of condemnation upon the Jews (see Isa. 8:14–15).

vv. 45–46—The chief priests and Pharisees got the point of the parable. In verse 46, we see why they wanted Jesus to be betrayed in a lonely place like Gethsemane, because they didn't want to have to deal with the crowds. The Pharisees saw Jesus as a dangerous revolutionary who was turning the crowds against them.

APPLY

v. 33—Just like Israel, God has given you a well-equipped vineyard (see Eph. 1:3). What kind of grateful response does he want from you?

vv. 38–39—Are you trying to hold on to the ownership of your life?

MEMORIZE

Matthew 21:42

Remember that Jesus is the foundation of the Church.

PRAY

A: Praise God for his patience in continually appealing to humanity.

C: Confess your failure to give God the fruit that belongs to him.

T: Thank God for including the Gentiles in his plan of salvation.

S: Intercede for someone who thinks that Jesus is only a good teacher and not God the Son.

TELL

How would you answer someone who said, "Jesus never claimed to be God"?

FEBRUARY 25

THE PARABLE OF THE WEDDING BANQUET

PRAY

Ask for God's grace to respond to him whenever he calls you to do something.

READ

Matthew 22:1–14; Luke 14:7–24

OBSERVE

The accounts in Matthew and Luke have some significant differences. The context in Luke is people taking the positions of honor at a feast. Jesus urges them to be humble and encourages them to invite the poor and needy to their banquets. He also has the original invitees in his parable turning down the invitation with creative excuses. Nevertheless, there is enough similarity to the parables to consider them together.

vv. 1–2—The context in Matthew is Jesus' teaching aimed at the hypocritical and blind religious leaders. The parable begins as most do in Matthew with, "The kingdom of heaven is like...." The king is clearly God the Father and, as the previous parable established, the son is Jesus.

vv. 3–7—The message here is very similar to the Parable of the Tenants of the Vineyard. The king, like the master, showed kindness to the people he invited, and they not only rejected his kindness, they persecuted those who delivered the message. The king responds to their rejection with rage and destroys them. It is a chilling picture of God's judgment of the religious authorities.

vv. 8–10—If the original invitees won't come, the king will invite other people (John 1:11–12). The "good and bad" may refer to the fact that many of the Gentiles were bad in the sight of the Jews.

vv. 11–14—The wedding clothes are a metaphor for righteousness (Isa. 61:10; Rev. 19:8). Both "good" and "bad" people must be clothed in the righteousness of Christ in order to share the heavenly banquet. *"Throw him outside, into the darkness, where there will be weeping and gnashing of teeth"* is a metaphor for hell (Matt. 8:12). The doctrine of election, that "few are chosen," is strong in Matthew. Jesus presented it in 11:27, but uses the term "the elect" with increasing frequency at the end of the gospel (24:22, 24, 31) as a designation for his disciples.

APPLY

v. 10—Do you think that there will be "bad" people in heaven; people not considered respectable?

vv. 11–12—Are you trusting in Christ's righteousness alone for your salvation?

MEMORIZE

Matthew 22:14

This presents the truth that many hear the message but few respond.

PRAY

A: Praise God that he graciously invites us to share the riches of his glory.

C: Confess the times that you have failed to respond to God's invitation.

T: Thank God for his mercy to "good" and "bad" people.

S: Pray that God would use you to present the invitation to someone this week.

TELL

Ask God for the opportunity to share the Gospel with someone you know isn't saved.

FEBRUARY 26

JESUS' OPPONENTS ASK THREE QUESTIONS AND HE ASKS ONE

PRAY

May you really see the humanity of Christ as he struggles with difficult questions and understand that the wisdom he received is available to you.

READ

Matthew 22:15–46; Mark 12:13–35; Luke 20:19–44

OBSERVE

Matthew and Mark are very similar in describing the grilling of Jesus in the temple. Luke doesn't include the question about the greatest commandment, but otherwise this is similar.

v. 15—These were not the questions of seekers, but the evil probes of people who were trying to destroy Jesus. Who knows how many hours were spent in back rooms dreaming up these trick questions? The commitment and resources of evil are something that the children of light must take seriously (Matt. 10:16; Luke 16:8).

vv. 16–18—The Pharisees, separatists who hated Rome, and the Herodians, people who owed their livelihood to the Roman government, were strange bedfellows. It's a measure of their common hatred of Jesus and their love of evil that they team up to attempt to trip him up. Notice that they try to set him up with flattery. They tell Jesus that he is an upright man who speaks the truth and is afraid of nobody—all of which is true! They were trying to get him to speak out against Rome, but Jesus saw through their charade and knew their insincerity. It's no surprise that they begin with a political teaser. If Jesus says that paying taxes to Caesar is wrong, the

Herodians would arrest him as a revolutionary, disloyal to Tiberius Caesar. If he says that paying taxes is right, the Pharisees could discredit him in the eyes of the masses as a Roman sympathizer.

vv. 19–22—The tax in question was known as the hated census, which every adult had to pay just for existing. It was one denarius, equal to one day's labor. In answering this question, Jesus establishes a principle that greatly influences history: that the state and God have their realms of authority. We need to understand that those realms are not totally separate, for Jesus will soon teach that the claims of God are all-inclusive (Matt. 22:37). But the overall teaching of the New Testament is that governmental authority is instituted by God (Rom. 13:1), and as long as the state functions responsibly (Rom. 13:4) obeying the state is obeying God. There are great advantages to having civil order.

vv. 23–33—The next question comes from the bitter opponents of the Pharisees, the Sadducees. The Sadducees were the theological liberals of Christ's day. Composed of mostly aristocratic priests, they attached more importance to the Pentateuch (Genesis through Deuteronomy) than to the rest of Scripture. They found no evidence for eternal life in those books, ignoring later references like Job 19:25.

Jesus condemned them for knowing neither the Scriptures nor the power of God. Paul instituted a near riot when he was brought before a combined group of Pharisees and Sadducees by saying that he was on trial because he believed in the resurrection of the dead (Acts 23:6–10).

The Sadducees' question is based on the Law of the Levirate (Deut. 25:5–10). The question is an exaggeration which attempted to make the whole idea of the resurrection seem ridiculous. As he often does, Jesus answers the question profoundly on two levels. First, he deals with the manner of the resurrection in heaven. The laws of this life no longer hold. Marriage holds no significance there because *agape* love relationships will be all-inclusive.

Interestingly, Jesus brings in the comparison to angels, whom the Sadducees also rejected, but whose existence is taught in the Scriptures (with twenty-eight references in the Pentateuch alone). The second level of Jesus' reply deals with the fact of the resurrection. Again, from the Pentateuch (Exod. 3:6), Jesus shows that Abraham, Isaac, and Jacob were still in existence when God spoke to Moses. Therefore, they must have been raised from the dead. Jesus' regard for the verbal inspiration of Scripture is impressive. His entire argument rests on one vowel which sets apart the verb "I am" from the verb "I was." It's no surprise that the crowds were impressed with his brilliant handling of his opponents.

vv. 34–40—The third controversy was with a scribe (lawyer), an expert in Old Testament law. Mark tells us that he was impressed with Jesus' answers. He asks the Lord a far more honest and important question than the other two. Jesus answers him by combining two key texts creatively. The first is the great creedal statement of Israel, the *Shema* ("Hear!") found in Deuteronomy 6:4. Every devout Jew wore a small leather case on his forehead and wrist called a phylactery in which the words of the *Shema* were written.

When Jesus quoted this great statement as the first commandment, the devout Jews in the audience would have been nodding their heads. But combining the *Shema* with Leviticus 19:18 is unique to Jesus. He was saying a profound thing: loving God, loving your neighbor, and loving yourself are all connected. The scribe finds himself agreeing with the man he had been sent to discredit (Mark 12:32–33) and the one he had been sent to judge was now judging him (Mark 12:34)! This paradox is true: whenever a mortal man sets out to judge the claims of Christ, he is inevitably judged by them.

vv. 41–45—This passage is often called "Christ's Unanswerable Question" since his listeners had to understand Christ's pre-existence as God in order to answer it. The reason David, inspired by the Spirit, could call the Messiah "Lord" is that the Messiah is the eternal God made flesh (John 1:1–3, 14). Jesus quotes Psalm 110:1. This is the Old Testament verse most frequently quoted in the New Testament. It is a prophecy of Christ's ascension when the Lord (*Yahweh*, God the Father) exalts "my Lord" (*Adonai*, the Messiah Jesus).

APPLY

v. 21—What is an example (besides taxes) of something that belongs to Caesar? How about something that belongs to God? Can you think of an example when the two might conflict?

v. 29—Are you coming to know the Scriptures and the power of God? Are you really trying to apply God's Word to your life?

vv. 37–39—How can you love the Lord more fully today and love your neighbor as yourself?

MEMORIZE

Matthew 22:37–39

These are Christ's great commandments.

PRAY

A: Praise God for his wisdom.

C: Confess your failure to love God with all your heart, soul, mind, and strength, and your neighbor as yourself.

T: Thank God for your government.

S: Ask for wisdom and anointing that you might know both the Scriptures and the power of God.

TELL

Share with someone today how much you love him or her because of Christ.

FEBRUARY 27

SEVEN WOES

There's a bit of the Pharisee in all of us. Ask God to help you see it today.

READ

Matthew 23:1–39; Mark 12:38–40; Luke 11:37–54, 13:31–35, 19:41–44, 20:45–47

OBSERVE

Matthew's section of woes is much more elaborate than Mark's or Luke's.

vv. 1–12—One of the major themes of Matthew's gospel is, *"Don't make a show of your piety"* (6:1–18). The scribes and Pharisees were the epitome of religious showmen: *"Everything they do is for men to see."* Jesus told the people that they were to obey the teaching of the Pharisees because they occupy the position of authority, but he had harsh words for those who don't practice what they preach. In verses 8–10, Jesus rejects the use of titles, a principle the Church has not followed throughout history. The conclusion of his introduction to the woes consists of familiar words, which we saw in Matthew 20:26 and Luke 14:11.

vv. 13–14—The first woe concerns the hard-heartedness of the scribes and Pharisees. They had rejected the message of the kingdom of heaven which Jesus declared, and they put an obstacle before those who wanted to respond to his message.

v. 15—They had a zeal for evangelism, but it was misguided. Like Jehovah's Witnesses today, they went to great lengths to win converts, but since their message is false, the person is still lost.

vv. 16–22—One of the most contemptible qualities of the religious leaders was their greed. They were lovers of money who would foreclose on a widow who missed a mortgage payment (Mark 12:40). While Jesus opposed most oaths in principle (Matt. 5:33–37), he was repulsed by hypocritical oaths which valued money above the temple.

vv. 23–24—The scribes and Pharisees were scrupulous tithers, even giving a tenth of the spices which were grown on the windowsills of their homes. Jesus endorses their practice of tithing, but faults them for ignoring more crucial issues: justice, mercy, and faithfulness. The expression "You strain out a gnat but swallow a camel" was considered hilarious by Jesus' contemporaries.

vv. 25–28—Woes five and six make the same point. It's easy to look good on the outside and impress people, but what matters is the inside. That's what God is concerned about.

vv. 29–39—The seventh woe is very personal to Jesus. He begins by establishing that the Scribes and Pharisees were the heirs of those who killed the prophets. Abel was the first righteous man to be killed in the Old Testament, and Zechariah was the last. It's clear that Jesus sees himself as their next victim. Christ's lament over Jerusalem is poignant and profound. Verse 39 looks back to Palm Sunday and forward to Christ's Second Coming.

APPLY

vv. 5, 12—Do you ever do things to impress other people? True humility isn't concerned with making an impression.

v. 23—Are you tithing? Are you also practicing justice, mercy, and faithfulness?

v. 28—Have you asked God to cleanse the inside of your life?

MEMORIZE

Matthew 23:12

This summarizes the danger of pride and the value of humility.

PRAY

A: Praise God for his wrath toward sin.

C: Confess your pride and hypocrisy.

T: Thank God for his mercy to those who repent.

S: Intercede for a proud Pharisee whom you know (maybe yourself!).

TELL

When people claim that the Old Testament is full of God's wrath and the New Testament is full of love and mercy, mention this passage!

FEBRUARY 28

THE LAST DAYS ACCORDING TO JESUS

Ask God for his Spirit's illumination to understand this very difficult passage.

Matthew 24:1–35; Mark 13:1–31; Luke 21:5–33

The prophecies in Matthew, Mark, and Luke are very similar. There is no question that these are some of the most difficult chapters in the Bible to understand. One reason it is hard for us is that the images Jesus uses come right out of Jewish history. An especially important concept in the Old Testament is the "Day of the Lord" when God would intervene decisively in human history. Read Isaiah 13:6–13 and Joel 2:28–32 for background. Many people have misinterpreted eschatology (the study of the End Times) in the New Testament by both neglecting the Old Testament source and ignoring the fact that Jesus prophesied several events besides his Second Coming. In Matthew 24, there are four prophetic themes:

1. The destruction of Jerusalem
2. The persecution of Christians
3. The great tribulation
4. The Second Coming of Christ

The difficult question is how they all fit together.

vv. 1–8—It's always crucial to study the context when trying to interpret Scripture. The context for Jesus' teaching about the End Times is the destruction of the temple. That marked the end of Jewish influence. Herod's temple was begun in 20 BC and was still unfinished fifty years later when Christ was speaking these words. It was one of the wonders of the ancient world. It was built on top of Mt. Moriah and needed a huge platform to support it. Some of the stones used for the foundation of the building were forty-feet-long by twelve-feet-high by eighteen-feet-wide!

The temple rivaled the Egyptian pyramids as a marvel of architecture. It's no wonder that the poor Galileans were impressed. Yet, despite its magnificence, Jesus' amazing prophecy of destruction was accurate. Within forty years, the Roman army under Titus thoroughly destroyed Jerusalem after a horrible siege in which over a million Jews starved to death. There were a myriad of false messiahs in the middle of the first century as well as many wars and natural disasters (the most famous being the eruption of Mt. Vesuvius and the destruction of Pompeii), but it may be a mistake to restrict the events described to one point in time. Based on the Old Testament distinction between the Present Age and the Age to Come (ushered in by the Day of the Lord), the prophecies could be the continuous experience of the Church between the resurrection and the Second Coming.

vv. 9–14—We generally associate persecution with the early Christians, but with the exception of John the Baptist, the disciples had not seen any real physical persecution up to this point. Within forty years, however, dying for the faith became a common experience. Christians were crucified, drowned, eaten by wild animals, and used as human torches. The accounts are gruesome. The Greek word for "witness" is "martyr." The "perseverance of the saints" (v. 13) is an important doctrine in the New Testament. Those who belong to Christ will hold fast because God holds them fast. It's no coincidence that Jesus links persecution with preaching the Gospel to Gentiles. As persecution scattered the church, the Gospel went with the dispersed believers (Acts 8:4).

vv. 15–22—The "abomination that causes desolation" (Dan. 12:11) refers to a specific horror story in the history of Israel. In the time between the Old and New Testaments, the Jews were ruled by a Syrian king, the egomaniac Antiochus Epiphanes ("the glorious appearance"). He attempted to destroy the Jewish religion, going so far as to commit the ultimate sacrilege, sacrificing a pig on the altar of the temple.

Luke 21:20 tells us that the sacrilege would be committed by encircling armies, the Romans who brought their standards bearing an image of an eagle (images being forbidden by the Second Commandment) into the temple. The tribulation and distress were incredible, as we already noted. Over a million Jews died. They even resorted to cannibalism within the walls of Jerusalem. Many Christians, however, because of Christ's prophecy in this passage, fled to the hills of Pella in Trans-Jordan and were saved. They were able to do this because Titus delayed his siege, hoping that Jerusalem would surrender. Perhaps this is what is meant by the shortening of the days. Clearly, as Luke points out, this tribulation would be at the hands of the Romans, and the events of 70 AD certainly fit.

vv. 23–35—Jesus warns that false messiahs will proliferate in those days, and it was true in the first century. The return of Christ will be sudden, like lightning. It will also be unmistakable, just as a collection of vultures (or Roman eagles) is hard to miss. Matthew quotes Isaiah 13:10 and 34:4 to present the signs that will appear in the sky. But another Old Testament reference that isn't quoted directly is from Daniel 7:13–14. As R. C. Sproul points out in *The Last Days According to Jesus*, the picture in Daniel is of the Son of Man in the presence of the Ancient of Days (God the Father) pronouncing judgment. The judgment he pronounced was of Israel, and from that time forward, Christianity was clearly and irrevocably distinct from Judaism. Sproul holds that the events described in Matthew 24:1–35 had to take place in the first century because verse 34 makes it clear that all these things had to take place within "this generation," which the Jews always understood as forty years. Sproul makes a strong case that all of the other conditions described in these verses were fulfilled in the first century.

APPLY

v. 33—Are you ready for Christ's return? If he were to return tomorrow, what would you change today? (Don't say, "Nothing") Why not do it now?

MEMORIZE

Matthew 24:14

Preaching the Gospel is "preparing the way of the Lord."

PRAY

A: Praise God who rules over history.

C: Confess your failure to eagerly await the Second Coming.

T: Thank God for preserving the elect.

S: Pray for understanding of the End Times.

TELL

This would be a great passage to discuss with a group that has different opinions.

MARCH

MARCH 1

MAJOR END TIMES MESSAGES

PRAY

Ask God to continue to give you insight into and application of his Word as it discusses last things.

READ

Matthew 24:36–51; Mark 13:32–37; Luke 17:22–37, 21:34–38

OBSERVE

Once again, Matthew's treatment is more complete, especially with the end-time parables. Mark is shortest, and Luke arranges the material in separate chapters, as he often does.

Matt. 24:36–41—The major message here is that nobody can put a timetable on Christ's return. Many of the end times books and tapes disregard the Lord's words. Every attempt throughout history to predict when Christ will return has been wrong because it is misguided. The reference to Noah indicates that it will happen when people least expect it. Even the incarnate Son of God in his emptying of himself (Phil. 2:7) did not know when he would return. Verses 40 and 41 are often interpreted as suggesting that the one who will be taken will be "raptured," that is, whisked away to meet Jesus in the sky. But the passage doesn't say that. The word "rapture" doesn't ever appear in Scripture. They will be "gathered" (v. 31), though how and where is not specified.

vv. 42–44—The other major message of the end times is "Be ready!" If we don't know when the Master will return, we must be ready at all times. Are you?

vv. 45–51—The way to be ready is to do our work to the best of our ability. The major responsibility of the Lord's servants is to be faithful (1 Cor. 4:2). The servant who ignores his responsibilities and betrays the Master's trust is showing his true colors. The returning Master will bring judgment and punishment rather than a reward.

APPLY

Matt. 26:42—Have you been influenced by books and teaching that attempt to suggest when Christ will return (the more modest ones suggest, "I'm confident it will be in my lifetime")? Be very wary of such prophetic teaching. It violates this clear message.

MEMORIZE

Matthew 24:36

This is a valuable antidote against those who set time tables.

PRAY

A: Praise God for the heights of his wisdom and knowledge (Isa. 55:9).

C: Confess your lack of preparation for the Lord's return.

T: Thank God that you can be faithful because of his Spirit's power.

S: Ask God to show you a situation in which you can faithfully serve him today.

TELL

When someone tells you that Jesus is coming back soon (which people often say), challenge that statement with Matthew 24:36.

MARCH 2

THE PARABLE OF THE TEN VIRGINS

PRAY

Ask God to prepare you to meet Jesus whenever that may occur.

READ

Matthew 25:1–13

OBSERVE

This parable is unique to Matthew.

v. 1—Jesus continues the themes articulated in Matthew 24. The first word of chapter 25, *Tote,* means "then" or "at that time" (NIV). This word links this chapter with what precedes it. The introductory formula is similar to other parables in Matthew—"the kingdom of God is like"—but it is placed in the future because this is an eschatological (end times) parable. The ten virgins would be very much like the bridesmaids in our modern weddings. They attend to the bride. One of their duties in ancient weddings was to welcome the groom. The bridegroom is identified in Matthew 9:15 as Jesus. It's even more clear in John 3:29. There are a number of other analogies of God's relationship with his people— father/child, shepherd/sheep, master/servants, king/subjects. The bridegroom/bride analogy is the most intimate. The kingdom of heaven is described in the gospels and Revelation as a wedding banquet, an extravagant celebration.

vv. 2–5—Some commentators see in the oil a symbol of the Holy Spirit, but that may be reading too much into the parable. The oil represents preparation. Notice that both the wise and the foolish virgins fell asleep. There is nothing wrong with sleeping as long as you are prepared.

vv. 6–9—The image of the lamps of the wicked going out is found in Proverbs 13:9 and Job 18:5. Verse 9 is not meant to teach Christian ethics (i.e., the importance of sharing) but to reinforce the point that we are to be single-minded in being prepared to meet the bridegroom.

vv. 10–12—Commentator Augsburger writes, "Three of the saddest sayings in the parables of Jesus are found here: 1) 'Our lamps are gone out'; 2) 'The door was shut'; and 3) 'I do not know you'" (Augsburger, *Matthew*, 278–279). The last statement is an echo of Matthew 7:23. Those who are not prepared to meet him don't really know Christ. Once the bridegroom returns, it is too late to get prepared.

v. 13—The bottom line of the parable is that we are to be always prepared. It echoes Matthew 24:42.

APPLY

v. 13—Are you prepared for Christ's coming? If Jesus returned tomorrow, would he find you involved meaningfully in his work, investing your time in eternal things?

MEMORIZE

Matthew 25:13

This a good complement to the verse you memorized yesterday.

PRAY

A: Praise the Bridegroom.

C: Confess that you have not prepared effectively for the Lord's return by being single-minded in your pursuit of God.

T: Thank God that he has surrounded you with other believers who are wise.

S: Pray for someone who is not prepared.

TELL

Discuss with your small group how you can best prepare for the return of Christ.

MARCH 3

THE PARABLE OF THE TALENTS

Pray for God to show you how he wants you to use your talents.

Matthew 25:14–30; Luke 19:11–27

Except for the difference in the value of currency (a mina was worth one-sixtieth of a talent) and the idea that the master in Luke is a king who is rejected by his new subjects, the parables in Matthew and Luke are very similar.

Matt. 25: 14–15—The situation presented in this parable is very similar to Matthew 24:45–51, where a master leaves on a journey and puts his servants in charge. A talent was originally a measure of weight but came to be associated with silver coinage. One talent of silver equaled 6,000 *denarii*. The *denarius* was the day's wage for a laborer. In today's currency, a talent would be worth three or four hundred thousand dollars. According to a biblical expert:

> Of course, the issue really at stake is not money but the stewardship of what has been given to individual disciples. Since this stewardship involves different 'amounts' entrusted to the disciples (five, two, one talent[s]), the 'talents' probably symbolize personal gifts and abilities rather than the Gospel itself. This is supported by the phrase 'to each according to his own ability' (perhaps picked up by Paul in Romans 12:3,6,7). (Hagner, *Word Biblical Commentary: Matthew 14–28*, 734)

vv. 16–18—The first word in Greek in verse 16 is "immediately." The emphasis is that the five-talent and two-talent servants went to work right away to put the money to profitable use.

vv. 19–23—The "long time" of the master's journey corresponds with the long time in 25:5 and the suggestion of delay in other end times parables. It's important to notice that the master's praise of the two-talent servant is identical to his praise of the five-talent servant. Even if we're not as gifted as someone else, if we are faithful, the Lord is just as pleased and will reward us the same.

vv. 24–30—What was the problem with the one-talent servant? For starters, he had a negative view of the master. He saw him as a "hard man," rather than as one who delighted to share his happiness. Secondly, the servant who buried his talent was ruled by fear. As we've seen in Matthew several times, fear is the opposite of faith. The master's reply uses the wicked, lazy servant's own words against him. If the servant believed that he was a hard man, harvesting where he had not sown, the least the servant should have done was to invest the money so that the master would have received interest. The unproductive servant will not be tolerated but cast out. This is a powerful warning to people who claim to be Christians but do not use their gifts. Jesus establishes productivity in God's kingdom as a measure of authentic belief!

APPLY

Matt. 25:21–23—What has God given you and how are you using it? How could you be more productive for his Kingdom?

MEMORIZE

Matthew 25:21 or 23

There is a reward for productivity in Christ's kingdom.

PRAY

A: Praise the Gift Giver.

C: Confess your failure to use your gifts fully.

T: Thank God that he blesses faithfulness.

S: Intercede for someone who thinks he or she is a Christian but is not faithful or productive.

TELL

Share with someone what you believe your gifts are and how you plan to use them.

MARCH 4

THE PARABLE OF THE SHEEP AND THE GOATS

PRAY

Ask God to convict you of the need to put hands and feet to your faith.

READ

Matthew 25:31–46 (this passage is unique to Matthew)

OBSERVE

v. 31—This parable fittingly concludes the section on last things because its setting is the Second Coming, which marks the end of history. The picture is the Great White Throne Judgment (Rev. 20:11–15).

vv. 32–33—Each of the end times parables has emphasized judgment, but this is the most comprehensive. "All the nations" will be judged. Michael Green comments:

> It tells me that I am accountable. I am free to live my life just as I please, but at the end I shall have to give account to the one who gave me my life. It tells me that judgment awaits everyone. There will be no exceptions. There will be no favoritism. There will be no excuses. It will be totally fair. It tells me that we are not all going the same way, as we would dearly love to think in this tolerant and pluralist age. We will not all end up in the same place. It is possible to be utterly lost, and Jesus warns us of that possibility in this, the last of his parables. (Green, *Matthew for Today*, 242)

There is no particular significance to the sheep and goats simile (Jesus did not think sheep were good and goats evil) except that they had to be separated by the shepherd at the end of the day. Goats, lacking the thick coat of sheep, had to be kept warmer than the sheep.

vv. 34–40—Notice that the Son of Man is also the King. It's hard to escape the doctrine of election in the words, *"Take your inheritance, the kingdom prepared for you since the creation of the world."* The blessed are rewarded because of their response to Jesus. Again, Michael Green's wonderful commentary summarizes the issue:

> It tells me that the heart of Christianity is relationship with Jesus himself, which shows itself in loving, sacrificial care for others, in particular the poor and needy. (Green, *Matthew for Today*, 242–243)

An anonymous writer paraphrased and parodied Jesus' words according to the usual response of "religious" people. It includes statements like, "I was hungry, and you formed a humanities club to discuss my plight; I was naked, and you debated the morality of my appearance." The key to serving Christ is to see him in needy people. St. Francis of Asissi's life was changed by this truth. He was the son of a rich merchant and lived in luxury. One day he saw a repulsive leper, and something compelled him to dismount from his horse and embrace the wretched sufferer. In his arms, the face of the leper transformed to become the face of Christ.

vv. 41–46—The opposite is also true. Those who fail to love Jesus Christ by not loving others are no children of his. This is a sobering truth. We should examine the genuineness of our relationship to Jesus, who said, *"Not everyone who says to me, 'Lord, Lord,' will enter the kingdom of heaven, but only he who does the will of my Father who is in heaven"* (Matt. 7: 21). We are not saved by our works, but our works are a much better indication of our relationship with Jesus than our words (James 2:18).

APPLY

vv. 35–36—How are you doing in helping those in need?

MEMORIZE

Matthew 25:40

PRAY

A: Praise the King who is the righteous Judge.

C: Confess your lack of care for the hungry, thirsty, stranger, naked, or imprisoned.

T: Thank God for opportunities to serve him by serving the needy.

S: Ask for an opportunity to put flesh to your faith this week.

TELL

Discuss with a Christian friend how you could both be involved in mercy ministry.

MARCH 5

THE PLOT AGAINST JESUS AND THE OUTPOURING OF LOVE

PRAY

In the midst of those who would destroy the cause of Christ, ask his help to give him your all.

READ

Matthew 26:1–16; Mark 14:1–11; Luke 22:1–6; John 12:1–11

OBSERVE

Matthew and Mark have a very similar structure: the chief priests and elders plotting against Jesus, the anointing at Bethany, then Judas' offer to betray Jesus. Luke has the plotting of the Jews and Judas as a continuous story, and John has the anointing story in which he specifies that Mary of Bethany is the one who anoints Jesus. The anointing stories in Matthew, Mark, and John are very similar. However, the anointing story in Luke 7:36–50 is so different that it appears to be describing another incident. We will treat it separately, with Luke's unique material.

Luke 22:1–2—The cross came as no surprise to Jesus. Though he wrestled with what he knew would be a spiritually and physically excruciating experience, he did not shy away from his fate. Why is it that we so often attempt to escape suffering?

vv. 3–5—The plot to arrest and kill Jesus was conceived at the highest levels of Jewish leadership. It's clear why a location like Gethsemane was sought—the authorities wanted to avoid a possible riot if they seized Jesus in the presence of the crowds who loved him.

vv. 6–13—In the midst of great evil, there is always greater grace from the Lord. The story takes place in the home of Simon the Leper. Clearly, it must have been

Simon the Former Leper, for a leper would not have been allowed in polite company, let alone the host of a dinner. We can assume that Simon was one of the many lepers healed by Jesus and that this dinner was his way of thanking the Lord. The "alabaster jar of very expensive perfume" represented the woman's inheritance from her parents. In Mark and John, its value is set at 300 *denarii*, a year's wages. The reaction to the beloved excess of her offering is an interesting study of how the gospels together present a more complete portrait than any one account. Mark writes that "some of those present" were indignant about her wasteful anointing (Mark 14:4). Matthew indicates that the disciples were part of that group (Matt. 26:8). John hones in on the primary objector, Judas, who was angry because he wanted to steal the money, not give it to the poor (John 12:6). All three gospels record Jesus' praise of the woman's beautiful offering. John also states that "the poor you will always have with you," a phrase that has been grossly misunderstood. Jesus was not discouraging active concern for the poor (cf. Matt. 25:31–46). He was saying that opportunities to serve the poor are never ending, while the window of opportunity to care for him was closing quickly. The woman's selfless love has been memorialized in the gospels, and Christ's prophecy has been fulfilled.

vv. 14–16—Judas' motives for betraying Jesus have been romanticized in works of fiction like the rock opera *Jesus Christ Superstar*. Some have written that Judas was trying to force Jesus' hand by having the Romans arrest him. But if we look carefully at John's account of the anointing and connect it with Matthew 26:15, it seems that Judas' motive was nothing more than pure greed. He was a thief who loved money, and he was willing to betray his master for thirty pieces of silver, the ransom for a slave.

APPLY

Matt. 26:2—Is there any legitimate suffering that you are trying to avoid?

v. 10—Have you ever made an extravagant sacrifice for Christ? What might it be?

MEMORIZE

Matthew 26:13

An act of self-giving love can have eternal consequences.

PRAY

A: Praise God for receiving our gifts.

C: Confess that you've too often valued money over Christ.

T: Thank Jesus for willingly going to the cross.

S: Pray for someone who worships money like Judas did.

TELL

Share with someone the significance of Christ's betrayal being the price of redemption.

MARCH 6

THE LORD'S SUPPER

PRAY

Ask God to give you a deeper appreciation for the significance of communion.

READ

Matthew 26:17–30; Mark 14:12–26; Luke 22:7–22; John 13:18–30

OBSERVE

The last four days of Jesus' life are so crucial to God's plan of redemption that all four gospels record almost every significant event. There is a great deal of similarity in the Last Supper accounts, but enough variation to give richness and additional detail to the story.

Matt. 26:17–19—The Passover Feast was on the first day of a week-long celebration called The Feast of Unleavened Bread, which recalled the events of the Exodus (Exod. 12:34). On that Thursday morning, all leaven had to be removed from the house in which the Passover was to be eaten. Passover was to be eaten within the city walls of Jerusalem if possible. Jesus was staying in the village of Bethany, just a short distance from the Holy City. Mark and Luke add to Matthew's portrait by telling us that Jesus instructed his disciples to look for "a man carrying a jar of water" (Mark 14:13; Luke 22:10). The man would not be hard to find; he would stand out in the street as glaringly as a man wearing a dress would today. It was women who carried water jars in Jesus' time. Some say that Jesus carefully arranged all the details for the Passover in advance, and this is an example of his organizational skills. Others believe that the particulars were revealed to him by the Holy Spirit, and this is an example of his sensitivity to the Spirit. It's not necessarily a dichotomy because both organization and discernment are gifts of the Spirit. It's impossible to decide with any degree of certainty from the text.

vv. 20–25—It's also hard to tell from the four accounts exactly how Jesus identifies his betrayer. Mark and Luke suggest that the identification wasn't totally clear. It was one of the twelve, the one who dips his bread with Jesus. The privilege of dipping bread with the host was usually the role of the guest of honor to the feast. If that's true, isn't it amazing that Jesus made Judas the guest of honor at the Passover even when he knew what the false disciple was about to do! However, it's possible (particularly from the tense of the Greek verb) that Jesus was simply saying that the betrayer was one of those eating with Jesus. That would more clearly explain why Judas (and all of the other disciples, according to the other gospels) asked if it were he. The question and answer may have been quiet and confidential, much like Jesus' conversation with the beloved disciple (John 13:23–28). It appears that only John and Judas knew that the latter was the betrayer.

vv. 26–30—The Passover Meal presented a number of elements, each of which was powerfully symbolic. There was unleavened bread, which as we already noted, symbolized that the Exodus required an emergency exit that did not afford the time for bread to rise. The Passover Lamb recalled the blood of the lamb that was shed to cover the doorposts in Egypt so that the Angel of Death would pass over the Jewish homes. A bowl of saltwater was placed on the table to symbolize the tears that the Jews shed as slaves in Egypt. Bitter herbs served much the same purpose. There was a paste called *charosheth*, a mixture of apples, dates, pomegranates, and nuts that reminded them of the mortar they had used for the bricks in Egypt. Lastly, there were four cups of wine to remind them of the four promises of Exodus 6: 6–7. In the context of this highly symbolic meal, Jesus took two of the elements—the bread and the wine—and reinterpreted them for his followers.

The bread now represents his body, which was broken that we might be whole. The wine now represents his blood, which is poured out as the eternal sacrifice for our sins, so that we might be forgiven. Bible commentator William Barclay writes:

> Here is another thing to note. There was one basic difference between the Last Supper and Sacrament which we observe. The Last Supper was a real meal; it was, in fact, the law that the whole lamb and everything else must be eaten and nothing left. This was no eating of a cube of bread and drinking of a sip of wine. It was a meal for hungry men. We might well say that what Jesus is teaching men is not only to assemble in church and eat a ritual and symbolic Feast; he is telling them that every time they sit down to eat a meal; that meal is in memory of him. Jesus is not only Lord of the Communion Table; he must be Lord of the dinner table, too. (Barclay, Commentaries, 342)

Jesus' statement in verse 29 is poignant and powerful. He knows that he is going to die and this will literally be his last supper. But he also knows that his death will usher in the kingdom of the Father, and his death will not end his fellowship with his disciples. Verse 30 is one of the few times that hymns are mentioned in the life and ministry of Jesus, though we can suppose that he sang with the disciples on many occasions.

APPLY

Matt. 26:28—Do you really believe that Christ's shed blood removes all of your sin? Believe it!

MEMORIZE

Matthew 26:26–29 is something you have heard many times if you have been part of the Church for very long. It would be helpful for you to memorize it and reflect on its meaning for your life.

PRAY

A: Praise God for the depths of his knowledge.

C: Confess that you have taken communion without properly considering its meaning.

T: Thank Jesus for his broken body and shed blood.

S: Pray for someone who has betrayed the Son of Man by their unbelief.

TELL

If you are a parent, try to explain the significance of communion to your child(ren).

MARCH 7

PETER'S DENIAL

PRAY

Ask God to give you strength through his Spirit that you might not deny your Lord.

READ

Matthew 26:31–35, 69–75; Mark 14:27–31, 66–72; Luke 22:31–38, 54–62; John 13:36–38, 18:15–18, 25–27

OBSERVE

Each of the four gospels separates Jesus' prediction of Peter's denial with the denial itself. The Synoptic Gospels have the two events in the same chapter, but John separates the prediction and fulfillment by four chapters. Once again, though, the four gospels combine to paint a complete portrait.

Matt. 26:31—Jesus saw his entire life in the context of Scripture and as a fulfillment of the Old Testament. Here he quotes Zechariah 13:7 to prophecy that his disciples would all desert him in his time of need. Luke adds that Jesus especially directed the promise to Peter, telling him that *"Satan has asked to sift you as wheat"* (Luke 22:31). Peter will fall, but Jesus prays that his faith will not fail and that after he repents, Peter will strengthen the other disciples.

v. 32—Jesus adds to his previous resurrection prophecies the specific fact that he would meet his disciples in Galilee. That's why not only the disciples, but five hundred believers were able to gather to see him at one time (Matt. 28:16–17; 1 Cor. 15:6).

vv. 33–35—One of the great moral flaws for the Greeks was *hubris*, blind pride, which was the downfall of such characters as Oedipus. The Bible agrees with that value system. Pride is odious to God (1 John 2:16) and precedes destruction (Prov. 16:18). Peter may have been the worst offender, but notice that the other disciples also proudly declared their loyalty, even if it meant their life. Not only does Jesus prophecy that all of them will fall away from him, but that Peter would deny him three times before the morning. Predictions don't get much more specific than that!

vv. 69—Before we condemn Peter, we would do well to remember that the temptation he faced in the courtyard was a temptation only one disciple of the twelve had the courage to encounter. It took guts to come that close when discovery meant that Peter would have probably hung on the cross next to his Master. Would you have had the courage to venture into that courtyard? If not, go easy on Peter. Also, realize that the source of this story was Peter himself. Peter's pride was turned to humility. He was willing to tell the story of his denial, saying in effect, "This is what I did, but Jesus never stopped loving me."

vv. 70–74—To the cultured people of Jerusalem, Galileans came from the wrong side of the tracks. They had an obvious accent that marked them as outsiders. Jesus' hometown, Nazareth, was seen as especially bad. John writes, *"Can anything good come from Nazareth?"* (John 1:46). Invoking a false oath was a serious sin, akin to blasphemy (Lev. 19:12). Jesus had told his followers not to take oaths at all (Matt. 5:34, 37). In effect, what Peter said was, "May God curse me if what I say is not true." It's a good thing that God doesn't answer some prayers! In a sense, Peter's denial was inevitable. His rash boasting and scorn of others (Matt. 26:33), his failure to devote himself to prayer in the Garden (Matt. 26: 43, 45), and his close association with Christ's enemies (Mark 14:54) all led to his downfall. The time for the Christian to fight temptation is before it is encountered. John adds a fascinating detail. One of Peter's accusers was a relative of Malchus, the servant whose ear Peter had cut off at the time of Jesus' arrest (John 18:26).

v. 75—To see our own weakness in Peter is good, but to overlook the seriousness of his sin is evil. Cole writes, "Light thoughts on sin ultimately lead to light thoughts on redemption, and ultimately rob the cross of its glory" (Cole, *The Gospel According to Mark*, 231). To add to the impact of the prophetic cock crow, Luke 22:61 says, *"And the Lord turned and looked at Peter."* Jesus was close enough to see Peter and perhaps even hear him, but at that moment Peter was far away from Jesus.

APPLY

Matt. 26:33—Do you struggle with spiritual pride? Remember that *"whoever exalts himself will be humbled, and whoever humbles himself will be exalted."* (Matt. 23:12).

MEMORIZE

Matthew 26:33

This is a great verse to remember in order to be warned against pride.

PRAY

A: Praise God who speaks the truth in love and warns us of the consequences of our actions.

C: Confess the times that you've denied the Lord.

T: Thank Jesus for praying for you (Rom. 8:34), just as he did for Peter.

S: Pray for courage to be in the arena where temptations are strong, but where God's grace is even stronger.

TELL

Lyman Coleman suggests that a great exercise would be to write a letter to Peter just after he leaves the courtyard and share your own experiences with him. Read that letter to a friend or your small group.

MARCH 8

GETHSEMANE

PRAY

Make Jesus' words, *"Yet not as I will, but as you will,"* your theme in prayer.

READ

Matthew 26:36–46; Mark 14:32–42; Luke 22:39–46

OBSERVE

Matthew and Mark's versions are nearly identical, but Luke's is compressed. Luke locates Jesus' fervent prayer on the Mount of Olives, but he doesn't specify the Garden of Gethsemane. He is the only evangelist to note that an angel ministered to Jesus (Luke 22:43).

Matt. 26:36–39—We see perhaps the most precious portrait of Jesus' humanity in this passage. Gethsemane is a beautiful garden on the Mount of Olives. It overlooks the East Gate of Jerusalem. It would have been a wonderful place to retreat from the busy city to spend time with the Father. Jesus must have gone there often because Judas knew that was where he would be. Jesus took all of the disciples with him to the garden, but only his inner circle of Peter, James, and John went further in with him. Jesus shares with his dearest brothers the depth of his sorrow as he considers his impending death. It was important to him that they be with him during this dark night of the soul. As someone who was fully human, the Lord did not look forward with joy to the painful death that awaited him. He was not a masochist who loved pain, and so Jesus prayed that if it were possible, the cup of suffering might be taken from him. The key to his prayer, and a phrase that should underline all of our prayers, were the words, *"Yet not as I will, but as you will."* The secret to effective prayer is to pray in the will of God (1 John 5:14). If we think about it carefully, asking for and receiving anything outside of God's will is sheer folly!

vv. 40–46—People will always disappoint us. In his hour of profound spiritual agony, Jesus' disciples couldn't even stay awake to pray with him. The struggle between a willing spirit and flesh that is weak is described throughout the New Testament, especially by the Apostle Paul (Rom. 7; Gal. 5). Jesus prays three times in Gethsemane, just as Paul does for his thorn in the flesh (1 Cor. 12). The olive presses on the Mount of Olives squeezed the olives three times, each more forcefully than the one before. It is not clear that this is a biblical formula for prayer, but it's not a bad rule of thumb. The tension is between these examples and other passages that tell us to keep on asking (Matt. 7:7; Luke 18:1–8).

APPLY

v. 39—What is the biggest request you have to ask God right now? Are you ready to pray as Jesus did, *"Yet not as I will, but as you will?"*

MEMORIZE

Matthew 26:41

Diligence and prayer are our best defenses against temptation.

PRAY

A: Praise the Lord who was obedient to the Father.

C: Confess the weakness of your prayer life and ask for God's help to improve.

T: Thank Jesus that he understands your temptations, having faced them himself (Heb. 4:15).

S: Pray about a difficult decision you are facing, being sure to surrender your will to the Father's.

TELL

Share with someone you trust an area in which you are struggling and ask them to pray with you.

MARCH 9

JESUS' BETRAYAL, ARREST, AND TRIAL

PRAY

Pray that your love for Christ and for others would be genuine today.

READ

Matthew 26:47–68; Mark 14:43–65; Luke 22:47–53, 63–71; John 18:1–14, 19–24

OBSERVE

Each of the gospel writers adds to the total picture of these climactic events.

vv. 47–50—The mob represents the different constituents of the Sanhedrin. It's unlikely that the priests were the ones carrying clubs because it was not lawful for priests to shed blood. There were soldiers as well (John 18:3) who would have carried swords. Gethsemane was very dark at night; that's why an insider was needed to correctly identify Jesus. Judas had planned the betrayal well. The kiss of peace and the salutation "Rabbi" were both natural signs between a disciple and his master that would arouse no suspicion. But Judas had a flair for the dramatic. In Mark 14:45, the Greek word for kiss is an intensive, "a kiss of earnest affection." This is one of the worst things in the whole grim story. It's amazing that a person who lived so closely with Christ for three years could be so cold and hypocritical!

vv. 51–54—The incident of the chopped ear is a fascinating study. Matthew, Mark, and Luke don't identify the disciple who struck the blow with his sword. They knew who it was, but it may have been dangerous to name him when their gospels were circulated. John, writing much later, could identify him as Peter (John 18:10) because Peter had been martyred years earlier. John also identifies the victim as Malchus, a slave of the high priest. Luke, in his medical precision, tells us that

Jesus healed the man's right ear (Luke 22:50–51). Since most people are right-handed, it must have been a wild scene for Peter to cut off Malchus' right ear! Can you imagine the conversation between Malchus and Caiaphas when the servant returned to his master's house?

Malchus: "One of his disciples cut off my ear with his sword."

Caiaphas: "But your ear looks perfectly fine."

Malchus: "Um, Jesus healed it."

It took determined evil for the high priest to see Jesus as someone who had to be killed. Matthew is the only evangelist to include the words, "All who draw the sword will die by the sword" and Jesus' comment that he could have called on twelve legions (72,000) of angels. Matthew indicates that the arrest was the fulfillment of Scripture. Luke specifies the verse Isaiah 53:12 (Luke 22:37). Luke 22:53 is a heavy statement, *"But this is your hour—when darkness reigns."* The power of darkness tried to snuff out the Light of the World, but it could not (John 1:5, 3:19).

vv. 55–56—Jesus is calm enough to comment on the irony of the situation. He wasn't leading an armed rebellion. They could have arrested him at any time (if they had a valid reason!), but they chose to do it in this secluded spot. The only disciples we hear anything about from this point until the resurrection are Peter and John. John stands at the foot of the cross with Jesus' mother. Peter courageously follows Jesus to Caiaphas' house but then loses his nerve. Interestingly, archeologists in Jerusalem believe that they may have found Caiaphas' actual house buried beneath thirty feet of history! The word "deserted" has the full meaning of abandonment.

vv. 57–68—Mark adds a unique detail in 14:51–52. Many commentators believe that the unclothed man was Mark himself. The Last Supper was held in his home, and he may have gone to bed after the meal. He was then roused from sleep by the mob and ran to warn Jesus at Gethsemane. This would explain why he only wore a linen garment. It was his bedclothes. In any case, the entire trial of Jesus before the high priest Caiaphas and the Sanhedrin was a farce. This kangaroo court broke all of its own rules. The Sanhedrin could only meet in the Hall of Hewn Stone within the temple precincts. Only there were their decisions valid. This makeshift group met in the high priest's home. They were not allowed to meet at night, nor during any of the great feasts. Witnesses were to be examined separately, and their testimony had to agree in every detail. Otherwise, the case was thrown out of court. Verdicts were to be pronounced individually, from the youngest to the oldest members of the court. At least one night had to pass before the death penalty could be given to allow the court to reconsider its decision and recommend mercy. The law completely forbade asking leading questions by which the person on trial might incriminate himself or herself.

Matthew makes it clear that Caiaphas' question was put to Jesus under oath (v. 63), which is one reason that the Reformed church has held that taking of lawful oaths is valid. Jesus cannot deny who he is. Anyone who believes that Christ never claimed to be God hasn't read this section or the rest of the gospels very carefully.

If Jesus were a man, his response to Caiaphas was blasphemy. Clearly the high priest and his cohorts recognized Jesus' words as a claim to deity.

Spitting on him and punching him were also violations of Jewish trial law. There were many ironic elements in this trial. The Sanhedrin couldn't even get their paid witnesses to agree on a lie. But they could have found any number of witnesses who would have freely said, "I was blind, but now I see," "I was lame but now my legs are strong," or "His teaching changed my life. I repaid all the money I cheated." The Sanhedrin was blind to the truth that Christ revealed because they sought lies. It was they who were on trial, not him. They accused him of blasphemy, but the ones who tore their garments and spit upon him were guilty of blasphemy.

APPLY

v. 51—Do you sometimes try to take things into your own hands? Why not step back and seek the Lord and his will before you act?

MEMORIZE

Matthew 26:52.

Jesus' revolution is spiritual and doesn't require physical weapons.

PRAY

A: Praise the Christ, the Son of God.

C: Confess the times you have deserted him and fled rather than face difficult situations.

T: Thank God for his patience with sinners.

S: Pray for someone you know who thinks Jesus is only a good man.

TELL

Discuss with a Christian friend whether violence is ever justified for Christians.

MARCH 10

JESUS FACES PILATE AND JUDAS FACES HIMSELF

PRAY

Ask God for the courage to act upon what you know is right.

READ

Matthew 27:1–26; Mark 15:1–15; Luke 23:1–25; John 18:28–19:16

OBSERVE

Matthew's is the only gospel to include Judas' suicide (though Luke mentions it in Acts). Luke includes Jesus' appearance before Herod, and John gives a fuller description of Pilate's deliberations. The four gospels give a complete picture of Jesus facing the politicians.

vv. 1–2—The Sanhedrin had given Jesus the death sentence, but they did not have the power to carry out capital punishment. For this they had to convince the Roman authority, represented by Pontius Pilate the procurator ("governor" in the gospels) of Judea, Idumea, and Samaria.

vv. 3–10—In Judas, we see a man who was conscience-stricken. But rather than repent before God and seek his forgiveness (which would have been granted even for Judas' heinous sin), the betrayer goes to the people who used him, perhaps expecting sympathy and understanding. His expectations were foolish, for these were cold-blooded men who saw him only as a pawn and had no concern for him once he had fulfilled his function. It's interesting that the chief priests, who so cavalierly broke the law in condemning an innocent man to death, observe the scruples of the law about blood money. Matthew, as usual, sees their decision as a fulfillment of prophecy, combining verses from Jeremiah and Zechariah to describe the purchase of the Potter's Field.

vv. 11–14—The Jews knew that the charge of blasphemy wouldn't work with Pilate, so they trumped up political charges: that Jesus claimed to be a king in opposition to Caesar and that he forbid the Jews to pay tribute to Caesar (Luke 23:2), a bold-faced lie. In John 18:36, Jesus tells Pilate that his kingship is not of this world, otherwise his servants would have fought. Between the initial interview and the gathering of the crowd (v. 17), Luke tells us that Pilate sent Jesus to Herod Antipas who had jurisdiction over Galileans (apparently, Herod was in Jerusalem for the Passover.) Herod could find no fault in Christ either, but he ridiculed him, dressed him up in an elegant robe to complete the mockery, and sent him back to Pilate. Luke's cynical observation is that Pilate and Herod became friends that day.

vv. 15–26—Pilate obviously admired Jesus and knew the Jewish leaders wanted to get rid of him because they were envious (v. 18). In John, when he presents Christ to the crowd, he says, *"Behold, the man!"* Pilate's wife also confirms Christ's innocence and relates a prophetic dream (could she or her husband have imagined that for centuries people would recite that Jesus "suffered under Pontius Pilate"?). Pilate had lots of reasons to free Jesus, but he was a politician who was most concerned with satisfying the crowds. His choice was between a murderer and revolutionary (Mark 15:17)—Jesus Bar-Rabban (Aramaic for "Son of the Teacher" was not his real name)—and Jesus Bar-Joseph, a carpenter's son who had been leading a revolution of love.

Some commentators have tried to make a major point about how the Palm Sunday crowd was fickle and turned against Jesus just four days later. But this was probably a different group from the Galilean pilgrims. This mob was no doubt led by the cronies of the priests, scribes, and Pharisees. To them, Barabbas was a patriotic hero. If some of the Palm Sunday crowd were there, they may have been disenchanted with Jesus when he failed to oppose the Romans violently.

The cry, *"Crucify him!"* is chilling, but even more eerie is the call, *"Let his blood be on us and on our children!"* The normal means of capital punishment for the Jews was stoning (Josh. 7:25). Beheading was the death penalty for a Roman citizen, as tradition tells us it was for Paul. Crucifixion was the penalty for a slave or a foreigner. The Romans may not have permitted the Jews to stone Jesus, fearing mob violence. For the Jews, crucifixion was an attractive alternative. Beside the Roman associations of shame via a slave's death, Deuteronomy 21:23 says that anyone hanging on a tree is accursed by God (Paul comments on this theologically in Gal. 3:13). Flogging (also known as scourging) was the beginning of Christ's horrible physical torture. It consisted of thirty-nine lashes with a leather cat o' nine tails which had embedded pieces of bone, glass, and metal. It ripped the back so badly that some people died from the beating.

How could Pilate do this to an innocent man? He didn't want Jesus to die; in fact, he publicly and symbolically washed his hands of the guilt of condemning Christ. But Pilate was still guilty. His sins were:

1. Moral relativism. In response to Jesus, Pilate says, "What is truth?" (John 18:38). For him, truth was no absolute that determined his behavior, but something to be ignored if it were inconvenient.
2. Conformity. Pilate went along with the crowd rather than stand up for a principle. In a real sense, that was Adam's sin too. Eve was enticed. Adam conformed.
3. Lack of courage. Pilate knew that what he was doing was wrong. He tries to blame it on the people (Matt. 27:24), but when you are in a decision-making position, you can't pass the buck.

His decision to hand Jesus over for scourging and crucifixion stands as one of the most cowardly acts in history.

APPLY

v. 14—Do you always try to defend yourself against unjust accusations? Why not try letting your life speak for you, as Jesus did.

v. 15—Where is conformity to the crowd a sin in your life?

v. 22—The ultimate question for every human being is, *"What shall I do, then, with Jesus who is called Christ?"* Is there someone to whom you should be asking that question?

MEMORIZE

Matthew 27:22

This is a key question and so many people's response.

PRAY

A: Praise the one who "was oppressed and afflicted, yet he did not open his mouth" (Isa. 53:7).

C: Confess the times you have conformed because of fear of the crowd.

T: Thank God that the blood of Christ's death is not upon you by grace through faith.

S: Pray that you may not be conformed to the world, but transformed by the Holy Spirit (Rom. 12:2).

TELL

Ask someone you trust to share with you an area in your life where there might be a conformity to the world (James 4:4). Thank them for their honest feedback.

MARCH 11

THEN THEY CRUCIFIED HIM

PRAY

That you might be touched in a new way by Good Friday, the day that was bad for Christ, but good for us.

READ

Matthew 27:27–66; Mark 15:16–47; Luke 23:26–56; John 19:17–43

OBSERVE

Each of the gospels adds significant details to the portrait of our Lord's passion.

vv. 27–31—Christ's prophecy in Mark 10:33–34 is fulfilled in these verses. The scarlet robe was worn by royalty. It was part of the mockery. The only charge that would have impressed the Romans was that this despicable Jew claimed to be a king. The thorns used for the crown were not the variety we are used to seeing on rose bushes. Those Palestinian thorns were three inches long and as sharp as spikes.

v. 32—It was customary for the condemned man to carry his cross to the place of execution. The longest route was chosen, through as many streets and alleys as possible, so that many people could see the fate awaiting opponents of Rome. Because of the blood loss due to the scourging and crown of thorns, Jesus must have faltered often. Since his arms were tied behind the crosspiece, the only thing to break the fall was the front of his body and his face. He must have been a bloody and swollen mess when Simon, the Passover pilgrim from Africa, was pressed into duty. As the flat of the Roman sword struck his shoulder, Simon must have resented both the Roman authorities and the criminal whose cross he was forced to bear. But something he saw in Jesus changed his attitude. We read in Acts 13:1 that one of the leaders of the Church in Antioch was "Simeon who was called Niger." Simeon is the Hebrew name for Simon, and Niger (black) was the common term (not a slander in those days) for a man who came from Africa. Mark 15:21 mentions that Simon was the father of Alexander and Rufus. Romans 16:13 mentions "Rufus, chosen in the Lord." The apostles would have known Rufus as the son of Simon, the first disciple to carry the cross for his Master.

v. 33—*Golgotha* is the Aramaic. *Calvary* is the Latin for the hill located outside the walls of Jerusalem that is still present today. It is shaped like a bald head, complete with two ditches that look like eye sockets. Two thousand years later, it still looks much the same.

v. 34—Wine mingled with myrrh (or gall) was usually offered by pious Jewish women in obedience to Proverbs 31:6. It was an act of mercy to the victim of crucifixion to dull the pain. But Jesus refused it because he wanted a clear head to experience what lay before him. The wine would also have broken his vow of Matthew 26:29.

vv. 35–44—It's amazing how closely the crucifixion of Christ parallels David's prophecy in Psalm 22, especially verse 16. At the time of David's writing, approximately one thousand years before Christ, the horrors of crucifixion ("they have pierced my hands and feet") were unknown. It didn't come on the world scene for another eight hundred years! The phrase in Matthew 26:35, "When they had crucified him," describes in stark terms one of the most abominable forms of torture ever invented. The wrists and ankles were fastened to the T-shaped beams with ropes or nails (the latter in Jesus' case, according to John 20:25). The body rested on a peg called a *sedile*, in order to prolong the agony. If the weight could not be supported by the *sedile*, or if a leg were broken (John 19:31–33), death would be swift, since death usually occurred by suffocation, the weight of the upper body collapsing the lungs.

Sometimes the victim would live for days until he was eaten by wild beasts or punctured by a spear. In the case of Christ, many believe that death was actually caused by acute anguish, which caused the pericardium to rupture, thus producing the mixture of blood and water that John saw (John 19:34–37). *"Come down from the cross, if you are the Son of God!"* is ironic since it is precisely the wrong challenge. As William Booth wrote, "It is because Jesus did *not* come down from the cross that we believe in him."

Pilate's last jibe at the Jews (see John 19:19–22) was true: He is the King, bloodied but unbowed. To show the universality of Jesus' death, the superscription, "This is Jesus, the King of the Jews," was written in Greek, Hebrew, and Latin—the common language, the religious language, and the legal language. Matthew's sources missed the crucial conversation Jesus had with the repentant thief that is recorded in Luke 23:39–43. In these marvelous verses, we see that even in the midst of the darkest evil mankind can produce, God's grace shines bright. Luke records the awesome word of grace, *"Father, forgive them, for they do not know what they are doing"* (Luke 23:34).

vv. 45–54—The sixth hour was noon, the ninth was 3 p.m. *Eloi, eloi, lama sabachthani* is the Aramaic translation of Psalm 22:1. This word from the cross contains much of the mystery and meaning in Christ's redemptive work. In commenting on this verse, Martin Luther wrote, "God forsaken of God? Who can understand it?"

Our best clue comes from 2 Corinthians 5:21. While on the cross, Christ took the penalty for all sin for all time. He became sin incarnate. Since the Father cannot abide sin in his presence (Rev. 21:27), for the first and last time in all eternity, the unclouded communion between the Father and the Son was broken. Jesus asked for something to drink, *"I thirst,"* (John 19:28) probably so that he could shout out his last words, *"It is finished!"* (John 19:30) and *"Father, into Thy hands I commit my spirit"* (Luke 23:46).

Matthew 27:51 tells us that after Jesus' last loud cry, there was an earthquake that tore the heavy curtain of the temple in two. The tearing of the curtain was powerfully symbolic theologically. It meant at least two things: 1) The curtain separated the Holy of Holies from the rest of the temple. Only the high priest could enter the Holy of Holies and only on the Day of Atonement. Christ's atonement means that every person has complete access to God freely and without an intermediary (other than Christ). 2) It also means that "the dwelling of God is with men" (Rev. 21:3). Just as every person has free access to God, so also God's presence is not confined to a holy place (it never was really).

Perhaps it was the earthquake that convinced the centurion or maybe he, like Simon of Cyrene, saw something in the face and manner of the Lord that showed his unique relationship with the Father. The centurion was a hard-bitten soldier who had seen many men die. But none ever died like this. The cross can speak to the heart of even the toughest person—a soldier, a gang leader, or hard-hearted people like you and me! The resuscitated saints (vv. 52–53) are an amazing mystery. We don't know what happened to them. We can only assume that they died again, but nobody knows when.

vv. 55–56—Devoted women disciples were crucial in the early church, just as they are today (Luke 8:2–3).

vv. 57–61—Joseph of Arimathea did a courageous thing by burying Christ's body. If discovered, he would have probably been expelled from the Sanhedrin and faced further persecution. His action fulfilled another prophecy, Isaiah 53:9. John 19:38 identifies Joseph as a secret disciple of Christ, who performed the royal burial with another secret disciple and Sanhedrin member, Nicodemus. Although these men cared for Christ after his death, they didn't stand up for him while he was alive, especially not during his trial, at least as far as we know from Scripture.

vv. 62–66—The fact that the chief priests and Pharisees posted guards at the tomb indicates their concern about the body of Jesus and possible resurrection rumors. Rather than quelling rumors of the resurrection, the posting of guards adds further credibility to the historical evidence for the resurrection.

APPLY

vv. 27–31—Are you afraid of being mocked for being a Christian? Consider what Jesus experienced.

v. 32—Are you willing to carry the cross of Christ by helping to bear the burdens of others? Where is one place where you could do that?

v. 51—Are you taking advantage of your free access to the Father?

MEMORIZE

Matthew 27:46

This communicates the marvelous mystery of Christ's atonement. You can also impress people that you've memorized a phrase in Aramaic!

PRAY

A: Praise God for his amazing grace shown in the cross.

C: Confess any sin you have been holding onto; lay it at the foot of the cross.

T: Thank God for the open access you have to his throne of grace.

S: Make use of that access and bring your deepest needs before him.

TELL

Share with someone one aspect of the crucifixion that you find especially meaningful.

MARCH 12

BUT HE ROSE ON EASTER!

PRAY

Pray that the power of Christ's resurrection might invade your life in a fresh way today and that you would *"always be prepared to give an answer to everyone who asks you to give the reason for the hope that you have"* (1 Pet. 3:15).

READ

Matthew 28:1–20; Mark 16:1–8; Luke 24:1–12; John 20:1–18

OBSERVE

The gospel writers give different details and perspectives on the resurrection of Jesus Christ. Matthew focuses on two women, Mary Magdalene and "the other Mary" (possibly the mother of James, the son of Alphaeus) and says little about Jesus' Judean appearances. The final scene is in Galilee.

Mark's account is the sketchiest. It's very likely that Mark's original ending has been lost. Scholars agree that Mark 16:9–20 is a frantic summary of the resurrection appearances in the other gospels with some odd words about handling snakes and drinking poison, and it was not part of the original text but added in the fifth century by a creative scribe. Mark's gospel ends with Mary Magdalene, Mary the mother of James, and Salome (perhaps another name for Joanna?) trembling and bewildered with fear.

Luke begins with the women (not named) and includes Peter's trip to the tomb (without including John). Luke then describes several appearances in Judea, which we will study when we examine the material unique to Luke.

John begins with Mary Magdalene, then moves to Peter and "the other disciple" (most believe it's John) and their race to the tomb. John features the greatest variety of post-resurrection appearances, some in Judea and some in Galilee. He does not include the ascension, unlike Matthew and Luke. We will concentrate on Matthew's account and include the variations in his basic story from the other gospels.

v. 1—All of the gospels are in agreement that the resurrection took place on the first day of the week, Sunday. This became known in the early Church as "the Lord's day" and eventually replaced the Jewish Sabbath as the day of worship and rest.

v. 2—Matthew is the only evangelist to record the violent earthquake. It is the second one that surrounded the events of Christ's death and resurrection (Matt. 27:51). The earthquake seems connected to the appearance of an angel of the Lord, who rolled back the tombstone and sat on it. This angel was tremendously strong. Even though the stones were round and rolled into place to seal the tomb, they were typically very large (five or six feet in diameter), and they lodged in a deep groove in front of the tomb. Their purpose was to guard the tomb and prevent the odor of the decomposing body from escaping, so they formed a snug fit and were not easily dislodged even by several men. The women could not possibly have moved the stone, which is why Mark 16:3 includes their comment, *"Who will roll the stone away from the entrance to the tomb?"*

vv. 3–4—As we've noted previously, the common reaction to angels in Scripture is appropriate fear. This one was brilliant in appearance and must have nearly blinded the guards.

vv. 5–7—The angel ignores the cowering guards and speaks to the women who loved Jesus. Because Jesus died just before the Sabbath (Friday at sundown), there had not been time to properly render the appropriate treatment to his body. The women had come in an act of tender service and were rewarded with the greatest news the world has ever heard! The angel's command to the women is the same one that God has for us today, *"Come and see"* (that Christ is risen and alive) and *"Go quickly and tell"* (the good news). Matthew doesn't include the incredulity of the disciples (Luke 24:11), nor does he include the footrace between Peter and John (John 20:4) or Peter's entry into the tomb. John probably did not enter because he was part of a priestly family and did not want to be ceremonially unclean.

vv. 8–10—The gospels are united in their witness that it was the women who first saw the risen Christ. Christianity shouldn't treat women as second-class citizens because our Lord did not. Paul tells us in 1 Corinthians 15:6 that more than five hundred people saw the risen Christ at the same time. The reason that was possible is that the women faithfully passed on Jesus' instructions to the disciples that they were to go to Galilee and meet him there.

vv. 11–15—The first attempt to explain away the resurrection began on the Resurrection Day. The plan that the chief priests and elders hatched with the guards was ridiculous in at least two ways: 1) The penalty for a Roman guard who fell asleep on his watch (or let a prisoner escape) was that his uniform would be set on fire with him in it. The Philippian jailer in Acts 16 was ready to fall on his sword rather than be set aflame when he thought that his prisoners had escaped. We can be very sure that the Roman centurions did not fall asleep on their watch. 2) Even if they had, who knows what transpires when they are sleeping? To say that the disciples stole the body while they were sleeping was a flimsy contrivance that would convince no thinking person. Throughout history, opponents of Christianity have centered their attack on the resurrection, because it is clearly the heart of the Gospel. Paul wrote:

> If Christ has not been raised, your faith is futile; you are still in your sins. Then those also who have fallen asleep in Christ are lost. If only for this life we have hope in Christ, we are to be pitied more than all men. (1 Cor. 15:17–19)

Although some medieval Jews promoted the idea that the disciples stole the body, few others have given that theory any credence. Would eleven of these twelve men go to tortuous deaths to defend a fact that they knew was a lie? To ask the question is to answer it. Other alternate explanations for Christ's resurrection include:

1. The Swoon Theory—Although it has been suggested several times throughout history, the most well-known proponent of this idea was Hugh Schoenfield in his book *The Passover Plot*. The basic theory is that Jesus was drugged on the cross and only appeared dead. He had carefully arranged with Joseph of Arimathea to bury him alive so that he would later revive and convince his disciples and others that he had risen from the dead. Medical knowledge in that day was primitive, so Jesus could have faked his death. Schoenfield's twist on the swoon theory is that Jesus planned to resuscitate, but the soldier's spear ruined his plan. However, he had a back-up plan, an accomplice (the gardener in John's gospel) who disposed of the body and made the resurrection appearances as Jesus' stand-in. This theory is absurd for several reasons. It purports Jesus to be a scheming liar. Even those who don't believe that Jesus is God generally agree that he was a person of fine character. The theory also doesn't square with the physical realities. All of the earliest accounts were emphatic about Jesus' death. The Roman centurions were professional executioners with much experience. Christ had been scourged (beaten thirty-nine times with a whip that had pieces of bone and metal that caused a massive loss of blood), had his hands and feet pierced and hung on a cross suffocating for three hours. Could he have lain in a cold tomb for thirty-six hours with no medical attention, food or water then burst through the tightly wrapped grave clothes or walk seven miles on tortured feet, and convince his disciples that he had conquered death? The swoon theory doesn't explain how the stone was rolled away or the body removed without the guard's knowledge. Schoenfield's hypothesis of the gardener stand-in suggests that the disciples, who had lived with Jesus every day for three years, couldn't distinguish between him and a stranger. As one writer puts it, "The theory is paltry, absurd, worthy only of rejection" (Thomas Thorburn, *The Resurrection Narratives and Modern Criticism*, 106).
2. The Hallucination Hypothesis—This is a more contemporary construction with the advent of modern psychology. The thesis is that Jesus never really

rose from the dead. The disciples and others experienced a mass hallucination. They couldn't stand to let the memory of this good man die, so they convinced themselves and others that he actually rose from the dead. However, psychologists know that hallucinations are individualistic and subjective. They are usually the experience of highly suggestible, hysterical personalities. Hallucinations are not shared by five hundred people, especially pragmatic types like fishermen and tax collectors. Furthermore, the resurrection was proclaimed immediately and vigorously just seven weeks after Christ's death. If his appearances were hallucinations, the authorities could have stopped all the preaching (and put an immediate end to the Christian faith) by placing Jesus' decomposing corpse on an ox cart and parading it down the main street of Jerusalem.

3. The Wrong Tomb Theory—The only one to seriously propose this notion was Kirssop Lake in his book *The Historical Evidence for the Resurrection of Jesus Christ*, published in 1907. Lake's thesis is that the neighborhood of Jerusalem had many rocky tombs. It was easy for the women to make a mistake and go to the wrong one. In Matthew 28:6, when the angel (Luke sees him as a gardener) says, *"He is not here.... See the place where they laid him,"* he actually pointed to another tomb. The women were frightened and confused and fled. This concoction is the weakest non-explanation of all. Matthew 27:61 says that the two Marys sat opposite the tomb where Jesus was placed on Friday. They would have carefully noted its location since they were planning to return on Sunday. Even if the women were mistaken, would Peter and John have made the same mistake? What about the grave clothes they saw? The theory fails to explain why the authorities didn't produce the body, fails to explain the stone, fails to explain the resurrection appearances. James Hanson writes, "If I had any doubts about the resurrection, Professor Lake's book would provide a most salutary correction to my skepticism" (Hanson, *The Resurrection and the Life*, 47).

There is no other logical or reasonable explanation for the events of Easter than that Jesus of Nazareth rose physically from the dead. The implications of this amazing historical fact are that Jesus is God in the flesh (Rom. 1:4) and what he said about himself is true (John 14:6). We have victory over sin and death through our faith in him (Rom. 8:2). The same Spirit who raised Christ from the dead is available to us (Rom. 8:2).

vv. 16–20—The conclusion of Matthew's gospel gives us one other inescapable imperative of the resurrection. We must proclaim the message of the risen Lord to the entire world! Isn't it amazing that though most of Christ's followers worshiped him on the mountain, some actually doubted! That is proof that, for the skeptic, no evidence can convince him of the truth. But for those who believe, Christ clothes us with his authority as we minister in his name. He calls us to make disciples of all nations, not just converts. Teaching those who receive Christ to obey all of his commandments is a crucial part of the missionary enterprise. The great promise is that he is always with us as we go in his name. What a great ending to this gospel!

APPLY

vv. 6–7, 19–20—The thrust of this crucial passage is that those who have seen the truth have an obligation to share it. Are you sharing your faith regularly? If not, get some training and do it!

MEMORIZE

Matthew 26:18–20

This is the Great Commission, Jesus' marching orders for his church.

PRAY

A: Praise the risen Lord, who reigns.

C: Confess your sinful silence as a witness.

T: Thank him for opportunities to share today.

S: Ask that he open the heart of a lost friend.

TELL

"Come and see" and "Go and tell."

MARCH 13

JESUS DRIVES OUT AN EVIL SPIRIT

PRAY

Ask that you might better understand the Holy One's authority in an encounter with evil powers.

READ

Mark 1:21–28; Luke 4:31–37

OBSERVE

We begin our study of the passages unique to the gospels other than Matthew with this story that appears in Mark and Luke. The accounts are almost identical. The only detail that the compassionate Dr. Luke adds is that the demon didn't injure the man when it was cast out.

v. 21—As you might remember, Capernaum was the new center of Jesus' ministry after he left Nazareth. His typical pattern early in his ministry was to teach in the synagogues.

v. 22—This observation is very similar to what Matthew states at the end of the Sermon on the Mount (Matt. 7:28–29).

vv. 23–24—What a condemnation of the synagogue that a demon-possessed man could worship there undisturbed until Jesus arrived! Notice that demons seem to work in groups (remember the legion of demons in the Gedarane demoniac we discussed earlier). God in the flesh was the ultimate threat to the kingdom of darkness, and they recognized it immediately. They also accurately admit who Jesus is (James 2:19).

vv. 25–26—Christ did not welcome the witness of demons. To the Jews, the character of the witness was all-important in accepting his message. Jesus doesn't engage in a debate. He simply exercises his authority to exorcise!

vv. 27–28—The common people recognized Christ's spiritual authority and perceived that it was from God. It was the religious people who wanted to attribute Christ's power to the evil one (Matt. 9:34).

APPLY

v. 22—Our authority comes from knowing and applying the Word of God to situations. It doesn't come from quoting men (like the teachers of the law did) but from knowing God.

vv. 23–24—Is your life a threat to the kingdom of evil? What, if anything, needs to change in order for the demons to see you as a formidable spiritual opponent?

MEMORIZE

Mark 1:22

We remember that Christ is the ultimate authority for your life.

PRAY

A: Praise God for his holiness and power.

C: Confess your lack of reliance on his power.

T: Thank him for overcoming the evil one.

S: Intercede for someone you know who is in the grip of evil.

TELL

Discuss with a Christian friend or small group how you see demons at work today.

MARCH 14

JESUS' QUIET TIME

PRAY

Ask for the same devotion to the Father that you see in the Son in this passage.

READ

Mark 1:35–39; Luke 4:42–44, 5:16

OBSERVE

Once again, Mark's and Luke's accounts are very similar. Luke includes the fact that the people of Capernaum wanted Jesus to remain with them.

v. 35—Luke 5:16 makes it clear that it was Jesus' custom to get off by himself before sunrise to pray. Notice the context of these verses. Jesus had just had an exhausting day, preaching and casting out demons in church, then healing people from all over the town of Capernaum all night. Nobody could have blamed him if he slept in. But it is clear that Jesus viewed prayer as his lifeline and the source of power for his ministry. He needed that connection with the Father through the power of the Spirit to do the work he had been given.

vv. 36–37—Simon Peter seemed to assume the role of ringleader of the disciples from early on. We can imagine that the "everyone" Simon and his companions mentioned were the residents of Capernaum who had even more friends and relatives for Jesus to heal.

vv. 38–39—Christ was and is never willing to restrict his ministry to any one group of people. He defines his primary mission as preaching. Healing was a way of confirming his ministry, but it was not his primary calling. Too often people want to come to Christ primarily because of the benefits they see in a relationship with him. Christianity is much more concerned with the message that Jesus came to announce.

APPLY

v. 35—Have you found the joy of those early morning hours with Jesus and his Word? Is your work dependent on the quality of your prayer life?

MEMORIZE

Mark 1:35

Remember the source of Jesus' strength.

PRAY

A: Praise God that he, the Ruler of the Universe, wants to meet with you.

C: Confess your casual attitude toward time with God.

T: Thank God for his Word and the gift of prayer.

S: Intercede for the day ahead.

TELL

Tell someone how important it is to spend time with God.

MARCH 15

THE POWER OF PARABLES

Pray that God would grow your understanding as you seek to hear these growth parables.

READ

Mark 4:21–29

OBSERVE

Though there are echoes of this teaching in the other Synoptics, Mark's treatment is unique.

vv. 21–23—This statement is used in Matthew 5:15 as an exhortation to let your good works be examples to men. Mark applies it, in this context, to the unspoken question the disciples were thinking (after Mark 4:12), *"Are parables meant to hide the truth from those outside?"* No, Jesus says. They are a lamp meant to illuminate the truth. If truth is temporarily hidden in parables, it is only so that it may be more fully revealed upon reflection. Truth cannot be suppressed, and falsehood will eventually be exposed. Jesus changed the metaphor from seeing to hearing, with the common invitation of verse 23. Keep in mind that "to hear" in biblical terms means "to obey."

vv. 24–25—Jesus presents a profound spiritual truth in these verses: you get what you give. It is expressed elsewhere in Scripture as "you reap what you sow." Many people act like the world—their parents, friends, teachers, employers—owes them a debt. They go through life critical and miserable. In every area of life, if you have a self-giving attitude, you will be richly blessed. If you reach out to your family in love, you'll be surprised at the response. A superficial study is often boring, while an in-depth examination of a subject can be thrilling. In his famous book *How to Win Friends and Influence People*, Dale Carnegie shows that the key to successful relationships is to be genuinely interested in other people rather than trying to make others interested in you. Carnegie writes, "All of us crave sincere appreciation, not cheap, insincere flattery. So treat others as you would have them treat you." This is just a restatement of the Golden Rule. Verse 25 presents the law of spiritual growth versus spiritual atrophy. A person can never stand still in the Christian life. You are either growing closer to Christ or moving farther away. One philosopher put it this way, "A man who ceases to become better ceases to be good."

vv. 26–29—There are three points to this parable:

1. People are necessary in God's plan as sowers of the Word, but they are helpless to produce spiritual growth. Only God can do that (1 Cor. 3:6).
2. Given God's blessing, growth is unstoppable. Just as a tree can split concrete pavement with its roots, in the end, nothing can stop the growth of God's kingdom.
3. When the time is right, God will intervene decisively in history and establish his rule.

APPLY

v. 24—What are some other areas where the principle of getting what you give holds true? In which areas do you need to give more? Make a specific commitment and form a concrete goal.

vv. 25–27—In what ways are you growing? It may be imperceptible to you, so ask someone who knows you well.

MEMORIZE

Mark 4:24

This is a very important biblical principle.

PRAY

A: Praise God as the source of all true growth.

C: Confess your failure to give generously to others.

T: Thank God for the areas of growth in your life.

S: Ask for help to grow in your weak areas.

TELL

Tell someone where you have seen growth in his or her life.

MARCH 16

JESUS HEALS A DEAF MAN IN GRAPHIC FASHION

PRAY

Pray for God's Spirit to make you flexible enough to respond to each situation uniquely as Jesus did.

READ

Mark 7:31–37

OBSERVE

Though there are similar healings in the other gospels, this story is unique to Mark.

v. 31—Jesus heads for home (the Sea of Galilee) but goes "through Sidon to the Sea of Galilee." He travels south by going due north! Some commentators think this text is in error and that Sidon shouldn't be mentioned at all. But this is another example of where an incidental detail tells us a lot. When you read the gospels, Jesus' ministry sometimes seems more like it was three weeks than three years. Obviously, the books are very selective and large blocks of time are omitted or compressed (see John 21:25). In this verse, one scholar sees a journey of eight months duration. It could have been a peaceful time spent with the disciples before the coming storm in Jerusalem. The region of the Decapolis is where Jesus healed Legion, the demon possessed-man, and where earlier the townspeople had asked him to leave.

v. 32—Like the story of the friends lowering the invalid to Jesus through a roof, this is another example of the faith of friends functioning on behalf of another. There were no trained Anne Sullivans to help the Helen Kellers of Jesus' day.

vv. 33–35—One thing you can predict about the healing ministry of Jesus—he was unpredictable! He seldom does the same thing twice. Notice his beautiful sensitivity here. He takes the man aside privately. Deaf people are often more embarrassed than blind people because the deaf can see the awkward reactions of others. Jesus shows consideration for his feelings. Knowing the man's condition, Jesus acts out the healing in a pantomime. The Lord wasn't afraid to touch people. His fingers in the man's ear suggest that the canal is opened. "Spit on the tongue" symbolizes the removal of the speech impediment. Looking up to heaven shows the source of the healing. The use of the Aramaic word *ephphatha* strongly suggests that the man and his friends were Jews. Many Jews had come into the Decapolis to hear Jesus in his early ministry (see Matt. 4:25), and the word was out that Jesus was back.

vv. 36–37—The fact that they were Jews would explain why Jesus asks for silence. The Jews had less respect for miracle workers than they did for teachers. The words, "He has done everything well" were never more true of a person. They point to Jesus' identification with the subject of Genesis 1:31.

APPLY

vv. 32–35—Jesus responded to each person individually because he was led by the Holy Spirit. Ask the Holy Spirit to lead you today so that you can respond individually and appropriately to each person you encounter.

MEMORIZE

Mark 7:37

This is a great statement about Jesus.

PRAY

A: Praise the one who does all things well.

C: Confess your tendency to rely on formulas in relating to people and pigeonholing them.

T: Thank God for all the good things he has done in your life in the past week.

S: Pray for sensitivity and insight into the people you are trying to reach for Christ.

TELL

Tell someone in your family how much you love them. Do it non verbally, as Jesus did to the deaf man.

MARCH 17

TWO TOUCHING STORIES

PRAY

Pray that you might experience Christ's second touch today.

READ

Mark 8:22–26; 12:41–44

OBSERVE

These two wonderful little stories are the last unique material in Mark.

v. 22—Bethsaida (also known as Bethsatha or Bethesda) was the site of several of Jesus' healing miracles (John 5:2) and has become associated with healing. It was the hometown of several disciples, including Peter (John 1:44). Blindness is one of the great maladies of the Near East. With the scorching glare of the sun and a host of communicable diseases that attack the optic nerve, it was not and is not an uncommon problem. In context, Jesus had just rebuked the disciples for their spiritual blindness (Mark 8:21). It is fitting that the next miracle should be the opening of a blind man's eyes.

vv. 23–25—This is the only time Jesus ever asked someone if they had been healed. This man was obviously not blind from birth because he knew what trees looked like. It is the only miracle that Jesus performed gradually. Perhaps there is a symbolic message here as well as the development of the man's faith. We can compare the first touch to our initial decision for Christ. That decision is real and important, but you don't see all of God's truth at once. It is natural for areas in both one's belief and practice to be fuzzy. It is only as Christ touches certain areas of our lives a second time that things clear up. We need to see the Christian life as a process of growth and not get impatient or discouraged when it takes a while for things to come into focus. That's the thesis of Keith Miller's book *A Second Touch*, which he bases on this passage. Real Christian discipleship is the result of being touched by Jesus on a daily basis.

v. 26—Christ loves the man in a thoughtful way by sending him home first. Perhaps a wife and children awaited him. They should be the first recipients of the good news, not a sensation-seeking crowd.

Mark 12:41–44—Once again, it's helpful to check the context. Just before this wonderful vignette, we see Jesus condemning the scribes and Pharisees for devouring widows' houses. Jesus always loved to teach by contrast, and what better contrast could he present to the vicious greed of the Jewish leaders than this poor widow. The very small copper coins she contributed were known as *leptons,* and they were worth about one-sixteenth of a penny in our currency. Several significant truths come from this mini-portrait:

1. The New Testament standard for giving isn't the tithe, although Jesus affirms its validity in Mattthew 23:23. The new standard is everything you have! We must be willing like the widow (and unlike the rich young ruler) to give everything to Christ, knowing that he will return to us what we need. Christian stewards shouldn't ask, "How much of my money should I give?" but "How much of your money should I keep?"
2. To be really meaningful, Christian giving must be sacrificial. Jesus doesn't deny that rich people put in large sums, but it was no sweat to them. Their giving didn't require faith. The widow's did. Jesus always commended this kind of reckless extravagance, like the woman who anointed him with perfume (Mark 14:3–9). Like the widow, the woman held nothing back.
3. It is beautiful that the one person whose giving to the temple Jesus commended gave only one-eighth of a cent. In gifts of money and of ourselves, it doesn't matter how much we have to give but whether we give it all to Christ.

APPLY

8:25—Where do you need the second touch of Christ today?

12:41–44—How much money are you giving for the work of Christ and his church? How much of yourself are you offering? Should you be giving more of either?

MEMORIZE

Mark 8:25

This reminds you of the importance of Jesus' second touch.

PRAY

A: Praise the Lord, who touches us and recognizes the smallest good deed.

C: Confess your greed and stinginess.

T: Thank God for all that he has provided—healing and material blessing.

S: Intercede for someone who needs Christ's second touch.

TELL

Discuss Christian giving with a friend or your small group.

MARCH 18

AN ORDERLY ACCOUNT

PRAY

Pray that you might learn something important from Zechariah's example.

READ

Luke 1:1–25, 57–80

OBSERVE

Luke gives a full background to the birth of John the Baptist.

vv. 1–4—Dr. Luke begins his gospel by establishing himself as a historian. He was a Gentile believer and part of Paul's missionary team. He was probably not present for much, if any, of what he writes in his gospel (he was an eyewitness to a lot of the events in Acts). Luke made a careful investigation and interviewed those who were Jesus' companions. The eyewitnesses he interviewed were "servants of the word," a phrase that only appears here in the New Testament. His desire is to write "an orderly account." The Greek word for orderly is also used only here. It describes "a logical and artistic arrangement" of the information pertaining to the life of Christ (Norval Geldenhuys, *Commentary on the Gospel of Luke*, 41). Theophilus means "lover of God." That may not have been his given name, and he may or may not have been a Christian; no one knows. The phrase, "most excellent Theophilus" probably indicates that he had an important position.

vv. 5–7—Herod ruled from 37–4 BC, and these events took place toward the end of that reign. The temple priests were divided into twenty-four divisions, of which Abijah was in the eighth. Each division was on duty only twice a year at the temple, for one week at a time. To be married to a wife who was also a descendant of Aaron (Levi) was considered a great blessing. But Zechariah and Elizabeth lacked the great human blessing of children, and they were old. This is a familiar story in Scripture.

vv. 8–10—There were so many priests that lots were cast to determine who would offer incense before the Lord in the Holy of Holies. A priest could only offer incense once in his lifetime, and some priests were never chosen.

vv. 11–25—For more than four hundred years, the people of God had not heard a direct word from the Lord. Zechariah's experience in the temple changed all that. In contrast to the popular depictions of angels, the biblical response to their appearing is overwhelming fear. An angel's first words are almost always, "Do not be afraid." They must be awesome to behold! The name John means, "The Lord is gracious." It goes without saying that any child would be a joy and a delight to this childless couple, but the angel's prophecy that "he will be great in the sight of the Lord" sets John apart. He may have been consecrated as a Nazirite, but the lack of mention of other parts of the vow (i.e., never cutting hair) argues against that interpretation (Num. 6:1–8). Luke is the gospel writer who focuses most on the Holy Spirit, and he introduces the third person of the Trinity here. John will be filled with the Holy Spirit and have the prophetic task of making the people ready for the Lord. Zechariah's response is similar to other believers who have been given extraordinary promises by an angel (Moses, Abraham, Sarah, Jeremiah, etc.). However, the priest is punished for his lack of trust. Could it be that God expected more from Zechariah because he had the scriptural accounts of these other people? The first part of the prophecy is fulfilled immediately. Elizabeth conceives and rejoices, almost with relief.

vv. 57–66—Just as an act of disobedience caused Zechariah's tongue to be bound, an act of obedience loosens it. In addition to the pregnancy of an old woman, Zechariah's healing caused his neighbors to anticipate that this child would be special.

vv. 67–80—Zechariah's "song" (actually it is a poem) of praise to the Lord is known as the Benedictus, from the Latin for the first words, "Blessed be." Zechariah's words were Spirit-filled and intended to be understood as a prophecy. Let's look at the four sections of this song:

1. Thanksgiving for the Messiah (vv. 68–70)—Despite being disciplined by the Lord, the elderly priest still begins with praise to the Redeemer. The horn was a symbol of strength, so the "horn of salvation" was a "mighty salvation" or a "strong savior." The reference to the house of David establishes clearly that Zechariah was talking about the Messiah.
2. The Great Deliverance (vv. 71–75)—The Benedictus seems to reflect the common understanding of the Messiah as deliverer from the oppressive evil powers who enslaved the Jews. But on closer examination, the deliverance does not seem so much political as spiritual. The Messiah would fulfill the covenant God swore to Abraham (Gen. 12:1–3) to bless Israel so that she can be a blessing. The result of the deliverance would be that God's people could serve him without fear in holiness and righteousness. These are certainly spiritual goals.

3. The Ministry of John (vv. 76–77)—We might have expected the excited father to focus his entire message on his son, but Zechariah only addresses John specifically in these two verses. There had not been a prophet among the Jews for centuries, so this was no small prediction. Not only would John be a prophet, he would prepare the way of the Lord (Isa. 40:3). John could save nobody, but he could prepare people for the Messiah by calling them to repentance.

4. The Messianic Salvation (vv. 78–79)—What a beautiful picture the Holy Spirit paints through Zechariah! Because of God's tender mercy, the Messiah will bring light to those in darkness and guide us on the path of peace. Peace, according to Barclay, "does not mean merely freedom from trouble; it means all that makes for a man's highest good" (Barclay, *The Gospel of Luke*, 14). The last verse in chapter one summarizes John's growing up years until he began his ministry.

APPLY

v. 18—Do you ever have difficulty accepting God's clear word to you? Have you seen any negative consequences as a result?

v. 69—Do you see your salvation as a source of great strength? Be on the offensive (don't be offensive) for Christ today.

v. 76—John's purpose in life was clear from the outset? What is your purpose, and are you fulfilling it?

MEMORIZE

Luke 1:68

This is the first verse of the Benedictus.

PRAY

A: Praise God for his mighty salvation.

C: Confess those times you've failed to hear/obey God's word.

T: Thank God for angels, John, and Jesus.

S: Intercede for those still living in darkness.

TELL

Explain to someone the tender mercy you have received from God.

MARCH 19

THE SONG OF MARY

Pray for faith like Mary's, which enables you to celebrate what you can't fully understand.

READ

Luke 1:39–56

OBSERVE

Mary's is the first "song" recorded in the Gospel of Luke.

vv. 39–45—Elizabeth was six months pregnant when the newly pregnant Mary went to visit her. John the Baptist responds to his Messiah in utero, the earliest evidence of a person's joy of salvation in Scripture! Once again, Luke describes Elizabeth as being filled with the Holy Spirit. Out of her fullness comes important words of blessing—Mary is blessed for believing God's Word. Jesus is the child of blessing, and Elizabeth is blessed to have the mother of the Messiah in her home.

vv. 46–55—Mary's song is known as the Magnificat (Latin for "glorifies/magnifies," the first word of the poem). There are a number of resemblances to the Song of Hannah (1 Sam. 2:1–10), which indicates that Mary was a student of the Old Testament. She begins by praising God for what he has done for her, a humble handmaiden of the Lord. In Greek, there is a different verb tense between "glorifies," which is Mary's continual action, and "rejoiced," which indicates that she rejoiced at a particular time—when Gabriel made his announcement that she was to be the mother of the Messiah. The middle of the Magnificat (vv. 50–53) describes a great reversal. The Messiah will invert the world's value system. The proud will be brought low, the rich will be sent away empty, but the humble will be lifted up and the hungry filled. The verse concludes with the fact that the Messiah is the fulfillment of God's covenant promises to his people, first announced to Abraham.

v. 56—Mary spends three months there, but leaves her kinswoman Elizabeth just before the birth of John the Baptist. Perhaps she didn't want to be part of the pandemonium that would accompany the prophet's birth, or maybe she didn't want to take the focus away from her cousin.

APPLY

v. 41—John's praise of the Messiah wasn't based on cognitive knowledge. Will you allow yourself to glorify the Lord today with your heart and emotions, not just your head?

vv. 51–53—Where do you see Mary's prophecy of the Great Reversal at work today in the spiritual sense?

MEMORIZE

Luke 1:46–47

Remember to praise God continually and rejoice in him.

PRAY

A: Praise the God who turns the world's values upside down.

C: Confess that you have sometimes reflected the world's value system rather than God's.

T: Thank God for the great things he has done for you.

S: Intercede for those who are proud and that the pride within you would be scattered.

TELL

Discuss with a friend how Christianity is really a revolutionary religion.

MARCH 20
THE BIRTH OF JESUS THE CHRIST

PRAY

Pray that this familiar story might speak to you with renewed power today.

READ

Luke 2:1–20

OBSERVE

vv. 1–5—As a historian, Luke sets Jesus' birth in the context of secular history. There are difficulties because we don't have a lot of records that have survived from that ancient period. There is no record of an official census conducted by Augustus Caesar, but he did reorganize the Roman administration. There are records in Egypt of censuses held every fourteen years, and actual documents survive for every census held between 20–270 AD (Barclay, *The Gospel of Luke*, 14). The historical record on Quirinius is even more spotty. There is a record of a census he carried out as governor of Syria in 6 AD (mentioned in Acts 5:37), but that is too late to be the one described in Luke 2:2. Jesus was probably born sometime between 6 and 4 BC (the people who revised the calendar made significant mistakes). Despite the historical difficulties, it is not difficult to say that God used the events of history (a census) to accomplish his purposes (the Messiah being born in Bethlehem to fulfill Micah 5:2).

vv. 6–7—The biblical account is simple and straightforward. There is no mention of Mary and Joseph traveling by donkey (they probably couldn't have afforded one). No innkeeper is identified in the story (the word translated "inn" probably referred to a guest room at a relative's house). The manger was a feeding trough for the animals, hardly the place we would consider appropriate for the Son of God!

v. 8—Shepherds were far down the totem pole of Near Eastern society. Their personal hygiene left a lot to be desired, as did their morals. They were considered unclean in the religious sense because they couldn't perform the ritual hand washings the law required before eating. These shepherds may have been a little higher class since they were probably caring for the temple flocks, animals that would be sold as appropriate sacrifices to religious pilgrims at a huge premium.

vv. 9–12—The shepherds have the usual reaction to an angel. But the angel's message, in addition to calming their fears, gives them cause for rejoicing. Notice that the first announcement of the Messiah's birth is "good news of great joy." We must never forget that the Christian message is, first and foremost, Gospel—good news that brings great joy! The child will be a Savior, Messiah (Christ, the Anointed One), and Lord; three awesome titles. This is the only place in Scripture where these three titles are used in one verse. He will be for "all the people," not just the Jews. This is the first statement of the missionary nature of Christianity. The sign was specific and unmistakable, just like all biblical prophecy (and unlike today's so-called prophets). The shepherds might find more than one new baby in Bethlehem wrapped in cheap strips of cloth, but they weren't likely to find more than one in a cattle trough.

vv. 13–15—The solo angel is joined by a company of the heavenly army (the real meaning of the word translated "host") that declares peace. The angels' job is to give glory to God, and that's the first thing they say (notice that they don't sing). This declaration has been mistranslated to suggest that Christ comes to give a generalized peace and goodwill to all men. The truth is very different. Peace comes only to those on whom God's favor rests, those who receive the Messiah and are given a right relationship with God because of him and his work. The shepherds are understandably anxious to see for themselves what has happened in Bethlehem.

vv. 16–20—We might wonder, if the shepherds told people what they had seen and heard, why weren't more people anticipating the life and ministry of the Messiah? The probable reason is that the shepherds told relatively few people, and they were not the movers and shakers of society. Furthermore, the testimony of shepherds was considered unreliable; at least not worthy of publishing in the *Jerusalem Times*. Mary keeps the events confidential, a good quality for the woman God chose to carry the awesome secret of his entry into human history in the flesh. How amazing to ponder that Mary gave birth to her own Savior. As the song "In the First Light" (written by Bob Kauflin) says, "As his mother held him closely, It was hard to understand; That the baby, not yet speaking, Was the Word of God to man."

APPLY

v. 10—Does your life reflect the truth that Christ's life is "good news of great joy"? How can you reflect that today?

v. 10—Do you believe that Christ is for all people? How is that reflected in your support of missionaries?

v. 14—Are you experiencing God's peace? Why or why not?

MEMORIZE

Luke 2:10–11

This is a great statement of why Christ came to earth.

PRAY

A: Give glory to God in the highest.

C: Confess that you have not always lived as though your relationship with Christ is good news.

T: Thank God for coming in the flesh for your salvation.

S: Intercede for a missionary who is trying to bring Christ to all the people.

TELL

Tell someone why the Lord's coming is good news of great joy.

MARCH 21

JESUS IS PRESENTED IN THE TEMPLE

PRAY

Pray that you might learn something from Simeon and Anna.

READ

Luke 2:21–40

OBSERVE

We learn more from Luke about Jesus' infancy than from the Jewish evangelists.

vv. 21–24—There are three different religious rites described in these verses. As a sign of God's covenant, every male infant was circumcised on the eighth day of his life (Gen. 17:12). It was also, according to Jewish custom, the time when his name would be announced. "Jesus" (Hebrew *Yeshua* or Joshua) means, "Our God saves" or "Savior" (Matt. 1:21). Every firstborn male was consecrated to the Lord (Exod. 13:2) and presented at the temple if possible. Luke doesn't mention it, but there was an offering of five shekels (about two ounces) of silver required to redeem the firstborn child of a couple. That must have strained Joseph's resources. We see that fact in the purification offering. After the birth of a son, a woman would be ceremonially unclean for forty days (Lev. 12:1–5). The required purification was a lamb and turtledove. However, if the woman was too poor, two pigeons could replace the lamb and dove (Lev. 12:6–8). This was known as the Offering of the Poor. How ironic that the Lord of the Universe is born into a family so poor that it can't afford the normal offering to accompany his birth!

vv. 25–27—Simeon is a representative of that group of Jews known as "The Quiet in the Land." "They had no dreams of violence and of power and of armies with banners; they believed in a life of constant prayer and quiet watchfulness until God should come. All their lives they waited quietly and patiently upon God" (Barclay, *The Gospel of Luke*, 21). Simeon was righteous, which described his right relationships with other people, and devout, which described his right relationship with God. "The consolation of Israel" was another term for the coming Messiah, who would bring comfort to his people after their great suffering (Isa. 40:1–2). Simeon is also described as having the Holy Spirit upon him. The Spirit moves him to go into the temple courts at just the moment when Joseph and Mary were presenting Jesus.

vv. 28–35—The Song of Simeon is known as the *Nunc Dimittis* ("Now Depart"), again for the Latin words at the beginning of his message. Leon Morris writes, "Simeon's *now* is important. He is ready to die peacefully *now* that he has seen God's *salvation,* i.e. the Baby through whom God would in time bring salvation" (Morris, *The Gospel According to St. Luke,* 88). That salvation is described as having been prepared for all people, a light of revelation for the Gentiles and the glory of Israel. Simeon continues in a more personal message to Mary to describe Jesus as a stumbling block for some and a stepping stone for others in Israel. He will reveal men's thoughts and cause a reaction. Many will speak against him. Mary would not be unscathed; the same sword that comes against Jesus will also hurt her. What an amazing, accurate prophecy when Jesus is only one month old!

vv. 36–40—Another character who made the temple her home was Anna, a prophetess and an eighty-four-year-old widow. Like Simeon, she lived a life of prayer and devotion to the Lord. She also gives the revealed message that Jesus will be the Redeemer. The passage is low-key concerning Mary and Joseph's reaction to these prophecies, but can you imagine what they thought and talked about as they returned to Nazareth? The concluding verse of this section describes Jesus' childhood much like verse 52 will describe his adolescence.

APPLY

v. 24—Do you ever assume that wealthy people have more to offer the kingdom of God than the poor? This passage should cure you of that false perception.

v. 34—Do you truly believe that everyone rises or falls depending on their view of and relationship with Jesus? How should that affect your desire to share your faith?

MEMORIZE

Luke 2:40

This is a model for how your children and grandchildren might grow up.

PRAY

A: Praise the God of all consolation.

C: Confess your tendency to think that rich people are more important.

T: Thank God for a quiet, faithful person you know.

S: Intercede for someone who is stumbling over the person of Jesus. Ask God for a chance to share your faith with that person.

TELL

Tell that individual about how Christ has been a light in your life.

MARCH 22

THE TWELVE-YEAR-OLD JESUS

PRAY

Ask that God might give you some of the insight and maturity Jesus had at age twelve.

READ

Luke 2:41–52

OBSERVE

This is the only account we have of Jesus' life between infancy and age thirty. It's very likely that Luke became a close friend of Mary because he reveals some of her most intimate experiences and thoughts.

v. 41—Nazareth is about eighty miles from Jerusalem, so it wouldn't have been too rigorous a journey, especially if one weren't pregnant. Since Joseph had relatives in Bethlehem who would provide free lodging, it wouldn't have been too expensive for them to make the annual trip for the Passover. This explains why Jesus felt very comfortable in Jerusalem at feast time when he was an adult.

vv. 42–44—It would not have been difficult for Jesus' parents to lose him. The practice of Jews traveling by caravan to and from Jerusalem was for the mothers and young children to leave first. The fathers and older children, who traveled much faster, would leave later and catch them by the end of the day. No doubt both Joseph and Mary thought that he was with the other parent and didn't discover his absence until they were reunited at the end of the day.

vv. 45–48—If you are a parent, imagine the anxiety and fear you would feel after searching for your child unsuccessfully for three days. It's not surprising that Mary would rebuke Jesus harshly when they finally found him. They probably didn't look for him in the temple courts because the typical twelve-year-old would find the rabbinical exchanges there boring and too difficult to follow. But instead, Jesus was discussing the law with expert teachers, and they were amazed at his understanding and answers to their questions. How many parents today are rearing children who value God's truth above everything else? It seems that most American parents would far rather see their children focused on sports or music or secular academics than in pursuing the knowledge of God and his Word.

vv. 49–50—In these verses, we have the first recorded words of Jesus of Nazareth. The Greek translated, *"Didn't you know I had to be in my Father's house?"* could also be translated, "about my Father's business." Whichever the translation, the message is the same. Even at this early age, Jesus knew that he had a special relationship with the heavenly Father. It was very unusual for a Jew to address God as, "My Father," especially without adding "in heaven." Even with the amazing revelations that accompanied Jesus' birth, his parents didn't fully understand his unique relationship with the Father.

vv. 51–52—Mary was very likely the source of much of the information that Luke and the other gospel writers recorded. We can picture her sharing this story with Luke and telling him how she treasured this experience. The concluding verse, which describes Jesus' teenage years, shows us that he grew mentally, physically, spiritually, and socially.

APPLY

v. 47—Jesus had to study just like you and I do. Are you serious enough about God's Word that people are amazed at your understanding?

v. 49—Do you love the Father's house like Jesus did? Do you look forward to worship? Are you serious about committing your time and energy to the Father's business?

v. 52—Jesus grew mentally, physically, spiritually, and socially. Of those four areas, where do you most need to grow in your life? Can you lay out a plan for growth that, with God's help, will make a difference in your body, mind, spirit, and relationships?

MEMORIZE

Luke 2:49

Remember Jesus' priority for his life.

PRAY

A: Praise God that he reveals himself to those who diligently seek him.

C: Confess your lack of commitment to his house and his work.

T: Thank God for the example of Jesus' balanced life.

S: Pray for your mental, physical, spiritual, and social growth.

TELL

Tell someone at least one goal that you have for each of those four areas.

MARCH 23

JESUS PREACHES AT HIS HOME CHURCH

PRAY

Pray for the ability to apply this passage effectively to your life.

READ

Luke 4:16–30

OBSERVE

This isn't the first sermon Jesus ever delivered. He had already begun his ministry in Capernaum (v. 23) before he returned to Nazareth. After his temptation, he began his ministry in the synagogues of Galilee and acquired a reputation as a teacher and healer (vv. 14–15).

v. 16—This is the earliest description in existence of synagogue worship. No one is certain when the synagogue (Greek "come together") began, but it was not highly developed before the destruction of the temple (70 AD). If the later customs were in place this early, the service would have begun with prayer, then a reading from the Law, then a reading from the prophets, which is when Jesus was invited to teach. He stood up as an expression of respect for the Word of God. Rabbis typically sat when they taught their students.

vv. 17–21—The scroll of the prophet Isaiah was handed to Jesus, but it appears that he chose the passage for his sermon. He read Isaiah 61:1–2, a messianic prophecy, but his initial remark had to surprise his friends and neighbors. The Jews all believed that someday God's kingdom would come with the Anointed One. But Jesus indicated that it wasn't some day, it was "today." Jesus shows that the ministry of the Messiah included preaching good news to the poor and caring for people in distress. One theologian writes, "The *acceptable year of the Lord* does not, of course, represent any calendar year, but is a way of referring to the era of salvation" (Morris, *The Gospel According to St. Luke,* 106).

vv. 22–30—Though the Nazarenes were impressed, they clearly weren't converted. Morris comments:

> They were astonished that someone from their own town, one whom they could call "Joseph's son," could speak like this. Notice that Luke speaks of astonishment, not admiration or appreciation. They wondered at his preaching, but they did not take it to heart. (Morris, *The Gospel According to St. Luke,* 107)

Jesus senses their skepticism and quotes two proverbs, *"Physician, heal yourself!"* and *"No prophet is accepted in his hometown."* It's his illustrations that inflame his neighbors, however. He quotes from the lives of two of the earliest prophets, Elijah and Elisha, who performed miracles for Gentiles, not Jews. This was too much for Jesus' neighbors. It would be like a modern preacher saying that God has a soft spot in his heart for the followers of radical Islam. The congregation turns into a lynch mob. They take him to the highest hill in town (a location that doesn't exist any longer) and attempt to throw him down the cliff. But it is not Jesus' time yet. The majestic Lord sheds his captors and walks right through the middle of the crowd, and none of the furious residents of Nazareth stop him! He must have been a pretty impressive physical specimen. Gang leaders have described particularly tough individuals who walked away from a confrontation because no one was willing to take them on.

APPLY

vv. 18–19—The church's task is to continue the ministry of Jesus. Which of the tasks in this passage might God be calling you to perform?

v. 22—Do you ever judge someone because of their background? Remember that God is not limited by human factors.

vv. 24–27—Remember also that God's work is not limited to the people we think he should concentrate on.

MEMORIZE

Luke 4:18–19

This is a great summary of the work of Christ.

PRAY

A: Praise God for his love for the unlovely, including you and me.

C: Confess that you've sometimes judged people by superficial standards.

T: Thank God that sinful people cannot thwart his purposes.

S: Intercede for a prisoner, blind person, or someone who is oppressed.

TELL

Tell someone who seems oppressed that you care about him.

MARCH 24

JESUS RAISES THE WIDOW OF NAIN'S SON

PRAY

Pray that God would give you Christ's heart of compassion.

READ

Luke 7:11–17

OBSERVE

Luke's is the only gospel that tells this story.

v. 11—Nain was about a day's journey from Capernaum (where Jesus healed the centurion's servant earlier in this chapter). This is the only place in Scripture that the city is mentioned. Most scholars believe that it is the modern Nein, about six miles southeast of Nazareth at the foot of Little Mt. Hermon. As many as one hundred and fifty people accompanied Jesus from town to town, as well as his disciples.

v. 12—Jesus and company enter Nain just as a large crowd is leaving the city. It's a funeral procession of the saddest sort. The focus of attention was a woman who had not only lost her husband, but had now lost her only son. There weren't a lot of economic or social prospects for a widow in the Near East at the time of Jesus (thus the early church's great concern for widows), and her neighbors must have really empathized with her. The large crowd is all the more impressive considering the fact that the custom of the day was to hire as many mourners as a family could afford, to weep and wail impressively. Morris quotes the *Ketuboth*, part of the rabbinical literature, which said, "Even the poorest in Israel should hire not less than two flutes and one wailing woman" (Morris, *The Gospel According to St. Luke*, 140). The widow of Nain couldn't have afforded much more than the minimum.

v. 13—Luke uses the strongest word possible in Greek to describe how Jesus' heart went out to the widow. It's also the first time since 2:11 that Luke uses the phrase "the Lord" in a narrative to describe Jesus. Barclay points out that Greek Stoic philosophers believed the primary characteristic of God was apathy—the inability to feel. If something can make us feel, they reasoned, it can influence us. If it can influence us, it means that, at least temporarily, it's superior. Since nobody is superior to God, he must be unfeeling (Barclay, *The Gospel of Luke*, 86). Jesus shows the fallacy of that thinking in this scene. It's because of his compassion that Luke identifies him as Lord. The writer of Hebrews underscores Christ's empathy when he writes, *"For we do not have a high priest who is unable to sympathize with our weaknesses…"* (Heb. 4:15).

vv. 14–17—Christ is not only empathetic. He is powerful. At his word, the dead boy is raised to life, one of three resuscitations Jesus performed (see also Jairus' daughter and Lazarus). These mighty acts of God are called resuscitations because each of those brought back to life subsequently died again. Jesus was the only one to experience a resurrection, which included his ascension into heaven. The people are understandably impressed and view Jesus as a prophet, high praise from Jews. But it is not high enough. Though they believed that God had come to help his people, they did not recognize that Jesus was God. News about Jesus spread throughout Judea, so that his fame was known throughout all of Palestine.

APPLY

v. 13—Who are you compassionate for? What would God have you do about it?

v. 16—Do you know anyone who thinks Jesus is only a great prophet or teacher? What arguments could you use to convince him or her that Christ is God?

MEMORIZE

Luke 7:13

Remember the heart of Jesus toward those who are hurting.

PRAY

A: Praise God for his compassion and power.

C: Confess your lack of compassion at times.

T: Thank God for his compassion toward you.

S: Ask God to use you to meet needs that you feel deeply about.

TELL

Discuss with your small group why compassion isn't weakness but strength.

MARCH 25

THE BELOVED EXTRAVAGANCE

PRAY

Pray that you would recognize how much you have been forgiven so that you may love extravagantly.

READ

Luke 7:36–8:3

OBSERVE

Though we looked at a similar situation in Matthew, Mark, and John, this anointing in Luke seems significantly different, especially the teaching and application Jesus gives. Luke's event also seems earlier in Christ's ministry. It may be that what takes place in the other gospels was a later copycat of what happened in Luke. Or Luke's account may be an amplification of the story in the other gospels (the fact that the host's name is Simon would support that, though it was a common name), but there is enough meat in this story to consider it on its own.

v. 36—Matthew and Mark identify the host as "Simon the Leper," apparently someone Jesus had healed. Luke's Simon is a Pharisee. It would seem that if it were the same person, Luke would have noted that he was a healed leper and Matthew and Mark would have identified him as a Pharisee.

vv. 37–38—Neither Matthew nor Mark identify their woman as a prostitute, John's woman is identified as Mary of Bethany. This woman is the only one described as wetting Jesus' feet with her tears. The anointing in Matthew and Mark is of Jesus' head (for burial). Mary in John 12 also anoints Jesus' feet and wipes his feet with her hair. For a Jewish woman to "let down her hair" was very unusual.

She usually did it only in the presence of her husband. Barclay notes, "The fact that this woman loosed her long hair in public showed how she had forgotten everyone except Jesus" (Barclay, Commentaries, 94).

v. 39—Simon's reaction is typical of a Pharisee. To him, a truly religious person keeps a careful moral checklist and distinguishes carefully between those who are acceptable and those who are not. He is quick to condemn the sinner.

vv. 40–43—Christ tells this mini-parable to indict Simon. Part of Jesus' teaching strategy was to tell a story that brought his listeners to agreement with the main teaching point. Simon couldn't dispute the message of this parable. Those who are forgiven of a greater debt are more grateful than those forgiven of a smaller debt.

vv. 44–47—Jesus then applies the parable in a powerful way to Simon and the woman. Simon is the one who thinks he is good and doesn't need to be forgiven of much. Yet he stands condemned as a bad host, who does none of the pleasantries that a good host should have done for his guest. The woman, who is aware of her sin, shows great kindness to the guest of honor. Christ's conclusion must be examined carefully. Jesus is not saying that she was forgiven because she loved much. A clearer translation would be, "Her many sins have been forgiven, *therefore* she loved much." Her love was proof that she had already been forgiven. Jesus' words to Simon are full of irony, much like his proverb, *"The healthy have no need of a physician."* It's those who think they have little need for forgiveness who experience little forgiveness and show little love. Like those who think they are healthy, they are deluded and fail to recognize the depth of their sin (which Jesus pointed out to Simon earlier). It's a spiritual reality that the closer a person is to God, the more she recognizes her sin.

vv. 48–50—Jesus pronounces her forgiveness for the benefit of the other guests. She had already been forgiven when she demonstrated saving faith in Jesus. The guests recognized that the prerogative to forgive sins only belongs to God. They should have made the logical connection that Jesus was claiming to be God himself in his statement to the woman.

8:1–3—This section is not a part of the previous story, but it's worthwhile to look at them together because they both describe how important the ministry of women was to Christ and the disciples. The women who traveled with Jesus included prominent and wealthy figures like Joanna and less notable women as well. But they were all servants who provided meals for Jesus and the disciples at their own expense. Christ's ministry would have been much more difficult without these women. Those with the gift of service contribute significantly to Christ's body today.

APPLY

v. 43—Do you honestly see your debts as great or relatively small? Ask God to help you see your sin from his perspective.

v. 47—Are you truly grateful for God's forgiveness? Show your gratitude by loving others extravagantly today.

MEMORIZE

Luke 7:47

Remember the "therefore" in this verse.

PRAY

A: Praise the God of mercy.

C: Confess the sins that you have previously minimized.

T: Thank God that his forgiveness is complete.

S: Intercede for someone who thinks he has little need for forgiveness.

TELL

This parable would be a great one to discuss with a group. It brings us back to the heart of the Gospel.

MARCH 26

THE PARABLE OF THE GOOD SAMARITAN

PRAY

Pray that you might go and do likewise!

READ

Luke 10:25–37

OBSERVE

This is one of the best known parables in the New Testament, unique to Luke.

vv. 25–29—The setup for the parable is very similar to the parables in Matthew—a teacher of the law (scribe) tries to test Jesus. He asks the most important question of all, the one every true religion tries to answer, "What must I do to inherit eternal life?" Notice that the question presupposes that eternal life is something you earn by doing. Jesus, who always asks questions that reveal a person's heart, asks the man to summarize his understanding of the Law. He responds with the Shema Israel (Deut. 6:4–5), which every Jew knew and recited daily. He adds Leviticus 19:18, which stresses loving one's neighbor as oneself. Jesus affirms his response, but adds the ominous words, "Do this and you will live." Jesus knew that nobody (but he) loves God with all their heart, soul, strength, and mind or their neighbor as themselves. The scribe wants to impress Jesus with his piety so he asks a follow-up question, "And who is my neighbor?" Christ's answer is an unforgettable classic.

v. 30—The road from Jerusalem to Jericho was notoriously dangerous. Jerusalem, near Mt. Zion, is 2,300 feet above sea level. Jericho, near the Dead Sea, is the lowest inhabited city in the world at 1,300 below sea level. In little more than twenty miles, the road drops 3,600 feet. The road to Jericho is a narrow, rocky pass. Robbers would hide behind an outcropping of rocks and accost the helpless traveler.

vv. 31–32—The priest and the Levite would have been concerned about ceremonial purity. If the poor victim was in fact dead and they touched him, they would have been unclean for seven days (Num. 19:11) and unable to do many of their religious duties. These men considered religion more important than relationships, especially with a stranger. The priests and Levites were men who played it safe, so they got as far away from the victim as possible.

Before we're too quick to condemn them, we should consider a famous experiment that was conducted at Princeton Theological Seminary. Three groups of seminary students were given the assignment of studying this parable in the library and writing a paper about it. After some time, one of the groups was told that their paper was due right away at another campus location, the second group was told that their paper was already late, and a third group was told that they had plenty of time. On the way from the library to the other location, a professional actor lay on the ground feigning great distress. None of the seminary students in the first two groups stopped to help him. Though it was an experiment designed to measure the effect of stress on the exercise of compassion, it indicates that many of us in this stress-filled world do no better than the priest and Levite when it comes to demonstrating genuine compassion for those who are hurting.

vv. 33–35—Morris comments:

> The audience would have expected a priest and a Levite to be followed by an Israelite layman. They would almost certainly now be expecting a story with an anti-clerical twist. Jesus' introduction of the Samaritan was devastating. In view of the traditional bitterness between Jew and Samaritan, a *Samaritan* was the last person who might have been expected to help. (Morris, *The Gospel According to St. Luke*, 189–190)

Samaritans were northern Jews who intermarried with Assyrians and corrupted the Jewish faith. Because they had once been part of the covenant people and fell away, they were even more despised than the "ignorant Gentiles." This Samaritan had a heart of compassion like Jesus. He put himself out physically and financially, caring for the injured man even beyond the initial crisis. He is a model of Christian social action.

vv. 36–37—Jesus' unavoidable conclusion to the scribe is also his word to us, *"Go and do likewise."*

APPLY

v. 27—Which do you have more trouble with, loving God with all of your being or loving your neighbor as yourself? What can you do today to improve in both relationships?

vv. 30–32—What excuses do you make to avoid caring for those who are hurting? Are there valid excuses?

v. 37—How will you "go and do likewise"?

MEMORIZE

Luke 10:36–37

This reminds you how important it is that love is a verb.

PRAY

A: Praise God for his marvelous Word.

C: Confess your failure to care practically for the needy.

T: Thank God for opportunities to serve him by serving others.

S: Pray for a particular need in your community.

TELL

Discuss with your small group how you can be involved in meaningful mercy ministry.

MARCH 27

ARE YOU A MARY OR A MARTHA?

PRAY

Pray that you might see yourself clearly as you identify with this story.

READ

Luke 10:38–42

OBSERVE

This little domestic drama is a corrective to those who might overemphasize the parable of the Good Samaritan—that good works epitomize what it means to be a Christian. It, too, is unique to Luke.

v. 38—The home of Mary, Martha, and Lazarus is more familiar to the readers of John's gospel, where it is mentioned several times. The village in which they lived was Bethany, about two miles from Jerusalem. It was a place where Jesus retreated to on many occasions to renew himself for his ministry. Martha appears to be the older sister and the one in charge of the home, if not its owner.

v. 39—Mary was devoted to Jesus. Every time she appears with Jesus (John 11:32, 12:3) she is at her Lord's feet, the place of a disciple.

v. 40—Martha recognizes Jesus' lordship. She appeals to his authority to get her younger sister to do what she wants. But notice the subtle rebuke in her words to Jesus, "Don't you care...." Martha is the model of the task-oriented person who feels that work comes first and relationships second. It wasn't wrong of her to want to serve Jesus. The problem was that she became distracted by what she thought had to be done. Her priorities were misplaced. If her gift was to serve in the kitchen, she should have done it without complaining. We get the impression that she was somewhat of a Martha Stewart, who wanted to impress Jesus with a big spread and demanded that her sister share her values and work ethic.

vv. 41–42—In Hebrew culture, repeating a person's name had the effect of softening the message. Jesus corrects Martha, but he does it gently. Jesus uses a play on words. Martha is anxious about many things. A simple meal—one thing—is sufficient. Mary has chosen the one thing, fellowship with her Lord, and it will last longer than any meal.

APPLY

v. 40—Do you have the tendency to get distracted with a lot of tasks and ignore intimacy with Christ?

v. 42—Remember that the time we spend with Christ will last for eternity, unlike earthly tasks.

MEMORIZE

Luke 10:41–42

Remember the importance of devotion to Christ.

PRAY

A: Praise God that he desires your fellowship.

C: Confess the times you have taken his fellowship for granted.

T: Thank God for the example of Mary and other people whose devotion to Christ is a model for you.

S: Pray that you will consistently choose what is better with your time.

TELL

Discuss with a friend or a small group the balance between work and worship.

MARCH 28

THE PARABLE OF THE RICH FOOL

PRAY

Ask for the courage to look honestly at the issue of greed.

READ

Luke 12:13–21

OBSERVE

Luke's gospel is the one that focuses most on the issue of money, especially the danger of worshiping money. This is a key passage communicating that message.

vv. 13–14—There were generally clear rules about inheritance in Jewish culture (Deut. 21:15–17), but occasionally there were gray areas. Rabbis gave opinions about disputed points of law, but it would require the agreement of both brothers in this situation for Jesus to arbitrate. The disinherited brother wants Jesus to take his side, and Jesus refuses. The term "man" is a mild rebuke. Leon Morris notes, "He came to bring men to God, not to bring property to men" (Morris, *The Gospel According to St. Luke*, 212).

v. 15—This powerful warning introduces the parable. "Be on your guard" is a good translation of the Greek word *phulassesthe*, which describes positive action taken to defend against an enemy. In this materialistic society, Christ's words have tremendous relevance. Americans often tend to judge a person's worth and success based on the number of and quality of his possessions.

vv. 16–20—The parable of the rich fool is perfectly directed at those who want to trade up to a bigger house, a more luxurious car, and, at times, a newer-model spouse. The American dream of a carefree retirement isn't Jesus' idea of heaven on earth. Isn't the motto "Take life easy; eat, drink and be merry" the goal of our senior years? But the materialist fails to recognize that life is unpredictable and there is a spiritual dimension whether we acknowledge it or not. "This very night your life will be demanded from you" is literally translated, "This very night *they require* your life from you," "a common construction among the rabbis to denote the action of God" (Morris, *The Gospel According to St. Luke*, 213). The implication of, "Then who will get what you have prepared for yourself?" is that the rich fool has cut himself off from even family who would inherit his bigger barns full of grain.

v. 21—The moral of the parable stresses priorities. Christ does not necessarily decry all wealth; it is selfish and uncaring wealth that he condemns. We must guard carefully against being materially rich and spiritually impoverished. Most people in America accumulate a great deal during their lifetime. Christ wants us to accumulate what really matters, treasure in heaven that cannot be taken away (Matt. 6:19–21). Most people are devoted to accumulating things that won't even last their entire time on earth. One of the fastest-growing industries in the United States is storage facilities that people use to warehouse all the stuff that wouldn't fit in their houses. This parable applies to America in a big way.

APPLY

v. 15—Have you been caught up in the mindset that possessions equal success? How can you change that way of thinking? (It's not easy!)

v. 18—How about the "bigger is better" ideology? Do you really need the latest and best furnishings and technology?

v. 21—Take an honest self-examination right now. How would you rank your dependence on material things (1–10) and on God (1–10)?

MEMORIZE

Luke 12:15

This is a crucial corrective to deliver you from the American way of death.

PRAY

A: Praise God that he is Eternal Spirit.

C: Confess your dependence on material things and your desire to have personal peace without hassles.

T: Thank God for this clear and powerful parable.

S: Pray that Jesus would reorient your priorities.

TELL

Share with someone any lifestyle decisions you have made as a result of this study.

MARCH 29

JESUS REVERSES THE STATUS QUO

PRAY

Ask for understanding and application of these difficult and challenging words.

READ

Luke 12:49–56, 14:7–33

OBSERVE

Though these passages are separated in Luke and have a slightly different subject, the theme is very similar. Jesus came to change the way people look at relationships, especially with God.

vv. 49–53—This passage is difficult to interpret with any degree of certainty, but interpret it we must. The metaphor of fire, biblically, almost always refers to God's judgment. Whether people like it or not, part of the reason Christ came to the earth was to make very clear the basis on which God will judge every individual— by his or her relationship to the Messiah. The baptism Christ refers to describes his upcoming suffering (Mark 10:38–39) and death. We tend to underestimate how much the upcoming cross influenced Jesus' thinking and teaching. Jesus is the cornerstone for some and the stumbling block for others (1 Pet. 2:6–8). We can all think of families who have been deeply divided because some trust in Christ as Lord and Savior and others in the same family reject him. Those who see Jesus as only a peacemaker have missed this crucial aspect of his ministry.

vv. 54–56—It's not abundantly clear how these verses are related to what precedes them. The best guess is that Jesus is continuing the theme of why he came. "This present time" is the decisive time of judgment he ushered in with his coming.

Though his contemporaries were good at gauging the weather based on the signs in the skies, they were blind to what was happening in their midst, despite the very clear signs Jesus gave them through his life and ministry.

14:7–11—The wedding customs in Jesus' day were different than ours. At a sit-down reception today, people are generally assigned to a table by the bride's family. In Christ's time, wedding guests were seated around a large table. An expert on that culture tells us:

> At banquets the basic item of furniture was the couch for three, the *triclinium*. A number of *triclinia* were arranged in a U-shape. Guests reclined on their left elbows. (This is the way Jesus and his disciples would have been arranged at the Last Supper.) The place of highest honor was the central position on the couch at the base of the U. The second and third places were those on the left of the principal man (i.e., reclining behind him) and on his right (i.e., reclining with the head on his bosom). After this there seems to have ranked the couch to the left, its most honorable occupant being in the middle, with the next places behind and before him as on the first couch. The third couch, with a similar arrangement of its occupants, would be on the right of the first, the fourth to the left of the second, and so on. (Strack and Billerbeck, *Commentary on the New Testament from the Talmud and Midrasch, Volume IV*, 618, quoted in Morris, *The Gospel According to St. Luke*, 231)

Jesus observed a wedding in which there was a mad dash for the places of honor, and he gives a piece of solid, commonsense advice. If you take a place of honor, you could get bumped when a more important person comes along. That would be the proverbial walk of shame. If you take a less-important seat, the host might invite you to take a more prominent place and you will be honored. The moral of the story, though, underlines the way Jesus' ethics contrast with the world's value system. The world says, "Blow your own horn and others will join in the music." Jesus says, *"Everyone who exalts himself will be humbled, and he who humbles himself will be exalted."* This is the most frequently quoted verse in the New Testament (Luke 18:14; Matt. 18:4, 23:12; 1 Pet. 5:6).

vv. 12–14—The principle is then applied to the person who throws a party. Most people like to invite a group of important people, including their closest friends and relatives. Implicit in this "social contract" is that those people will invite you to their shindigs. It's the "You scratch my back, I'll scratch yours" philosophy that is so prominent in contemporary society and business. But Jesus rejects the status quo. If you invite the needy and hurting who can't reciprocate, God will reward you in heaven. Notice that, once again, Jesus appeals to the concept of eternal reward as a motivation for our behavior on earth.

vv. 15–24—Jesus' party program is illustrated and expanded upon in the Parable of the Great Banquet. The parable is introduced by the exclamation of a person at the table with Jesus who got the message. The happiest person will be the one who is invited to the feast in heaven! Jesus describes a great earthly banquet in which many people were invited. The custom, in an era without watches, was to confirm the invitation by sending a servant to announce when the banquet was ready. But the people who had initially accepted the invitation all decided to beg off.

Their excuses were transparently lame. No self-respecting Jew bought a field or a yoke of oxen without first inspecting and testing them. Though the law protected the newlywed from military service in the first year, he and his bride were not discouraged from socializing. The homeowner who invited these disappointing guests then sends the servant to invite the poor. When there is still more room after the disenfranchised accept the invitation, the servant is told to be more assertive—to persuade the homeless who lived on the streets to join the party. The host concludes that none of the ungrateful invitees will even get a taste of his wonderful food.

Not only does this parable illustrate the teaching of verses 12–14, it is a theological commentary on God's rejection of the religious elite in Israel. Jesus came and invited them to God's party, but they turned him away (John 1:11). Jesus then went to the Jewish outcasts (the poor, crippled, blind, and lame) and finally to the Gentiles (those outside the city). The heavenly feast will feature a cast of unlikely guests! The theme of surprise and the reversal of people's ingrained opinions is strong in Jesus' teaching.

vv. 25–33—This is the strongest passage in Scripture about the cost of following Jesus Christ. Some people are troubled by Jesus' command to *hate* family members and even ourselves. The Greek word *miseo* can mean "to love less." The parallel passage in Matthew 10:37 makes it clear that this is Jesus' intended meaning. And the intended meaning is very challenging and counter cultural. In an age in which people make an idol of family and in which self-love is considered the key to happiness, Christ demands first place with no challengers to his position. Following him will not be easy, for there is suffering down the path of any true disciple. The illustrations of building a tower and going to war simply expand on these truths. In order to make an informed decision for Christ, we've got to count the cost. That cost includes the willingness to give up everything we have for the surpassing worth of following him (Phil. 3:8).

APPLY

12:49–50—Have you diminished Christ's role as Judge in your own mind (John 5:27)? How does the fact that Jesus is our judge impact the way you live your life?

12:51–53—Has faith in Christ produced any divisions within your family? How can you deal with the reality of that situation in a way that honors and pleases God?

14:11—Can you think of any ways in which you have exalted yourself? How does Jesus want you to humble yourself instead?

14:12–14—Have you ever considered giving a party and inviting needy people? Are you willing to do it?

14:26—Do you love Jesus even more than you love your family? One of the ways you can love him more is by caring about your family's spiritual growth more than their worldly success.

MEMORIZE

Luke 14:33

Remember the uncompromising demands of discipleship.

PRAY

A: Praise God that he is a jealous God who will not take second place.

C: Confess that you have not always put him in first place.

T: Thank God for the opportunity to reorient your priorities today.

S: Pray that you will put Jesus first, before every other relationship, including your love for yourself.

TELL

Discuss with your small group how these tremendous demands can be lived out in the crucible of your daily experience.

MARCH 30

REPENT OR PERISH

PRAY

Pray that you might not grow weary of hearing the hard words of Jesus.

READ

Luke 13:1–9

OBSERVE

Luke is the gospel that most emphasizes God's grace see Luke 15), but it also speaks the truth about judgment (see John 1:14, last phrase).

v. 1—We don't have any other information about this incident. These Galileans were presumably offering their sacrifices in Jerusalem, the only appropriate place to sacrifice. A strong likelihood is that they were revolutionaries because the men of Galilee had a reputation for being hotheads, prone to become involved in political causes. Barclay mentions that about this time Pilate was building an aqueduct to improve the water supply to Jerusalem. He was using temple funds, which infuriated the Jews. When a mob gathered, Pilate had his soldiers mingle with them, dressed in civilian garb. The soldiers descended on the crowd and ended up killing a number of them. Perhaps the greatest number were Galileans (Barclay, *The Gospel of Luke*, 177). Whatever their offense, to kill them in the midst of the act of sacrifice was particularly brutal and cold-blooded.

vv. 2–5—The common understanding at the time of Christ was that bad things happened to bad people. Disaster and tragedy were the payment for sin. Jesus dispelled that quid pro quo relationship. He cited another example that is even more obscure than Pilate's slaughter, a tower that fell on a group of Judeans near the pool of Siloam. In both cases, Jesus declared that those who lost their lives were no worse sinners than their countrymen who were spared. The bottom line for Jesus is that all men are sinners who need to repent. The clear implication is that God's judgment is much more to be feared than Pilate's (Matt. 10:28). So often, people approach the problem of evil in the world with the presupposition that people are good. A popular book asks, "Why do bad things happen to good people?" Jesus makes it clear that there are no good people. The tougher philosophical question is why a holy God allows good things to happen to evil people. He is gracious, but he is also a just judge who will condemn those who do not repent.

vv. 6–9—The Parable of the Fig Tree takes the focus from sins of commission to sins of omission. The issue for Jesus is whether we bear good fruit or not (Matt. 7:19–20). Like us, the fig tree had the best of situations in which to thrive. A vineyard had good soil, and the tree would receive the best of care from the vinedresser. Typically, if a fig tree has not produced fruit after three years, it is not likely to ever bear fruit. The owner is justifiably unhappy with the tree, but he is persuaded to give it one more year. God is patient with those who are just taking up space (Rom. 2:4), but there will be a day of reckoning, the final judgment, when each person's fruit (or lack thereof) will be exposed (1 Cor. 3:12–15). Of course, the most important fruit of all is trusting in Jesus Christ alone for justification and cooperating with his Spirit for sanctification (Rom. 14:9–12).

APPLY

vv. 1–5—How would you summarize Jesus' teaching on the problem of evil in this passage?

v. 6—What fruit are you bearing? Think of one specific thing that you could do that would please God and bear fruit for his kingdom today.

MEMORIZE

Luke 13:5

This is a simple but powerful word concerning the need for repentance.

PRAY

A: Praise God for his patience.

C: Confess your failure to bear fruit.

T: Thank God that you have the chance to produce spiritual fruit today.

S: Pray that God would lead you and empower you to do that one specific thing.

TELL

Tell someone you trust to act as your "fruit inspector." Invite honest feedback.

MARCH 31

JESUS HEALS TWO HURTING PEOPLE ON THE SABBATH

PRAY

Pray for a healthy balance between keeping the rules and loving people.

READ

Luke 13:10–17, 14:1–6

OBSERVE

Though these occur in different settings, they are similar in tone and message.

v. 10—This is the last time in Luke's gospel that we see Jesus in a synagogue. He moves his ministry to the more receptive territory outside the synagogue.

v. 11—The woman's deformity is described by A. Rendle Short as "spondylitis deformans; the bones of her spine were fused into a rigid mass" (Short, *Modern Discovery and the Bible*, 91). But Dr. Luke tells us that the root of her problem was spiritual, not physical. An evil spirit had crippled her.

vv. 12–13—Jesus' word of healing precedes his healing touch. Perhaps his word exorcised the spirit and his touch brought physical healing. She straightens up for the first time in eighteen years and praises God. There is no indication that she believed in Jesus or identified him with the God whom she praised.

v. 14—The ruler of the synagogue was like a master of ceremonies. He decided who did what in the service. Perhaps he objected to Jesus usurping the floor, but he certainly viewed the Sabbath law as more important than mercy toward a suffering person. Notice that he addresses the people rather than Jesus. Perhaps he considers Jesus to be beyond hope of correction.

vv. 15–17—Apparently, the ruler of the synagogue was just the spokesman for the Jerusalem mafia. Jesus addresses them, not just the ruler. He calls them *hupokrites*, play actors, who do everything for show. Jesus reminds them of the provision in the Mishnah, the rabbinical commentary on the law, that required Jews to be merciful to animals on the Sabbath. Jesus contrasts their kindness to animals with their lack of mercy toward this daughter of Abraham. The language Jesus uses is very strong—it could be translated, "Then *must* not this woman...." Luke's commentary is that the people delighted in Jesus while the religious professionals were humiliated. This is one major reason that they set out to kill him.

14:1–6—In the next chapter, it is clear Jesus is being carefully watched. He is invited to the home of a prominent Pharisee for the Sabbath meal. Perhaps the man with dropsy (an abnormal accumulation of fluid) was planted at the dinner by the Pharisees. Even though Jesus knows their agenda, he reaches out to them again. He wants them to commit on the side of mercy, but they remain silent. Open wells were common in Palestine, and the Old Testament had provisions for dealing with animals that fell into a well (Exod. 21:33). Jesus will not allow their adherence to man-made laws to inhibit his mercy and heals the man just as he had healed the crippled woman. Christ took the law seriously, but he did not view it as supreme: *"The Sabbath was made for man, not man for the Sabbath"* (Mark 2:27).

APPLY

13:14—Do you ever let someone's man-made rules stand in the way of caring for people? Maybe you've been taught "Never talk to strangers" (which has some wisdom), but do you hide behind that to ignore people in need?

14:1—Are you willing to do the right thing even when you could be rejected for it?

MEMORIZE

Exodus 20:8–9

The Fourth Commandment prohibits work, not mercy.

PRAY

A: Praise the Lord of the Sabbath.

C: Confess the times you've kept man-made rules rather than the law of love.

T: Thank God for his healing power.

S: Ask God to use you to bring healing to others.

TELL

Tell someone who is hurting that Jesus is the Healer.

APRIL

APRIL 1

PARABLES OF LOST THINGS

PRAY

Pray that your understanding of the Parable of the Lost Son would deepen and change your life.

READ

Luke 15:1–32; Matthew 18:10–14

OBSERVE

Matthew includes the Parable of the Lost Sheep. The other two parables about lost things are unique to Luke. Though it has commonly been called The Parable of the Prodigal (Wasteful) Son, in the context of this chapter the best known and loved of Jesus' parables should be named The Parable Of the Lost Son, or The Parable of the Two Lost Sons.

vv. 1–2—It is crucial to our understanding of these parables (especially the third one) to notice carefully the occasion which prompted Jesus to tell these stories. Jesus is rebuked by the Pharisees and scribes for welcoming sinners and eating with them, the Middle Eastern sign of acceptance.

vv. 3–7—The message of the Parable of the Lost Sheep is very simple. A shepherd cares deeply and particularly about every member of his flock and will go to great lengths to save even one lost sheep. In his book *A Shepherd Looks At the Twenty-Third Psalm,* Philip Keller points out that a lost sheep is extremely vulnerable. Not only is it nearly defenseless against predators, if it falls (becomes *cast),* it cannot right itself. When a sheep is lost, the shepherd is desperate. The spiritual implication is obvious in verses 5–7—Jesus is the Good Shepherd (John 10:14), and when he rescues a lost sinner, there is great rejoicing in heaven.

vv. 8–10—Christ doesn't want anyone to miss the message, so he tells another parable with the identical message, this time in a domestic setting.

vv. 11–12—He saves the most dramatic and complex parable for last. The Church is indebted to Dr. Kenneth Bailey, Professor of New Testament at several Near Eastern universities, for his groundbreaking work on the parables as seen from the eyes of a Middle Eastern peasant. His book *The Cross and the Prodigal* will provide much of our deeper understanding of this parable. Bailey interviewed tribal people in Palestine, where the culture has changed little since the time of Jesus. The dialogue went like this:

"Has any son ever asked for his inheritance early in your village?"
The herdsmen answered, "Never! It would be impossible!"
"Why?" responded Bailey.
"Because it would mean that he wants his father to die!"

It is an expression of the father's amazing love that he permits this unprecedented and unloving request.

vv. 13–16—For a Jewish boy, feeding pigs is the pits. To wish for the food the pigs ate indicates how much he had fallen from his pre-famine life of luxury.

vv. 17–19—Bailey asked the villagers what would happen if a son disgraced his father, left the village, and later tried to return. The custom was that the young men of the village would meet him with sticks, stones, and manure and pelt him unmercifully. If the father agreed to talk with him, it would be only after the son had sat for several weeks outside the home and endured the continued abuse of the village. The father would then beat him severely and, if he were supremely merciful, take him on as a slave with no rights whatsoever.

v. 20—This is the climax of the parable. Notice that unlike the sheep and the coin, the father does not go searching for the son. He waits until the son makes the decision to head home. It's crucial that we recognize who the father is in this story. It is not God the Father, it is God the Son. Jesus is the one who welcomes sinners and eats with them. When Bailey's Muslim friends learned the Parable of the Lost Son, their perceptive question was, "If the cross is central to Christianity, where is the cross in the best-loved Christian parable?" Bailey finds it in this verse. Middle Eastern fathers never run; it is undignified. The more important the landowner, the heavier he is because he can hire someone to do all his physical work (the Hebrew word for holy, *kabod*, means "heavy.") If the father were to be so lacking in self-respect as to run, especially after a disgraced son, the wrath of the community would be turned upon him. He would receive all of the physical and emotional abuse of the villagers. That's what Jesus did for us lost sons and daughters as he hung on the cross and took the abuse for our sin.

vv. 21–24—The son gives his prepared speech, but the father brushes it aside. His joy is boundless. He calls for a grand feast to celebrate the symbolic resurrection of his son. He said, *"In the same way, I tell you, there is rejoicing in the presence of the angels of God over one sinner who repents."*

vv. 25–32—The older brother clearly represents the Pharisees and scribes. The problem with the older brother is that he doesn't really know the father. He sees the father as a taskmaster who demands hard work from him and shows little appreciation. That is generally the emotional perspective of the legalist. The older brother refuses to acknowledge his relationship with the younger brother. He is "this son of yours" not "my brother." Notice that the older brother judges his younger brother harshly. There is no mention of prostitutes in the story, but he assumes the worst of his sinful brother. The father corrects his faulty theology in verse 31 and his relational problem in 32 ("this brother of yours"). But we can assume that the older brother is unmoved and unpersuaded. The parable ends without a conclusion, but Bailey powerfully points out that we know the end of the story. The older brother (the Pharisees) kills the father (Jesus).

APPLY

v. 7—Do you celebrate a new believer with great rejoicing, or do you hold back your approval until he proves himself?

vv. 22–24—Are you rejoicing in Christ's extravagant love for you? It's the best way to keep from being like the older brother.

v. 28—Have you ever resented the grace that another Christian has experienced?

MEMORIZE

Luke 15:10

This verse helps us to remember the joy in heaven when a sinner repents.

PRAY

A: Praise the God who welcomes sinners.

C: Confess any failure to rejoice over new believers.

T: Thank God for accepting you, his lost son/daughter who was found.

S: Pray for a lost one whom you know.

TELL

Tell that lost one that she has a savior who wants to welcome her home with great rejoicing.

APRIL 2

PUTTING POSSESSIONS IN PERSPECTIVE

PRAY

Ask God to help you apply his standards toward the way you handle money.

READ

Luke 16:1–15, 19–31

OBSERVE

These two parables continue Luke's concentration on the dangers of uncaring wealth and the relative unimportance of money.

vv. 1–9—This is a difficult parable to interpret. At first glance, it appears that Jesus is approving of dishonesty, but a deeper look is required. The rich man was probably an absentee landlord who put a steward or manager (Greek *oikonomos*, "house law") in charge of his lands. The fields were leased to farmers who were required to pay a certain amount of the produce as their rent. This manager had been ripping off his master for some time, and when the owner finds out about it, he demands that the steward produce the books and resign. The manager knows himself well. He has neither the body for manual labor nor the stomach for begging.

He comes up with a clever plan. With the complicity of the farmers, who aren't models of honesty either, he sets up a scheme to get partial payment for the owner and lots of good will for himself. Morris suggests that the steward may have asked the farmers for what they would owe the master without interest, since charging interest to fellow Jews was against the law. In that case, the owner would have to settle for the reduced payment or declare himself to be guilty of usury. But there is nothing within the story to suggest this scenario. Perhaps Jesus wants people to react with shock to the story, in order to get their full attention. The statement, *"The people of this world are more shrewd in dealing with their own kind than are the people of the light"* is reminiscent of Jesus' words in Matthew 10:16, *"Be as shrewd as snakes and as innocent as doves."*

The moral of the parable is found in verse 9. Jesus uses a negative story to provide a positive message. "Worldly wealth" in the NIV is a poor translation of the Greek. The King James' "unrighteous mammon" is literal and more accurate. His point is very similar to Matthew 6:20–21. What we give to others becomes our treasure in heaven. Here, Jesus personalizes the gift and tells us that those whom we bless with money on earth will welcome us thankfully into heaven. People and relationships are much more important than money.

vv. 10–12—To protect against the possibility that someone could interpret his parable as condoning the steward's dishonesty, Jesus gives another application. When someone like the steward is found to be dishonest in small things, you can be sure that he is not to be trusted with big things. If we can't handle money well, God will not entrust us with things that really matter.

v. 13—This parallel to Matthew 6:24 is further evidence that the Parable of the Unjust Steward is an illustration of the financial principles of Matthew 6.

vv. 14–15—Not only were the Pharisees self-righteous—they were greedy (Matt. 23:25). Jesus is not saying that money itself is detestable in God's sight, but the love of money (1 Tim. 6:10).

vv. 19–21—The Parable of Lazarus and the Rich Man further reveals God's condemnation of greed and uncaring wealth. Some have speculated that this parable is based on a real-life story since Lazarus is the only person given a name in Jesus' parables. The rich man (sometimes called *Dives*, Latin for "rich man") is described in the most luxurious terms, and Lazarus' earthly condition could hardly be more pitiful.

vv. 22–25—Eternity is the scene of the Great Reversal. We need to be careful not to read too much into the parable and conclude that Lazarus went to heaven because he was poor and *Dives* went to hell because he was rich. Jesus is not expounding on how one enters heaven (by faith) but rather illustrating that our situation on earth is not the last word, or even the most important thing. The Jews assumed that a person was rich because he was favored by God and that the poor were cursed. Jesus makes it abundantly clear that nothing could be further from the truth.

vv. 26–31—We also need to be careful not to press the details of a parable too hard. Other clear narrative portions of Scripture confirm that hell is a place of terrible torment as verse 24 describes (Mark 9:48). But no didactic portion of Scripture suggests that people in hell have a window to heaven and vice versa. We can't conclude, therefore, that people in hell are able to view the situation in heaven. They may be able to, but this is a story, not a didactic lesson. The lesson we can deduce is that *Dives* and those like him have little concern about eternity. To his credit, even in hell the rich man is concerned for his brothers (Matt. 5:47).

We sometimes think like *Dives*. If unbelievers could only witness a miracle, they would be converted. But we forget that even some of the people who saw the resurrected Christ did not believe (Matt. 28:17). Abraham makes it clear that there is plenty of evidence in Scripture to commend belief. If people ignore or deny it, they won't be convinced by a miracle.

APPLY

vv. 10–12—Are you scrupulously honest in your handling of finances? Could Jesus sign your tax return? When you borrow someone else's property do you return it in as good or better condition?

v. 14—How is your love relationship with money? Many people in our society love things and use people rather than loving people and using things.

vv. 19–21—Have you made the mistake of equating wealth with value?

MEMORIZE

Luke 16:11

This verse will help you to remember God's perspective on stewardship.

PRAY

A: Praise God as the King of Heaven.

C: Confess that money is often too important to you.

T: Thank God for Moses and the prophets and all of Scripture.

S: Pray for a *Dives* whom you know.

TELL

Tell someone close to you how you want to relate to money from now on.

APRIL 3

ON DUTY AND THANKFULNESS

PRAY

Pray that you would be humble and thankful today.

READ

Luke 17:7–19

OBSERVE

vv. 7–10—Jesus had just spoken about having small faith which can do great things (17:6). Believers with that kind of faith might be tempted to spiritual pride. Jesus tells the Parable of the Unworthy Servants to guard against thinking of ourselves too highly. Everyone in his society was familiar with the proper etiquette for servants. It was laughably ludicrous to imagine a servant coming in from the fields and having his own meal before waiting on the master. The servant's first priority is serving his master. So we also, when we obey our Master, should not be proud and expect praise. We've only done our duty. Though Jesus warns us against pride and expecting congratulations for obeying God, the other side of the coin is that our Master is very gracious, and he does celebrate his servants. The good news is that we can look forward to meeting our Master face to face and hearing these words, *"Well done, good and faithful servant! You have been faithful with a few things; I will put you in charge of many things. Come and share your master's happiness!"* (Matt. 25:23).

vv. 11–13—The lepers stood at a distance because they were commanded to by law (Lev. 13:45–46). We shouldn't read too much into the title "Master." It was a term of respect used for any man higher on the social pyramid, and lepers considered themselves on the bottom.

v. 14—Jesus' response to these lepers is different than his interactions with other people with this dread disease. He doesn't touch them but tells them to go to the priest, whose job it was to certify when lepers were healed (Lev. 14:2 ff.). This required a major step of faith on their part, and as they head toward the priest, they are healed. God often requires us to take a step of faith in order to experience healing.

vv. 15–19—It's a commentary on the horror of leprosy that Jewish and Samaritan lepers lived together. Normally, they would avoid each other at all costs. Luke's gospel particularly makes a point of affirming these despised half-breeds. Luke has a heart for the alien and the disenfranchised. The major point of this story, though, is the importance of gratitude. Were the other nine lepers thankful for their healing? Undoubtedly. But only one returned to express his thankfulness. He praises God for the healing and throws himself at Jesus' feet in an act of worship. Jesus sees real faith in that act. Christ's final words are the most important of all because this man not only received physical healing, which is temporary, but he also received spiritual healing, which is eternal.

APPLY

v. 10—Are you continually looking for a pat on the back from God or from others? One person has said, "There is no limit to the good that we can do if we don't care who gets the credit."

v. 19—What is the connection between thankfulness and genuine faith? Does your expression of gratitude reflect your belief that God is the source of "every good and perfect gift" (James 1:17)?

MEMORIZE

Luke 17:17

Use this as an encouragement to regularly express your thanksgiving to God.

PRAY

Today, spend your entire prayer time in thanksgiving. It may be helpful to think of something to thank God for that begins with each letter of the alphabet or to take a mental inventory of the past week and remember his blessings.

TELL

Encourage your small group to have a prayer time in which you concentrate on thanksgiving.

APRIL 4

TWO IMPORTANT PARABLES AND A LIVING PARABLE

PRAY

Pray to apply these parables to your life today, just as Zacchaeus applied the second parable.

READ

Luke 18:1–14, 19:1–10

OBSERVE

v. 1—Whenever a parable is introduced with a statement like this, it's very important to keep it in mind when interpreting the message of the parable. The purpose of this parable is to teach the importance of persevering in prayer.

vv. 2–7—Christ is not saying that the judge is like God. In fact, the magistrate is opposed to God and God's people (v. 4) and is, in fact, an unjust judge (v. 6). Jesus' point is that if even an uncaring and unfair judge can be influenced by a widow who won't take no for an answer, how much more will God bring justice to his chosen people? Unlike the judge, God will see that they get justice, and quickly. The last verse gives an eschatological element to the parable. When Jesus returns, will he find the kind of faith that is represented by faithful, persistent prayer to the Father?

v. 9—Once again, Luke introduces the Parable of the Pharisee and the Publican with a very helpful comment. This is directed to those who are confident of their own righteousness.

vv. 10–14—The NIV translates verse 11, *"The Pharisee stood up and prayed about himself."* The Greek of the verse could also be translated, "prayed to himself." It's clear that his prayer was not addressed to the God of the Bible, who commands us to come before him humbly. Any time we exalt ourselves in prayer, we are praying to ourselves, not to God. God does hear the prayers of repentant sinners, even notorious sinners like tax collectors. The familiar message is that those who bow before God will be lifted up, while those who stand proud will be brought down.

19:1-2—Zacchaeus was a Jew. His name in Hebrew means "pure" or "righteous." Up until the day Jesus passed through Jericho, his name was an ironic joke. The chief tax collector took a cut from all of the other tax collectors before passing to the Romans what they required. He was probably even more despised than the average tax collector, who was seen by the Jews as a turncoat and a thief. Jericho would have been a particularly good location for tax collectors because it was located on a major trade route from Jerusalem to the East. It is still a beautiful oasis surrounded by desert.

vv. 3–4—Zacchaeus had, no doubt, heard of Jesus' reputation. His height was an impediment, but it's also very likely that the crowds would not be eager to part and let him stand in the front of the line. In fact, there were probably more than a few residents of Jericho who would have been eager to use the jostling of a crowd as an excuse to plant their elbows into Zacchaeus' ribs.

vv. 5–7—The little man may have been hard to spot in the sycamore-fig tree, but the keen eyes of Jesus had no trouble. Perhaps he had been told about the diminutive tax collector earlier, or it may have been a direct revelation of the Holy Spirit, but Jesus calls him by name and invites himself to Zacchaeus' house. This time, the general public and not just the religious elite are miffed at Christ's fraternization with this lowlife.

v. 8—The attitude of the townspeople probably changed dramatically when they heard what Zacchaeus was going to do as a result of his encounter with Jesus. Chances are that his reparations wiped out his large fortune, for he had ripped off a lot of people. Like the previous parable, Zacchaeus was a repentant publican.

vv. 9–10—Christ is not declaring that Zacchaeus was saved because he repented but that the publican's repentance was clear evidence that he had experienced salvation. We must never forget that Christ's primary purpose in coming to earth was to seek and save those who were lost, like you and me.

APPLY

18:1—Are you persistent in prayer? What should you keep on asking for?

18:11—Are you ever guilty of spiritual elitism?

19:8—Is there anything God might want you to do as an act of repentance?

19:10—Do you have a heart for lost people?

MEMORIZE

Luke 19:10

This is a statement of Christ's purpose for his life and for his Church.

PRAY

A: Praise God that he is the Hound of Heaven.

C: Confess any spiritual pride.

T: Thank God for having mercy on you, a sinner.

S: Ask God to deliver you from the sin of pride and to give you a deep desire to share Christ with lost people.

TELL

Tell someone who is lost that Jesus loves them and came to earth to seek and save them.

APRIL 5

THE ROAD TO EMMAUS AND THE ROAD TO HEAVEN

PRAY

Pray that the love and power of the risen Christ would fill you to overflowing today.

READ

Luke 24:13–53

OBSERVE

The Cleopas described in this story may be the same person as Clopas, who is mentioned in John 19:25. If so, his companion may be his wife, Mary. They would have been Jesus' aunt and uncle, since Mary's sister was also named Mary!

vv. 13–16—Emmaus is a village seven miles west of Jerusalem. Some commentators suggest that since it was late in the day, the twosome were walking directly toward the sun, which blinded their eyes. That is why they didn't recognize the risen Jesus. But the passage emphasizes that they were *kept* from recognizing him. "Perhaps Luke wants us to gather, as Ford suggests, 'that we cannot see the risen Christ, although he be walking with us, unless he wills to disclose himself'" (quoted in Morris, *The Gospel According to St. Luke*, 337).

vv. 17–24—Jesus was the master questioner. We should learn from his approach because a good question can reveal a great deal. Cleopas and the anonymous disciple give a pretty good summary of Jesus' life, ministry, and death, but they only see him as a prophet, though they hoped he would be the redeemer. They had even heard the rumors of his resurrection, but they don't appear to be convinced.

vv. 25–27—What an exciting Bible study that would have been! When Christians interpret the Old Testament Christologically, we are only following the example of our Lord.

vv. 28–29—It doesn't appear as though Jesus was play-acting. He would have continued on if the men had not invited him to stay. The same is true today. We must invite Jesus into our hearts to eat and live with us (Rev. 3:20). He knocks at the door, but we must open it. Of course, the only way we are led to invite him in is if the Spirit draws us to him first (John 6:44). The place where they stayed was probably the home of one of these disciples.

vv. 30–35—Since their guest was obviously a learned rabbi, they asked him to take the role of the host and bless the meal. The breaking of the bread is probably not a reference to communion. Only the twelve were present for that special meal. But the larger group of followers shared many meals with Jesus, and it could be that his familiar act of blessing stirred their memories and was part of the eye-opening process. We need to remember that Jesus is our unseen guest at every meal. Once they recognized him, Jesus was whisked away. Though it was already late, Cleopas and the other disciple hurried back to Jerusalem to tell the twelve what had happened. By this time the women's rumor had been substantiated by Peter. That is another conversation that would have been worth hearing!

vv. 36–43—This is apparently Christ's first resurrection appearance to all of the disciples (except Thomas, John 20:24). Luke gives a more expanded account of Jesus' dialogue than John. It also appears that Jesus had encouraged the other disciples to touch his wounds even before Thomas demanded it. Jesus had used food before as a proof that the one brought back to life was not a ghost (Mark 5:43).

vv. 44–49—Jesus repeats the Bible study he had given to the two on the road to Emmaus, but he supplies a crucial application. Since he is the Messiah who rose from the dead, the message of repentance and forgiveness in his name must be preached, beginning in Jerusalem. This passage is very close to what Luke writes in Acts 1:1–8, but it could be that Jesus repeated his instructions at another later date.

vv. 50–53—It seems that Christ's ascension from Bethany was not his final act of being "carried up into heaven." Matthew 28 tells us that Jesus ascended from a mountain in Galilee, where Jesus had told his disciples to meet him (and probably where five hundred gathered—1 Cor. 15:6). The details aren't completely clear in Scripture. In any case the Gospel of Luke ends where it begins, in the temple (1:9). However, unlike Zechariah, these believers are praising God continually for all that they have witnessed.

APPLY

v. 16—Do you fail to perceive Jesus' presence with you? He is present in the power of the Holy Spirit.

vv. 47–48—Are you committed to proclaiming the Gospel to all nations? What part does God have for you in that process?

v. 53—Christ may not want you to hang around the Church all the time, but he does want you to praise God continually.

MEMORIZE

Luke 24:48

Like the disciples, you have witnessed marvelous things in the Gospel of Luke.

PRAY

A: Praise the risen Lord, who has entered his glory.

C: Confess your slowness of heart to believe all that the prophets and apostles have spoken.

T: Thank God for his presence with you continually.

S: Pray that you may be more aware of his presence today and in the days to come.

TELL

Discuss with a friend or your small group how you could be more involved in taking the message of repentance and forgiveness in Jesus' name to all nations.

APRIL 6

THE PROLOGUE TO JOHN'S GOSPEL

PRAY

Pray that these profound words would have a profound impact on your life.

READ

John 1:1–18

OBSERVE

Almost everyone agrees that the Gospel of John was written by the "beloved disciple" (John 13:23), the younger brother of James and one of the "Sons of Thunder" (Mark 3:17). John was probably the only one of the original disciples who did not meet a violent death. He was exiled by the Roman emperor (probably Domitian) to Patmos, an island off the coast of Greece, from which he wrote the book of Revelation. The Gospel of John was probably written from Ephesus, where most scholars believe he spent the majority of his life and ministry after the resurrection. Almost everyone agrees that the Gospel of John was written after the Synoptics.

There is disagreement over whether John had Matthew, Mark, and Luke to use as sources. If he did, he didn't rely on them, because the fourth gospel is very different. It is less concerned about giving a chronological outline of the life of Christ and more concerned about the spiritual significance of Jesus' words and deeds. John is written for Greeks, so he eliminates some of the material that would appeal more to readers steeped in the Hebrew mindset. For example, there are no parables in the book of John. The concept of the "word" (Greek *logos*) was a key idea in Greek philosophy, so John introduces his gospel with it. The symbol used for John is the eagle, the only animal that can look directly into the sun and not be blinded.

John writes of glorious things, and light is a dominant metaphor in this book. Its purpose is clearly stated in John 20:31: *"But these are written that you may believe that Jesus is the Messiah, the Son of God, and that by believing you may have life in his name."*

vv. 1–5—A major tenet of the quasi-Christian cults (Jehovah's Witnesses, Mormons, Christian Science) is that Jesus is not God. How do these groups that deny the Trinity deal with these verses? Not only does Scripture affirm that the Word (who is undeniably Jesus Christ—1:14–18) was in the beginning with God, and that all things were made through him, verse 1 states it strongly (in Greek): "God was the Word." It doesn't say that he was *a* God but *the* only God. Christ is the source of life and light. A better translation than "the darkness has not understood it" is "the darkness has not overcome it." John uses the title "Word" (Greek *logos*) in an attempt to communicate effectively to those who were familiar with Greek philosophy. Barclay writes:

> Greek thought knew all about the *Logos*; it saw in the *Logos* the creating and the guiding and the directing power of God, the power which made the universe and which keeps the universe going. So John came to the Greeks and he said: 'For centuries you have been thinking and writing and dreaming about the *Logos*, the power which made the world, the power which keeps the order of the world, the power by which men think and reason and know, the power by which men come into contact with God. Jesus is that *Logos* come down to earth.'" (Barclay, Commentaries, 13–14)

vv. 6–9—John's gospel sees John the Baptist as a key figure, sent from God. His role was to witness to the light.

vv. 10–13—The ultimate irony at the coming of Christ is that the world he made didn't recognize him, and the people he had called to be his own rejected him! But there were some who received him. The Greek word for "receive" is the same word used in Matthew 1:24 when Joseph "took" Mary home as his wife. It describes an intimate relationship. Those who receive the Word also believe in his name. This describes much more than intellectual assent to the facts of Christ's life. It means trusting in him, putting your present life and your eternal destiny into his total care. Those who receive him and believe in his name are given the *right to become* children of God. Contrary to popular belief, not everyone is a child of God (see also Rom. 8:14–17). We are all God's creations, but we are adopted into God's family when we receive and believe in God's Son. Nobody is a child of God based on the family he or she was born to or even a human decision, but based on God's reception.

v. 14—This is the miracle of Christmas, the incarnation. The supreme communication of God to humanity is the Word, who takes on human flesh. There are two Greek words for the human skin—*soma*, which is the more exalted term, usually translated "body" and *sarx*, which is the less-exalted term, usually translated "flesh." John uses the latter term. He wants to make it very clear that Jesus took on the same flesh and bones that you and I have. He was not a spirit masquerading as a man as the Docetists and Gnostics claimed. The Greek words translated "made his dwelling" is literally "tented." Jesus was only here for a brief period, but what a campout it was! He has the glory of the Father, but he is fully man. The description "full of grace and truth" is seen throughout the Gospel. Jesus tells people the truth, but he does it in a gracious way.

vv. 15–18—The apostle again quotes the Baptist, who refers to Christ's pre-existence. Jesus was the supreme expression of the grace of God, and we receive blessing upon blessing from him. Christ's grace and truth fulfills and surpasses the law that was given through Moses. Jesus has fully revealed the unseen God. He is God made visible, and he has revealed God's nature to us.

APPLY

vv. 1–2—How would you answer a Mormon who claims that the Bible never says that Jesus is God?

v. 4—Light in Scripture represents goodness and guidance. Where do you need Christ's guidance today? Where do you need Christ's light to expose the darkness and lead you into goodness?

v. 12—Can you clearly present to someone what it means to receive Jesus Christ, to believe in his name? If not, reread the section above.

v. 14—Do you tend to err on the side of grace or the side of truth? How can you be more balanced?

v. 16—What are some of the blessings you have received from the grace of Christ?

MEMORIZE

John 1:1

This is a basic truth about Jesus' deity.

PRAY

A: Praise the Word, who communicates the fullness of God.

C: Confess your failures to bear witness to the light.

T: Thank God for one blessing after another.

S: Pray for someone who is living in darkness.

TELL

Tell someone what you think it means to be "full of grace and truth."

APRIL 7

JOHN THE BAPTIST'S WITNESS ABOUT JESUS

PRAY

Pray that you might share John the Baptist's perspective on Jesus.

READ

John 1:19–34, 3:22–36

OBSERVE

John's gospel gives major attention to John the Baptist's attitude toward Jesus. The other gospels focus more on what the Baptist does, this gospel on what he says.

vv. 19–23—John's answer to the fact-finding delegation from Jerusalem is strong in his denial that he is the Messiah. John uses the term "the Jews" seventy times in this gospel, and it always describes a group of people who are in opposition to Jesus. The questions about Elijah and the Prophet refer to Old Testament prophecies (Mal. 4:5; Deut. 18:15), which said that a great prophet would arise to usher in the reign of the Messiah. John denies that he is that prophet, but he is wrong. Jesus identifies him as the Elijah prophesied in Scripture (Matt. 11:14, 17:12). John's false humility kept him from fully recognizing who he was, but he was not completely clueless. He quotes Isaiah 40:3, a passage which clearly talks about preparing the way for the Messiah.

vv. 24–28—Baptism was not understood to be for Jews but for Gentile converts. There were prophecies that suggested baptism might be practiced in the Messianic age by the Prophet (Isa. 52:15; Ezek. 36:25; Zech. 13:1), but John denied that he was that prophet. This baptism would be a cleansing and a preparation for the people of God. John believed that the Jews needed this baptism, but he sidesteps the question. Instead, he points to the one who would baptize with the Holy Spirit and with fire (Matt. 3:11). The work of untying sandals was the job of the lowest slave, but John says that he is not even worthy to be Christ's slave.

vv. 29–34—John the Baptist is the first one to identify Jesus as the Lamb of God. He is most likely referring to the passover lamb, which delivered the people of Israel (Exod. 12:21). It sounds strange for John to say that he did not know Jesus, his cousin. It becomes clearer in verses 32–34 that John didn't know him as the Messiah and Son of God until the event of Jesus' baptism when the Holy Spirit descended upon him in the form of a dove. God had revealed to John that this would be the sign of the one who would baptize with the Holy Spirit.

3:22–26—This is the only indication in Scripture that Jesus ever baptized anyone. John 4:2 tells us that it was actually Jesus' disciples. One of the arguments for the authority of the Bible is its irrefutable, common-sense approach to descriptions. John was baptizing at Aenon "because there was plenty of water." The Jew (or Jews in some manuscripts) approaches John to provoke a rivalry between John and Jesus. If John were ministering in the flesh he could have been threatened that the new prophet was baptizing more people.

vv. 27–30—John's response is perfect. He can't resent Jesus or be jealous because each person receives only what God gives. Jesus is the bridegroom, but John is only a groomsman. John's statement should be the confession of each one of us: "He must become greater; I must become less."

vv. 31–36—John acknowledges that Jesus came from heaven and has authority above every earthly speaker. Once again, this gospel presents the irony of people ignoring a message sent directly from heaven. God the Father has sent God the Son and sent God the Holy Spirit to fill the Son completely with God's Word. The final verse of chapter 3 makes it clear that the stakes are eternal—those who trust in the Son have eternal life (a present condition that continues forever); those who reject him will experience God's wrath eternally. The Church can never forget this ultimate message.

APPLY

1:26–27—Are you ever guilty of partisanship, believing that your church or leader is better or more important than someone else's? There should be no envy or rivalry between Christians and churches who are all on the same team.

1:29, 3:36—Are you sure that the Lamb of God has taken away all of your sin? Have you trusted in the Son of God as your Savior, who gives eternal life? If not, what is standing in the way?

3:30—What needs to take place in your life for Jesus to become greater and you to become less?

MEMORIZE

John 3:30

This is a great statement of our proper relationship with the Lord.

PRAY

A: Praise the Lamb who was slain.

C: Confess your pride and lack of humility.

T: Thank God for revealing himself fully in Jesus.

S: Pray for someone who has rejected the Son, that this rejection wouldn't be permanent.

TELL

Tell that person who Christ is and what he has done for you.

APRIL 8

THE FIRST DISCIPLES

PRAY

Pray that you would have the same response in following Christ today as his first disciples did.

READ

John 1:35–51

OBSERVE

The Synoptic Gospels take an overall look at Christ's calling of the disciples. John's description is more particular and in-depth. John also shows that Jesus knew them before he called them.

vv. 35–39—It's important to recognize that some of Jesus' disciples were first followers of John the Baptist. When he identified Jesus as the Lamb of God, he must have known that his disciples would soon want to follow the one who was greater. Jesus asks Andrew and the unnamed disciple (many think it was John himself) what they want. He asks us much the same question. If we want money or fame, he is not the teacher for us. But if we want to know Truth and Meaning, we will follow him. "Rabbi" is a Hebrew word meaning "my great one." John is writing for a Greek audience, and he translates it as *didaskalos*, "teacher." For the disciples to ask Jesus where he was staying was to indicate that they didn't want to have a casual conversation on the side of the road but a serious encounter. Jesus invites them to stay with him. The fact that John knew the exact hour (4 p.m.) supports the idea that he might have been the other disciple. It would have been noteworthy to remember the exact time he first learned about Jesus.

vv. 40–42—The Billy Graham Association calls this passage "Operation Andrew." The first thing a would-be disciple should do when discovering the Messiah is to bring those closest to him to Jesus. Simon receives his new name early in his relationship with Jesus. *Petros* in Greek and *cephas* in Aramaic both mean "rock." We would nickname him Rocky.

vv. 43–46—Philip also may have been the unnamed disciple, and the call in verse 43 is a follow up to the previous day's encounter. We just don't know. In any case, these first disciples were all Galileans who were following John the Baptist in Judea, east of the Jordan (a long way from home). It's not surprising that the charisma of John had attracted men from Galilee, which was a hotbed of Messianic expectation. Nathanael ("gift of God") voices the skepticism about Nazareth/Galilee shared by his contemporaries (John 7:41–42; Matt. 26:71–73; Mark 6:1–6; Acts 24:5). Philip's response to his doubtfulness is perfect: "Come and see." That's what we need to encourage people to do with the Gospel of Jesus Christ. Check it out for yourself. Then you'll have an intelligent basis on which to accept or reject it. The problem with most people is that they're not willing to expend the effort to discover the truth.

vv. 47–51—Jesus' praise of Nathanael may have been prompted by Psalm 32:2. His knowledge of Nathanael is supernatural and results in a response of profound praise. To call Jesus the Son of God and King of Israel may not have been as high an attribution as we would interpret. Nathanael may have seen him as the next king who would conquer the Romans. In replying to Nathanael, Jesus uses the formula for the first time that is used throughout John, "Amen, amen" or "Truly, truly." The NIV translation, "I tell you the truth" fails to capture the force of repeating the Amen, which is not recorded in the other gospels. Jesus expands the vision of his disciples by calling himself the Son of Man. Of all the titles given in the Gospel of John so far—Rabbi, Lamb of God, Lord, Messiah, Son of God, and King of Israel—Son of Man may be the most exalted. It comes from the prophecy of Daniel 7:13–14. Yet it also ironically conveys a sense of humility and identification with humanity. Jesus' description of what will happen to the Son of Man is certainly a description of great things to come. It is probably a reference to Jacob's ladder (Gen. 28:10ff.) but meant to suggest that the Son of Man is the intermediary between heaven and earth, a major theme in John.

APPLY

v. 38—What do you most want from Jesus?

v. 46—Are you ever guilty of judging someone by where they come from?

v. 46—Can you present compelling evidence of the truth of the Gospel to those whom you invite to, "Come and see?" If not, get a copy of Paul Little's *Know Why You Believe* and master its contents.

MEMORIZE

John 1:47

This is one of the highest expressions of praise you could give to another person.

PRAY

A: Praise the Son of God, King of Israel, Son of Man.

C: Confess that you've judged others superficially.

T: Thank God that he knows all about you and still loves you.

S: Pray for chances to share this truth.

TELL

Tell someone what you've learned about the term Son of Man.

APRIL 9

JESUS' FIRST MIRACLE

PRAY

Pray that Jesus would show you something in the story of his first miracle that applies to your life.

READ

John 2:1–12

OBSERVE

vv. 1–2—John's chronology is pretty general throughout his gospel. He often begins a narrative with, "The next day...." In the early chapters, some see an echo of the days of creation, but it's hard to see it clearly. The third day mentioned could be Tuesday, but is probably Wednesday. The days are being calculated from the time Jesus first called his disciples. The custom at the time of Christ was for weddings of a virgin to take place on Wednesday and a widow on Thursday. Weddings were lengthy affairs, much longer than our weddings today. Cana is only mentioned in John's gospel (4:46, 21:2). It is located "in Galilee" to distinguish it from another Cana in Syria. This city is very close to Nazareth, so it was not surprising that Mary was a friend of the family. (When my family toured Cana in 1990, we saw a local winery called, "Cana Wedding Wine!") Joseph is not mentioned, and most commentators conclude from the omission that he was dead by this time. Jesus probably grew up with the bride and/or groom, which is why he and his disciples were also invited.

vv. 3–5—For the wine to run out was a profound social failure for everyone involved. Hospitality, particularly at a wedding, was such a sacred obligation in the

Middle East "that it rendered the bridegroom's family liable to a lawsuit" (Morris, *The Gospel According John*, 179). Mary wants to spare her friends that embarrassment, so she approaches her son, confident that he can do something about the problem. Jesus' response to Mary is somewhat difficult to interpret. The Greek phrase is stark—"What have I to do with you, woman? My time has not yet come." But Barclay points out that the Greek word *gunai* (woman) is not necessarily "rough and abrupt. It is the same word as Jesus used when on the Cross. He addressed Mary as he left her to the care of John (John 19:26)." Barclay further interprets Christ's words as an idiom which meant, when spoken gently, "Don't worry; you don't quite understand what is going on; leave things to me and I will settle them in my own way" (Barclay, Commentaries, 83). Whatever the right translation, Mary doesn't seem put off as she instructs the servants to do whatever Jesus says. The servants' reaction isn't recorded, but can you imagine what they thought when the master of the banquet tasted the water they had drawn and declared it the best wine of the wedding?

vv. 6–10—The six water jars (which were used for foot and hand washing) were very large, holding at least twenty gallons of water. When Jesus changes the water into wine, the addition of one hundred gallons of wine would have probably solved the problem, no matter how large the crowd! The most wonderful aspect of this story is what the wedding master of ceremonies says to the bridegroom, "You have saved the best till now." Not only does Jesus provide an abundance, he provides the very best. The seventeenth-century British poet Richard Cranshaw describes the miracle at Cana with a beautiful metaphor: "The modest water saw its God and blushed."

v. 11—Miracles in John are always "signs" which point to who Jesus is. This was his first miracle (unrecorded in the other gospels). John sees it as a revelation of his glory (1:14), which prompts a response of faith from the disciples.

v. 12—It seems as though Jesus' family has a positive relationship with him, since they went to his headquarters in Capernaum. But that is not necessarily the case. By chapter 7, it is obvious that his siblings don't believe in him (7:5) and are even contemptuous and challenging (7:3–4).

APPLY

v. 4—Do you have a sense of God's timing in your life? Some activities are appropriate for certain times and not for others (Eccles. 3:1–8).

v. 10—Do you believe that Jesus wants only the very best for you, and in abundance? Where do you see his lavish, quality provision for your life?

MEMORIZE

John 2:10

This verse will help you to remember the quality of Christ's care for you.

PRAY

A: Praise the God of abundant quality.

C: Confess any complaining you have done about your circumstances.

T: Thank God that he's given you the very best, and plenty of it.

S: Pray that you would see his glory today.

TELL

Tell someone how many and how good God's gifts have been to you.

APRIL 10

NIC AT NIGHT

PRAY

Ask that you might understand and appreciate the love of God, which gave you new birth.

READ

John 3:1–21

OBSERVE

v. 1—Nicodemus was not only a Pharisee (a "separated one") but a member of the Sanhedrin, the Jewish ruling council. The Sanhedrin was composed of seventy Jewish elders who ruled on all religious matters. They did not have civil authority unless the Roman occupational rulers lent their clout.

v. 2—Nicodemus probably came at night to avoid being seen by his fellow religious leaders. He addresses Jesus respectfully as Rabbi and further praises him by accurately observing that no one could do the miracles Jesus was doing unless it was by God's power.

vv. 3–4—Jesus had a way of disarming people by cutting to the chase. He and Nicodemus could have sat around for a long time exchanging compliments, but there was something much more important to talk about. The word translated "born again" is actually a play on words. It could also be rendered, "born from above." Nicodemus takes the former sense and responds quite literally that physical rebirth is impossible.

vv. 5–8—Jesus concentrates on the spiritual reality he was trying to convey to Nicodemus. Some see in the expression "born of water and the Spirit" a reference to baptism, but Jesus is more likely describing the necessity of being born physically and spiritually. Verse 6 supports this understanding. The Spirit/wind analogy is also a play on words. The Greek word for wind, *pneuma*, is also the word for "spirit." The same is true of the Hebrew word *ruah*. Just as the wind is invisible but we know that it is blowing by the effects it causes, so it is with the Spirit of God.

vv. 9–15—Nicodemus' problem is that he lacks spiritual discernment. He has seen Christ's miracles, by his own admission, but he fails to see the deeper reality. Christ's earthly ministry points to heavenly realities, for he was sent from heaven. Jesus speaks an amazing prophecy of the cross early in his ministry. The snake that Moses lifted up in the desert is a reference to Numbers 21:4–9, when the Lord sent poisonous snakes to punish the complaining Israelites. Moses was instructed to put a bronze serpent on a pole, and anyone who was bitten and looked at the pole would live. Fredrikson notes:

> So the Son of Man has come to be lifted up on a pole. This one who sits with Nicodemus has made his descent into flesh and in obedience will die. This amazing and costly sacrifice calls forth the response of faith. Whoever will behold (him) with eyes of faith will be given everlasting life and will not languish and die in the wilderness. This is God's amazing provision for our salvation. (Fredrikson, *John*, 85)

vv. 16–18—It is not clear in the Greek text whether verses 16–22 are a continuation of Jesus' words to Nicodemus or John's commentary upon them. In either case, the message is the same. John 3:16 is one of the best known and loved statements of the Gospel. It is important to understand it in context of verses 17 and 18. God's purpose in sending his one and only Son was to save sinners, not condemn us. But Christ's coming presented a crisis—those who believe/trust in him are not condemned, but those who reject God's provision are already condemned by their lack of faith. No one can be neutral about Jesus Christ.

vv. 19–21—The light analogy, which was introduced in 1:4–9, is expanded here. Not only is the Light God's revelation, but he is also God's judgment. Light represents goodness and truth. Everyone whose heart is changed so that they love goodness and truth will come to the light. But those who persist in doing evil hate the light and avoid it. Most people don't seek God for the same reason a criminal does not seek a policeman. They don't want to be exposed and convicted. People often use intellectual problems as a smokescreen to explain why they won't come to Christ when the real reason is moral. They don't want his direct light to illuminate and reveal the darkness in their lives.

APPLY

v. 8—Have you been born of the Spirit? What effects do you see of his work in your life?

v. 17—In approaching unbelievers, do you emphasize that Christ came to save them, not to condemn them?

v. 21—Are you regularly allowing the light of God's Word to reveal your thoughts, words, and deeds?

MEMORIZE

John 3:16

Learn this verse if you don't already know it.

PRAY

A: Praise God for the wind of the Spirit.

C: Confess the darkness in your life.

T: Thank God for his marvelous light (Ps. 119:105).

S: Intercede for someone lost in darkness.

TELL

Tell someone that coming to Christ is primarily a moral rather than an intellectual decision.

APRIL 11

THE WOMAN AT THE WELL

PRAY

Pray that you would be full of grace and truth as you encounter people like the woman at the well.

READ

John 4:1–42

OBSERVE

At the time of Jesus, Palestine was divided into three main sections. To travel from Judea to Galilee, the most direct route would be through Samaria. But most Jews, who despised Samaritans, would travel across the Jordan River to the east and then come west after passing Samaria, a much longer route. Jesus traveled directly through Samaria for more reasons than efficient travel!

vv. 1–2—The Lord didn't want a controversy about baptism to deflect his ministry into unproductive areas, so he left Judea and returned home.

vv. 4–6—Jacob's well had a rich history. Jacob had bought the land for one hundred pieces of silver (Gen. 33:19) and built an altar there he named El Elohe Israel, "The Mighty God of Israel." Jacob bequeathed the land to Joseph on his deathbed (Gen. 48:52), and Joseph was buried there (Josh. 24:32). The well was more than a hundred feet deep, so water couldn't be drawn from it without a bucket.

vv. 7–9—The first surprising thing about this story is that Jesus spoke to the woman who came to draw water. Jews did not speak to Samaritans unless it was absolutely necessary, and men in Jesus' culture did not speak to single women unless it was a well-chaperoned, proper social situation. The next surprising thing is that the woman came all the way to Jacob's well to draw water. She lived in Sychar, which was more than half a mile away, and there were wells that were much closer. Barclay surmises, "May it be that she was so much of a moral outcast that even the village women drove her away from the village well, and she had to come here to draw water?" (Barclay, Commentaries, 139). Various writers have made a big deal about Jesus asking her for a drink, stressing that it's important to establish common ground when attempting to share your faith, etc. The reality is that it was twelve noon, and Jesus was probably very thirsty.

vv. 10–15—Like his conversation with Nicodemus, Jesus is speaking on one level, and the woman is hearing on another. Christ is describing spiritual thirst. "Living water" was understood in physical terms to be running water, but Jesus is making a Messianic claim. God is the one who offers the "fountain of life" (Ps. 36:9). Later, Jesus describes the Holy Spirit as the source of living water (John 7:38–39).

vv. 16–19—Jesus' first words are full of grace. Now he is full of truth. Though he may have inferred by her coming so far to draw water that she was a social outcast, there is no way he would have known that she had lived with six men if it had not been supernaturally revealed to him. She recognizes accurately that he is a prophet, for no ordinary man would know that type of information.

vv. 20–24—To take the focus from her personal life, the woman attempts to engage Jesus in a religious debate. Jesus doesn't take the bait. He has more important things to talk about than where people should worship God. The key to worship isn't where but how—true worshipers seek the Father in spirit and truth. Jesus makes a major theological point. God the Father is spirit, and he must be worshiped spiritually and truly. (The Mormons claim that God has a physical body, so they must ignore this passage.)

vv. 25–26—This is the first unambiguous declaration in the New Testament from Jesus that he is the Messiah.

vv. 27–30—The woman was so excited about this conversation that she left her water jar at the well. Her witness was honest and simple and stirred the interest of the townspeople.

vv. 31–38—The disciples had gone into Sychar to buy food and had probably eaten already. They were properly concerned that Jesus eat as well, but he turns the conversation in a spiritual direction once again. What truly sustains him is doing God's will. His experience with the woman at the well confirms his conviction that souls are ripe for the harvest. The application of the proverb cited in verse 37 isn't immediately clear. Who are the "others" Jesus refers to who have done the hard work? It may be the plural of majesty (like the Queen of England saying, "We are not amused") and Jesus is referring to himself only. J. A. T. Robinson argues that the others are John the Baptist and his followers (Robinson, *The Priority of John*, 510–515). Others consider that it is the work of the prophets or even points forward to the work of the Church. It's impossible to be sure.

vv. 39–42—The residents of Sychar take a balanced approach. They have an open mind to the woman's testimony, despite her moral failures. But they check out the evidence on their own and come to a firm conclusion that Jesus is indeed the Savior of the world. It doesn't appear that Jesus performed any miracles among them or even provided additional prophetic insights. They were convinced by his teaching.

APPLY

v. 10—Do you ever try to arouse interest by making a spiritual observation about a common experience?

v. 16—Do you have the courage to confront someone with God's truth when it is appropriate?

v. 24—How Spirit-filled and truth-focused is your worship? At your next worship service, ask the Spirit to enable you to worship fully and listen carefully to the Word of God in order to apply it to your life.

MEMORIZE

John 4:24

This is a key statement about the nature of God and worship.

PRAY

A: Praise God, who is spirit and truth.

C: Confess your failure to be a bold and sensitive witness.

T: Thank God for the Spirit's infilling, which gives you power.

S: Ask the Lord for a needy person to share with today.

TELL

Tell someone about the evidence for the Christian faith, and challenge him or her to check it out. Have a good book like C. S. Lewis' *Mere Christianity* handy to lend out.

APRIL 12

TWO MIRACULOUS HEALINGS IN CAPERNAUM AND JERUSALEM

PRAY

Pray that Christ's healing power would be real to you today.

READ

John 4:43–5:9

OBSERVE

The healing of the official's son has some similarities to the healing of the centurion's servant (Matt. 8:5–13). Both young men are healed in Capernaum, and both are long distance healings. But Christ's conversations with the two men are very different. The healing of the paralytic is unique to John.

vv. 43–45—The message here is similar to that of Matthew 4:12–17, Mark 1:14–15, and Luke 4:14–15. John adds that the Galileans gave Jesus a warm welcome because they had seen what he had done at the Passover feast (John 2:23).

vv. 46–47—The second notable miracle Jesus performs is in the same city as the first, Cana. The royal official (Greek *basilikos*, which can be translated "king") was probably a man of high standing in the court of Herod Antipas, tetrarch of Galilee. His home was Capernaum, but he traveled twenty miles to see Jesus, which indicates the desperate nature of his concern and the reputation Jesus had amassed.

vv. 48–50—Jesus often challenged people when they came to him, to test the genuineness of their faith. He didn't want people to come to him only as a miracle worker. But Christ was always impressed when a person persevered despite his challenge (Matt. 15:21–28). Jesus declared that the son would live, and the official had the faith to accept Christ's word. A less secure person might have tried to persuade Jesus to travel with him to Capernaum.

vv. 51–54—Though the man had faith in Jesus' ability to heal, it's obvious that it was not saving faith. It was only after the miracle that he and his household trusted in Christ. To some extent, Christ's lament in verse 48 was and is true. Many people will follow him if their lives experience only blessings from God.

5:1—The time is unclear, especially since the festival is unnamed.

v. 2—The NIV calls the pool in Jerusalem Bethesda ("house of mercy"), but there is strong manuscript evidence for Bethzatha ("house of olives"). The Jewish historian Josephus wrote that there was a section of Jerusalem known as Bethzatha. This site has been excavated and the colonnades exposed (it is more than thirty feet below modern Jerusalem). In Christ's time, it was a deep enough pool of water that swimming would have been possible.

v. 3—The best manuscripts of John don't include verse 4: *"From time to time an angel of the Lord would come down and stir up the waters. The first one into the pool after each such disturbance would be cured of whatever disease he had."* This explanation, while accurate, was probably added by a later scribe who wanted to provide some background for verse 7.

vv. 5–6—Can you imagine lying beside a pool every day for thirty-eight years? The man probably was close to the community of fellow sufferers and obviously had some caring people who would transport him to the pool. On the surface, Jesus' question seems ridiculous. Who wouldn't want to be delivered from that kind of life? But, as always, his question is truly insightful. Many people have learned to wallow in their unhappy circumstances, especially when others sympathize. Misery loves company, as the saying goes. To be healed would bring new responsibilities and challenges and profound changes.

v. 7—The man's initial response seems to confirm that he's not totally unhappy with his circumstances. He has a rationalization/explanation, but his problem is not his legs but his eyes. He sees only the limitations of his present situation. He doesn't see the person in front of him who can transform him and his circumstances.

vv. 8–9—There had to be some degree of willingness in the paralytic in order for him to even attempt to rise. His little faith is rewarded with a great miracle. The healing story ends with the ominous note, *"The day on which this took place was a Sabbath."* We'll look at the reaction to the healing tomorrow.

APPLY

4:48—Are you learning to walk by faith rather than by sight? *"Blessed are those who have not seen and yet have believed"* (John 20:29).

v. 6—Do you want to be well? If Jesus were to ask you that question today, what would he be referring to? Are you willing to trust him for your healing?

MEMORIZE

John 4:48

This is a warning against seeking signs.

PRAY

A: Praise Yahweh Rapha, the God who heals.

C: Confess any unhealthy patterns in your life.

T: Thank God for the healing you have experienced.

S: Ask him to heal one particular area that is hindering you.

TELL

It would be interesting to discuss with your small group examples that you have seen of people who don't really want to be well. Could some of you also be examples of this approach/avoidance conflict?

APRIL 13

THE TRUTH BEHIND THE MIRACLE

PRAY

Pray for deeper understanding of the life that is possible in Jesus Christ.

READ

John 5:10–29

OBSERVE

A unique aspect of John's gospel is that he often tells the story of what happened after Jesus' miraculous healings. The Synoptics typically end the story with the miracle itself.

vv. 10–14—We see a familiar pattern. The Jewish authorities were more concerned with their interpretation of the law than they were with a person's welfare. Verse 13 reveals an interesting truth. The man had no idea who Jesus was. God's healings don't always depend on the faith of the person in need but on his sovereign action on their behalf. Christ's warning to the man in verse 14 seems to contradict what he later teaches (John 9:1–3). Jesus didn't equate sickness with sin, but he did warn the man of something worse than physical illness if he did not come to faith. Jesus was more concerned with souls than with physical bodies.

vv. 15–18—The Jews persecuted and eventually killed Jesus because they thought that he was guilty of lawlessness and blasphemy. The irony is that they were the ones who defied God's law of love, and they were the ones who cursed God's name by refusing to acknowledge God the Son. Though some pious Jews had referred to God as their heavenly Father, Jesus most likely used the Aramaic word *Abba*, which is translated "Daddy." It suggested a relationship of intimacy that scandalized his hearers.

vv. 19–23—None of the people who listened to Jesus on the day he healed the paralytic could say that he didn't say he was the Son of God, as modern liberal scholars claim. Jesus claims a unique filial relationship in which:

1. He does what the Father does.
2. The Father loves him and shows him all that the Father does.
3. The Son gives life to whomever he chooses, just like the Father does.
4. The Father has turned over all judgment to the Son.
5. Whoever does not honor the Son does not honor the Father.

Most Christians are familiar with four of these five truths. Many don't realize the significance of #4—"From thence (his place of glory in heaven) he (Jesus, not God the Father) shall come to judge the quick (living) and the dead." No person, when he or she is judged by the Lord Jesus Christ, will ever be able to say, "But you don't understand! You didn't go through all the things that I went through." Hebrews 4:15 says otherwise.

vv. 24–29—The expression, "believes him who sent me" is unusual. It is much more common in the New Testament to believe *in* someone. Jesus may be trying to emphasize believing what the Father is saying through the Son. The emphasis is on the content of God's revelation in Christ—"my word." This section is very emphatic. Jesus uses the expression, "Amen, amen" ("Truly, truly" or "I tell you the truth"—NIV) twice more. "Listen carefully to what I'm about to say" would be a good paraphrase of the impact of this expression. The Gospel of John emphasizes that judgment occurs in the here and now (John 3:18). But this passage points to the future. The time is coming (at the return of Christ) when the voice of the Son will usher in the resurrection. "Those who have done good" and "those who have done evil" need to be understood in context. It's not salvation by works—the good or evil depends on one's relationship with the Father and the Son. It is impossible to do good if you do not believe on the Son. Conversely, if your trust is placed on him, it is impossible for your life to be evil, even though you commit evil acts.

APPLY

v. 10—Are you more concerned that a person is breaking the rules that you have set for yourself or that the person is someone Christ cares about?

v. 24—Have you "crossed over from death to life" intellectually and emotionally? Don't allow your former way of thinking to hold you captive.

MEMORIZE

John 5:22

This will help you to remember a key attribute of Christ, that he is the judge of every person.

PRAY

A: Praise the unity of Father and Son.

C: Confess times when you've valued rules more than people.

T: Thank God for new life.

S: Ask him to show you what he's doing so that you can cooperate with his work.

TELL

Share with a Christian friend the importance of seeing Jesus as our judge.

APRIL 14

THE TESTIMONY ABOUT JESUS

PRAY

Pray that you might understand the importance of credible testimony.

READ

John 5:30–47

OBSERVE

vv. 30–32—To the Jews, valid testimony was all-important, both in their law courts and in their synagogues. In speaking effectively to his culture, Jesus takes seriously the weight they gave to testimony and presents in this passage an almost legal summation. He begins by stating an obvious legal principle held by the Jews —self-testimony is invalid. We need to remember that when witnessing to others. Our testimony can be helpful, but it is certainly not indisputable. There are all kinds of people testifying to all kinds of religious experiences, and most unbelievers will place our testimony in the same subjective category that they place the testimony of Muslims, Mormons, or Maoists.

vv. 33–35—John the Baptist was highly respected by the Jews, so his testimony had weight. But even here, Jesus makes it clear that human testimony—even by a well-regarded person—was not conclusive. Nevertheless, God did speak through John, and he prepared people for the salvation that Jesus offered. John was a source of light, though he himself said he was only a witness to the true light (John 1:8).

v. 36—Jesus' God-ordained work was more a persuasive testimony than John's. Nicodemus was spiritually discerning when he said, *"Rabbi, we know that you are a teacher who has come from God. For no one could perform the signs you are doing if God were* *not with him"* (John 3:2). When attempting to discern the validity of a teacher, look at the fruit of all that he is doing, including the result of his works. A bad tree cannot produce consistently good fruit, nor will a good tree produce bad fruit.

vv. 37–40—The most powerful testimony possible is from God himself, and Jesus claims that the Father has given his stamp of approval to Jesus. The explicit witness is the Old Testament Scriptures, which clearly describe the Messiah. Jesus fulfilled all of those Scriptures, but the Jews refused to come to him. Their rejection of him caused them to reject what the Scriptures teach about him.

vv. 41–44—Jesus continues to speak the truth to his audience. He has the unique ability to penetrate behind our facades and see our hearts. The problem with Christ's contemporaries is the same problem with our contemporaries. They don't have the love of God in their hearts. If someone has that love, they will be drawn to Love Incarnate, Jesus Christ. Most people's inability to receive Christ is a heart, not a head, problem. They "loved darkness instead of light because their deeds were evil" (John 3:19).

vv. 45–47—Jesus repeats the message that the Scriptures, especially the books of Moses (the first five books of the Old Testament), describe him. It takes spiritual discernment to see the Messiah in the Pentateuch, but he is there, over and over again. Once again, their problem was lack of belief.

APPLY

v. 31—How should the fact that self-testimony is the least reliable affect the way we witness? This emphasizes that knowing what the Scriptures teach is more important than having a dramatic testimony.

v. 42—How should the fact that people have a heart problem more than a head problem affect the way we witness? Should we do more praying or talking?

MEMORIZE

John 5:46

This verse would be especially helpful when witnessing to Jewish people.

PRAY

A: Praise God for revealing himself.

C: Confess your heart problems.

T: Thank God for the Scriptures.

S: Intercede for someone who believes that all truth is relative.

TELL

Discuss with your small group the Old Testament prophecies which point to Christ.

APRIL 15

JESUS, THE BREAD OF LIFE

PRAY

Pray that you would be fed by the bread of life today.

READ

John 6:22–40

OBSERVE

John's gospel doesn't use parables, but it uses physical symbols to communicate spiritual truth. They are a kind of acted-out parable. This is the first of the great "I am" passages in John.

vv. 22–25—The setting for the teaching is that after Jesus had fed the five thousand, the crowds were looking for him. They knew that Jesus hadn't entered the boat with his disciples when they set off on the Sea of Galilee (Tiberias), so they wondered how he had gotten to the other side of the lake. They didn't know about his midnight walk on water.

vv. 26–27—As he often does, Jesus chooses not to answer their question but explores a deeper issue with the crowd. Christ diagnoses their spiritual illness —"their god is their stomach" (Phil. 3:19). They were pursuing Christ not because they believed that he was the Messiah and not even because they were impressed by his miracles, but because he put food in their bellies. Christ repeatedly contrasted the value of temporal things with eternal things. As in Isaiah 55:2, Jesus points out that earthly food does not ultimately satisfy our hunger. He alone can provide us with food that endures.

vv. 28–29—Like many people today, the Jews were quick to define their relationship with God in terms of works that they must do. Jesus makes it clear that the work God wants is to trust in his work, the one whom he sent into the world for our salvation. Christianity is unique among the major world religions in that it is not a system of rules and requirements but a relationship with the God who became flesh.

vv. 30–33—How ironic that the people demand a sign on the day after Jesus had just fed five thousand people with five small loaves and two fish. It's clear that they see Jesus as their meal ticket and want him to continue to provide their bread. They use the example of manna (Exod. 16:4) to challenge Jesus. He doesn't take the bait. Christ points out that it was God, not Moses, who provided the manna. That same God has provided heavenly manna in the person of Jesus, bread that offers to satisfy more than physical hunger.

vv. 34–39—The expression "I am the bread of life" has an unusual construction in Greek. The usual way of saying it would be *"Eimi ho artos tes zoes,"* but Jesus adds the emphatic personal pronoun *"Ego"* at the beginning. The literal translation would be, "I myself am the bread of life." Each of the "I am" sayings in John uses this same *Ego eimi* formula. It's a claim to deity, to being the "I am" (Exod. 3: 14). For the people of Jesus' day, bread was the essential food. Without it, physical life would have been impossible. The Greek language distinguishes between physical life (*bios*) and spiritual life (*zoe*). Jesus uses the latter word to describe himself. Jesus, the bread of life, satisfies our ultimate spiritual hunger and thirst. He makes it clear in this passage that it is the Father who decides who will come to Jesus. All those whom the Father gives to Jesus will never be turned away because Christ came to carry out the Father's decisions. Those who come in genuine faith will never be lost. The Reformed doctrines of Irresistible Grace and the Perseverance of the Saints are clearly taught here. Paul was not the first one to teach the doctrine of election!

v. 40—One commentator writes:

> There is no contradiction between the gift of life now and resurrection in the future. The duality of present and future participation in the kingdom of God is fundamental to the proclamation of Jesus in all four gospels, in this no less than in the other three, as also in the proclamation about Jesus in the rest of the New Testament. (Beasley-Murray, *John*, 92)

APPLY

v. 27—Is the focus of your life gaining temporary things or that which endures?

v. 35—Is Christ satisfying your hunger and thirst, or are you looking to things which never can satisfy?

MEMORIZE

John 6:37

This is a clear statement of how God takes the initiative in our salvation.

PRAY

A: Praise the Bread of Heaven, who satisfies the hunger of your soul.

C: Confess your pursuit of things that don't satisfy.

T: Thank God for calling you to himself.

S: Pray for someone who believes that he or she chose Christ.

TELL

Discuss with a friend or small group whether there is any other way to understand Jesus' teaching here other than the reality of election.

APRIL 16

MANY WOULD-BE FOLLOWERS DESERT JESUS

PRAY

Pray that God would give you the ability to understand this hard teaching and apply it to your life.

READ

John 6:41–71

OBSERVE

This is a continuation of the message we examined yesterday.

vv. 41–51—In another parallel to the Jews who received the manna, the crowd begins to murmur against Jesus. They perceive his claim to be "the bread that came down from heaven" to be blasphemous. After all, they thought, this is a mere man. We know his parents, how can he claim a heavenly origin? It would, indeed, be a blasphemous statement if Jesus were a mere man. That's why C. S. Lewis' statement in *Mere Christianity* is so true. Jesus cannot be simply a good teacher or even a prophet but not God. If a mere human being said the kind of things Jesus did, we would have to consider him a megalomaniac or even a lunatic. Do good teachers claim to be able to raise people up on the last day? Do they claim to be the only one who has ever seen God? Do they claim to be the source of everlasting life for those who trust in them? Has any other religious leader ever claimed to give his flesh for the life of the world? Notice the verb tense in verse 47. The promise isn't that those who believe will have eternal life in the future, but that they possess it here and now. For the Christian, a new quality of life begins at conversion and continues forever.

vv. 52–59—In verse 41, the Jews grumbled, but now they argue sharply among themselves. If Jesus were a mere human, offering his flesh for his followers to eat would not only be blasphemous, it would be repulsive. Clearly, Christ's language here is symbolic just as it was when he called himself the bread of life. Jesus uses the graphic word for flesh (*sarx*) rather than the more polite term for a body (*soma*). His words are intended to shock and to make his listeners consider a deeper reality.

John's gospel does not contain a description of the Last Supper. His focus in the Upper Room is upon the foot washing. This teaching seems clearly sacramental in nature. Roger Fredrickson writes:

> The bread that is eaten and the blood that is drunk are separate realities, signs of Jesus' life and death. It was through his flesh that Jesus lived out a life of holy obedience. In eating his flesh we partake of this life of surrender and begin to manifest his life in all those fleshly places into which we are thrown or called—at sales conventions, on used car lots, laundering our clothes, making love and bearing children, watching TV and going to church. It is in our temptations and defeats, our joys and our victories, that we are to bear in our bodies the marks of the Lord Jesus (Gal. 6:17). But we are also to drink his blood. How abhorrent this was to the Jews who had been forbidden by law to partake of blood. But in this act we appropriate, or take into ourselves, his life sacrificed, his expiation, and his atonement. In accepting his life poured out we are reconciled to God and live in grace as forgiven sinners. The Son of Man, the one who has identified himself with us, offers this incredible feast of life. We shall become like him as we continue to feed on him. (Fredrickson, *John*, 137)

vv. 60–71—Seeing that some of his followers were having problems with the difficulty of his human sacrificial language, Jesus doesn't try to minimize the difficulty of believing in him but adds to it! He claims that they will see him ascend into heaven and that his words are spirit and life. He repeats the message that only those whom the Father has enabled can come to him. It is too much for some of his would-be followers. Many of them decide to leave. Christ's question to the Twelve is phrased in such a way that he is hoping for a positive answer, *"You do not want to leave too, do you?"* Once again, impulsive Peter comes through with the perfect response. But even his powerful confession of faith does not deter Jesus from expressing another painful truth. Even among his closest followers there is a *diabolos*, a devil, who seeks to accuse the Master.

APPLY

v. 54—How seriously do you take communion? Jesus is not teaching salvation by taking communion, but that his supper, taken in faith, is a sign that we are saved and will experience his glorification.

vv. 68–69—Is Christ truly the last word for you? Do you believe that he has ultimate truth for your life?

MEMORIZE

John 6:47

This verse will help you to remember that your eternal life is a present reality.

PRAY

A: Adore the Lamb of God, whose broken body makes you whole and whose shed blood gives you forgiveness.

C: Confess any grumbling about your circumstances.

T: Thank God for his Word, which is spirit and life.

S: Intercede for someone who has turned back from following Christ.

TELL

Discuss with a friend or your small group a hard saying of Jesus that you need help to understand.

APRIL 17

JESUS AT THE FEAST OF TABERNACLES

Pray for the discernment of Christ to know how to answer your opponents.

John 7:1–24

Though John, like the other gospels, acknowledges Jesus' Galilean roots, the focus of Jesus' ministry in John is Jerusalem, the capital city. From John 7:10 until the resurrection, John's gospel is set in Jerusalem, the spiritual center of Jesus' (and John's) world.

v. 1—It's important to note at the outset that Jesus knew that there was a death sentence pronounced against him in Jerusalem. His words and actions are more understandable with that realization in mind.

v. 2—The Feast of Tabernacles, also known as the Feast of Booths, was an eight day campout for the Jews. It was the third major feast (after Passover and Pentecost) and occurred around the middle of October. Its historical significance was to remember the time in the wilderness when God's people lived in tents. Those who celebrated the festival had to erect a temporary dwelling to remember the time of the sojourn. Its agricultural significance was to celebrate the harvest. It was the most joyous of all the feasts. Zechariah 14:16–19 sees this feast celebrated by all of the nations when the Day of the Lord arrives. The symbolism of this great feast will become more significant when we get to verse 37 tomorrow.

vv. 3–9—One of the supreme ironies of the gospels is that Jesus' own family didn't believe in him before his death and resurrection. It's a testimony to how normal and genuinely human authentic holiness really is that Jesus' family didn't see him as peculiar or odd, even though he was sinless. His brothers seem here to be goading Jesus into making a public splash, much like Satan's second temptation (Matt. 4:5–7). Jesus doesn't react. The NIV translation does a great job of clarifying Christ's response to his brothers. In other versions, it seems like Jesus is deceiving them when he says, *"My time has not come."* The NIV distinguishes between the more common Greek word for time (*chronos*) and the word for quality time or opportune time (*kairos*). Jesus wasn't telling his brothers that he wouldn't go to the feast at all; he just didn't sense God's timing to go at the beginning.

vv. 10–13—Jesus also wanted to sense the lay of the land, so he entered Jerusalem quietly, wanting to discover what people were saying about him. He must have been discouraged, because the three main opinions circulating were:

1. He's a danger. The people asking, "Where is that man?" were not asking out of curiosity but out of evil intent.
2. He's a good man. Like a lot of people today, this was probably the majority opinion, but it is an insult itself. If Jesus was not God, he was not good.
3. He deceives the people. These people also were part of the coalition seeking to eliminate the Word of God made flesh.

If one probes beneath the surface, these same opinions still exist concerning the person of Jesus.

vv. 14–18—Christ's contemporaries were frequently impressed by the power and perceptivity of his teaching (Matt. 7:28–29). The literal Greek of verse 15 is, "How does this man (a term of contempt) know letters having never learned?" The term "letters" refers to knowledge of the Bible, and the idea that Jesus had never "learned" meant that he had never studied under a rabbi. In fact, the Bible (the Old Testament) was readily available in the form of scrolls in the synagogues, and every Jewish boy would have the opportunity to study on his own. Jesus made the most of that opportunity, and, from the amount of Scripture he quotes in teaching, it's obvious that he memorized large portions of the Bible. But he stresses in this passage that it was not just his study that informed his message. The Father directly communicated his truth to and through Jesus. A clear sign of whether someone desires to do God's will is his or her reaction to Jesus' teaching. Those seeking the truth will embrace the words of Christ.

vv. 19–24—Jesus never teaches in abstract terms. He always applies his message to his listeners. Christ pierces to the heart of the issue—the hostile attitudes people held against him (which we observed above). The Jews prided themselves on keeping the law of Moses, but they kept it selectively. Christ's argument here is that they will circumcise a child if the eighth day falls on the Sabbath. This is clearly not a life-saving medical procedure. But Jesus healed a man who had been crippled for thirty-eight years on the Sabbath (John 5), and the leaders turned the crowd against him, calling him a lawbreaker. Christ's warning to them in verse 24 is an important caution to us as well. One of the reasons we should be careful about judging is that we often see only part of the picture and we judge by mere appearances. Once again, Jesus isn't prohibiting judging. He's teaching us to do it carefully and accurately. One of the greatest sins in our society is that people are judged and rejected based on their physical appearances.

APPLY

v. 6—Do you seek God's timing for your decisions and actions?

v. 24—How can you be more careful and accurate in the judgments you make?

MEMORIZE

John 7:24

Use this verse to discourage yourself from making snap judgments based on appearances.

PRAY

A: Praise God for his truth.

C: Confess the times you've judged based on superficial criteria.

T: Thank God for his timing in your life.

S: Pray that you would hear his inner voice today, just as Jesus did.

TELL

Share with someone or your small group a time when God clearly showed you his perfect timing.

APRIL 18

JESUS, THE LIVING WATER

PRAY

Pray that streams of living water would flow from within you today.

READ

John 7:25–52

OBSERVE

Yesterday's teaching at the Feast of Tabernacles continues.

vv. 25–36, 40–43—The issue in this passage continues to be, "Who is this Jesus, really?"

1. Some of the crowd marvels at the fact that the authorities haven't arrested him yet. Could he be the Messiah? As soon as they ask that question, they answer it for themselves because they know that Jesus came from Galilee and they think that the Messiah's origins should be unknown. This portion of the crowd is apparently ignorant of the prophecy of Micah 5:2 which others in the crowd knew (v. 42). Jesus answers the question of origins in a more profound way. They think they know where he came from (Galilee), but he really came from God and was sent by the Father.
2. Many in the crowd trust in Jesus. Their reasoning is sound. Could the Messiah do any greater works than Jesus had already done? The faith of this group was the final straw for the Pharisees, who send temple guards to arrest Jesus when they hear that people are receiving him as the Messiah.
3. Others in the crowd are earth-bound. When Jesus prophesies his ascension

in verses 33–34, they conclude that he must intend to live among the Gentiles if he's going where they cannot find him.

4. Another group of the people are truly impressed by Jesus' teaching and conclude that he must be the Prophet (v. 40). The Prophet they referred to is the one promised in Deuteronomy 18:15–22. Over time, this Prophet had become associated with the promise of Elijah (Mal. 4:5), who would prepare the land for the Messiah.

5. Still another group of people see Jesus as more than the Prophet; he is the Anointed One, the Messiah. But those believers were opposed by those who did know the Micah prophecy that the Messiah must come from Bethlehem. Apparently, no one was willing to do the homework to ask Jesus where he was born! How interesting that people will make life-changing decisions based on incomplete information. It's still happening today!

vv. 37–39—It's important to understand the context of the Feast of Tabernacles to fully understand Jesus' crucial teaching in these verses. For the first seven days of the feast, the priest led a procession to the pool of Siloam, where he filled his golden pitcher with water as the crowd sang, *"With joy you will draw water from the wells of salvation"* (Isa. 12:3). Then the crowd followed the priest back to the temple carrying branches and twigs in their hands (symbolizing the huts their forefathers built in the wilderness). They proceeded to the altar and sang, *"Save now, I pray, O Lord; O Lord, I pray, send now prosperity"* (Ps. 118:25). The priest then poured the water into a silver funnel, through which it flowed onto the ground, as a symbol of fertility. On the last day of the feast, this ritual was not performed, but the crowd circled the altar seven times to celebrate God's gift of water at Meribah (Num. 20:1–13), when Moses struck the rock in the wilderness.

It is out of this background that Jesus speaks. Christ makes the grand claim that he is the source of living water (water that will not stop flowing) to all who are thirsty and believe in him. John makes it clear that this living water comes in the form of the Holy Spirit, who wells up from within those who receive Jesus by faith. The Spirit refreshes, renews, and gives us life. The Holy Spirit did not begin his ministry after Christ's ascension. He is eternal and works throughout history. In contrast to the Old Testament, when the Spirit "came upon" believers, Christians are given the Spirit as a constant possession, a seal of our salvation (Eph. 1:14–15) and the source of spiritual power (Eph. 3:16).

vv. 45–52—The common people, represented by the temple guards, always had a much greater appreciation for Jesus than the religious elite. Christ's teaching had so impressed the guards that they took the unprecedented step of disobeying the orders of the chief priests to arrest Jesus. The Pharisees try to intimidate the guards by pulling rank—"We're the ones in the know, and none of us believes in Jesus. Why are you listening to the ignorant mob?" They don't know that one of their own was honest enough to check him out on his own. He is a secret believer. Nicodemus raises a key point of the law in verse 51, but he is shouted down by the Pharisees, with their implied condemnation of Nicodemus if he follows this Galilean.

APPLY

vv. 37–38—The Holy Spirit dwells within every believer, but the New Testament urges us to "be filled with the Spirit" (Eph. 5:18). This filling will produce the streams of living water flowing from within. We must first confess our sins and repent of them, then simply ask the Spirit to fill us to overflowing!

MEMORIZE

John 7:38

This is a key reminder of the awesome presence and power of the Holy Spirit.

PRAY

A: Praise the indwelling Holy Spirit.

C: Confess your sins and repent of them.

T: Thank God that he can do in you today "immeasurably more than all we ask or imagine" (Eph. 3:20).

S: Ask him to do just that.

TELL

Discuss with a Christian friend or your small group the role of the Holy Spirit in our lives.

APRIL 19

JESUS, THE LIGHT OF THE WORLD

PRAY

Pray that the light of Christ will guide you today.

READ

John 8:12–30

OBSERVE

John 7:53–8:11 was almost certainly not part of the original Gospel of John. It doesn't appear in the oldest manuscripts of the gospel, and when it does appear (fifth century AD), it is inserted in different places. It was added by a copyist who took on the forbidden role of co-author. Most scholars believe that this could have been an authentic story about Jesus that was passed down by oral tradition. Eusebius, who wrote in the fourth century, quoted Papias as having, "expounded another story about a woman who was accused before the Lord of many sins" (quoted in Morris, *The Gospel According to John*, 883). Since this story, like Mark 16:9–20, was not part of the original gospel, it's not included in this New Testament devotional. It's not a bad story to read and meditate upon by any means, but it shouldn't be studied or taught as though it were Scripture. John 8:12 follows very naturally after 7:52.

v. 12—Let's concentrate on this, the second of Jesus' "I myself am" sayings in John. Light is the dominant image in the entire Bible. In Genesis, God says, "Let there be light," and order comes out of chaos. In Revelation, the Holy City does not need the sun or moon because the glory of God is its light, and the Lamb of God is its lamp. In between, nearly every book of Scripture deals with light in some fashion or another. The major symbolic significance of light in Scripture, however, is in these meanings:

1. Light symbolizes guidance and direction. *"Your word is a lamp to my feet and a light for my path"* (Ps. 119:105).
2. Light symbolizes good versus darkness, which is evil. *"The light shines in the darkness, but the darkness has not understood (or overcome) it"* (John 1:5).
3. Light signifies truth versus the darkness of lies. *"God is light; in him there is no darkness at all. If we claim to have fellowship with him yet walk in the darkness, we lie and do not live by the truth."*
4. Light represents life. *"In him was life and that life was the light of men"* (John 1:4). Just as light is essential to plant life, the light of God is essential to spiritual life.
5. Light represents the presence of God as we see in the burning bush, the pillar of fire by day, and in the Transfiguration.

When Jesus says, *"I am the light of the world,"* he means all of these things. He brings guidance, goodness, truth, life, and the presence of God into our dark world.

vv. 13–30—We have explored the other themes in this section in previous studies —the testimony to Jesus from the Father, his preexistence and ascension, prophecies of his death and resurrection, and the faithfulness of his message to the one who sent him.

APPLY

v. 12—Which aspect of Christ's light do you most need—guidance, goodness, truth, life, or his presence?

MEMORIZE

John 8:12

This is a great "I am" saying.

PRAY

A: Praise the Light of the World.

C: Confess your darkness.

T: Thank God for his guidance, goodness, truth, and presence.

S: Pray that your light might so shine before others that they give glory to the Father (Matt. 5:16).

TELL

Tell someone how God's light of guidance made a difference in your life at a particular time.

APRIL 20

CHILDREN OF ABRAHAM, CHILDREN OF THE DEVIL

PRAY

Ask for the ability that Jesus had to speak the truth to others, whatever the cost.

READ

John 8:31–59

OBSERVE

This is the climax of Jesus' teaching at the Feast of the Tabernacles. It is crucial to understanding who he is and who he clearly presented himself to be.

vv. 31–32—It's not enough to simply know Christ's teaching or even to present it to others. Only those who hold to his teaching—that is, "remain steadfast in living out its implications"—are truly his disciples. This truth is liberating. It sets us free. It's like getting good directions when you've been lost and frustrated. It's like a breath of fresh air when you've been imprisoned among sweaty miscreants. It's like the first day of summer for a student who has been bored with school.

vv. 33–36—His Jewish listeners respond too literally to Jesus' statement, so he sets them straight. He isn't referring to physical slavery. It's spiritual. *"Everyone who sins is a slave to sin"* is a New Testament theme, echoed prominently by the Apostle Paul (Rom. 6-8). The only way for a slave of sin to be set free is by a relationship to the Son, who has a special place and status with the Father. He alone gives genuine freedom. People think that they can pursue freedom in other ways (sensual pleasure, substance abuse, doing their own thing, etc.), but the end result is always slavery.

vv. 37–41—Jesus continues to come back to what is in the peoples' hearts. He knows that they are ready to kill him and attributes it to the voice of their father (whom he will soon identify). They think he's referring to their earthly fathers and reiterate the claim that Abraham is their spiritual father. Jesus counters that if Abraham really were their father they wouldn't respond negatively to the truth he has told them. They appeal to a higher court and claim that God himself is their only Father.

vv. 42–47—Christ speaks the hard truth in no uncertain terms. Once again, his reasoning is simple. If they were children of God, they would receive the message that has come from God in the person of God's Son, and they would love him. The reason they want to kill him is that they are actually being led by their true spiritual father, the Devil, who is the father of lies. Satan is the origin of all murderous intentions because he has no regard for the sanctity of life that God has given. Nobody is spiritually neutral, according to Jesus. Those who are not following Christ are following Satan.

vv. 48–58—Jesus' opponents bring out the heavy artillery. They accuse him of being a Samaritan (Galilee was just south of Samaria), the worst slur a Jew could make on a fellow Jew. Then they suggest that he is demon-possessed, which is not an original accusation (see Matt. 12:24). With impeccable logic, Jesus answers that a demon-possessed person would not honor the Father. By implication, it is those who dishonor him who are led by the Evil One. Christ continues to assert the truth, which is difficult for earthly eyes to see. The one who keeps his word will never die spiritually. Jesus' opponents think they are raising the discussion to a ridiculous level when they ask, *"Are you greater than our father Abraham?"* They are not prepared for the answer. The heavenly Abraham rejoiced at the prospect of Christ's incarnation. When he saw it happen, he was glad. Christ affirms his pre-existence in no uncertain terms, literally, "Before Abraham was, I am" (the NIV adds, "born" for clarification, but it somewhat weakens the starkness of the declaration). Not only are the verbs provocative, the term "I am" (as we have already noted) is a direct claim to deity. It's no surprise that the children of the devil pick up stones to kill Jesus for blasphemy, but the time is not right, and Jesus slips away from the temple.

APPLY

v. 32—Is there an area of your life in which you need Christ's truth to set you free?

v. 44—In this age of tolerance it is considered the height of arrogance and bad manners to suggest that someone else is wrong in their religious beliefs. Jesus says that they are not only wrong but that they are controlled by Satan. Do you have the courage to tell someone honestly that their beliefs are wrong?

MEMORIZE

John 8:32

This will help you to remember the source of true freedom.

PRAY

A: Praise God, who is the Truth.

C: Confess the lies you have believed and your lack of courage to expose them.

T: Thank God for the truth that has set you free.

S: Pray for someone who is bound by lies.

TELL

Tell someone with whom you have a strong relationship that what they believe is false and that all lies have their source in the evil one. Don't do this arrogantly but humbly, using Christ as your source of truth.

APRIL 21

THERE IS NONE SO BLIND AS HE WHO WILL NOT SEE

PRAY

Pray for the eyes to see God's truth in his Word today.

READ

John 9:1–41

OBSERVE

A common pattern in the book of John is for Jesus to make a crucial statement (i.e., *"I am the light of the world"*) and then illustrate it in action. It also works from the opposite direction—that he performs an action (usually a miracle) and then uses it as an illustration for his teaching. In this chapter, both things happen. *"I am the light of the world"* is Christ's sixth major discourse in John. The healing of the blind man is his sixth major healing.

vv. 1–3—The disciples reflected the theology common to their culture—that illness, especially severe disabilities, were a punishment from God for particular sins committed by a person or his or her ancestors. Despite the book of Job and other Old Testament teaching to the contrary (Ps. 130:3), this view persisted. Jesus didn't completely reject the connection between sin and God's punishment (Luke 13:1–5), but he certainly qualified it. Sometimes God does punish and correct us for our sins in this life (Heb. 12:5–11), but misfortune is not always the result of sin, and in some cases (like Job), the most righteous people experience the worst that life has to offer.

vv. 4–5—Jesus was profoundly aware that his time on earth was passing quickly. He was determined to shine God's light into the world as much as possible before his death.

vv. 6–12—This is yet another example of Jesus' creativity in healing. Though Jesus had used saliva before (Mark 8:22–25), this is the first time he used a mud pack. Some see in the mention of the ground a reference to Genesis 2:7, where people are made from the dust of the earth. If that is intentional, we can discern in Christ's action a work of re-creation. The Pool of Siloam is where the water had been drawn for the Feast of Tabernacles. The Hebrew name for the pool means "sent," a very important verb in John. Jesus is sent by the Father, the Holy Spirit is sent by the Son, and believers are sent by the Spirit.

vv. 13–34—Another common pattern in John is that the Pharisees object to Christ healing on the Sabbath, and they launch an investigation. Like many legalists today, they baptize their particular understanding of the law (Christ effectively refuted their interpretation of the Sabbath on several occasions), then they use it as a grid with which to judge others. "Jesus could not be from God because he heals on the Sabbath"—case closed.

But some of the Pharisees question the party line: *"How could a sinner perform these miracles?"* The formerly blind man simply believes that Jesus must be a prophet. The skeptical Pharisees interrogate the parents of the man born blind. But they represent those who are afraid to stand for the truth because they might experience persecution. In this case, it was expulsion from the synagogue, which meant loss of salvation to most Jews (as it does in some denominations today).

The second dialogue between the blind man and the Pharisees is priceless. The man with new sight does not share the fear of his parents. He is a good witness, who tells his personal experience. *"Whether he is a sinner or not, I don't know. One thing I do know. I was blind but now I see!"* He is not afraid to put the needle to the Pharisees—"Why do you want to hear it again? Do you want to become his disciples, too?"

His question reveals another of their prejudices. They won't consider that Christ could be the Messiah because they don't know where he comes from. Only someone from an approved background could possibly be God's man. The formerly blind man proves to be a far superior theologian to the Pharisees (vv. 30–33), but they reject him according to the same theological error the disciples held at the beginning of the chapter.

vv. 35–41—The moral of the story is given in this tender final scene between Jesus and the man he healed. Christ is not content with only healing his body, he wants the man to experience a total spiritual healing. It's clear from Jesus' usage here that he recognized "Son of Man" as a messianic title (Dan. 7:13–14). The conversion of the formerly blind man is simple but profound. He is now able to see with the eyes of faith, while those who have had 20/20 vision all along remain spiritually blind.

APPLY

v. 30—Are you willing to be as bold in your witness as the man with new sight?

MEMORIZE

John 9:25b

Use this as a perfect answer when someone asks how Christ has changed your life.

PRAY

A: Praise God for his light.

C: Confess any tendency you have to make people fit into your mold.

T: Thank God for opening your eyes.

S: Pray for someone who is spiritually blind.

TELL

Ask someone who knows you well if there are any blind spots in your life.

APRIL 22

I AM THE GOOD SHEPHERD

PRAY

Pray that you may have renewed appreciation for the one who laid down his life for you.

READ

John 10:1–42

OBSERVE

There are actually two "I myself am" statements in this chapter, the third and fourth in the Gospel of John. Though the fourth is better known, we shouldn't ignore the third.

vv. 1–10—The people of Palestine have always had an ambivalent relationship with shepherds. Because Israel is largely rocky rather than verdant, shepherds have to cover large distances every year to feed their flocks. Some shepherds took advantage of their mobility and had a casual attitude toward the possessions of others, removing whatever was not nailed down. These men gave shepherds a bad name. But many shepherds were admired for their self-sacrificing love for their sheep.

God is frequently pictured as this kind of shepherd in the Old Testament. Jesus identifies with the Father in this chapter. There were actually two different kinds of sheepfolds—one used in the city, where several flocks might be penned together, and one in the countryside, where each flock spent the night with its shepherd. Jesus refers to the city sheepfold in verses 1–3 and the country fold in verses 7–10. Important insights from these verses include:

1. Jesus knows his sheep. Shepherds had descriptive names for each of their sheep that set them apart and enabled them to always keep track of the flock. To know another person by name in the Middle East implies a close relationship.
2. His sheep know the voice of Jesus. Only sick sheep will follow a stranger. We need to distinguish between Christ's voice and the word of false shepherds. Cult members fail to do this.
3. In the country pen, the shepherd became the actual gate for the sheep. He slept across the entrance to the pen and had each sheep pass under his staff in the evening and morning. Jesus cares personally and particularly for every one of his sheep.

The thief may refer to false prophets or even to Satan, who comes to steal and kill and destroy what rightly belongs to the shepherd. The one who is the gate for the sheep protects them and provides the fullest life possible for his sheep. In verse 10, Jesus repeats the word that the NIV translates "to the full." The Christian life is the only existence that is super-abundant. As Mel Gibson says when he is portraying William Wallace in the movie *Braveheart,* "Every man dies. Not every man really lives."

vv. 11–18—*"I [myself] am the good shepherd"* flows directly from *"I am the gate for the sheep."* This metaphor pictures the fold attacked by a wolf predator. Most shepherds owned their flocks, but some owners hired workers to tend their flock. When that was the case, the hired worker would rarely risk his life for sheep that weren't his. Good shepherds are marked by their willingness to die in a battle to protect their sheep. Jesus takes this historical fact and gives it deeper theological meaning. He lays down his life for his sheep, just as the Father has authorized him to do. It is a voluntary act—no one takes his life from him. Jesus could have called down twelve legions of angels to save him from the cross (Matt. 26:53–54), but it was the Father's will for him to lay down his life to fulfill the Scriptures. Jesus also points forward beyond the cross to other sheep, "not of this sheep pen." This seems to be a clear prophecy of the gathering of the Gentiles into Christ's fold.

vv. 19–21—The same division continues between Jews who saw Jesus as destructive and demon-possessed and those who were impressed by his miracles.

vv. 22–39—The Feast Of Dedication (Hanukkah) celebrates the amazing rebellion of the Jews under the Maccabees, who gained independence from the Romans for a short time in the second century BC. Contrary to false teachers who say that Jesus never claimed to be God, he acknowledges to his Jewish questioners that he is both Messiah and God's Son. He sets before them his miracles as attestation. But he immediately acknowledges that they cannot believe because they are not his sheep. Verses 27–30 are some of Jesus' strongest statements concerning God's election of believers and the perseverance of those saints. His statement, "I and the Father are one" was particularly incendiary to the Jews. They picked up stones to kill him because they recognized accurately that this statement was a claim to deity. Jesus argues from the lesser to the greater. Psalm 82:6 calls believers "gods," though it makes it clear that they are mere men. How much more does God exalt "his very own" whom he "sent into the world?"

vv. 40–42—Jesus wisely alternated intense times like those at the temple with times of refreshment. The fellowship with believers who had been baptized by John must have been like an oasis.

APPLY

v. 10—Are you experiencing life to the fullest? If not, what needs to change?

MEMORIZE

John 10:10

This verse is a poignant reminder that Christ wants the very best for you.

PRAY

A: Praise the Good Shepherd who lays down his life for his sheep.

C: Confess the times you've behaved like a hireling and fled persecution for your faith.

T: Thank God for the abundance of your life.

S: Pray for whatever needs to change in order for you to experience the fullness Christ wants for you.

TELL

If you ever hear someone say "Jesus never claimed to be God," cite this chapter.

APRIL 23

I AM THE RESURRECTION AND THE LIFE

PRAY

Pray that the same power that raised Lazarus (and Jesus) from the dead will empower you today.

READ

John 11:1–44

OBSERVE

The fifth "I am" statement of Jesus is the most powerful of all.

vv. 1–6—This is the first mention in Scripture of Lazarus, the brother of Mary and Martha (we encountered the sisters in Luke 10). The reference to Mary anointing Jesus' feet with perfume is a forecast of John 12. It's clear that Jesus was close to this family who lived close to Jerusalem. It seems strange that Jesus would wait for two days before going to Bethany. But he had an acute sense of God's timing and purposes. He knew beforehand that the end result would not be death and that he, God's Son, would be glorified in what happened with Lazarus.

vv. 7–10—The disciples perceive that a return to Jerusalem could be a suicide mission, given the recent reception Jesus received there (10:31–33). Christ's enigmatic statement about twelve hours of daylight has at least a double meaning:

1. Conscious of the Father's timing, Jesus knew that he had a certain amount of work to accomplish. Barclay notes, "If a man chooses to serve God, then that man's day will not end before God wishes it to end" (Barclay, Commentaries, 97).

2. Keeping in mind that light is a dominant image in John's writing, Jesus
   points his disciples to the inevitable clash between his goodness and the
   evil that awaits in Jerusalem.

Christ senses that the climax is not far off, and he will walk boldly into Jerusalem
in the light God has given him to confront the darkness.

vv. 11–16—Jesus, who is full of grace, tries to gently tell his disciples that Lazarus
is dead. "Fallen asleep" in first century Israel meant much the same as "passed
away" does to us, although the former expression was somewhat more capable of
being misunderstood. Sure enough, the disciples misunderstand, and Jesus has to
be full of truth with them. Thomas, the twin, doesn't say much in the gospels (this
is the first time his speech is recorded, and he is quoted only in John), but when he
does speak, he has something important to say. His bravado here is very similar to
what Peter will express in a few days. We can assume that both disciples were
ashamed of their failure to live up to their boast. That may be one reason that
Thomas isn't with the other disciples when Jesus appears to them in the upper
room following his resurrection.

vv. 17–27—As we've seen, Martha was the more assertive of the sisters and had a
somewhat controlling personality. We can read a pretty clear rebuke in her words
to Jesus in verse 21. The NIV translation of verse 22 is problematic. It appears that
Martha is expressing faith that Jesus could raise Lazarus from the dead, but the
rest of the passage emphatically denies that she believed that. Leon Morris points
out that verses 21 and 22 could be translated, "If you had been here my brother
might not have died, for I know that God gives the things you ask" (Morris, *The
Gospel According to John*, 549). Jesus is patient with Martha when she qualifies each
of the strong statements he makes about Lazarus rising from the dead. Notice her
response to Jesus' "I am the resurrection and the life" statement. Christ speaks
first about a physical resurrection and secondly about a spiritual resurrection.
Martha ignores both aspects of the resurrection and affirms that he is the Messiah
and the Son of God. We sometimes can discern what people believe more by what
they don't say than by what they do say.

vv. 28–37—Mary is the sister who is more demonstrative emotionally. Every time
she appears in Scripture, she is at the feet of Jesus! She uses the same words as
Martha, but her tone was probably different. Jesus, who was marvelously empathetic, is touched by her grief and the grief of her friends. Even though he knew he
was going to raise Lazarus from death, he weeps. (John 11:35 is the second-
shortest verse in the Bible.)

vv. 38–40—It's time to take action. At this point, Jesus loses patience with
Martha's lack of faith. The eternal housekeeper is more concerned about offending
her friends with an unpleasant odor (King James, "But Lord, he stinketh") than
she is concerned about seeing God's glory displayed through Jesus.

vv. 41–44—The initial impression we get of Jesus' prayer is that it was said to
impress the crowd. That would certainly violate Jesus' own teaching in Matthew
6:5–6. Once again, Leon Morris' interpretation is very helpful. He writes:

This does not mean that his prayer was primarily for the crowd to hear. That would make it an artificial thing, and in any case, as we do not know when it was spoken, we have no reason for thinking the crowd heard. As Wright says, "The Evangelist does not say that *Jesus' prayer* was for the sake of the multitude; but that *his thanksgiving* was for their sakes. Jesus, in other words, would always have people know that he did nothing of himself." (Wright, 561)

Jesus called Lazarus by name because there could have been a parade of resuscitated corpses if he had simply said, "Come out!" Christ's command to the crowd to take off Lazarus' grave clothes was a gesture of compassion. It was important for his friends and neighbors to see for themselves that Lazarus wasn't a ghost or some other-worldly creature. His humanity would be reaffirmed for them as they touched him.

APPLY

vv. 11–14, 21–27—Are you full of grace and truth as Jesus was? We need the Holy Spirit's guidance to know when to be patient and when to correct someone who is mistaken.

vv. 25–26—How sure are you that you are living an eternal life and will be with Christ forever?

v. 35—Ask the Spirit to give you the gift of empathy to "weep with those who weep."

MEMORIZE

John 11:25–26

PRAY

A: Praise the Resurrection and the Life.

C: Confess any doubts you have about the resurrection.

T: Thank God for his power at work in you.

S: Pray for someone who doesn't believe in the resurrection.

TELL

Tell that person why you believe in the resurrection. Use the notes from February 20.

APRIL 24

THE PLOT TO KILL JESUS

PRAY

As you study the events that led to Jesus' death, pray to appreciate the importance of his life.

READ

John 11:45–57, 12:20–50

OBSERVE

We've studied Jesus' anointing and triumphal entry, which occur between these two passages.

vv. 45–48—What an amazing response to the raising of Lazarus! Though many believe, some go to the Pharisees to report the danger of Jesus' growing popularity. Rather than the Sanhedrin seriously examining what Jesus has done to see whether he is someone they should follow, they perceive him as a threat to their establishment. They are mostly concerned that they will lose their place as top dogs in the vassal state. It is very often religious leaders who are most opposed to Jesus, even today.

vv. 49–53—Caiaphas' statement in verse 50 is profoundly ironic. He means that it is expedient for them to sacrifice this itinerant preacher to stay out of trouble with the Romans. God fulfills the high priest's statement in a way that Caiaphas never imagined. Jesus would be the atoning sacrifice for not only the nation of Israel but every nation in history.

vv. 54–57—As we've seen previously, Jesus wasn't afraid of the death order. He was acutely conscious of God's timing and waited for the *kairos* moment to make his appearance in Jerusalem (Palm Sunday).

12:20–22—The request from the Greek pilgrims is the ideal statement from a seeker, *"We would like to see Jesus."* The Lord will reveal himself to anyone who really wants to see him.

vv. 23–26—Jesus taught a very similar truth in the Synoptic Gospels (Matt. 10:39; Mark 8:35; Luke 9:24). Here, he adds the image of a kernel of wheat. The seed that "dies" produces much fruit. Christ's death results in a host of believers who experience new life. Just as he was a servant, willing to die to serve the Father, so those who follow him must also be willing to do whatever it takes to serve our Lord.

vv. 27–33—The ultimate reason Jesus came to the earth was to die. Though he didn't look forward to the pain of the cross (remember his anguish in Gethsemane), he was willing to make that sacrifice. Once again, God the Father endorses the ministry of God the Son with a voice from heaven. Interestingly, only those with the ears of faith heard it clearly. Jesus indicates that his death on the cross will be a judgment against Satan, the prince of this world (Col. 2:15). At the same time that Satan is judged, those who trust in Jesus will be lifted up and set free from sin, in union with Christ.

vv. 34–36—Jesus always distinguishes between an honest question and an antagonistic one. He had clearly taught previously that he was the Son of Man and the Christ (Messiah). He urges the skeptical crowd to take advantage of the Light that he was while he was still available. If they put their trust in him, they would become sons of light.

vv. 37–50—People haven't changed much since the time of Christ. They still have the same responses to Jesus that we see in these verses. 1) Those who have known and seen Christ's works but still don't trust him as their Lord and Savior. The quotes from Isaiah make it clear that this unbelief is the will of God. Morris comments:

> But when John quotes "he hath blinded their eyes…," he does not mean that the blinding takes place without the will or against the will of these people. So with the hardening of their heart. These men choose evil. It was their own deliberate choice, their own fault. Make no mistake about that. Throughout his gospel, John has insisted upon the seriousness of the decision forced on the Jews by the presence of Jesus, on their responsibility, and on their guilt. He is not now removing all that. What he is now saying is that the hand of God is in the consequences of their choice (*cf.* The threefold 'God gave them up' in Rom. 1:24, 26, 28). (Morris, *The Gospel According to John*, 604)

2) Some believe in Christ but are afraid to stand up for him because they are more concerned about what people think than what God thinks. Are these people genuine Christians? Only God knows, but Matthew 10:32–33 would argue against their salvation. Jesus makes it clear that our response to him is our same response

to the Father. 3) The person who does not accept or obey Christ's words will be condemned by those very words on the Day of Judgment.

APPLY

v. 24—Are you truly willing to die for Christ? What about dying to your own ambitions and desires?

v. 26—Where do you see Jesus working today? That is where he wants you to serve him.

MEMORIZE

John 12:26

This is a powerful verse about service.

PRAY

A: Praise the Seed who fell to the ground.

C: Confess your unwillingness to let go of control of your life.

T: Thank God for opening your eyes to believe his Word.

S: Intercede for someone who is spiritually blind.

TELL

Discuss with a friend or your small group your understanding of John 12:42–44 and Matthew 10:32–33.

APRIL 25

LORD OF THE BASIN AND TOWEL

PRAY

Pray to have the opportunity to wash someone's feet (metaphorically) today.

READ

John 13:1–17, 31–35

OBSERVE

This is another powerful enacted parable in John's gospel.

v. 1—As we noted earlier, John does not record the Passover meal/Lord's Supper like the Synoptic Gospels. His focus is on what Jesus did before the meal. Perhaps the foot-washing was Christ's way of responding to the dispute among his disciples as to who was the greatest. It would end the debate! There is a question about the proper rendering of the last phrase of verse 1. The Greek phrase *eis telos* can either be translated "to the end/last" or "to the fullest extent." Most commentators argue for the latter translation, but in either case, it means that what follows is a demonstration of how much Jesus loved his disciples as they neared the cross.

vv. 2–5—The reference to Judas' betrayal lets us know that this is the Last Supper. In verses 3–5, we see clearly from John's language that this is an enacted parable of the incarnation. Jesus took off his outer clothing (he shed his heavenly garments—Phil. 2:7a), wrapped a towel around his waist (took on the garments of a servant—Phil. 2:7b), and washed his disciples' feet (he humbled himself—Phil. 2:8).

vv. 6–11—We could count on impulsive Peter to reject the servant role that Jesus assumed because Peter had a hard time with the idea of Jesus as the Suffering

Servant (Matt. 16:21–22). MacGregor writes, "Peter is humble enough to see the incongruity of Christ's action, yet proud enough to dictate to his Master" (Mac-Gregor, *A Historical and Theological Investigation of John's Gospel*, 426). Jesus gently but firmly corrects Peter, telling the disciple that he will understand the significance of this washing later. Christ's explanation makes it clear that the deeper significance of the foot-washing is that Christ's spirit will cleanse the baptized believer from daily sin.

vv. 12–17—The resumption of his place is a forecast of Christ's resurrection and ascension. The lesson of the foot-washing is simple. If Jesus came not to be served but to serve (Matt. 20:28), shouldn't we also humble ourselves and serve others in his name?

vv. 31–35—Jesus saw himself glorified even before the cross and resurrection because of his obedience. Judas' betrayal was part of the process of Christ's exaltation. It's in the context of Jesus' imminent departure that he gives the New Commandment. By far, the most frequent "one another" command in the New Testament is "love one another." When all else is said and done (and a lot more is usually said than done!), the world will know who are the true disciples of Christ by their authentic *agape* love for one another. The measure of that love is that it is to reflect the love that Jesus has shown us. That is certainly the highest possible standard to which we should aspire.

APPLY

v. 14—Are you regularly washing the feet, literally or figuratively, of someone else? What service is Jesus calling you to perform?

vv. 34–35—Are there any brothers or sisters in Christ that you are having difficulty loving? Ask God to fill you with the Holy Spirit so that you might demonstrate the fruit of the Spirit to those people.

MEMORIZE

John 13:34–35

This is the new commandment Jesus gives us.

PRAY

A: Praise the Servant Master.

C: Confess your reluctance to serve and to love.

T: Thank God for cleansing you from your sin.

S: Pray for that person (or those persons) whom you find difficult to love.

TELL

Tell those persons that you love them by your actions toward them the next time you see them.

APRIL 26

A PROMISED HOME IN HEAVEN AND COMFORT ON EARTH

PRAY

Pray for the presence and power of the Holy Spirit as you study the Word he inspired.

READ

John 14:1–31

OBSERVE

John 13–17 is known as The Upper Room Discourse. It contains crucial teaching from Jesus about the Holy Spirit. The theme that connects all of chapter 14 is Jesus' desire to comfort his disciples.

vv. 1–4—Christ's disciples would no doubt be troubled by his prophecy that he was leaving them to go to a place where they cannot come (John 13:33). Jesus makes it clear that while they can't come immediately, they will come eventually, if they trust in him (which is the same as trusting in the Father). The word in verse 2 translated "rooms" in the NIV is translated "mansions" in the KJV. It describes a permanent dwelling place and has the sense of a custom-designed room. We can't go too far with speculation, but it suggests that Jesus is preparing a unique place for each one of us. John emphasizes the Second Coming of Christ less than the other gospel writers, but it is unmistakable in verse 3.

vv. 5–11—Thomas, possibly the most transparently honest of the disciples, speaks up to raise the objection that they don't know where Jesus is going or the way to get there. Jesus answers with the sixth "I myself am" statement. He is the only Way to heaven; he is the ultimate Truth of God; and he is the source of Life abundant and Life eternal. Jesus claims exclusivity—there is no other way to God. This is a claim that is incendiary in our age of toleration in which the only absolute is that no one can claim absolute truth. But Christians are not claiming to be superior or exclusive, it is Jesus who makes this claim. To deny it and say that there are many roads to heaven is to deny Christ's words and his claim to truth. It will not be a popular message, but it's a message that genuine Christians cannot compromise. Philip expresses for the disciples, who are truly slow learners, their desire to see the Father. Jesus patiently reiterates that if they have seen him they have seen the Father. The evidence for his claim is found in Jesus' words and works.

vv. 12–14—Jesus makes one of the most amazing statements in the Bible in verse 12. How could we ever do greater things that Jesus did? Have you walked on water lately? Any luck feeding the entire church (let alone five thousand men plus women and children) with two dinner rolls and five sardines? The only logical way to interpret this verse is that Jesus is talking about the quantity of good deeds rather than the quality. Because those who trust in Christ are a worldwide multitude, millions of people now trust in him through the witness of believers. Hundreds of thousands of people have been healed in the name of Jesus in hospitals dedicated to him. Millions are fed in his name every week. He promises to answer the prayers of those who minister and pray in his name, in order to bring glory to the Father.

vv. 15–21—Jesus sends his Holy Spirit to those who love him and obey his commandments. Love and obedience are inseparable. Dietrich Bonhoeffer once wrote, "Only he who believes is obedient, and only he who is obedient believes. It is quite unbiblical to hold the first proposition without the second" (Bonhoeffer, *The Cost of Discipleship*, 63). The word Jesus uses for the Spirit in verse 16 is the Greek *parakletos*, which means "the one called alongside." Interestingly, the two opponents in a Greek courtroom were *diabolos*, the prosecutor (the devil), and *parakletos*, the defense attorney. This advocate not only comes alongside us as our defender against the evil one, he remains with us and lives within us. This is God's greatest gift!

vv. 22–27—In addition to comforting us and defending us, the Holy Spirit is our teacher, who reminds us of all that Jesus said and taught. It is he who gives us peace, even in the midst of trouble. The world defines peace as the absence of conflict. The Holy Spirit's peace is the presence of God in the midst of conflict. We are able to be unafraid because of the peace of the Spirit.

vv. 28–31—Some cults have argued from Jesus' words in verse 28 that he is not God since he says that the Father is greater than he. That is an extremely myopic view. Philippians 2 makes it very clear. Jesus was and is always God in his very nature (Phil. 2:6). However, at his incarnation, he voluntarily "made himself nothing," taking on the nature of a servant and giving up some of his heavenly prerogatives (Phil. 2:7). It is only in this limited sense and for this limited time that "the Father is greater than I." At his ascension, Jesus resumed his place in heaven (Phil. 2:10–11).

APPLY

v. 6—Are you willing to courageously testify that Jesus is the only way to God?

vv. 15–21—Are you disobeying the Lord in any way? This disobedience short-circuits your connection with the Holy Spirit. He will not abandon you, but he will not use you fully until you confess that sin.

v. 27—Ask God for his peace in the midst of whatever difficulties you are experiencing.

MEMORIZE

John 14:15

This is a crucial equation for disciples.

PRAY

A: Praise the Spirit of Truth who lives with you and is in you.

C: Confess and repent of any disobedience.

T: Thank God for his peace.

S: Pray that you would do great things for God today.

TELL

If you are having a struggle obeying God's Word in a particular area, share it with a trusted Christian friend who will pray with you and keep you accountable.

APRIL 27

I AM THE VINE AND YOU ARE THE BRANCHES

PRAY

Pray that you might abide in Christ and bear much fruit today.

READ

John 15:1–17

OBSERVE

This passage contains the seventh (the perfect number) and final "I myself am" statements in John's gospel.

vv. 1–3—When Jesus says, *"I am the true vine,"* he is making a thinly veiled statement about the nation of Israel. Just as the national symbol of the USA is the eagle, the national symbol of Israel was the vine. The nation had failed to bear fruit, and Jesus (along with his followers) would replace it in the eyes of the gardener. The Divine Gardener, as we've already seen a number of times, disciplines us so that we can be more fruitful. Not only does he completely remove that which is unproductive, he lovingly removes even the good that stands in the way of the best. Joseph Garlington gives a wonderful illustration of how a father's love is shown by discipline in his article, "The Pruning Process" (Garlington, *New Wine Magazine*, May 1980, 9). He married a widow with three sons who didn't want to call him dad. They referred to him as Reverend Garlington, but "most of the time they just called me 'him' as in, 'Go get *him* for dinner.' Then the boys did something that required discipline." He writes, "I called them together and read the Scriptures in Proverbs regarding discipline. Then we went down into the game room where I administered their punishment. The next day they began to call me Dad."

Discipline is a mark of love, and God is not a sentimental parent.

vv. 4–8—The key to bearing fruit is to "remain" or "abide" in Christ. The Greek verb tense means "keep on remaining in me." Christ wants an unbroken connection with us. He makes the stark statement, "apart from me you can do nothing." Does that mean that we can't go to work, drive a car, or do homework? Of course not. Unbelievers do all those things. What we cannot do is bear fruit that lasts (v. 16). If we practice the presence of God in our daily lives, he will produce lasting results in us, and in others through us.

vv. 9–17—Genuine love reflects the model of Jesus Christ. Jesus has loved us obediently and sacrificially (vv. 10, 13). The greatest measure of his love is to sacrifice one's life for a friend. Jesus loves us joyfully and wants us to have complete joy (v. 11). Few things have harmed the cause of Christ more than religious people with long faces. The wonderful message of this passage is that Jesus not only loves us, he likes us and calls us his friends. Jesus wants to bless his friends. He tells us to ask for whatever we need in his name, and the Father will respond. Verse 16 is a strong statement of election. Notice that Christ chose us for a purpose—that we would bear fruit for eternity. It's the most loving thing that we can do for someone.

APPLY

v. 2—When you go through hard times, remember that it might be God removing something good to prepare you for something better.

v. 4—Are you remaining in Christ? Are you aware of his presence throughout the day?

v. 11—Are you an example of Christian joy? You are the first gospel some people will read.

MEMORIZE

John 15:5

This verse can help you remember the importance of abiding in Christ.

PRAY

A: Praise the Vine and the Gardener.

C: Confess your wandering spirit.

T: Thank God for his great promises in this passage.

S: Pray that you might be aware of Christ's presence throughout the day.

TELL

If you are a parent, explain to your children how discipline is an expression of love.

APRIL 28

IF THEY PERSECUTED ME, THEY WILL PERSECUTE YOU

PRAY

Pray that you might be able to apply this difficult word to your life in the twenty-first century.

READ

John 15:18–16:4

OBSERVE

Jesus moves immediately from love in the preceding passage to hatred in this section.

vv. 18–21—As the branches are intimately related to the vine in joy and love, so also are servants related to their master in the way people treat them. Because Christians are identified with Christ, those who hate him will also hate us. We should expect nothing else.

vv. 22–25—Another inevitable analogy is that those who hate Jesus also hate the Father because they are one. Because Christ came to reveal the Father and he revealed him perfectly, they are without excuse. Even those who saw Christ's miracles turned from him. This was a fulfillment of Psalm 35:19 and Psalm 69:4, both of which describe those who hate without cause.

vv. 26–27—The Holy Spirit's testimony will accompany the testimony of the Church about Jesus Christ. In context, the implication is that people will reject his testimony as well.

16:1–4—Jesus warns us about persecution so that when it comes we won't be taken by surprise. The prophecy of verse 2 certainly came true in the early church, even in the person of Saul of Tarsus. If we are warned about opposition we should be prepared to weather the storm.

APPLY

v. 20—In the US, persecution isn't likely to take the first-century form of physical abuse. What are some more subtle types of persecution? Are you experiencing any? If not, why not (see 2 Tim. 3:12)?

MEMORIZE

John 15:18

This verse can give us great comfort when people reject us because of our faith.

PRAY

A: Praise the Spirit who tells us hard truth.

C: Confess your unwillingness to experience rejection for Christ.

T: Thank God that the Spirit comforts us.

S: Pray for courage to stand up for Christ whatever the cost.

TELL

Share with a Christian friend your perspective on persecution, and listen to his or her response.

APRIL 29

THE WORK OF THE HOLY SPIRIT

PRAY

Ask that the Spirit will turn any of your grief into joy today.

READ

John 16:5–33

OBSERVE

This is a key passage for our understanding of the Holy Spirit's person and work.

vv. 5–7—Can you imagine how difficult it would have been for the disciples to hear Jesus say, *"It is for your good that I am going away."* But it's true for the Church because the incarnate Christ could only be one place at a time. The Holy Spirit is omnipresent and therefore able to minister to believers all over the world.

vv. 8–11—This is the only place in Scripture which describes the Spirit's ministry to the world. The Spirit convicts people of the sin of unbelief (which then enables them to turn to Christ). The Spirit shows people that righteousness comes only from Christ's atoning work. He also is God's instrument of judgment against Satan, which was accomplished at the cross.

vv. 12–15—This is the Spirit's ministry to believers, to guide us into all truth. He is that still small voice that reminds us of what Christ teaches us through his Word. Verse 14 describes both the process of inspiration of the writers of the New Testament and the process of illumination of the readers of the New Testament.

vv. 16–33—Jesus' enigmatic comment in verse 16 is troubling to his disciples. Though it isn't one hundred percent clear, it seems that Jesus is preparing them for what is about to happen in Jerusalem:

1. He will go to the cross, all alone (v. 31). The world will rejoice while the disciples mourn.
2. He will rise again and see them once more. It will be like a new birth—pain followed by joy.
3. He will return to the Father after triumphing over the world, and he will leave his peace (in the midst of trouble) with his followers.

APPLY

vv. 8–11—Recognize that it's only the Holy Spirit who can convict people of sin. Our job is to share God's truth. His job is to bring people to conviction and repentance.

v. 13—Be sure to remember to ask the Spirit to lead you into all truth as you study the Word he inspired.

MEMORIZE

John 16:33

Remember that as Christ has overcome the world, so will we (Rom. 8:37).

PRAY

A: Praise the Spirit who comforts and convicts.

C: Confess your sin of unbelief.

T: Thank God for guiding you into all truth.

S: Pray for whatever you need in Jesus' name (16:24).

TELL

Share with a brother or sister how God has given you peace in the midst of trouble.

APRIL 30

CHRIST'S HIGH PRIESTLY PRAYER

PRAY

Pray that your prayer life would be enriched by the example of Jesus.

READ

John 17:1–26

OBSERVE

This prayer probably takes place in the Upper Room before Jesus prays in Gethsemane (18:1).

vv. 1–5—Jesus first prays for himself. His first petition is crucial—that the Father and Son are glorified. John Piper writes:

> Redemption, salvation, and restoration are not God's ultimate goal. These he performs for the sake of something greater: namely, the enjoyment he has in glorifying himself. (Piper, *Desiring God*, 33)

Verse 2 tells us who is the source of eternal life; verse 3 tells us what it is—knowing God through Jesus Christ. Jesus' ascension would restore Jesus to his preincarnate glory.

vv. 6–19—Christ's prayer in these verses is specifically directed to his disciples. Keep in mind that there were many more than the twelve who trusted in him and followed him. In keeping with the strong note of election struck in verse 2, Jesus defines his disciples as "those whom you gave me out of the world." The Greek word for the church, *ekklesia*, literally means "those called out" of the world. But notice that the disciples aren't taken out of the world (v. 15). They are to be salt and light, *in* the world but not *of* it. Jesus wants neither isolation (not in it, not of it), nor imitation (not in it but of it), nor assimilation (in it and of it), but transformation (in it but not of it). Christ indicates that a primary purpose for his disciples was to glorify him (v. 10). He prayed (and prays—Rom. 8:34) for our protection (vv. 12–16) and for our sanctification.

vv. 20–26—The prayer changes at this point from petitions for those who followed him around 30 AD to all those who would hear (and read) their message and put their trust in Christ. Notice how tremendously important it was to Jesus for his followers to be united. If we are one, just as the Father and Son are one, the world will know that the Father sent the Son and that the Father loves us as he loves the Son.

That is an awesome responsibility! Some have argued that this unity precludes different denominations. This is the strongest passage to support that position, but it's not thoroughly convincing. Jesus isn't talking about the outward structure of the Church but the inward attitude of the Church. True believers must be one in heart and mind even if we are physically separate. The Church's witness depends on our unity. Verses 24–26 are wonderful promises for the future. Jesus prays that believers, too, will be glorified and will see his glory in heaven. He also promises that he will continue to make himself known so that future believers might experience his love in the power of the Holy Spirit.

APPLY

v. 10—Is your life goal to glorify God and enjoy him forever?

vv. 15–16—Jesus wants us to be "in the world" but not "of the world." What does that mean to you in practice?

v. 23—What are some ways that you can express your unity with members of your own church? Other churches?

MEMORIZE

John 17:22

This will help you remember that Jesus has glorified you so that you might be one with other believers.

PRAY

A: Praise the Righteous Father.

C: Confess those things you've done that have not contributed to the unity of the church.

T: Thank God for the gift of unity and the promise of glorification.

S: Ask for sanctification.

TELL

Discuss with a Christian friend or a small group what Christ's prayer for unity should mean to twenty-first-century Christians.

MAY

MAY 1

THE RISEN CHRIST APPEARS TO HIS DISCIPLES

PRAY

Ask God to make you open to what Jesus means when he says, *"As the Father has sent me, I am sending you."*

READ

John 20:19–21:25

OBSERVE

We've covered John 18:1 through 20:19 in our study of the passages common to the gospels. In the events surrounding Jesus' death, John parallels the Synoptic Gospels more closely than anywhere else. His account of Jesus' post-resurrection appearances adds a great deal to our understanding of those incredible days!

vv. 19–23—Though R. C. Sproul cautions us against assuming that the risen Christ passed through the door and into the room where the huddled disciples sat (Sproul, *Knowing Scripture*, 46), it's hard to see any other intention from John's language. He seems to be describing a supernatural appearance, though Jesus immediately calms their fears by showing his hands and side. Before the dramatic appearance of the Holy Spirit at Pentecost, Jesus gave him to his followers in a quiet but dramatic fashion. Their spiritual power and authority as leaders of the infant Church would enable them to exercise church discipline.

vv. 24–29—We mentioned earlier that one of the reasons Thomas may not have been with the other disciples is that he was dealing with his own grief at disappointing his Lord (John 11:16). Though Thomas is a pragmatist and empiricist, when proof is offered, his response is perfect when he says, *"My Lord and my God!"*

As a message to future believers, Jesus emphasizes that faith is believing what is not seen (Heb. 11:1), not requiring proof.

vv. 30–31—As we noted in the introduction to John (April 6), the great purpose of this gospel is articulated in verse 31. Every part of John's gospel fits into this purpose.

21:1–14—It seems like the disciples weren't exactly sure what they were to do after they met the risen Lord, so they did what was natural and went fishing. It's no mystery why John recognized that it was Jesus on the shore. The circumstances were very similar to what they had experienced three years before (Luke 5:5–7).

vv. 15–17—There is a wonderful parallelism in the way Jesus restores Peter. Just as The Rock denied Jesus three times when he turned to jelly in the courtyard, he is asked three times to affirm his love for the Master. Christ's initial question *"Simon, son of John, do you truly love me more than these?"* is difficult to pinpoint. Jesus could mean:

1. Do you love me more than the other disciples love me? It would seem odd that Jesus was asking Peter to compare his love with another person's.
2. Do you love me more than you love the other disciples? This is possible, for Jesus commanded us to love him more than anyone else and Peter's connection with the other disciples seems to be solidly established despite his denial.
3. Do you love me more than you love these boats and nets? It might have been a temptation for Peter to return to the simple life of fishing rather than the complicated path of following Christ.

It's impossible to be sure what Jesus meant, but options 2 and 3 seem more likely. Some commentators make a big deal about the fact that John changes the Greek words for love (from *agape* to *phileo*) and sheep (from *arnia*—lambs—to *probata*—sheep) in the three questions, but it was John's common practice as a writer to vary his language when describing something. For example, his title as Beloved Disciple sometimes uses the word *agape* and other times *phileo*. The variation isn't meant to describe someone or something different. Key things to note in this dialogue are that Peter knew who Jesus was—"Lord, you know all things." Jesus makes it clear that a way we show our love for him is by taking care of his children.

vv. 18–19—Jesus predicts that Peter's life will end as his master's did—at a cross. Tradition says that Peter was crucified in Rome in the mid-60s AD, asking to be crucified upside down because he didn't feel worthy to die in the same way as his Lord. The verb tense of "Follow me!" has the force of, "Keep on following me!" Morris writes, "Peter had followed Christ, but not continuously in the past. For the future he was to follow steadfastly in the ways of the Lord" (Morris, *The Gospel According to John*, 877).

vv. 20–24—Jesus doesn't tell us anyone's story but our own (a fact C. S. Lewis emphasizes in his *Chronicles of Narnia*). According to tradition, John was the only disciple who was not martyred, dying in exile on the island of Patmos at the end of the first century. It appears that someone other than John wrote the last phrase of verse 24. It was most likely an elder from the church at Ephesus, where John served for many years.

v. 25—As we close our study of the gospels, it's interesting to consider that these books are only snapshots of the Savior. The gospel writers selected stories from Jesus' life that most conveyed the message the Spirit wanted to communicate through them. Jesus' life was far richer than even these rich portrayals. Maybe we'll see the videos in heaven!

APPLY

20:29—Do you have the faith to believe that God is at work even when you don't see it?

21:15–17—How does Jesus want you to take care of his sheep? Is there a ministry in the Church that you are gifted to fill which involves caring for people?

MEMORIZE

John 21:25

Remember that Jesus is always bigger than we picture him.

PRAY

A: Praise God that he is gracious to forgive and restore us.

C: Confess the times you've betrayed him.

T: Thank God for the gospels and that he provides more than we expect.

S: Ask God to direct you to that caring ministry he has prepared for you.

TELL

Without using words, tell someone that you love Jesus. Do it by caring for them.

MAY 2
THE ACTS OF THE HOLY SPIRIT

PRAY

Ask God for a fresh experience of the Holy Spirit as you study Acts.

READ

Acts 1:1–26

OBSERVE

Acts is the sequel to Luke's gospel. The message of Acts is a confirmation of what Jesus promised in John—the ministry would continue in the Church by the power of the Holy Spirit. Though the familiar name of this book is "The Acts of the Apostles," it is more profoundly "The Acts of the Holy Spirit." The book records what happens when the Holy Spirit fills people. E. M. Blaiklock gives a stirring overview of Acts in his commentary:

> The story moves rapidly from episode to episode. It shows the Church in birth and being, in experiment and action, as devoted minds sought after and apprehended truth, shaping policy and purpose in the process. It reveals the growing vitality of the Christian faith as it outgrew prejudice and limitation. It tells of men, who had known horizons little wider than those of Palestine, conceiving bold projects of world evangelism, and moving out in the strength of indomitable faith to reach the nations with their story. (Blaiklock, *The Acts of the Apostles*, 11)

Dr. Luke probably wrote this book sometime between 60 and 70 AD. A unique aspect of Acts is the first-person narrative in several chapters (16:10–17, 20:5–21:18, and 27:1–28:16). Luke was an eyewitness to much of what he wrote, and he would have heard direct reports from Paul, Peter, and the other apostles about the rest.

vv. 1–3—Theophilus ("lover of God") is referred to as "most excellent Theophilus" in Luke 1:4. It's very likely that he was a Roman official who was either a committed Christian or a serious inquirer. Verses 2 and 3 are a summary of the end of Luke.

vv. 4–8—This is the first time we read of Jesus' promise that they would be "baptized with the Holy Spirit." The disciples are still somewhat bound by their pre-Christian worldview. They want the glory of Israel to be restored by her Messiah. Jesus suggests that this will happen at his return, but they should be more concerned about what they do before then. He doesn't suggest that they consider sharing the Gospel. He says, "You *will* be my witnesses." They (and we) are to begin where they are (Jerusalem), move out from there to the surrounding area (Judea), go to another area in the same country (Samaria), and finally make it to the entire world.

vv. 9–11—In Scripture, a cloud is a sign of the presence of God. The two men in white might be the same angels who were at the empty tomb (Luke 24:4). They indicate that Christ's return will be bodily and visible, just as his ascension was.

vv. 12–14—The list of the eleven disciples, soon to be apostles ("those sent out"), includes "Judas, son of James." This is a name we haven't seen before. It is most likely the one called Thaddeus ("big chest") in the Synoptics. Judas was a very common name. He was probably given a nickname to distinguish him from Judas Iscariot. With the passing of the betrayer, he reclaimed his given name. Notice that the resurrection had made believers of Jesus' brothers. Jesus appeared to his brother James (1 Cor. 15:7) who became a prominent leader in the early Church and wrote the New Testament book bearing his name.

vv. 15–22—There's no question that Peter has now lived up to the name Jesus gave him. He is the leader of the disciple band. Notice that the number of believers was again up around one hundred twenty from the low point (John 6:66) when many couldn't handle Jesus' teaching. Some commentators see a conflict between Matthew 27, which states that Judas hung himself, and this account in Acts. The two are easily harmonized. Judas hung himself, but his body fell to the ground, hit a rock, and burst open. Both accounts refer to it as the Field of Blood. Peter applies Scripture adroitly, calling for Judas' replacement. From this point on, an apostle was defined as someone who had seen the Lord. Peter lays out the job description clearly—to be "a witness with us of his resurrection."

vv. 23–26—The disciples used Scripture (Ps. 69:25 and Ps. 109:8), prayer, and common sense (it should be someone who knew Jesus) to select two candidates. The casting of lots (probably two stones with Barsabbas' and Matthias' names written on them) was a biblical option (Lev. 16:8), at least prior to the coming of the Spirit in power. Some commentators try to make a case against the casting of lots, saying that Matthias was never heard of again. That's true of most of the other disciples/apostles.

APPLY

v. 8—What is your strategy for witnessing in your hometown, your region, your state, and to the ends of the earth?

v. 14—Is there anyone with whom you are joining together constantly in prayer? If not, why not?

MEMORIZE

Acts 1:8

This is another statement of the Great Commission.

PRAY

A: Praise the ascended Christ.

C: Confess your reluctance to witness.

T: Thank God for the gift of the Spirit's power.

S: Ask God to fill you with his power today.

TELL

Share the good news of the risen Christ with someone in your Jerusalem.

MAY 3

THE RUSH OF A MIGHTY WIND

PRAY

Ask that the power of the Holy Spirit would be more than an intellectual conviction for you. Pray that he would empower you to glorify the Father and the Son.

READ

Acts 2:1–13

OBSERVE

It's crucial to remember that the Holy Spirit did not *come* at Pentecost. The Spirit is eternal, and he (not *it*) has been at work in the world since creation (Gen. 1:2). The Spirit came in power on the day of Pentecost and from that point on, he takes up residence in those who believe in Jesus Christ.

vv. 1–3—Pentecost was one of the three great Jewish festivals. Every male Jew living within twenty miles of Jerusalem was legally bound to attend. The word "Pentecost" means "the fiftieth." Another name for Pentecost was The Feast of Weeks, because it fell on the fiftieth day, a "week of weeks" after Passover. It commemorated the giving of the law on Mt. Sinai. As the law was the dominant reality of the Old Testament church, the Spirit becomes the dominant reality of the New Testament church. Its agricultural significance was that it was "the day of the first fruits" since it marked the beginning of the wheat harvest. At the first Pentecost after Christ's resurrection, we see the first fruits of the new creation.

Pentecost marks the birthday of the Christian Church. What a birthday party it was! There were no wax candles, but the believers became like human candles as tongues of fire were distributed and rested on each one of them. A mighty wind came, but instead of blowing out the candles, it caused them to be more on fire!

Both of these manifestations were the fulfillment of Scripture. Jesus used the same word (*pneuma*) for "the Spirit" and for "wind" in John 3:8. The Holy Spirit's work is usually unseen and unpredictable, but it is very powerful. Verse 2 tells us that the Spirit filled the whole house in which the believers were standing. The same Holy Spirit can fill us completely as well. In Ephesians 5:18, Paul writes, *"Do not be drunk with wine, but be filled with the Holy Spirit."*

vv. 4–13—The third physical evidence of the Holy Spirit at Pentecost was the speaking in other tongues. The Greek word is *glossalalia*, and it appears that there are two types of *glossalalia* in the New Testament. In this passage, the believers speak in languages they did not know. Pilgrims to Jerusalem from many different countries (the population in Jerusalem during the feasts often swelled from 250,000 to 2,000,000) heard the Spirit-filled believers speaking in their native languages. In 1 Corinthians 14, Paul describes *glossalalia* as an ecstatic utterance that cannot be understood without someone who has the gift of interpretation.

The theological significance of speaking in tongues at Pentecost was to reverse the curse of the Tower of Babel described in Genesis 11. At Babel, different tongues brought division and disorder. At Pentecost, the gift of tongues brought unity and joy. At Babel, confusion and chaos reigned supreme. At Pentecost, the Christian Church was born and Christ reigned supreme. At Babel, men attempted to erect a monument to their pride. At Pentecost, men and women surrendered their pride and relied on the Holy Spirit. There were scoffers, as there always are. Peter will answer them in the passage we study tomorrow.

APPLY

v. 2—Jesus said, *"How much more will your Father in heaven give the Holy Spirit to those who ask Him!"* (Luke 11:13). Ask the Father to fill you with the Holy Spirit today.

MEMORIZE

Acts 2:2–3

PRAY

A: Praise the mighty Spirit.

C: Confess your timid faith.

T: Thank God for the birthday of the Church.

S: Ask for the fullness of the Spirit.

TELL

Discuss why God sent the Spirit in such a dramatic way at Pentecost.

MAY 4

THE FIRST CHRISTIAN SERMON

PRAY

Ask God to help you apply this sermon to your life today.

READ

Acts 2:14–40

OBSERVE

The most impressive thing about Pentecost wasn't the rush of the mighty wind, the tongues of fire, or the speaking in tongues. It was the power of the Holy Spirit in one person, the Apostle Peter.

vv. 14–21—Peter begins his message with a common sense observation, *"These men aren't drunk.... It's only nine in the morning!"* He then shows the crowd that this is a fulfillment of Joel 2:28–32, the promised outpouring of the Spirit in the last days. The Spirit is given to *all* people. Pentecost is a missionary event. From that time on, the Church knew that God, the Father of our Lord Jesus Christ, is the God of all nations, not just the nation of Israel.

vv. 22–23—The Apostle isn't afraid to confront his listeners. They had seen Jesus' miracles but rather than praising God, they crucified him. Though this was part of God's predestined plan, they are nevertheless guilty for their part in it. He even repeats in verse 36: "whom you crucified."

vv. 24–36—The basic *kerygma* (proclamation) of the early Church included these truths:

1. God sent Jesus, the Messiah from the house of David, to earth.
2. He lived a sinless life and died an atoning death at the hands of evil men.
3. Jesus rose from the dead by the power of God.
4. He was exalted to the right hand of God.
5. The ascended Lord pours out the Holy Spirit.
6. The crucified, resurrected, and ascended Jesus is both Lord and Messiah.
7. Forgiveness of sins (salvation) comes by putting your trust in him.

vv. 37–40—A sure sign that the Holy Spirit was moving in Peter's listeners is that they were convicted of sin and wanted to do something about it. Peter tells them to change their minds (the literal meaning of "repent") and be baptized for the forgiveness of sins. When they do, they will receive the gift of the Holy Spirit. The Spirit is given at conversion not at some later time. This is a promise for families. The first hearers took it seriously. We'll see several family baptisms in Acts. A loving and effective preacher doesn't comfort the people with peace when there is no peace. A loving preacher warns his listeners that they're in danger if they miss the message of salvation.

APPLY

v. 37—Have you been "cut to the heart" lately by a sermon? If not, why not?

MEMORIZE

Acts 2:38

This is the New Testament formula for adult conversion.

PRAY

A: Praise the ascended Lord.

C: Confess your sins and ask for forgiveness.

T: Thank God for the promise to save your family.

S: Intercede for your children (if you are a parent) or for your parents (if you are a child).

TELL

Is there a friend who is an unbeliever whom you could lovingly warn?

MAY 5

THE FIRST CHRISTIAN CHURCH

PRAY

Ask God to teach you as you learn about the life of the first Christian church.

READ

Acts. 2:41–47

OBSERVE

v. 41—The first example of large-scale evangelism is a ringing success as Peter's message results in three thousand new believers. It's important to recognize that those new believers were probably a microcosm of Jerusalem at Pentecost. Some would have been from places as far away as Rome. With their newfound faith, they decided to remain in Jerusalem to be discipled. That explains to a great degree the unique sharing ministry of the first Christian church.

vv. 42–47—A church of three thousand people would have been difficult to manage. The disciples wisely decided to divide the church into a number of smaller groups that met in homes. There were four major aspects of the church's life and witness that should be present in every contemporary believer and church as well. These activities form an easy to remember acrostic, since the Church is the bride of Christ:

1. Worship—*"They devoted themselves ... to prayer.... Everyone was filled with awe.... Every day they continued to meet together in the temple courts ... praising God...."* The first Christian church worshipped every day and worship was at the heart of their common experience.

2. Instruction—*"They devoted themselves to the apostles' teaching."* John Stott writes: "We note that those new converts were not enjoying a mystical experience which led them to despise their mind or disdain theology. Anti-intellectualism and the fullness of the Spirit are mutually incompatible, because the Holy Spirit is the Spirit of truth. Nor did those early disciples imagine that, because they had received the Spirit, he was the only teacher they needed and they could dispense with human teachers. On the contrary, they sat at the apostles' feet, hungry to receive instruction, and they persevered in it." (Stott, *The Spirit, the Church and the World*, 82)

3. Fellowship—*"They devoted themselves … to the fellowship, to the breaking of bread…. All the believers were together and had everything in common. Selling their possessions and goods, they gave to anyone as he had need…. They broke bread in their homes and ate together with glad and sincere hearts."* The Greek word *koinonia* occurs several times in this passage. It is translated "fellowship" in verse 42, but "in common" in verse 44. Fellowship is sharing our common life in Jesus Christ in the power of the Holy Spirit. This would probably have been the most notable thing about the first church in history. Since the pilgrims had no jobs in Jerusalem, their brothers and sisters who lived in the Holy City were willing to provide for them by selling their own possessions. The love of this church was impressive.

4. Evangelism—*"… enjoying the favor of all the people. And the Lord added to their number daily those who were being saved."* There was no evident program of evangelism, but people were breaking down the doors to become part of this body. The amazing love the believers had for each other had to be attractive to the watching world. But it was *the Lord* who added to their number daily. An important part of his working had to be through the devoted prayers of the church. Stott writes, "He did not add them to the Church without saving them (no nominal Christianity at the beginning) nor did he save them without adding them to the Church (no solitary Christianity either)" (Stott, *The Spirit, the Church and the World*, 87).

APPLY

vv. 41–47—In which of these areas—worship, instruction, fellowship, evangelism—do you most need to grow? Where does your church most need to grow?

MEMORIZE

Acts 2:47b

This is a goal for your church.

PRAY

A: Praise the God who changes lives.

C: Confess your lack of devotion.

T: Thank God for the gift of Christian fellowship.

S: Ask God to show you the area in which you most need to grow.

TELL

Tell a close brother or sister in Christ that if they have a need, and you have the resources to meet it, you will gladly meet their need.

MAY 6

A HEALING PROVIDES A HEARING

Ask God to give you an opportunity to bless someone and share the Gospel.

READ

Acts 3:1–26

OBSERVE

This is the first healing miracle performed by the Church after Christ's ascension.

v. 1—In the early days of the church, people continued to worship in the temple as we saw in the passage yesterday. It was only after the fall of Jerusalem that Christian worship became distinct from temples and synagogues.

vv. 2–10—It took a real step of faith for Peter to confidently command the beggar to walk. Peter could not have been certain that the power of Christ would enable this healing, but he believed and God honored his assurance. The sheer joy of the beggar must have been a tremendous encouragement to Peter and John and the church. The story is told that when Francis of Assisi went to Rome, one of the cardinals took him on a tour of the Vatican. When they arrived at the vault where the church's wealth was stored, the cardinal boasted to Francis, "The Church can no longer say, 'Silver or gold I do not have,' can we?" Francis' reply was, "Neither can the Church say to the poor of this world, 'In the name of Jesus Christ of Nazareth, walk'!"

vv. 11–23—Peter uses the amazement surrounding the healing as an opportunity to place the focus exactly where it belongs—on the power of God. Once again, we see the essentials of the early church's *kerygma*. God sent his servant Jesus; the author of life was put to death by your evil; God raised him from the dead; by the power of Jesus this miracle took place; repent and come to the Lord in faith. Peter promises a dual benefit for those who repent and turn to God. Forgiveness is described as "your sins may be wiped out," which comes from the writing practice of that day. Barclay writes, "Ancient writing was upon papyrus, and the ink used had no acid in it. It therefore did not bite into the papyrus as modern ink does; it simply lay upon the top of it. To erase the writing a man might take a wet sponge and simply wipe it away" (Barclay, *The Acts of the Apostles*, 32). The second promised blessing is "that times of refreshing may come from the Lord." God not only wipes away our sins. He wipes away our guilt and gives us renewal, relief, and refreshment.

vv. 24–26—Peter had already quoted Moses predicting the Prophet who would come from among the people. He adds Samuel and Abraham as two other prophetic strands in the Old Testament. It was important for the Jews to see that the ministry of Jesus Christ was fully attested to by the Old Testament. Peter effectively speaks their language.

APPLY

v. 6—Do you see a connection between reliance on silver or gold and lack of spiritual power?

v. 12—Are you careful to give the glory to God when people notice things you've done?

MEMORIZE

Acts 3:6

Remember the riches that really matter.

PRAY

A: Praise the God of Abraham, Isaac, and Jacob.

C: Confess all of your sins so that they may be wiped out.

T: Thank God for his healing power.

S: Intercede for someone who needs that power, either physically, emotionally, relationally, or spiritually.

TELL

Does God still heal today? Discuss that question with a friend or your small group.

MAY 7

OBEYING GOD RATHER THAN MEN

PRAY

Ask God for wisdom and courage for when to disobey human authorities.

READ

Acts 4:1–22

OBSERVE

This is the first fulfillment of Jesus' prophecy, *"If they persecuted me, they will persecute you also"* (John 15:20). It would be far from the last.

vv. 1–4—The priests and the Sadducees were allies since many of the priests were more liberal theologically, and the Sadducees were politically connected with the Romans. They bring the captain of the temple guard as their muscle when they confront Peter and John. Since they couldn't refute the preaching of the resurrection, they wanted to censor it. Throwing Peter and John into prison was ineffective because the Church always grows through persecution. Another two thousand men are added to the Church.

vv. 5–12—The meeting with the Sanhedrin fulfills another promise the Lord made to his disciples: *"When they arrest you, do not worry about what to say or how to say it. At that time you will be given what to say, for it will not be you speaking, but the Spirit of your Father speaking through you"* (Matt. 10:19–20). The Spirit speaks through Peter in a powerful way. Contrary to the law's demand, Peter doesn't even know the charge against him and John. He assumes that they were arrested because of their healing of the crippled man rather than their preaching of the resurrection. He then proceeds to preach the resurrection! Notice that Peter personalizes Psalm 118:22.

The psalm reads, "the stone *the* builders rejected." Peter makes it, "the stone *you* builders rejected." If this were not bold enough, he makes the uncompromising assertion that Jesus is the only one who offers salvation. Bruce writes:

> From the once despised but now glorified Jesus, and from him alone, could true salvation come—not merely healing from a physical affliction, such as the cripple at the Beautiful Gate had received, but healing from the spiritual disease of sin and deliverance from coming judgment as well. (Bruce, *The Book of Acts*, 100–101)

vv. 13–22—When the opponents of Christianity can't squelch the Gospel by argument or lies, they try to do it with force. Because of the Sanhedrin's connections to Roman power, their threats were not idle warnings. But Peter and John would no longer be intimidated. The man who had cowered in the courtyard stands tall in the Sanhedrin and declares that they will obey God rather than them. The biblical position toward disobedience is that we are commanded to submit to ruling authorities (Rom. 13:1) except when they command us to do something God forbids (e.g., the Hebrew midwives who refused Pharaoh's order to kill Jewish boys—Exod. 1:15–21) or forbid us to do something God commands (such as witnessing to the resurrection of Christ or praying to God—Dan. 6:5–24). Though good public opinion would preserve the apostles' lives for a while, it wouldn't constrain the evil authorities for long.

APPLY

v. 12—This is another uncompromising statement of Christ's unique sufficiency. Are you bold enough to proclaim it in the face of societal opposition?

vv. 19–20—Are you obeying the ruling powers in their proper sphere of authority—like observing the speed limit? Is there an area in which a law clearly violates Scripture and God would want you to disobey?

MEMORIZE

Acts 4:12

PRAY

A: Praise the stone the builders rejected who has become the capstone.

C: Confess your lack of boldness.

T: Thank God for the Spirit who gives us the words to say.

S: Intercede for those proclaiming the Gospel in hostile lands where threats are very real.

TELL

Discuss with your small group when civil disobedience is appropriate for Christians.

MAY 8

THE EARLY CHURCH AT PRAYER

PRAY

Ask to find some people to pray with who believe in the power of prayer like the first Christians did.

READ

Acts 4:23–37

OBSERVE

Like Acts 2:41–47, we can see powerful models in the early Church for what God wants us to be and do.

vv. 23–31—There are some wonderful aspects to the prayer meeting of this early Church that we can learn from.

1. When they were released from prison, Peter and John went first to the Church to share their joy with the Body of Christ. It's not that their families were unimportant, but the Church was the priority in their human relationships! This is an important truth to remember in our contemporary church when the exaltation of the family threatens to take on cult-like proportions.
2. The Church believed in and focused on the sovereignty of God. When we affirm that God is in control, we can trust him to take control of every situation.
3. These believers prayed the Scriptures. One way that we can be certain that we are praying in God's will is to use his Word in prayer. At least one

person (the passage suggests that they all knew it) had memorized Psalm 2:1–2 .

4. They not only knew Scripture, they knew how to apply it to their historical situation. Herod and Pontius Pilate were the rulers who gathered together against the Lord's Anointed. But notice that the Church saw this as part of God's sovereign plan (v. 28), not some horrible tragedy.

5. They applied God's Word and its promises in bold, faith-filled prayer. Can you imagine what it must have been like when the Holy Spirit actually shook the building where they were meeting? What a dramatic answer to prayer!

vv. 32-37—These verses are largely a reiteration and reemphasis of the Acts 2:41–47 passage. Calvin writes poignantly in his commentary on Acts about this passage:

> We must have hearts harder than iron if we are not moved by the reading of this narrative. In those days the believers gave abundantly of what was their own; we in our day are content not just jealously to retain what we possess, but callously to rob others.... They sold their own possessions in those days; in our day it is the lust to purchase that reigns supreme. (Calvin, *Acts 1–13*, 130)

Geneva in the sixteenth century sounds a lot like America in the twenty-first century, doesn't it! This passage also introduces a major character in Acts, Barnabas, the Son of Encouragement. Joseph of Cyprus was a Levite, a member of the priestly tribe who was now part of the diaspora—Jews living in other countries. Levites in the New Testament were distinguished from priests by their function. Their role was to assist the priest in the worship service. Joseph probably had another job in Cyprus, but came to Jerusalem for Pentecost to assist in the worship services at the temple. He would have been very knowledgeable in the Old Testament Scriptures. Barnabas must have been a man of some means. Though he was from Cyprus, he apparently owned land in Jerusalem (or nearby), which he was able to sell. Verse 37 shows his generous spirit. It is also an important note of foreshadowing for what is to follow in chapter 5.

APPLY

v. 24—Do you trust in the sovereignty of God? How does this theological truth affect your life?

vv. 29–30—Are you praying boldly?

vv. 32–34—Are you willing to hold lightly to your possessions? Do you see anyone in need who could use something you own or the money from its sale?

MEMORIZE

Acts 4:31

This verse is a reminder of what can happen when God's people pray.

PRAY

A: Praise the Sovereign Lord.

C: Confess your selfishness and greed.

T: Thank God for providing you with an abundance.

S: Ask God to enable you to speak his Word with great boldness.

TELL

Pray for an opportunity to share God's Word boldly with someone.

MAY 9

LIVING A LIE CAN KILL YOU

PRAY

Pray for the ability to look honestly at your practice of telling the truth.

READ

Acts 5:1–11

OBSERVE

People who say ,"The God of the Old Testament is full of wrath and judgment, but the God of the New Testament is loving and merciful" must not read passages like this!

vv. 1–2—Ananias and Sapphira wanted to impress the Church with their generosity. Their deception was a matter of degree.

vv. 3–4—Peter makes it clear that this was more than an exaggeration, they "lied to the Holy Spirit." Any time we shade the truth we violate the Spirit of truth. When Peter says, "You have not lied to men but to God," we need to understand it much like David's statement in Psalm 51:4, "Against you, you only, have I sinned." David also sinned against Bathsheba and Uriah (and the entire nation of Israel, just as Ananias and Sapphira sinned against the church) but in the ultimate sense, our sin offends a holy God.

vv. 5–11—Some commentators suggest that Ananias' death was psychosomatic, a heart attack brought on by the stress of being found out. But it's unlikely that this would happen twice. Peter would not have been so bold as to declare Sapphira's fate if he had not been confident that this was the judgment of God. It's no surprise that "great fear seized the whole church and all who heard about these events." If God began to strike down all those who lied to the Church (in their baptismal, church membership, or church officer vows, for example) how many contemporary churches would be decimated? The bottom line is that God considers telling the truth as more crucial than we do.

APPLY

v. 8—Are you aware of any lies you have told recently? God wants you to confess, repent, and correct what you've said. Will you have the courage to do that?

MEMORIZE

Acts 5:4c

PRAY

A: Praise the Spirit of Truth.

C: Confess your tendency to shade the truth.

T: Thank God for his mercy and patience.

S: Ask God to guard your tongue today.

TELL

Tell someone whom you have deceived that you're sorry and correct the record.

MAY 10

SIGNS, WONDERS, AND WISDOM

PRAY

Pray that God would give you the wisdom of Gamaliel.

READ

Acts 5:12–42

OBSERVE

God uses an unbeliever to advance his kingdom.

vv. 12–16—Solomon's Colonnade was one of two beautiful sets of columns surrounding the temple area in a very visible area. The believers who had hidden in the Upper Room before Pentecost were now embolded. Everyone was welcome, but unbelievers didn't join them. It's likely they were afraid after they heard the news of Ananias and Sapphira. The apostles continued Jesus' healing ministry. Peter's shadow was as powerful as the hem of Jesus' garment had been.

vv. 17–26—Luke pinpoints the motives of the high priest's posse—they were jealous of the apostles. They try to silence the Gospel and fail again. This is the first of several jailbreaks performed by angels. Can you imagine the looks on the faces of the temple guards when they saw the apostles standing in the temple court, teaching the people? They must have been livid, but they were smart enough in their public relations not to get rough with the apostles and risk a riot.

vv. 27–33—The Sanhedrin had threatened them before (4:21) but it had no effect on these courageous witnesses. Further intimidation was ineffective also. Peter repeats the proclamation of the early church: you killed Jesus; God raised him from the dead; he is exalted as Prince and Savior; he offers forgiveness; he sends the Holy Spirit to those who believe and obey. The response of the Sanhedrin is predictable given their response to Jesus: "Let's kill them."

vv. 34–39—Gamaliel, who was the teacher of the Apostle Paul (Acts 22:3), shows why he was so highly respected. He uses the concrete examples of the revolutionaries Theudas and Judas the Galilean, whose followers dispersed when they were killed. If the apostles were only operating on their own steam, they would certainly fail like the others. However, if God is behind them, no one can stop them and those who try will be fighting God himself. One commentator notes of Gamaliel's words:

> Such advice was typically Pharisaic in both temper and content. It picked up the leading point in their theology, namely, that God rules the world by a wise providence that is over all. Everything, they said, was in God's hand except the fear of God, by which they meant that God is sovereign and the human part is simply to obey and to leave the issue with him. (Williams, *Acts: A Good New Commentary*, 97)

vv. 40–42—Gamaliel persuaded the Sanhedrin to drop the charge of blasphemy whose penalty was death. But disobedience to the Sanhedrin still had a price, and it was severe. As we saw on March 10, flogging (scourging) was a terrible torture. Notice the apostles' reaction to their beating. They rejoice that they had been counted worthy to suffer for Christ. They also refused to obey yet another warning against speaking about Jesus. We are blessed because they didn't!

APPLY

v. 20—Are you seeking to tell people the full message of the new life in Christ?

v. 41—Do you count it an honor to be put down because of your faith?

MEMORIZE

Acts 5:41

Use this as encouragement when you suffer as a Christian.

PRAY

A: Praise your Prince and Savior.

C: Confess your lack of boldness.

T: Thank God for the perseverance of the apostles.

S: Ask God for wisdom like Gamaliel showed.

TELL

The next time you hear someone make a hasty judgment, urge them to be more patient, just as Gamaliel urged the Sanhedrin.

MAY 11

THE FIRST DEACONS ARE CHOSEN AND OPPOSED

Pray that the deacons in your church would be like Stephen.

READ

Acts 6:1–15

OBSERVE

Like any organization, the early Church became more organized as it grew.

vv. 1–4—The Church was growing explosively! The first chapters of Acts indicate that:

1. It began with three thousand new believers on the day of Pentecost (2:41).
2. The Lord added to their number daily (2:47).
3. After the crippled beggar was healed, the number rose to five thousand men (probably eight thousand or more members, 4:4).
4. After the awesome display of God's power in the judgment of Ananias and Sapphira, "more and more men and women believed in the Lord and were added to their number" (5:14).

As we indicated on May 5, many of these new believers were from lands far from Israel. Though the Church had provided for these Grecian Jews by selling their possessions, apparently this mercy ministry was not effectively reaching the widows. John Stott recognizes:

A vital principle is illustrated in this incident, which is of urgent importance to the Church today. It is that God calls all his people to ministry, that he calls different people to different ministries, and that those called to "prayer and the ministry of the word" must on no account allow themselves to be distracted from their priorities. (Stott, *The Spirit, the Church and the World*, 121)

The word translated "wait on tables" is *diakonia*, from which we get the word "deacon." Though their ministry was primarily caring for physical needs, the first deacons were men identified by their wisdom and spirit-filled lives.

vv. 5–7—Each of the men chosen had a Greek name, so the disciple band (the one hundred twenty five rather than the twelve) may have chosen them because they would have a natural affinity and care for the Hellenistic widows. We only hear of two of these deacons again, Stephen and Philip. But we can assume that the others went about their ministry quietly and effectively, for the problem is never mentioned again. The deacons freed up the apostles to preach the Word, and the preaching had great success. Another large number of people believed, including many priests, who would have been very difficult to reach apart from an outpouring of the Holy Spirit.

vv. 8–15—It wasn't only apostles God used to perform miracles. He used Stephen, a deacon full of God's grace and power. As always, God's person faces opposition. The Synagogue of the Freedmen was composed of freed slaves and their descendants. Since the word for synagogue is singular, it appears that these were foreign Jews from four locations who formed a synagogue in Jerusalem. Since they had come out of slavery they were probably more fervent about their faith than most Jews. They first attempt to debate Stephen (as did Jesus' Jewish opponents). When they could not prevail against Stephen's wisdom, they used false witnesses (like the ones at Jesus' trial) and accused Stephen of speaking against the law and the temple (the same accusations leveled at Jesus). But these lies could not discourage this Spirit-filled deacon. He stood before the Sanhedrin with the face of an angel. We'll look at Stephen's trial over the next two days.

APPLY

v. 3—What responsibilities could the leaders of your church turn over to you? Where are you gifted to serve the Lord?

MEMORIZE

Acts 6:2

This verse will help you remember the vital importance of delegation in the church.

PRAY

A: Praise the Spirit who fills and calls.

C: Confess your reluctance to respond to his call.

T: Thank God for deacons.

S: Ask God to clearly reveal your ministry to you.

TELL

Tell one of the deacons in your church how much you appreciate their crucial ministry.

MAY 12

STEPHEN'S SERMON

Pray to appreciate the importance of knowing salvation history.

Acts 7:1–53

Like Peter, Stephen uses the situation as an opportunity to proclaim the Gospel.

v. 1—The charges were that Stephen spoke words of blasphemy against Moses and against God (6:11). That charge, in itself, shows how off-target Stephen's accusers were. They called words spoken against Moses blasphemy, indicating that they had put Moses on a pedestal above that of a human being. The other accusation was that he spoke against the temple, another indication of their misplaced worship.

vv. 2–8—Stephen begins his discourse on salvation history with Abraham, the first person God sent into the Holy Land. Abraham was also the first to observe the covenant of circumcision, crucial to Jewish understanding of the law. Stephen sees himself in the lineage of faith passed down from Abraham, Isaac, and Jacob.

vv. 9–16—The most important son of Jacob was Joseph, whom God rescued from Egypt and who rescued Israel. Stephen connects Jacob and Joseph to Abraham because they were buried in the tomb Abraham had provided in Shechem.

vv. 17–34—Since Stephen had been accused of subverting the law of Moses, the majority of his sermon is devoted to the lawgiver and deliverer. The details of Moses' birth, preservation, education, murder of the Egyptian, flight to Midian, and experience of the burning bush are well known (at least to those who saw the movie *The Prince of Egypt* or *The Ten Commandments*).

vv. 35–50—Now Stephen applies the scriptural history lesson to his hearers. Though Moses was sent to be their ruler and deliverer, the people of Israel rejected him (just as the Sanhedrin rejected Christ). Then, when he prophesied that a prophet would be sent (Jesus Christ), they refused to listen to Moses and worshipped idols (just as Stephen's listeners idolized the law and temple). While in the desert, God gave them the tabernacle as a testimony to his presence. It remained until Solomon built the temple. But God himself says (Isa. 66:1–2) that he does not live in houses made by men.

vv. 51–53—The powerful conclusion of Stephen's message is that his listeners were just like their forefathers. He echoes the words of Moses, that this is a stiff-necked people (Exod. 32:9), which indicated their stubborn unbelief. Though Stephen's opponents insisted on circumcision, they were uncircumcised in their hearts and ears (Lev. 26:41; Deut. 10:16; Jer. 6:10; Ezek. 44:7). The New English Bible translates this expression, "heathen still at heart and deaf to the truth." We can almost hear the words of Jesus in Luke 11:50–51 when he said that his genera-tion would be held responsible for killing all the prophets from Abel to Zechariah. Not only did they kill all the prophets, they killed the one they prophesied about. Stephen repeats Jesus' judgment that they had not obeyed the law they were given and he adds a new condemnation, that they "always resist the Holy Spirit!" What courageous preaching!

APPLY

vv. 2–53—Are you able to summarize salvation history like Stephen did? If not, how can you improve your knowledge of the Old Testament?

MEMORIZE

Acts 7:48a

This verse will help you to remember that God's presence goes beyond buildings.

PRAY

A: Praise the God of Abraham, Isaac, and Jacob.

C: Confess your stubbornness.

T: Thank God for his work through history.

S: Ask God for the courage of Stephen.

TELL

Share with a friend or your small group how you see God working in history.

MAY 13

THE FIRST CHRISTIAN MARTYR

PRAY

Ask to see Jesus interceding for you as he did for Stephen.

READ

Acts 7:54–60

OBSERVE

Stephen is the first of literally millions of people who have died because of their faith in Christ. His name, *Stephanos*, is the Greek word for "crown," and no human wears one more nobly. The Greek word *marturia*, from which we get the English word "martyr," is translated as "witness." The blood of the martyrs is the seed of the Church.

v. 54—David John Williams comments on this verse:

> By the time Stephen had finished speaking, the roles of those involved in this trial had effectively been reversed. It was as though the Sanhedrin were on trial and his was the speech for the prosecution. With Stephen thundering against them, it is highly unlikely that they would have allowed him to go on, even had he intended to do so. No charge was more hateful to the Jew than that he had broken the law (cf. John 7:19), and no such charge could have been made with greater force than Stephen had made it against the Sanhedrin. (Williams, *Acts: A Good New Commentary*, 132)

vv. 55–56—Stephen's vision of heaven is truly amazing. He sees the glory of God, which in itself is awesome. But he also sees Jesus *standing* at the right hand of God.

This verb is extremely significant. In the Apostles' Creed, we recite that Jesus "sitteth at the right hand of God the Father Almighty." It is the judge who sits, and all judgment has been given to the Son (John 5:22). But in this case, the judge becomes the defense attorney, who stands to intercede for his client. Stephen had been confessing Christ before men, now he sees Christ confessing Stephen before the throne of heaven!

vv. 57–60—Yelling at the top of their voices inflamed the anger of the members of the Sanhedrin and momentarily drowned out the witness of Stephen. But not even the stoning of Stephen could silence his message. Stephen's death must have had a profound effect on the man who held the cloaks of the executioners, Saul. The young Pharisee heard a powerful message which tied Old Testament history to the coming of the Messiah, Jesus. Though Saul initially rejected this message, it must have been planted in his mind waiting for Jesus to address him on the road to Damascus. Saul also heard the beautiful witness of the Spirit of Christ speaking through Stephen, as Stephen's prayer echoes the words Jesus spoke from the cross, *"Lord, do not hold this sin against them,"* and, *"Lord Jesus, receive my spirit."* St. Augustine, commenting on this passage, wrote, "The Church owes Paul to the prayer of Stephen."

APPLY

vv. 55–56—Do you visualize Jesus Christ interceding for you before the Father? That is the truth of Scripture, according to Romans 8:34.

v. 60—Are you able to forgive your enemies to the extent that you pray, "Lord, don't hold this sin against them?" Jesus asks you to pray for those who persecute you; that is gracious praying.

MEMORIZE

Acts 7:56

Stephen's amazing vision of heaven applies to you.

PRAY

A: Praise God and his glory.

C: Confess your fear of rejection or persecution.

T: Thank God for Stephen and modern martyrs.

S: Intercede for those facing death for Christ overseas.

TELL

Discuss with your small group what it means to you that Christ is actually praying for us.

MAY 14

THE CHURCH IS PERSECUTED AND SCATTERED

PRAY

Pray for eyes of faith to see God's Spirit bring good out of evil.

READ

Acts 8:1–25

OBSERVE

Jesus had told his followers to make disciples of all nations and to be his witnesses in Jerusalem, Judea, Samaria, and to the ends of the earth. It's interesting that it takes persecution to activate the Great Commission.

vv. 1–4—The stoning of Stephen initiates the first great persecution of Christians, in Jerusalem. Notice that everyone except the "professionals," the apostles, were scattered and yet the Word was preached everywhere they went. Even though Stephen's death would result in good for the church, it was appropriate to mourn deeply for him (Matt. 5:4; 1 Thess. 4:13). Paul's actions in persecuting the Church stayed with him, even after he had been forgiven (1 Tim. 1:12–16). It isn't wrong to remember past sin (as a warning against future sin) as long as the sting of guilt has been removed. It's when we dwell on past sins and are unable to forgive ourselves that we nullify the grace of God.

vv. 5–8—Philip is the second notable deacon who acts as an evangelist and healer. We will see more of his Spirit-led ministry tomorrow.

vv. 9–13—Simon the Sorcerer (sometimes known as Simon *Magus* (the Greek word for "magic" or "sorcery," closely related to the Magi of Matthew 2) realized that a greater power than his had arrived in Samaria. It's impossible to know the degree of sincerity of his belief, but Luke records it as if it were authentic.

vv. 14–17—It is very significant, in light of Acts 1:8, that the Gospel had taken root in Samaria. Peter and John would have been seen as the lead apostles at that time and they are dispatched to fellowship with the new Samaritan believers. Some have argued that this passage teaches that we should have a "second blessing," in which we are baptized in the Holy Spirit after we receive Christ. It is very dangerous to argue a theological principle from a narrative account, as John Stott points out in his book *The Baptism and Fullness of the Holy Spirit*. Stott believes that this was a unique kind of "Samaritan Pentecost" in which God used the apostles to bring unity between the church of Jerusalem and their Samaritan brothers and sisters. It is not meant to be normative.

vv. 18–25—The attempt to buy the power of God has become known as "simony," after the magician. Peter's response doesn't necessarily mean that Simon was unsaved, though it's possible that Simon's baptism was just an attempt to figure out the apostles' power and that he faked his conversion. He could have been an immature Christian who had a lot of growing to do. The witness of church history argues against Simon Magus' salvation. In the decades following these events, he was shown to be a determined opponent of apostolic Christianity. It seems that his interest was based on an attempt to prosper from the Gospel, and when that door was closed, Simon bitterly rejected the faith (Erhardt, *Christianity Before the Apostles' Creed*, 85). For Peter and John to preach the Gospel in Samaritan villages reflects a genuine change in their hearts. These were the same men who wanted to call down fire from heaven to consume a Samaritan village (Luke 9:51–54) when they were walking with Jesus.

APPLY

v. 4—Do you sometimes think that you're not trained well enough to share the Gospel? Notice that it was not the apostles who took the Word of God beyond Jerusalem.

vv. 18–19—Be careful not to present the Gospel to someone in terms of what's in it for them. Faith in Christ is not a commodity to be purchased because of the benefits it provides.

MEMORIZE

Acts 8:4

PRAY

A: Praise the Lord because he cannot be bought.

C: Confess that you have sometimes been distracted by spectacular pagans like Simon.

T: Thank God that true spirituality cannot be counterfeited.

S: Intercede for someone who is following a power other than Jesus.

TELL

Tell someone that it's not up to the professionals (pastors, missionaries, etc.) to grow God's Church. The witness of laypeople is crucial.

MAY 15

PHILIP AND THE ETHIOPIAN EUNUCH

PRAY

Pray to receive insights on how to effectively share your faith. Phillip provides a good model.

READ

Acts 8:26–40

OBSERVE

The Gospel begins its travels "to the ends of the earth" with this encounter.

v. 26—When the Lord calls us, through one of his messengers or through the Holy Spirit, he doesn't generally tell us what we will encounter, only where he wants us to go. Like Philip, we have the choice whether to obey in faith or not.

v. 27—The male servants who attended ancient queens were often castrated to remove any possibility of inappropriate behavior between them and royalty. The Jewish faith of Candace and her CFO may go back a thousand years to Solomon's visit by the Queen of Sheba (1 Kings 10), a trade partner with Ethiopia. The man had probably gone to Jerusalem for Pentecost.

vv. 28–29—It's unclear whether the Spirit's instruction to go to the Ethiopian's chariot was an audible voice or an inward prompting.

vv. 30–31—When God has planned a divine encounter for us, it is often so obvious! But we still have to seek and respond to his leading, as Philip did.

vv. 32–35—The authoritative interpretation of Isaiah 53 is given in this passage. There's no question the prophet was writing about the Messiah Jesus, the silent lamb who was slain for us.

vv. 36–38—The little details that the Bible so often provides are delightful. Why does Philip baptize the Ethiopian eunuch? Because they pass some water! There would have been a pretty large retinue traveling with the treasurer and the act of baptism stamped him as a Christian and gave him opportunities to spread the Gospel with his fellow travelers. The church in Ethiopia has been strong throughout much of history.

vv. 39–40—The verb Luke uses is *harpazo*, which the NIV translates "suddenly took away." This is the same one used by Paul to describe the taking up of Christians in 1 Thessalonians 4:17. It seems that Philip was miraculously transported on a "supersonic ride" (Horton, *The Book of Acts: A Commentary*, 112). Philip worked his way up the Mediterranean coast, preaching the Gospel until he reached the city which would become his home (Acts 21:8).

APPLY

vv. 26–29—Are you open to God's communication? Unconfessed sin, such as the unwillingness to follow, can block the flow (Ps. 66:18).

MEMORIZE

Acts 8:29.

God can give us precise direction like that if we listen carefully.

PRAY

A: Praise the God who guides.

C: Confess your unwillingness to follow.

T: Thank God for leading you.

S: Intercede for someone who needs to have the Scriptures explained.

TELL

When God leads you to that person, explain that the Bible points to Jesus.

MAY 16

SAUL'S CONVERSION

PRAY

Pray to see someone come to Christ who is as far from the Lord as Saul was.

READ

Acts 9:1–31

OBSERVE

Not all conversions are as dramatic as Saul's, but his is wonderful.

vv. 1–2—Some commentators have suggested that the zeal Saul showed at the stoning of Stephen resulted in his rising in the ranks of the Sanhedrin. If so, his road trip to Damascus to persecute Christians would only add to his reputation. The high priest didn't have direct authority over the synagogues in Damascus, but his letter carried a lot of weight. It appears that the believers in Damascus had not separated from the synagogues, but instead preached the "way of salvation" from within. "The Way" was the first name for Christians, probably coming from John 14:6.

vv. 3–9—The expression, "I saw the light" comes from this famous encounter. It was intense enough to temporarily blind Saul. Jesus so identifies with his body, the Church, that to persecute members of the Church is to persecute him. E. M. Blaiklock comments:

> Saul's whole mind and conduct were based on the certainty that the impostor (Jesus) was dead. If that were not so, the whole foundation crumbled beneath his feet. Then, in the mid-course of his mad career, he saw Jesus, so clearly, so unmistakably, that he

could not disbelieve. He saw; he heard; he knew; and there was no alternative but to surrender. (Blaiklock, *The Acts of the Apostles,* 87)

It's clear that Jesus has a plan for Saul. The initial chapters of that plan await him in Damascus. Blindness and fasting would have prepared him for what he was about to hear. It's very likely that during these three days, Paul saw the visions referred to in 9:12 and in 2 Corinthians 12:1–4.

vv. 10–19—Straight Street is still the main east-west thoroughfare in Damascus. The man who went to Damascus "breathing out murderous threats against the Lord's disciples" is now involved in humble prayer. Ananias' initial reluctance to introduce himself to Saul isn't surprising. This would have been tantamount to signing his own death warrant. Christ's plan already includes Saul/Paul's ministry to the Gentiles and the suffering he will encounter in that ministry. Ananias responds to the Lord's reassurance wholeheartedly, calling Saul his brother, laying hands on him, and baptizing him. The scales that fell from Saul's eyes were literal, but also symbolized the crust of his previous spiritual rigidity falling away through the baptism of the Holy Spirit.

vv. 20–25—For a man who came to arrest believers to so quickly preach that Jesus is the Son of God is an amazing transformation. It's no wonder that his listeners were astonished and also no surprise that the leaders of the synagogue wanted to take him out of the picture. As a former Pharisee, Saul's conversion would have been a powerful threat to the rulers of the synagogue. They didn't want to kill him within the city where their treachery would cause people to question them. Instead, they wanted to ambush him as he left the city and kill him in the deserted countryside. Saul must have had a Christian sympathizer on the inside of the Jewish establishment. The basket Saul was lowered in was the larger Gentile *sphuris.*

vv. 26–31—Like Ananias, the disciples were afraid that Saul was a double agent who would infiltrate their ranks in order to create even more havoc. Barnabas, the Son of Encouragement, reached out to Saul in faith and vouched for him. Saul was uniquely qualified to debate the Grecian Jews since he had a classical Greek education in Tarsus where he grew up. With his training under Gamaliel in Jerusalem, he would have been a formidable opponent in any debate, especially with the Holy Spirit empowering his words. With the primary persecutor now an eloquent defender of the Gospel, the Church in Israel had a brief time of peace and prosperity.

APPLY

v. 6—Do you have a sense of what Jesus wants to do with your life? Seek him!

MEMORIZE

Acts 9:4

When people persecute you, they are really persecuting Jesus.

PRAY

A: Praise the Lord who changes lives.

C: Confess any spiritual blindness.

T: Thank God for his light.

S: Ask God for Saul's boldness in declaring the truth.

TELL

Share with a Christian friend a dramatic conversion story that is encouraging.

MAY 17

AENEAS AND TABITHA

PRAY

Pray that the healing of people two thousand years ago can have an impact on your life today.

READ

Acts 9:32–43

OBSERVE

Luke makes an abrupt transition from the ministry of Saul/Paul to the ministry of Peter. Peter will be the focus of Acts from 9:32 through chapter 12, and then he will fade into the background as Paul takes center stage. Luke wants to make it clear that Peter had a crucial part to play in the spreading of the Gospel and the inclusion of the Gentiles.

vv. 32–43—When persecution was rampant, the apostles stayed in Jerusalem. Now that a period of peace reigned, they were free to travel the countryside. Lydda is twelve miles south-east of Joppa, which is the closest seaport to Jerusalem on the Mediterranean coast. Peter could be following up believers Philip had led to Christ. Aeneas was a Greek Christian. Tabitha is Aramaic, while Dorcas is Greek for "gazelle." What a wonderful one-sentence biography of Tabitha, "who was always doing good and helping the poor." Let's look at these healings together. Both incidents highlight Peter's identification with Jesus. Stott points out four factors which suggest that Luke deliberately emphasized the similarities between Jesus' healings and Peter's (Stott, *The Spirit, the Church and the World*, 183–184):

1. Both miracles followed the *example of Jesus*. Peter's words to Aeneas, *"Get up and take care of your mat"* are very similar to Jesus' words to the paralytic, *"Get up, take your mat and go home"* (Mark 2:11). Peter's words to Tabitha are almost identical to Jesus' words to the little girl in Mark 5:41. In fact, if Peter spoke Aramaic (which he probably did) there would only be one letter's difference between *"Talitha kuom!"* (little girl, get up) and *"Tabitha kuom!"*

2. Both miracles were performed by the *power of Jesus*. To the paralyzed Aeneas, Peter says, "Jesus Christ heals you." With the dead woman, Peter prays in obvious dependence on the power of Christ to raise her.

3. Both miracles were signs of the *salvation of Jesus*. Peter uses the same command with Aeneas and Tabitha—*anastethi*, "Get up!" It's the same verb Peter uses several times to describe God raising Jesus. This usage is hardly an accident. Because of the salvation effected by Christ's death and resurrection, Peter is able to offer new life to both of these hurting individuals.

4. Both miracles resulted in the *glory of Jesus*. When the paralytic was healed, "all those who lived in Lydda and Sharon saw him and turned to the Lord." Tabitha's resuscitation *"became known all over Joppa, and many people believed in the Lord."*

APPLY

v. 34—The power that raised Jesus from the dead is available to you. God may not want you to raise the dead, but his Spirit can do amazing things that are in his will for you.

v. 36—Will you follow the example of always doing good and helping the poor?

MEMORIZE

Acts 9:34

This verse is a vivid reminder of who heals.

PRAY

A: Praise the Healer.

C: Confess your lack of faith.

T: Thank God for healing you've experienced.

S: Intercede for someone who needs Christ's healing touch.

TELL

Share with a friend where you need healing (physical or spiritual) and ask for prayer.

MAY 18

CORNELIUS AND PETER

Pray to hear God's inner voice as Peter and Cornelius did.

Acts 10:1–33

OBSERVE

Gentile evangelism continues as Peter reaches a Roman soldier's family.

vv. 1–2—Caesarea was an important Roman outpost on the Mediterranean. The Italian Regiment was composed of one thousand soldiers, one tenth of a legion. Cornelius commanded one hundred men and "his responsibilities corresponded to those of a modern army captain.... Centurions were the backbone of the Roman army" (F. F. Bruce, *The Book of the Acts*, 215). As noted previously, every mention of centurions in the New Testament is positive. Cornelius was a "God-fearer," a Gentile who observed Jewish law and customs but wasn't circumcised (perhaps out of fear of rejection). He went beyond mere observance to a devoted generosity.

vv. 3–8—It's clear in verse 30 that the vision came to Cornelius while he was praying. As always, the first response to angels is fear, something centurions didn't usually experience. Some versions translate Cornelius' address to the angel as "Sir," which is a possible variation of the Greek *kurie*. But "Lord" is better because Cornelius knows that this is a divine visitation. The angel's language about a memorial offering is very similar to the descriptions in Leviticus, of which Cornelius would have been familiar. The fact that Peter was staying with a tanner, a profession usually shunned by the Jews because of its involvement with dead bodies, suggests that he may already be somewhat open to the Gentiles.

vv. 9–16—Blaiklock comments:

> The kindly tanner made his guest comfortable on the roof, spreading a leather awning, hung by its four corners over his couch. Dinner tarried, and Peter fell asleep at prayer...The last impress on the tired man's drowsy mind was the drooping awning, and the sky at its four sides. Out of this was fashioned the imagery of the dream which was to have historic consequences. (Blaiklock, *The Acts of the Apostles*, 95).

Peter's response is typical of the impulsive apostle (Matt. 16:22; John 13:8). The repetition of the message three times was also familiar (John 21:15–17).

vv. 17–26—Peter's perplexity about the vision wouldn't last long. God's Spirit was moving quickly to include the Gentiles in the body of Christ. Apart from the Spirit reassuring him, Peter would have been nervous about receiving three strangers, one of whom was a soldier. Though it was an interlude of peace, persecution against Christians could break out at any time. Peter wisely takes six brothers in Christ with him (11:12) on the thirty-mile journey from Joppa to Caesarea. The apostle corrects Cornelius for falling at his feet in worship; Jesus never corrected those who worshiped him.

vv. 27–33—Though Peter's vision concerned only food, it's clear that he got the wider message that it applied to relationships with Gentiles in general. The fact that Cornelius had a corroborating vision had to be encouraging to Peter.

APPLY

vv. 3, 9—Do you listen to God when you pray?

v. 28—Is there anyone you consider impure with whom you wouldn't associate?

MEMORIZE

Acts 10:15

PRAY

A: Praise the Lord who makes all things clean.

C: Confess your failure to listen to him.

T: Thank him for cleansing you.

S: Ask God to make you open to people who seem impure to you.

TELL

Try to share a concise presentation of the Gospel as Peter does in this passage.

MAY 19

PETER'S SERMON AND DEFENSE

Pray that you might be as articulate as Peter in proclaiming and defending your faith.

READ

Acts 10:34–11:18

OBSERVE

vv. 34–43—Peter's new realization that God accepts people from every nation would soon be tested, but for the time being, he preaches the *kerygma* of the early Church to a group of Roman expatriates. We see the same key elements in the proclamation: God sent Jesus, who is Lord of all; Jesus went about doing good and doing miracles; they crucified him; God raised him from the dead; all who believe in him receive forgiveness in his name.

vv. 44–48—Once again, as at Samaria, a mini-Pentecost occurs. The new believers receive the Holy Spirit, speak in tongues, are baptized, and are instructed by Peter. The Great Commission and Acts 1:8 are being fulfilled.

11:1–3—The reaction of the men steeped in Judaism is predictable. How dare you eat with the heathen? To Middle Easterners, eating with someone was a way of accepting a person's lifestyle.

vv. 4–17—Peter doesn't attempt to deny the rumors but places them in the context of God's new revelation. His recitation is largely a recapitulation of the account in chapter 10. The one addition is his quote of Jesus' words, *"John baptized with water,* *but you will be baptized with the Holy Spirit."* Peter makes it clear to his Jewish brothers that if they fail to accept this new revelation they are guilty of opposing God.

v. 18—The conclusion of Peter's Jewish audience is right on target. However, as we'll see later, it didn't remain as the church's unanimous decision for long.

APPLY

vv. 34–44—Could you summarize the Gospel as effectively as Peter does in these verses?

MEMORIZE

Acts 10:34–35

The Gospel is for people of every tongue and nation.

PRAY

A: Praise the Judge of the living and the dead.

C: Confess your tendency to usurp the role of judge.

T: Thank God for forgiveness in Jesus' name.

S: Intercede for religious people who don't know Christ.

TELL

Share your summary of the Gospel with a friend and invite feedback.

MAY 20

ANTIOCH, WHERE THE DISCIPLES WERE FIRST CALLED CHRISTIANS

PRAY

Ask God to use you as he did the anonymous men from Cyprus and Cyrene.

READ

Acts 11:19–30

OBSERVE

Though the Church had declared that God had granted salvation to the Gentiles, the lessons are not easily unlearned.

vv. 19–21—It's possible that the Jewish Christians who had been scattered after Stephen's death didn't know about the Gentiles being granted repentance into eternal life. That could explain why they preached only to the Jews. But the fact that some of the diaspora, men from Cyprus and Cyrene, preached to the Greeks suggests that the others chose to close the door on the Gentiles because of their own prejudices. The good news is that the Lord works despite the partisanship of some of the dispersed Jews to honor the preaching of those who included the Gentiles.

vv. 22–26—The fact that the Church in Jerusalem sent Barnabas indicates that they weren't trying to conduct a witch hunt among the new believers in Antioch. He was "the Son of Encouragement" and, true to his name, he builds up his new brothers and sisters. God honors his faithfulness by bringing another harvest of new converts. Barnabas, in his humility, realizes that he needs help to disciple the believers at Antioch. He finds his friend Saul and they team up to teach a great number of young Christians. The word "Christian" literally means "Christ one," and this is the first time it is used.

vv. 27–30—Claudius reigned as Emperor from 41–54 AD. Though historians don't record one particular famine during this time, there were severe famines in various parts of the empire, especially Judea, which fulfilled Agabus' prophecy. The offering the disciples take up for the Church in Jerusalem becomes an important New Testament theme. God uses it to unite the Church, and Paul saw it as a symbol of Gentile-Jewish solidarity (Rom. 15:27). Saul and Barnabus make a second trip to Jerusalem to deliver this offering (Gal. 2:1–10).

APPLY

v. 23—Is there someone who needs your encouragement today?

v. 29—Is there someone who needs your practical help today?

MEMORIZE

Acts 11:24

This is a model of who God wants you to be.

PRAY

A: Praise the God whose hand is with us.

C: Confess your discouraging words.

T: Thank God for growing your church numerically and spiritually.

S: Intercede for someone who is discouraged.

TELL

Tell that discouraged person that he or she is special and that you care.

MAY 21

PETER AND HEROD

Pray in faith believing so that when your prayers are answered you're not surprised.

READ

Acts 12:1–25

OBSERVE

Up until now, only the Jewish religious authorities were involved in persecuting the church. Now, the Roman political authorities get involved as well, which was more serious.

vv. 1–4—Herod Agrippa I was the grandson of Herod the Great, who was king when Jesus was born. He shared many of his grandfather's characteristics. After the emperors Caligula (who gave him the title of king) and Claudius had given him large portions of Palestinian territory, his kingdom was as large as his grandfather's. He would have been familiar with Jesus, and his followers since his uncle, Herod Antipas, had examined Jesus (Luke 23:7). He was known to be anxious about preserving the *pax Romana* in Palestine and therefore disliked minorities who threatened to disturb it. James was beheaded, in keeping with Jesus' prophecy about him (Mark 10:39). It looked like Herod planned the same fate for Peter after a showy, public trial.

vv. 5–19—This is the second angelic jail break in Acts. It was so surreal that Peter initially thought it must be a dream or vision. When Peter comes to his senses, he goes to the church's usual meeting place—the house of Mary, the mother of Mark (the gospel writer). How ironic that the church, which had been "earnestly praying to God for him," refused to believe that it was Peter at their door, the answer to their prayers! The James who Peter refers to is Jesus' brother, already a leader in the Church at Jerusalem. Peter wisely finds another place to stay that is less well known to the authorities. Herod gave the usual penalty to guards who let a prisoner escape. They would have been set on fire in their uniforms.

vv. 20–24—Herod had become a Jew to ingratiate himself to the people he governed. He followed the law carefully. His failure to rebuke this blasphemy from Gentiles brought God's immediate, retributive justice. Even as powerful a man as Herod couldn't thwart the spread of the Gospel.

v. 25—This is a footnote to the story of Peter and Herod. Barnabas and Saul had come back to Jerusalem from Antioch with the gift for the church. They will soon set out on their first missionary journey with Mark as their companion. The young man's participation would prove to be controversial.

APPLY

vv. 5, 15–16—Do you really believe God will answer your prayers? Do you wait expectantly?

v. 23—Are you quick to acknowledge that anything good in you comes from God?

MEMORIZE

Acts 12:5

This verse helps us to remember the importance of earnest prayer and earnest belief.

PRAY

A: Praise the Lord who sets us free.

C: Confess your lack of earnestness in prayer.

T: Thank God for answered prayer.

S: Intercede for someone you know who is in prison.

TELL

Write a letter to that imprisoned person.

MAY 22
THE FIRST MISSIONARY JOURNEY

PRAY

Ask for the courage and faith of Barnabas and Paul.

READ

Acts 13:1–12

OBSERVE

Barnabas and Saul return to where they had taught new believers (12:25–26).

v. 1—The leaders of the Church at Antioch were amazing. In addition to Barnabas and Saul, there was Simeon called Niger. Most scholars believe this was Simon of Cyrene, the man forced to carry Jesus' cross (Luke 23:26) and the father of two church leaders, Alexander and Rufus (Mark 15:21; Rom. 16:13). Lucius of Cyrene may have been Luke himself. Lucius would have been his Roman name, and it is likely that he, too, was Black since he came from Africa. Most of the physicians in the first century were slaves, some of whom gained their freedom. Manaen was a *syntrophos* of Herod the tetrarch (Antipas), the son of Herod the Great and the uncle of the man who was trying to kill the apostles. The Greek word *syntrophos* may mean that he was "brought up with" Herod Antipas, or that he was his foster brother, or an intimate friend. He was probably Luke's source for information about Herod's court. The Antioch Church was led by an ethnically and culturally diverse group.

vv. 2–3—The commissioning of Barnabas and Saul is a model for how churches should call missionaries. Before they even began to pray, these two men had shown themselves to be faithful and gifted over the period of a year. Then the Church worshiped the Lord, fasted, and prayed. The Church sensed the Holy Spirit was calling Barnabas and Saul to be set apart. Then they laid hands on them to bless them and sent them off. The passage doesn't say so, but we can also safely assume that they provided for their needs as they took off on the first missionary journey.

v. 5—Seleucia was the seaport about fifteen miles from Antioch. From there, Barnabas, Saul, and John Mark sailed to the island of Cyprus (modern Turkey), Barnabas' native country. Salamis was a commercial city on the east coast of Cyprus where Jews who were fleeing Roman persecution would have first settled. They concentrated on preaching in the synagogues.

vv. 6–13—Paphos was the provincial capital of Cyprus. Paul's missionary strategy often included influencing the most influential city in a region. Luke describes Sergius Paulus, the ruler of the island, as an intelligent man despite his attraction to occult practices. The court wizard was named Bar-Jesus (Aramaic), which is literally "son of salvation." But he could have been promoting himself as the spiritual offspring of Jesus of Nazareth and suggesting that his tricks were inspired by the Messiah. His Greek name was Elymas Magos which means "skillful magician or sorcerer." There is no doubt why Elymas would oppose Barnabas and Saul. They threatened his livelihood. This is the first of several people who speak against gospel witnesses for economic reasons. Saul (who was the first king and the tallest of Hebrews) now becomes Paul, which is the Greek word for "short." He may have been small in stature, but Paul stood very tall in the courage department. Filled by the Holy Spirit, Paul causes Elymas' physical condition to match his spiritual condition as the hand of the Lord strikes the sorcerer blind. The result is that the proconsul becomes a believer, which would have had an impact on all of Cyprus.

APPLY

v. 2–3—Have you ever worshiped, fasted, and prayed about a big decision?

MEMORIZE

Acts 13:3

This verse helps us to remember how churches should call missionaries.

PRAY

A: Praise the God of judgment.

C: Confess your tendency to make peace with evil.

T: Thank God for courageous people like Paul.

S: Intercede for someone blinded by the occult.

TELL

Here is yet another example for those who think the New Testament God is only full of love and mercy.

MAY 23

THE JOURNEY CONTINUES

PRAY

Pray for the grace of Barnabas, the courage Mark lacked, and the eloquence and wisdom of Paul.

READ

Acts 13:13–52

OBSERVE

There are subtle but important messages between the lines of this passage.

v. 13—Notice that Luke now refers to "Paul and his companions." Previously, it was "Barnabas and Saul," from now on it is "Paul and Barnabas." The Son of Encouragement knew that his role was to train and then support the brighter and more eloquent Paul. As the old saying goes, "It takes more grace than I can tell; to play the second fiddle well," but Barnabas rejoiced in his secondary role. The missionary band moves from Barnabas' home country to Paul's. Luke mentions John Mark's return to Jerusalem almost in passing, but it was significant and eventually led to the breakup of Paul and Barnabas. Paul saw it as a desertion (15:38). There are several reasons commentators give for Mark's return:

1. He was homesick. His mother apparently had a wonderful home, the location of the Upper Room and the headquarters of the disciples.
2. He resented the fact that the partnership of Barnabas and Saul now became Paul and Barnabas. Barnabas was his cousin.
3. He was afraid. The trip from Perga to Pisidian Antioch required climbing

over the Taurus mountains, which were infested with bandits and a dangerous climb. We'll never know for sure, but we'll look at the ramifications of Mark's desertion when we examine chapter 15.

vv. 14–15—Paul always began in the synagogues until he was kicked out. At first, the synagogue at Pisidian Antioch seemed very open to his message.

vv. 16–41—Paul's message is yet another version of the *kerygma* of the early church: Jesus is the Messiah, son of David; the rulers of Jerusalem rejected him and killed him; God raised him from the dead; forgiveness of sins is offered in his name. Paul includes the ministry of John the Baptist, whose fame must have reached Asia Minor. Paul includes a variety of quotes from the Psalms (2:7, 16:10) and the prophets (Isa. 55:3; Hab. 1:5). What he says about David is worth noting: *"For when David had served God's purpose in his own generation, he fell asleep."* Paul contrasts David's death and decay with Jesus' resurrection, but it is, nevertheless, a wonderful epitaph for David.

vv. 42–48—At the return engagement, the jealous Jewish leadership poisoned the crowd against Paul and Barnabas. Paul tells them that since they have rejected the truth about eternal life, the Gospel will now be preached to the Gentiles, who rejoice. Notice the strong statement of election in verse 48: *"All who were appointed for eternal life believed."*

vv. 49–52—Whenever Paul entered a city, a revival and a riot broke out. The mob chased Paul and Barnabas from the region. They must have heard Jesus' teaching (Matt. 10:14), for they shook the dust off their feet. They were filled with joy not only because some Jews and many Gentiles believed, but because they had been "counted worthy of suffering disgrace for the Name" (Acts 5:41).

APPLY

v. 36—What do you need to change to fulfill God's purpose for your life?

MEMORIZE

Acts 13:36

PRAY

A: Praise the God of all nations.

C: Confess that you haven't been concerned about God's purposes but your own.

T: Thank God for appointing you for eternal life.

S: Ask God to help you fulfill his purpose for today.

TELL

Discuss with a friend or your small group what God's purpose for your generation might be and how you fit into that purpose.

MAY 24

PAUL AND BARNABAS COMPLETE THEIR FIRST MISSIONARY JOURNEY

PRAY

Pray for humility, discernment, and courage to live a misunderstood life.

READ

Acts 14:1–28

OBSERVE

Paul and Barnabas continue their journey in Asia Minor in the region known as Galatia, to which Paul later addressed an epistle.

v. 1—Iconium was one hundred miles southeast of Pisidian Antioch. It is now the fourth largest city in Turkey and known as Konya. When Paul and Barnabas visited, it was a Greek city and a center of agriculture and commerce. Their initial synagogue ministry was effective both to Jews and Greeks.

vv. 2–7—Paul and Barnabas were "wise as serpents and harmless as doves" (Matt. 10:16). When they heard about the plot to stone them, they fled to safety. They were not deserting the Iconian believers because they had spent a good deal of time with them, not only preaching the Word but confirming it by signs and wonders. The people of that city could not claim that they had failed to hear a persuasive presentation of the Good News about Jesus. Luke calls Paul and Barnabas "apostles" in verse 4. They were not part of the original twelve and, as far as we know, Barnabas never saw the risen Lord, a qualification for apostleship. Luke is probably using the word in its generic sense, "one who is sent out." That definition fit Paul and Barnabas perfectly, although Paul argues for his authentic apostleship later (1 Cor. 9:1–2). The towns they retreated to, Lystra and Derbe, were not important trade towns or centers of population. It could be that Paul and Barnabas needed a quiet place to regroup.

vv. 8–18—Paul's healing of the man with crippled feet was very similar to Jesus' healing of the paralytic at the pool of Bethsaida (John 5:1–9) and Peter's healing of the crippled beggar at the Beautiful Gate (Acts 4:1–9). The difference is that the Greeks in Lystra wanted to make gods of Paul and Barnabas, with priestly sacrifice and all. Rudyard Kipling presents a similar situation in his wonderful story *The Man Who Would Be King*. But unlike Danny, a would-be deity, Paul and Barnabas reject the superstitious worship and urge the Greeks to turn from false gods and dumb idols to the living God. John Stott remarks, "Like Jesus, Paul remained unmoved. His steadfastness of character was upset neither by flattery nor by opposition" (Stott, *The Cross of Christ*, 233).

vv. 19–20—As a testimony to the fickleness of mob psychology, a group of Jews manages to turn the crowd against Paul and they become a lynch mob, actually a stoning mob. Though Paul faced death numerous times, this was apparently the only time he was stoned (2 Cor. 12:25). What type of courage did it take for him to return to Lystra after a mob had tried to kill him?

v. 21—The ministry in Derbe, a sixty-mile walk from Lystra, was profitable but uneventful. Once again, we have to marvel at Paul traveling that far after coming close to death. Barnabas' encouragement had to be an important ingredient in his healing and perseverance.

vv. 22–25—It is Paul and Barnabas who do the encouraging of the believers and churches that were a result of their journey. Notice that they planted churches, not missionary societies or Bible studies. These new believers needed to know the truth—that the Christian life is not a walk in the park, but an arduous trek full of hardships. We see the beginnings of church government in verse 23, as the apostles appoint (some manuscripts say "ordained") elders. Paul and Barnabas show the importance of following up new converts. Even though these apostles were faithful, the book of Galatians shows that many of these young believers were seduced by the Judaizers, whom we will encounter in the next chapter.

vv. 26–28—The two missionaries had quite a story to report to their sending church. It's not reading too much between the lines to suggest that Antioch was a place where Paul and Barnabas received physical and spiritual healing and were recharged for further mission work.

APPLY

v. 6—Are you wise in not allowing yourself to be easily neutralized by those who oppose your faith? Jesus doesn't want us to be naïve where evil is concerned.

v. 22—On the other hand, are you willing to experience hardships when they come? A faithful Christian can't avoid them.

MEMORIZE

Acts 14:22b

We must go through many hardships to enter the kingdom of God.

PRAY

A: Praise your Protector.

C: Confess your desire for a comfortable, wrinkle-free existence.

T: Thank God that hardships produce character.

S: Intercede for a brother or sister who backs away from difficulties.

TELL

When you share the Gospel with someone, be honest. Don't suggest that "When you come to Jesus, all your problems will be solved." Sometimes they've just begun!

MAY 25
THE JERUSALEM COUNCIL

PRAY

Ask for the ability to apply this ancient dispute to your life today.

READ

Acts 15:1–35

OBSERVE

The council in Jerusalem set the pattern for the next several hundred years as church councils debated and decided key elements of doctrine.

vv. 1–6—The Jewish believers who insisted that Gentile converts must be circumcised and obey the Mosaic law were known as the Judaizers. From verse 5 we see that at least some of them were Pharisees, who were trying to incorporate the new wine of Christianity into the old wineskin of Judaism. They became Paul's bitter opponents, often undoing the good work he had done. The conflict they raised in Antioch was so significant and so difficult to resolve that the church leaders sent Paul and Barnabas to Jerusalem to consult with the apostles and elders of the church in Jerusalem. These church leaders received the missionaries warmly.

vv. 7–11—Peter's speech is a masterpiece. He begins with his own experience (as we saw with the household of Cornelius) and makes an important theological point. There is no distinction between believers whose hearts have been purified by faith. (Paul emphasizes this in Gal. 3:28 and Eph. 2:11–22). Peter goes on to make the powerful point that since none of his Jewish brothers were able to keep the law, why should they lay this burden on Gentile believers? Peter's articulation of salvation by grace is the first use of those terms in Scripture. This will, of course, become Paul's major theological theme.

v. 12—Paul and Barnabas' experience of God's signs and wonders among the Gentiles confirmed everything Peter had said.

vv. 13–21—James, the brother of our Lord, takes a moderating position. He rejects the idea that the Gentiles should take on the entire yoke of Moses, but he specifies certain behaviors that they should avoid. These were particularly egregious to the Jews—eating food sacrificed to idols, sexual immorality, and eating the meat of strangled animals and animal blood. His defense is that the law of Moses has been preached in every city, so the Gentiles should at least be familiar with it. Like most compromises his position is weak. Though it has the virtue of rejecting "faith plus the law" salvation, it still suggests that right standing with God involves some observance of the law. Anything that is added to justification by faith alone subtracts from it.

vv. 22–29—The letter sent from Jerusalem to the Gentile believers followed James' position. The apostles and elders don't make it a matter of salvation to avoid food sacrificed to idols, the meat of strangled animals, animal blood, and sexual immorality. They conclude, "You would do well to avoid these things." The problem is that they include an item of moral law—no sex outside of marriage—with three items of ceremonial law. The logic of that position is not convincing and didn't last for long. To be fair, others suggest that James was just advocating courtesy from the Gentiles toward Jewish scruples, a position Paul affirms in 1 Corinthians 8 and Romans 14. Some interpreters believe that the specific *porneia* (the Greek word for "sexual immorality") was incest, which made it more like a ceremonial provision.

vv. 30–35—The crisis had passed, but it's possible that the compromise of the Jerusalem Council, with its inclusion of even a few legalistic provisions, opened the door for the Judaizers to wreak havoc in the Gentile churches. But for the time, at least, peace reigned.

APPLY

v. 1—Are there any extra-biblical laws that people today add to the Gospel? Some people think if you smoke cigarettes, watch R-rated movies, or drink alcohol, you can't be saved. What should your response be to people who say that, or who believe that people who do those things are second- class Christians?

MEMORIZE

Acts 15:11

This is the best statement made at the Jerusalem Council.

PRAY

A: Praise God, who justifies freely.

C: Confess your own list of laws you use to judge others.

T: Thank God for freedom in Christ.

S: Intercede for your elders, deacons, or other church officers. Ask that the decisions they make will be faithful to God's Word and full of wisdom.

TELL

What is your position on the decision of the Jerusalem Council? (The position taken above is by no means the majority opinion.) Discuss it with a friend who is also doing the study or your small group.

MAY 26

PAUL AND BARNABAS SEPARATE

Pray for God to give you wisdom to know when to stay together and when to separate from friends in ministry.

READ

Acts 15:36–16:5

OBSERVE

This passage is full of gray areas which are not easy to evaluate.

vv. 36–41—As we saw earlier, John Mark's decision to turn back when they reached Asia Minor (Cilicia) was not a casual matter to Paul. Whatever the reason, Paul saw it as desertion. Barnabas, the Son of Encouragement, probably urged Paul to give the young man another chance. The fact that he was Mark's uncle no doubt influenced his opinion. These two great men had recently seen a compromise effected in Jerusalem, but they were unable to find a middle ground in this decision. They had a "sharp disagreement," but it must not have been too ugly or the Church would not have commended Paul and Silas to the grace of the Lord. Though the text doesn't say so explicitly, we can assume that they also blessed Barnabas and Mark as they sailed away.

Team Barnabas goes back to his hometown and Team Paul returns to his native country as well. Barnabas and Mark are never mentioned again in Acts. Luke's narrative follows Paul from this point on. But it seems that in the providence of God, this split actually resulted in both teams bearing fruit. We don't know what ultimately happened to Barnabas, but Paul's attitude toward Mark was eventually transformed (see Col. 4:10 and 2 Tim. 4:11). Paul's reference to Barnabas in Colossians 4:10 is positive and suggests that a healing of the relationship took place that the Bible doesn't record.

16:1–5—One reason that the Spirit led Paul and Barnabas to Lystra previously might have been the valuable young protégé who was living there. Timothy's mother was a Jewish Christian (as was his grandmother—2 Tim. 1:5) but his father was Greek and apparently an unbeliever. What are we to make of Paul's decision to circumcise Timothy? Was he overly influenced by the Jerusalem Council to make concessions to Jewish sensibilities? Didn't this even go beyond the Council's ruling and contradict the strong position Paul took earlier (Acts 15:1–2)? It's questionable whether Paul in his later career would have done the same thing, especially after all of his battles with the Judaizers. John Stott presents the other position. He writes:

> Little minds would have condemned him for inconsistency. But there is a deep consistency in his thought and action. Once the principle had been established that circumcision was not necessary for salvation, he was ready to make concessions in policy. What was unnecessary for acceptance with God was advisable for acceptance by some human beings. (Stott, *The Cross of Christ*, 254)

In any case, the good news is that the churches grew in number and strength.

APPLY

v. 39—How do you know when it's appropriate to part company with fellow believers? This is not an easy question!

v. 3—Do you think Paul was right to circumcise Timothy?

MEMORIZE

Acts 16:5

Keep in mind that, by God's providential grace, twice as many churches were strengthened!

PRAY

A: Praise the God who works all things together for good.

C: Confess any times when you've broken fellowship over nonessentials.

T: Thank God for both Paul and Barnabas.

S: Intercede for any church splits that you're aware of.

TELL

Once again, it would be profitable to discuss with someone whether you believe Paul was right in splitting with Barnabas and circumcising Timothy.

MAY 27

THE MINISTRY TO THE PHILIPPIANS

PRAY

Pray to be as sensitive to the Spirit as Paul was.

READ

Acts 16:6–40

OBSERVE

With the mission to Macedonia (Greece), the Gospel is planted for the first time in European soil.

vv. 6–8—Paul, Silas, and Timothy traveled from the southeast to the northwest corners of Asia Minor. It's unclear why they were prevented from preaching the Gospel in the province of Asia, but it is clear that Peter later evangelized that region (1 Pet. 1:1).

vv. 9–12—Paul had a dream of a man of Macedonia asking for help, but he submitted it to his brothers. They concluded together that God called them to preach the Gospel in Macedonia. Luke joined the group in Troas. Verse 10 begins the first "we" section in Acts. Samothrace is a rocky island in the Aegean Sea whose peak rises to five thousand feet. Neapolis is the modern port of Kavalla. The one-hundred-fifty-mile journey from Troas was completed in two days if there was a favorable wind. On their way back, it took five days (20:6). The walk from Neapolis to Philippi was ten miles along the famous *Via Egnatia*, whose massive paving stones are still visible. Philippi was given its name by Philip of Macedon in the fourth century BC. After two centuries as a Greek colony, it became a Roman colony settled by retired soldiers. Though they stayed there several days (probably weeks—v. 18), and there were many converts, Luke focuses on just three.

vv. 13–15—There may not have been a synagogue in Philippi. Ten men were required and Paul's initial audience was women. Lydia was an upper-class businesswoman as a dealer in purple goods. She was a "worshiper of God," holding Jewish beliefs without actually becoming a Jew. On that Sabbath morning she became a Christian. She and her household were baptized, one of five household baptisms in the New Testament (Acts 10:33, 16:33, 18:8, and 1 Cor. 1:6). One of the arguments for infant baptism comes from these household baptisms. The faith of the head of the house dictated the behavior of the rest of the household, which included slaves and their children. Children would have been baptized at the same time as the head of the house. To suppose that not one of these five households contained infants or children strains credibility.

vv. 16–24—The slave girl had a *pneuma puthona*, a spirit of a python. Stott comments:

> Apollo was thought to be embodied in the snake and to inspire "pythonesses," his female devotees, with clairvoyance, although other people thought of them as ventriloquists. Luke does not commit himself to these superstitions, but he does regard the slave girl as possessed by an evil spirit. (Stott, *The Spirit, the Church and the World*, 264)

It's likely that she predicted the future much like so-called clairvoyants do today with general statements based on the gullibility of the recipients. In any case, her demon did have accurate theological knowledge (James 2:19). Paul, like Jesus, would not receive such a witness and exorcises the demon. Though Luke doesn't say it explicitly, since this story is told between that of Lydia and the Philippian jailer, we can assume that she was converted and became part of the Church in Philippi. This was the second time Paul threatened someone's prosperity (cf. Acts 13:8) and the reaction was similar. The slave girl's owners had the political clout to get Paul and Silas thrown in jail. They cleverly concealed their economic reasons for hating the missionaries. Instead they used the people's anti-Semitism ("these men are Jews") and their racial pride ("us Romans"). The severe flogging would have been similar to the scourging Jesus received before his crucifixion. It was the first of five times that Paul would be scourged (2 Cor. 11:24). All of this was manifestly illegal, especially against Roman citizens like Paul and Silas.

vv. 25–40—Despite their pain, Paul and Silas were praying and singing hymns in prison. They must have had a major impact on the other prisoners. When the Holy Spirit caused an earthquake to open everyone's chains, all the prisoners stayed put, apparently at Paul's request. This so impressed the jailer that he realized that the God they were praising must be the real thing. His classic question is, *"What must I do to be saved?"* Paul's reply is also classic, *"Believe in the Lord Jesus and you will be saved —you and your household."* (This verse was instrumental in my own conversion!) The jailer not only found his life preserved, he found abundant and eternal life, as did his household. Paul was a man of principle, and he would not go away quietly. He wanted the authorities to recognize their gross injustice and apologize. After leaving the jailer's home, Paul and Silas fellowshipped at Lydia's house, the meeting place of the Church at Philippi, which was Paul's favorite church. It was a church of great diversity, with the families of a rich merchant, a middle-class officer, and a poor slave girl.

APPLY

v. 9–10—Do you submit your sense of the Spirit's leading to a group of Christian brothers or sisters who can confirm or question your leading? It's a wise practice.

v. 15—As a believer in the Lord, God wants you to practice hospitality (Rom. 12:13).

v. 25—Why not try praying and singing when circumstances are rough?

MEMORIZE

Acts 16:31

This is a one-sentence response to the question, "What must I do to be saved?"

PRAY

A: Praise God, who saves all different kinds of people.

C: Confess your tendency to complain rather than sing.

T: Thank God for saving you.

S: Intercede for a family that needs salvation.

TELL

Share with someone what it means to believe in the Lord Jesus and be saved.

MAY 28

IN THESSALONICA AND BEREA

PRAY

Pray to be like the Bereans, and examine the Scriptures to see if what this devotional says is true.

READ

Acts 17:1–15

OBSERVE

Paul and company continue along the *Via Egnatia* to other Macedonian cities.

vv. 1–4—Thessalonica (modern Saloniki) was named after Alexander the Great's sister. It is one of the great cities in Greece. The familiar pattern repeats itself. Paul argues from the Scriptures that Jesus is the Christ and persuades some Jews and a large number of God-fearing Greeks.

vv. 5–9—But the rest of the pattern is that the unbelieving Jews stir up a mob against Paul. They play the political card, but the charge is a little different this time—that they are promoting another king (Jesus) and defying Caesar's decrees. Paul expands on this brief account in 1 Thessalonians 2:14–15. He indicates that the Thessalonian believers were faithful, suffering *"from your own countrymen the same things those churches (in Judea) suffered from the Jews who killed the Lord Jesus and the prophets and also drove us out."* Furthermore, the faith of these believers "has become known everywhere" (1 Thess. 1:8). Once again, however, Paul and Silas are forced to flee the city to preserve their lives, and their host Jason is a great help.

vv. 10–15—Berea was sixty miles to the south of Thessalonica. Timothy joined Paul and Silas there and the trio found a wonderful reception for the Gospel. F. F. Bruce notes:

> Their procedure, "examining the Scriptures daily to see if these things were so" (RSV), is worthy of imitation by all who have some new form of religious teaching pressed upon their acceptance. (Bruce, *The Book of the Acts,* 347)

But the Thessalonian Jews were not about to let this peaceful situation alone. They stirred up the crowds, and Paul was whisked away again. The uprising must not have been as severe as in other cities for Silas and Timothy were able to stay. That's a significant factor when we look tomorrow at what happened in Athens.

APPLY

v. 11—Are you examining the Scriptures to see if what this devotional says is true? Don't accept anyone's teaching just because they say so. Make sure it conforms to sound interpretation of God's Word.

MEMORIZE

Acts 17:11

PRAY

A: Praise the Christ of Scripture.

C: Confess that you've treated the Bible too casually.

T: Thank God for preserving his Word.

S: Intercede for a Christian who isn't studying Scripture carefully.

TELL

Tell that person because Christ preserves us, we can freely seek to be faithful students. (2 Tim. 2:15).

MAY 29

PAUL IN ATHENS

Ask that you might approach intellectuals as wisely as Paul did.

Acts 17:16–34

This is the only city Paul visits alone. It's also the only place where there is no subsequent evidence of a church.

v. 16—Athens was the philosophical, intellectual, and cultural center of the ancient world. Its Acropolis featured in the architectural majesty and beauty of the Parthenon. The Areopagus was a marketplace where ideas were also bought and sold. Paul is not overwhelmed by the beauty of the artwork but by the profusion of idols. The preposition translated "full of" idols in the NIV can also mean "under" idols, for Paul no doubt saw it as oppressive.

vv. 17–21—Paul began in his usual locale, the synagogue, but also realized that the intellectual frontier in Athens was the Aeropagus, the open air market. Epicurean and Stoic philosophers would have been polar opposites; the Epicureans argued for the importance of pleasure and the Stoics for the importance of discipline in creating self-sufficiency. The Epicureans were similar to the Deists in American history, believing that the gods exist but they have little interaction with people. The Stoics were enthusiastic pantheists, embracing all of the gods and their virtues. Their initial reaction to Paul was that he was a *spermologos*, literally a "seed word" philosopher (NIV "babbler") who "picked up scraps of learning here and there and purveyed them where he could" (Bruce, 351). They brought him to the Court of the Areopagus, a venerable institution which attempted to judge and exercise some control over the propagation of new ideas in Athens.

vv. 22–23—The Greek word Paul uses to describe the men of Athens can be translated "superstitious" as well as "religious." It is not a complimentary term. Paul wisely begins where they are, with the statue "to an unknown God," before telling them about the God he knows.

vv. 24–31—Paul's address on Mars Hill (which still stands in Athens) does not follow the typical pattern of the early church's *kerygma*. In speaking to idolaters and pantheists, Paul seeks to establish the nature and character of the one God. The main points of his message are:

1. God is the Creator of the Universe. Any attempt to limit him to a man made building or statue is folly.
2. God is the Sustainer of Life. The Greeks generally saw their gods as remote and uninvolved, only entering human history to create mischief or to complicate matters. The true God cares for his people. We depend on him; he doesn't depend on us.
3. God is the Ruler of Nations. He is sovereign over all of history and has established human societies so that people would seek their authentic ruler. Paul shows his knowledge of Greek philosophy by quoting Epimenides, a sixth-century BC poet, who wrote, "in him we live and move and have our being."
4. God is our Father. As his offspring, it is absurd to fashion him from lifeless gold or silver or stone.
5. God is our Judge. Though he overlooks the ignorance of those who don't know better, now that he has been clearly revealed, he demands that people change their minds (repent). The Judge is the one who was raised from the dead, Jesus Christ.

vv. 32–34—The mention of the resurrection caused an immediate division of the house into scoffers, agnostics ("we want to hear you again"), and believers. Though there is no evidence of a church being planted in Athens, Paul's visit cannot be judged as a failure. There were a number of believers, including a prominent philosopher, Dionysius.

APPLY

v. 23—Are there any cultural idols you can point to as evidence of the emptiness of modern philosophy? What about the nihilism of modern music, the emptiness of modern art, etc.? How can you effectively address people who are caught up in these philosophies?

vv. 30–31—God commands all people everywhere to repent. Do your friends know this?

MEMORIZE

Acts 17:30

PRAY

A: Praise God who made himself known.

C: Confess your failure to speak effectively to your culture.

T: Thank God for Paul's example.

S: Intercede for someone caught up in empty philosophy.

TELL

Look for an opportunity to talk with someone who holds a pagan philosophy.

MAY 30

THE CORINTHIAN CHAPTER

PRAY

Ask God to lead you to partners in ministry who increase your effectiveness.

READ

Acts 18:1–17

OBSERVE

The missionary team continues to grow with the addition of Aquila and Priscilla.

v. 1—Corinth is fifty miles west of Athens, situated on an isthmus which made it a focal point of sea trade between the East and the West. It was one of the most important cities politically that Paul ever visited and served as the capital of Achaia. Though it had a long history of warfare and competition for its commerce, Julius Caesar re-established it as a Roman colony in 44 BC, naming it *Laus Julia Corinthiensis*, "Corinth the praise of Julius." It had a reputation "for a degree of sexual license remarkable even in classical antiquity" (Bruce, *The Book of Acts*, 367). The Latin poet Horace called it a city where "none but the tough could survive" (Horace, *Epistles*, 1.17.36).

vv. 2–3—Aquila and Priscilla are Latin names. Priscilla is the diminutive of Prisca, the name Paul uses in his letters to describe this remarkable woman. Suetonius, the Roman historian, records the edict of Claudius which expelled the Jews from Rome, though some historians differ. This is the first indication we have of Paul's secular vocation as a tentmaker, a term that has come to describe those who work at a secular job to provide for themselves and their families while also serving in the ministry. In a sense, every Christian should be a tentmaker.

vv. 4–6—Some commentators emphasize that Paul was unsuccessful in Athens because he was a Lone Ranger there without his Tonto. Whether or not that's true, he certainly benefited from the arrival of Silas and Timothy and was able to concentrate on his synagogue ministry. Paul's rejection of the Jews in Corinth and his vow to go to the Gentiles from now on was not a firm shift in policy. He went back to the synagogue when he went to Ephesus.

vv. 7–8—His ministry in the synagogue was not in vain, for its ruler became a believer. Nevertheless, Paul's new center was the home of Titius Crispus, most likely a Roman citizen. He is mentioned again in 1 Corinthians 1:14 along with the household of Stephanas, the first converts in Achaia (1 Cor. 16:15). It's obvious that Luke shared only selected portions of a very fruitful and long (for Paul) ministry in Corinth.

vv. 9–17—The vision Paul received had to be encouraging, especially when the Jews took him to court. God used a probable nonbeliever in Gallio as his instrument of justice. It's difficult to understand why the Jews turned on Sosthenes. Perhaps he didn't present the case against Paul as convincingly as they had hoped. If he is the Sosthenes of 1 Corinthians 1:1, it's possible that he was already showing Christian leanings, much like his predecessor.

APPLY

v. 5—Is there some way God wants you to help those who preach the Gospel?

MEMORIZE

Acts 18:6

Sometimes God calls us to "shake the dust off our feet" and move on.

PRAY

A: Praise God for his justice.

C: Confess your tendency to be a Lone Ranger.

T: Thank God for partners in the Gospel.

S: Pray for someone who has been unjustly accused.

TELL

Tell someone who has supported and encouraged you how important they are to you.

MAY 31

TEAMWORK IN EPHESUS

PRAY

As May comes to a close, pray for diligence to faithfully study God's Word all summer.

READ

Acts 18:18–19:20

OBSERVE

A new missionary joins the team, a silver-tongued preacher named Apollos.

vv. 18–23—Cenchrea was one of the Corinthian ports. We don't know what vow Paul took there; the rest of Scripture doesn't give a clue. Shaving the head to accompany a vow was common among pious Jews. Ephesus was the major port city of Asia Minor (Turkey). Though the prohibition against preaching in Asia (16:6) was apparently lifted, Paul didn't spend much time there, despite a more positive reception in the synagogue than usual. Paul returned to Antioch, which would have been the end of his second missionary journey. Then he began his third missionary journey by traveling on land throughout Asia Minor, ministering to the churches of Galatia and Phrygia.

vv. 24–28—Alexandria was the Athens of ancient Egypt. It was here that the Septuagint (the Greek translation of the Hebrew Scriptures) had been translated in 200 BC. Alexandria later became a center of Christian scholarship and the major location for copying the New Testament. There was a large Jewish population there, which included Apollos (a Greek name). Though he was learned and eloquent, his theology was deficient. He hadn't experienced the baptism of Jesus.

Two laypeople, Priscilla and Aquila, quietly take him aside and fill in the blanks. Luke puts Priscilla's name first, which suggests that she was more the teacher than Aquila. After his training, Apollos was ready to go to Corinth to continue the ministry Paul, Priscilla, Aquila, Silas, and Timothy had begun. Apparently, Silas and Timothy had remained to pastor the Corinthians.

19:1–7—The early missionaries worked as an effective team. Paul followed up the people Apollos had preached to and baptized them in the name of Jesus. Another mini-Pentecost occurs in Ephesus among twelve men.

vv. 8–12—The same pattern occurs in Ephesus as Corinth. Paul preaches in the synagogue until stubbornness and ridicule reign. Then he moves to a secular location where there is great fruit for the kingdom. He stays in Ephesus longer than any other location. Like Peter (Acts 5:15), Paul's healing ministry imitated Jesus (Mark 5:27) in that even clothing that touched him was effective in healing the sick.

vv. 13–20—The example of the seven sons of Sceva shows the folly of doing spiritual battle without the proper weapons. God brought good even out of that somewhat comical/tragic situation. People realized that it is only the power of Jesus that is greater than the power of evil and they turned in their occult materials. Fifty thousand drachmas is the equivalent of about five million dollars in our currency. That's a lot of sorcery scrolls!

APPLY

18:26—Do you have the humility necessary to accept correction? It's important for growth.

19:13—Never try to hitchhike on the coattails of someone else's relationship with Christ!

MEMORIZE

Acts 19:20

This verse reminds us that when evil is defeated, the Gospel spreads.

PRAY

A: Praise the God of power.

C: Confess your pride

T: Thank God that *"he who is in you is greater than he who is in the world"* (1 John 4:4).

S: Intercede for someone who is in the world.

TELL

If you think a teacher has mishandled Scripture, gently share your view and ask for clarification.

JUNE

JUNE 1

THE RIOT IN EPHESUS

Pray to keep your head when others around you are losing theirs.

READ

Acts 19:21–41

OBSERVE

vv. 21–22—Paul planned to go to Jerusalem but didn't make it until Acts 21. This is the first time he expresses his desire to go to Rome. As best we can tell, he only arrived there as a prisoner. Erastus and Gaius Aristarchus (v. 29) are two helpers we haven't encountered before. There were many more.

vv. 23–27—Unbelievers are usually tolerant toward Christianity until it affects their lifestyles or hits them in the wallet. Demetrius the silversmith is the third person to oppose Christianity because it threatened his personal economy. Like the owners of the slave girl in Philippi, he wraps his concern about money in another flag—this time religious zeal. The Greek god Artemis (Diana in Roman mythology) was the queen of the hunt. But Artemis of the Ephesians was the ancient mother goddess of Asia Minor. Commentator F. F. Bruce writes:

> Her temple at Ephesus was one of the seven wonders of the ancient world; her image, enshrined in that temple, was believed to be of heavenly workmanship; it appears to have been a meteorite in which the semblance of a many-breasted female was discerned. (Bruce, *The Book of Acts*, 397–398)

Archeologists have found miniature shrines of the temple in terra-cotta but not in silver.

vv. 28–34—Like most mobs, there was a lot of energy without a lot of understanding. Luke observes that *"most of the people didn't even know why they were there."* But like sports fans who endlessly chant, "We're number one," the Ephesian crowd shouted the praises of Artemis for two solid hours. Paul's friends wisely urged him not to address the crowd. His reasoned arguments would not have been heard in the midst of the craziness, and he risked serious violence against his person if he spoke up. The Alexander who tried to speak may have been the metalworker Paul warns Timothy about in 1 Timothy 1:19 and 2 Timothy 4:14, a man who blasphemed and caused Paul a great deal of harm. He seemed to be on the side of the angels in this situation.

vv. 35–41—Like the proconsul Gallio in Corinth, an anonymous city clerk provides the voice of reason. Paul was careful not to disparage a particular pagan deity, though he certainly dismissed the reality of all idols. That was being "wise as a serpent" (Matt. 10:16). The city clerk points out that the Roman courts were well-equipped to deal with grievances. The emperors were not pleased with riots for any reason, and the implicit threat of Roman repercussions may be what ultimately defused the mob.

APPLY

vv. 30–31—Do you listen to the advice of others before you make a risky move? Proverbs 12:15 reads, *"A wise man listens to advice."*

MEMORIZE

Acts 19:30

Even Paul made mistakes and needed the advice of others.

PRAY

A: Praise the One True God.

C: Confess the pride that has kept you from listening to others.

T: Thank God for good advice you've received.

S: Intercede for those who love money more than the truth.

TELL

Tell someone whose advice has been helpful how much you appreciate him or her.

JUNE 2

PAUL'S THIRD MISSIONARY JOURNEY CONTINUES

PRAY

Pray that you might understand and imitate the kind of love Paul had for people.

READ

Acts 20:1–38

OBSERVE

The historical record is unclear as to whether this is the last time Paul was able to travel freely as a missionary, but it is certainly the end of his missionary journeys in Acts. In chapter 21, he will head to Jerusalem and his arrest.

vv. 1–6—Like Jesus (see Luke 9:51), Paul's face was set steadfastly to go to Jerusalem. Before he did so, he wanted to make one last round of his churches to encourage them. Luke compresses almost ten months into these few verses. It is very likely that Paul wrote Romans and the Corinthian letters during this period. He also was accompanied by even more partners in ministry, all young men who had joined him from those churches. Luke also joined him. Acts 20:5 begins another "we" section. He went from Ephesus in Asia Minor to Macedonia, to Greece, back through Macedonia, and then to Troas. As we noted previously, the sailing trip from Philippi to Troas took more than twice as long against the wind.

vv. 7–12—Even great missionary preachers can be long-winded. Luke suggests as much when he writes that Paul "talked on and on." It's encouraging to subsequent preachers that even a speaker as great as the Apostle Paul bored someone to death! Eutychus is the poster boy for all those who fall asleep in church. God didn't judge him harshly. God's Spirit moved through Paul to bring him back to life.

vv. 13–16—Luke gives another rather breathless travelogue of the trip from Troas, hopping from coastal towns to islands to another coastal town, Miletus. Paul took part of the journey on foot, probably relishing the quiet to prepare himself for the return to Jerusalem, where he would present the offering from the Gentile churches (Rom. 15:30–33).

vv. 17–38—Paul asked the Ephesian elders to come to him at Miletus because he knew that if he went back to Ephesus, he would not be able to leave quickly. These were the brothers the apostle had known the best because he spent the most time with them. He wanted to encourage them and to have their support as he faced his destiny.

We see some beautiful things about Paul in this tender farewell address:

1. He not only taught publicly, but he also went house-to-house as a caring pastor.
2. He was going to Jerusalem because he believed that the Spirit was clearly leading him in that direction. He knew that death was a possibility. Verse 24 sounds very similar to what he later writes to the Philippians (3:8, 14).
3. He preached the whole will (or "counsel" in some translations) of God and was therefore not to blame if people rejected the truth.
4. He warned the church leaders continually to beware of false teachers who would invariably come.
5. He didn't take money from the churches he founded, but he preferred to meet his own needs through the hard work of making tents. Some of Jesus' teaching that was not recorded in the gospels was passed on to Paul. He shares a quote from Jesus that is not found elsewhere in Scripture, *"It is more blessed to give than to receive"* (Acts 20:35).
6. Paul was not a Stoic who said his farewells without emotion. There may have been a tear in his eye when he said that they would not see him again. There were certainly tears when he knelt to pray with his dear elder friends.

APPLY

v. 24—Do you see the task of your life as testifying to the Gospel of God's grace? It is.

v. 28—If you're a church leader, are you a faithful shepherd?

v. 35—How does your life reflect the truth that it is more blessed to give than to receive?

MEMORIZE

Acts 20:27

Remember the task of being a spokesperson for God.

PRAY

A: Praise the God of grace.

C: Confess that you've often forgotten your life's task.

T: Thank God for reminding you of your life's task in this passage.

S: Ask God for an opportunity to testify to his grace today.

TELL

As St. Francis is reported to have said, "Preach the Gospel to everyone. If necessary, use words."

JUNE 3

THE TRIP TO JERUSALEM

PRAY

Pray to have the courage to follow God's direction for your life as Paul did.

READ

Acts 21:1–16

OBSERVE

There is a difficult theological issue in this passage that we must address.

vv. 1–6—The trip from Miletus to Tyre was more than four hundred miles. Paul and company had wonderful fellowship with the disciples living in Tyre. Luke is using the term "disciples" much like he uses "apostles"—in the generic sense. It is not the twelve, or even the 120 who live in Tyre, but "learners" who follow the Lord Jesus Christ. We will deal with verse 4 when we discuss verse 11.

vv. 7–9—How wonderful that they could stay with Philip, who is now known as "the evangelist." His ministry earlier in Acts was a model of Spirit-led evangelism, and his sensitivity to the Spirit had also been given to his four daughters, who were prophets.

vv. 10–16—It is another prophet, however, who speaks to Paul. We can assume, though he comes from Judea and not Antioch, that this is the same Agabus who prophesied the famine in Acts 11:28. In graphic fashion, reminiscent of the Old Testament prophets (1 Kings 11:29ff, Isa. 20:3ff, Ezek. 4:1ff.), Agabus predicts that Paul will be bound over to the Gentiles. Both in verse 4 and verse 11, Luke emphasizes that it is the Holy Spirit who revealed these truths. Paul had earlier said that the Spirit compelled him to go to Jerusalem, "not knowing what will happen to me there" (Acts 20:22). It seems like the Spirit's message to Paul and his message to believers in Tyre and to Agabus are in conflict.

John Stott considers several possible ways of resolving the dilemma, and he rejects the ideas that the Spirit changed his mind or that these men only thought that they were inspired by God. Stott writes:

> The better solution is to draw a distinction between a prediction and a prohibition. Agabus only predicted that Paul would be bound and handed over to the Gentiles (Acts 21:11); the pleading with Paul that followed is not attributed to the Spirit and may have been the fallible (indeed mistaken) human deduction from the Spirit's prophecy. For if Paul had heeded his friends' pleas, then Agabus' prophecy would not have been fulfilled! It is more difficult to understand 21:4 in this way, since the "urging" itself is said to be "through the Spirit." But perhaps Luke's statement is a condensed way of saying that the warning was divine while the urging was human. After all, the Spirit's word to Paul combined the compulsion to go with a warning of the consequences (20:22–23). (Stott, *The Spirit, the Church and the World*, 333)

Stott's analysis seems to be the best explanation. Though none of Paul's friends wanted him to be arrested, when they saw that he seemed as determined to go to Jerusalem as Jesus was, their conclusion was, "The Lord's will be done."

APPLY

v. 11—Be careful when someone says, "The Lord told me …" or "The Spirit says…." The interpretation of the message isn't always obvious.

v. 14—Are you prepared to say, "The Lord's will be done," even if it means a difficult path?

MEMORIZE

Acts 20:13

This is a powerful statement of a man sold out for Christ.

PRAY

A: Praise God's sovereign will.

C: Confess that you've too often prayed, "My will be done."

T: Thank God for people who care about you.

S: Intercede for someone facing a difficult decision.

TELL

Tell that person that you are praying for him or her.

JUNE 4

PAUL IS ARRESTED

Pray that you might be able to understand the advice the church leaders give to Paul.

READ

Acts 21:17–36

OBSERVE

This passage begins a pilgrimage for Paul that was very similar to his Lord's.

vv. 17–21—By this time (mid-50s AD), the Church in Jerusalem was more organized, with elders in place. Since the Jewish Christians numbered in the thousands, there must have been quite a few elders to oversee their spiritual welfare. James the brother of Jesus was identified as the leader of the church, and he and the elders received Paul's missionary band warmly. Luke doesn't mention it at this point (he does in Acts 24:17), but Paul also presented the offering from the Gentile churches that was so important to him. To Paul, it tangibly expressed the unity of Gentile believers with their Jewish brothers and sisters. The Jerusalem believers praise God for the abundant harvest among the Gentiles but rather quickly (at least from Luke's words) present their problem to Paul. The false rumor had circulated throughout Jerusalem and even in the church that Paul was telling Jews who lived in the *Diaspora* to abandon the law of Moses, including circumcision. Though Paul had freed Gentile converts from the yoke of the law (in keeping with the Jerusalem Council), he had not urged Jews to abandon the law. In fact, as a concession to Jewish sensibilities, he had Timothy circumcised since he was going to minister among the Jews. Lloyd Ogilvie comments:

> Most of us are able to withstand criticism from our enemies. It is when fellow Christians criticize us that it hurts deeply…. What probably hurt most was that the Church leaders had not silenced the criticism. They knew what Paul had been doing. Why hadn't James or some of the others squelched the rumors and criticism long before the Apostle arrived back in Jerusalem? Had no one said, "That's enough! We believe in our brother Paul and know that these rumors are false. There will be no further criticism of his ministry. We trust that the apostle has faithfully kept what we all agreed upon together." Could it have been that the leaders were not sure? Often we allow criticism around us when we are secretly suspicious ourselves. (Ogilvie, *Acts*, 304)

It is difficult not to wonder whether, despite the compromise of the Jerusalem Council, James and the others had lingering doubts about Paul's approach. There is at least a difference in emphasis between the letters of Paul and the book of James, which Luther called "a right strawy epistle," because the Reformer read it as denying justification by faith alone. We'll explore that when we arrive at the book of James.

vv. 22–26—Ogilvie's analysis of the proposal from the Jerusalem church is again worth considering:

> Whatever the case, the leaders chose not to make a defense for Paul among the believers, but asked him to do it for himself. He would have to solve the problem. We wonder why the leadership of the Jerusalem church was not as decisive with the critics as they were with Paul then they told him what to do to diffuse the criticism. "Therefore do what we tell you" (v. 23) is not exactly a permissive suggestion but a command! Paul was told to participate in a compromise for unity. Again we wonder: did Paul groan inside at the necessity of proving his integrity? (Ogilvie, *Acts*, 304–305)

If he did groan, there's no indication of it in Acts or anywhere else. F. F. Bruce writes, "A truly emancipated spirit such as Paul's is not in bondage to its own emancipation" (Bruce, *Acts*, 432). Though Paul had already taken a view of purification recently (Acts 18:18), he joins four Jewish Christians in their purification rites and even pays their offering, fulfilling all the demands of the law. James hoped that this would convince the Jewish critics of the sincerity of Paul's personal observance of the law.

vv. 27–36—The strategy of appeasement backfired. It may have placated some of the Jewish Christians within the church, but it put Paul directly in the line of fire of some Jews from Asia Minor who were in Jerusalem for the feast of Pentecost. Using a couple of inflammatory lies, they quickly aroused the city against Paul. Jewish fervor ran especially high at feast times. It seems clear that they would have killed him on the spot if the Roman soldiers had not arrived. Luke's comment in verse 30, "they dragged him from the temple, and immediately the gates were shut," has as much theological as historical importance. The events surrounding Paul's life would be some of the major factors that closed the temple and synagogue to Christians and confirmed the division that continues to the present. The mob's cries, "Away with him!" sound eerily like the cries that were heard in the same city some twenty-five years earlier.

APPLY

v. 21—Have you ever been hurt by fellow Christians who have failed to defend you against unjust accusations? How does God want you to respond to them?

vv. 27–29—What groups do you think are most critical of the Church today? What, if anything, could be done to lessen the animosity? Is there anything you could do to help?

MEMORIZE

Acts 21:30b

This was a watershed moment in the history of the church.

PRAY

A: Praise God, who orders history.

C: Confess any times you have failed to defend your brothers or sisters.

T: Thank God for when police keep order justly.

S: Intercede for Christians who suffer for righteousness' sake.

TELL

Discuss with a Christian friend or your small group whether you think Ogilvie's analysis of the failures of the Church in Jerusalem is accurate.

JUNE 5

PAUL'S DEFENSE BEFORE THE CROWD IN JERUSALEM

PRAY

Pray that you might be as loving toward your enemies as Paul was toward his.

READ

Acts 21:37–22:29

OBSERVE

John Stott points out that Paul's experience once again parallels Jesus'. The Lord faced five trials in which he was called upon to defend himself—before Annas, the Sanhedrin, King Herod Antipas, and twice by Pilate. Paul defended himself before the crowd, the Sanhedrin, King Herod Agrippa II, and the two procurators, Felix and Festus (Stott, *The Spirit, the Church and the World*, 336–337). This is Paul's first defense, and it is impressive in several respects.

vv. 37–39—The Roman commander Claudius Lysias thought that Paul might be the Egyptian false prophet who led a large army to the Mount of Olives and promised them that the walls of Jerusalem would fall down at his command. Though his army was largely captured or killed, the false prophet escaped. Lysias thought that Paul might be him, given the huge uproar. The fact that Paul spoke flawless Greek and was a Roman citizen had to impress the commander.

vv. 40–22:2—God had chosen the right spokesman, for Paul also spoke Aramaic eloquently, and that quieted the crowd. Commentator Bruce notes:

> If an audience of Welsh or Irish nationalists, about to be addressed by someone whom they regarded as a traitor to the national cause, suddenly realized that he was speaking

to them not in the despised Saxon tongue but in the Celtic vernacular, the gesture would no doubt call forth at least a temporary measure of good will. (Bruce, *Acts*, 439)

vv. 3–22—This is the first time Paul gives his testimony in Acts in his own words. He wisely crafts his words to appeal favorably to his audience. Though he does not de-emphasize the life-changing person of Jesus, he places his conversion solidly in a Jewish context that his hearers can appreciate. Look at how he does it:

1. *"I am a Jew … brought up in this city."*
2. *"Under Gamaliel I was thoroughly trained in the law of our fathers and was just as zealous for God as any of you are today."*
3. *"I persecuted the followers of this Way to their death … as also the high priest and all the Council can testify."*
4. *"Ananias … was a devout observer of the law and highly respected by all the Jews living there."*
5. *"Then he said, 'The God of our fathers has chosen you to know his will and to see the Righteous One'."*
6. *"These men know that I went from one synagogue to another to imprison and beat those who believe in you. And when the blood of your martyr Stephen was shed, I stood there giving my approval and guarding the clothes of those who were killing him."*

Despite saying all the right things, Paul says one wrong thing (to the crowd's ears): *"Go, I will send you far away to the Gentiles."* Their fanatical hatred of the Gentiles was the reason they wanted to kill Paul. His mention of God's new covenant incensed the racist crowd. Stott writes:

In their eyes, proselytism (making Gentiles into Jews) was fine, but evangelism (making Gentiles into Christians without first making them Jews) was an abomination. It was tantamount to saying that Jews and Gentiles were equal, for they both needed to come to God through Christ, and that on identical terms. (Stott, *The Spirit, the Church and the World*, 348)

vv. 23–29—This was the first time, but not the last, that Paul's Roman citizenship would come in handy. This time it spared him a flogging. Once again, the hero of the story is a centurion, who reports the facts to Lysias. The commander is impressed that the citizenship he himself had to purchase with big bucks was Paul's by birthright.

APPLY

vv. 3–21—When you're sharing your faith with someone, it is perfectly acceptable to tailor the message to your audience. That's part of what Paul meant when he wrote, *"I have become all things to all men so that by all means possible I might save some"* (1 Cor. 9:22).

MEMORIZE

Acts 22:10

It's not included in the original story (Acts 9), but it's a great thing for every Christian to ask our Lord.

PRAY

A: Praise God, who changes lives.

C: Confess that you haven't always wisely sized up your audience when sharing your faith.

T: Thank God for chances to witness regardless of the reception.

S: Ask God for the opportunity to speak the truth in love to someone today.

TELL

Tell that person the Gospel in language he or she can understand.

JUNE 6

PAUL BEFORE THE SANHEDRIN

PRAY

Pray that you might be as clever as Paul when faced with opposition.

READ

Read Acts 22:30–23:11

OBSERVE

v. 30—The Roman commander was not a theologian and certainly didn't understand the fine points of Judaism, so he wisely takes Paul before the Sanhedrin to figure out just why the people were so upset with him.

vv. 23:1–5—Why was Ananias so disturbed by Paul's opening statement? He had certainly heard similar statements from defendants before the Sanhedrin previously. Many Jews, like Paul (Phil. 3:6) and the rich young ruler (Mark 10:20), could claim that they were never guilty of breaking one of the outward observances of the law. Stott writes, "The most likely explanation is that Ananias understood Paul's words as a claim that, though now a Christian, he was still a good Jew, having served God with a good conscience all his life" (Stott, *The Spirit, the Church and the World*, 351). Ananias' command to strike Paul in the mouth was not only offensive, it was illegal. Paul hadn't even been formally charged with a crime.

The apostle's anger is understandable even though it differs from the way Jesus responded when the soldiers struck him on the head again and again (Matt. 27:30, Luke 22:63–65). It also contrasts with what Paul had recently written to the Corinthians: *"When we are cursed, we bless; when we are persecuted, we endure it"* (1 Cor. 4:12). Perhaps the cumulative weight of unfair treatment finally caused Paul to crack a little bit. We can hardly condemn him for that. We might wonder how he failed to know that it was the high priest who gave the order. Several different explanations have been offered, but the most satisfying is that Paul had terrible eyesight, and his reference to a whitewashed wall "may have been not so much a reference to hypocrisy as an uncouth allusion to a white-robed figure across the court whom Paul could only dimly perceive" (Stott, *The Spirit, the Church and the World*, 352). In any case, Paul had the humility and obedience to apologize when he realized that he had violated Exodus 22:28.

vv. 6–11—Commentators are divided on Paul's strategy of dividing the Pharisees and Sadducees. F. W. Farrar writes:

> We cannot defend his conduct. He was a little unhinged, both morally and spiritually by the wild and awful trials of the day before. The claim still to be a Pharisee was hardly worthy of St. Paul. (Farrar, *The Life and Work of St. Paul*, 541)

W. M. Ramsay persuasively argues that Paul's strategy was not only brilliant but authentic:

> If one party (the Pharisees) was more capable of being brought to a favourable view of his claims than the other (the Sadducees), he would naturally and justifiably aim at affecting the minds of the more hopeful party. Paul was claiming, moreover, to represent the true line of development in which Judaism ought to advance. (Ramsay, *St. Paul*, 83)

It could be that Paul wanted to continue his dissertation on the resurrection of the dead, focusing on the resurrection of Christ, but the violent argument prevented any further speech. It was one thing to see a mob go berserk, but Claudius Lysias must have been stunned to see priests and lawyers threatening to tear each other (and Paul) limb from limb. How intriguing that Paul has to be taken to a Roman barracks to protect him from a church meeting. We can assume that Christ's appearance to Paul in his cell was another vision, like he had experienced in Acts 18:9 and 22:17. Stott writes:

> It would be hard to exaggerate the calm courage which this assurance must have brought to Paul during his three further trials, his two years' imprisonment and his hazardous voyage to Rome. (Stott, *The Spirit, the Church and the World*, 353)

At crucial periods of Paul's life, the Lord communicated just what he needed to sustain him. We can trust him to do the same for us.

APPLY

vv. 3, 5—Have you lost your temper lately? Are you humble enough to apologize to those you may have hurt?

v. 4—Do you show proper respect to those in authority even when you disagree with them?

MEMORIZE

Acts 23:11

It is the Lord's gracious assurance to Paul.

PRAY

A: Praise the risen Christ.

C: Confess your anger and its effects on others.

T: Thank God for his sovereign plan in your life.

S: Intercede for someone who doesn't believe in the resurrection.

TELL

If you've offended someone by your anger, go and ask his or her forgiveness.

JUNE 7

THE PLOT TO KILL PAUL AND HIS TRANSFER TO CAESAREA

PRAY

Pray that you might take seriously the forces of evil, yet not be intimidated by them.

READ

Acts 23:12–35

OBSERVE

vv. 12–15—Luke doesn't specify which Jews formed the conspiracy, but it's a safe guess that it was mostly Sadducees. Bruce writes:

> This plot bespeaks the fanatical devotion of the conspirators, for Paul would be guarded by Roman soldiers, and an attempt to assassinate him, whether it succeeded or not, would inevitably involve the assassins in heavy loss of life. (Bruce, *Acts*, 57)

Sometimes the forces of evil are more dedicated to their cause than the forces of good, which is to our shame (Luke 16:8).

vv. 16–22—We are given a fascinating glimpse into Paul's family life, which is unknown besides this brief mention of his nephew. Who was this nephew, and how did he receive such prompt news of the plot to kill his uncle? Bruce points out that a possible translation of verse 16 could be, "But Paul's sister's son heard the plotting, having been present (*paragenomenos*), and he entered into the fortress and reported it to Paul" (Bruce, 457). It could be that Paul's sister still lived in Tarsus but sent her son to Jerusalem to be educated, much like her brother had been. It's also possible that the young man studied under Gamaliel, which might explain his entrée to the Sanhedrin (especially if the wise teacher kept the boy's relationship with Paul under wraps). Whatever the case, God used this courageous young man to preserve Paul's life. The commander was wise to keep this news to himself so that he could thwart their plan without getting involved with their machinations.

vv. 23–25—Lysias took no chances. The force he sent to Caesarea would be more than enough to protect Paul against forty knife-wielding fanatics. The commander's letter to Felix is thoroughly unbiased, finding nothing in Paul deserving death or imprisonment but giving his accusers a chance to present their case. The trip to Antipatris was thirty-five miles, which had to be a difficult march for the infantry at night. Since they had left the assassins far behind, they walked back to Jerusalem the next morning and left Paul in the capable hands of the seventy cavalrymen. Felix asked Paul which province he was from because the governor would have consulted the ruler of Syria or Anatolia if Paul were from one of the client kingdoms. Since Paul was a Roman citizen, a Roman procurator could properly hear his case. Herod's palace was the headquarters of the Roman administration and would have provided nicer accommodations than what Paul received in Jerusalem. This was his real handing over to the Gentiles that Agabus foretold in 21:11.

APPLY

v. 16—It's not wrong to "tattle" when a moral principle is being violated.

v. 22—It's also important to know when to keep things confidential.

PRAY

A: Praise God, who preserves his elect.

C: Confess your failure to keep the right things confidential and the times you have told the wrong things.

T: Thank God that he gives wisdom when we ask for it (James 1:5).

S: Ask about a situation in which you're not sure whether to speak or keep silent.

TELL

If there's something you should share with someone who needs to know it, share it. If there's a secret you've been entrusted with, be sure to keep it confidential.

JUNE 8

PAUL'S TRIAL BEFORE FELIX

PRAY

Pray that if you're ever unjustly accused of anything, you can answer your accusers eloquently.

READ

Acts 24:1–27

OBSERVE

Like Jesus, Paul has done nothing wrong, but evil cannot stand true goodness.

vv. 1–9—It shows how important it was to the Jewish establishment to squelch Paul that the high priest himself traveled to Caesarea, which took him more than sixty miles through Gentile territory. The authorities came with all the firepower they could muster, including a slick Roman lawyer. Barclay writes, "Tertullus began his speech with a passage of almost nauseating flattery, every word of which he knew and Felix knew was quite untrue. He went on to state things which were equally untrue" (Barclay, Commentaries, 184–185). Every charge he makes against Paul is either a lie or, at best, a half-truth. But they were fairly effective fabrications. Paul never stirred up a riot. It was angry Jews who stirred up people against him again and again. One thing Rome would not tolerate was civil disorder, so this was a serious charge. Describing Paul as a "ringleader of the Nazarene sect" lumped him with a number of false messiahs who were insurrectionists. Again, Rome had seen the havoc these cult leaders could bring. Though Felix wasn't particularly concerned about the temple being defiled, he knew that the priests were all Sadducees, the pro-Roman party. It was an attempt to sway the court by saying in essence, "We're on the same side. This man is an outsider." Even Tertullus' claim that they seized Paul was false. The scene in the temple court was far more intense and dramatic than a normal arrest.

vv. 10–21—In contrast to Tertullus, Paul's *captatio benevolentiae* (capturing the good will) to Felix is a model of restraint. His defense is simple and powerful. He never argued with anyone in the temple, stirred up a crowd, or created any disturbance. They can't prove any of their charges because none of them happened. Paul acknowledges that he is a follower of the Way, but points out that there is a great deal of agreement between the doctrines of Judaism and Christianity. Some commentators criticize Paul for not presenting the Gospel clearly at this trial, but he is wise to show restraint. He will have a chance to present the claims of Christ later to Felix. The trial wasn't about theology but to determine whether Paul was a revolutionary.

vv. 22–23—It's obvious from Felix's response that the Jews did not prove their case and that Paul was more persuasive than the professional lawyer. Felix puts Paul under a benevolent house arrest until Lysias arrives. If the commander ever did get to Caesarea, Luke didn't record it.

vv. 24–26—Felix was not a "most excellent" governor. He was ambitious and unscrupulous. He began life as a slave in Rome. His brother Pallas was a favorite of Nero, and through the influence of Pallas, Felix became a freedman and then a governor—the first slave in history to ever be procurator of a Roman province. Like Nero, he was ruthless and paranoid, once hiring assassins to kill his closest supporters. Druscilla was his third wife (his second was the granddaughter of Antony and Cleopatra). Though Druscilla seemed to be a genuine seeker, when Paul began to speak about righteousness, self-control, and the judgment to come, it hit too close to home for Felix. An indication of his lack of character is that he would have released Paul if he had given the governor a bribe. Felix was removed from office for mishandling a conflict that occurred between Jews and Greeks. The Jews were winning until Felix dispatched the Roman troops. At his encouragement, they sacked and looted the homes of the wealthiest Jews in Caesarea. The Jews appealed to the emperor, whose patience with Felix was exhausted. Only Nero's friendship with Pallas saved Felix from execution. He kept Paul in prison for two years because he wanted to curry favor with the Jews, who hated him. Scholars believe that several of Paul's epistles were written during this period of his Caesarean imprisonment.

APPLY

v. 13—Are you living in such a way that no accusation made against you can stick? If not, what do you need to change?

v. 16—Beyond visible offenses, is your conscience clear before God? This doesn't mean that you are sinless, but that you confess your sins regularly and promptly.

MEMORIZE

Acts 24:16

This is a great aspiration.

PRAY

A: Praise the God of our fathers and mothers.

C: Confess any sins you're aware of.

T: Thank God for those like Paul who won't sugar-coat the Gospel to get a convert.

S: Ask God to show you anything you need to do to have a clear conscience before man. Do you need to confess to someone?

TELL

It's important to have an accountability partner or group who can keep you honest and help you keep your conscience clear.

JUNE 9

PAUL AND FESTUS

PRAY

Pray that God will show you how this encounter applies to your life today.

READ

Acts 25:1–27

OBSERVE

vv. 1–5—Porcius Festus was a man of better character than Felix. It was common for a new procurator to make the rounds of his province, especially going to prominent cities like Jerusalem. Though he was inexperienced, Festus did not allow himself to be hoodwinked by the bloodthirsty Jewish leaders. Exerting his Roman authority, he invited them to come to Caesarea and place Paul on trial again.

vv. 6–12—The charade of a trial was played out once more because Felix had failed to declare Paul not guilty. Once again, the Jews brought their charges, and Paul defended himself ably. But this seemed more like a preliminary hearing. As the new administrator, Festus wanted to build a bridge to the Jews and thought that having a full-blown trial in Jerusalem before the supreme religious court would do it. Festus would retain the power of judge. He knew it didn't matter to Rome where the trial was held. But it made a great deal of difference to Paul. The apostle knew that the same men who tried to kill him two years earlier still wanted his blood. He also knew that nothing good would come of a trial in Jerusalem even if he made it there alive. Remembering the Lord's promise that Paul would testify about him in Rome, Paul appealed to Caesar, the right of every Roman citizen. Festus gladly granted the request, since he didn't know what to do.

vv. 13–27—The dilemma facing Festus was that he had to send Paul to Rome with a specific charge against him. Enter King Herod Agrippa II and his sister Bernice, who would later become the consort of the Emperor Titus. Agrippa was the son of Herod Agrippa I, king of Judea from 41–44 AD. When Agrippa I died, his son was too young to be appointed king by the Emperor Claudius. But four years later, at age twenty-one, Agrippa II was given a small kingdom near Lebanon and the right to appoint the Jewish high priest. In 53 AD, Nero added to his territory substantially, and the young king changed the name of Caesarea Philippi ("The Emperor Philip") to Neronias. Agrippa was an authority on Judaism. Surely he would have the right advice for Festus. The procurator lays out the situation for the king, admitting that he doesn't have a clue as to how to proceed. Bruce writes:

> There is probably quiet humor in Luke's description of the "great pomp" with which they assembled; Luke had a very true sense of values, and knew that in his friend and teacher Paul there was a native greatness which did not need to be decked with the trappings of grandeur that surrounded his distinguished hearers. History has vindicated Luke's perspective. Most people nowadays who know anything about Agrippa and Bernice and Festus know of them as people who for a brief space of their lives crossed the path of Paul and heard him speak words which might have brought great blessing to them had they been disposed to pay serious heed to them. All of these Very Important People would have been greatly surprised and not a little scandalized had they been able to foresee the relative estimates that later generations would form of them and of the handcuffed Jew who stood before them to plead his cause. (Bruce, *Acts*, 484)

APPLY

v. 23—What really matters in the long run, fame or faithfulness?

MEMORIZE

Acts 25:12

God uses a secular proconsul as his instrument to get Paul to Rome.

PRAY

A: Praise God who works in history.

C: Confess times you've chosen acclaim over faithfulness.

T: Thank God for his plan for your life.

S: Intercede for someone caught up in status.

TELL

Tell someone close to you what you think really matters in life.

JUNE 10

PAUL TRIES TO PERSUADE KING AGRIPPA

PRAY

Pray that those in authority would seriously consider the Gospel.

READ

Acts 26:1–32

OBSERVE

This is the fifth and final time Paul speaks in a trial situation in Acts.

vv. 1–3—The motion Paul made with his hand would have been a formal salute to the king, which was mandated by Roman jurisprudence as was the *captatio benevolentiae,* which Paul again delivers in honest and restrained fashion.

vv. 4–8—In speaking to someone knowledgeable about Judaism, Paul makes the crucial point that Jesus the Messiah is the fulfillment of the hope of the Old Testament, a hope that even twenty-first century Jews are longing to see.

vv. 9–11—What could be more persuasive than a person who had once zealously persecuted Christianity becoming its ardent defender? Verse 10 is the first clear indication that Saul was part of the death sentence for many Christians. Previously, we only knew that he put them in prison. The memory of this horror never left the apostle (1 Tim. 1:13).

vv. 12–18—As in the gospels, different details emerge in each retelling of the story of the road to Damascus. The proverb spoken in verse 14, *"It is hard for you to kick against the goads,"* is taken from agricultural life. A young ox was usually trained on a one-handed plow. The plowman had a long staff with a sharpened end, which he held close to the ox's heels. Every time it attempted to kick, it was jabbed with the spike. Barclay writes, "The young ox had to learn submission to the yoke the hard way and so had Paul" (Barclay, Commentaries, 195). We also see, for the first time in this account, that Jesus promised to protect Paul as he sent him on his mission to the Jews first and then to the Gentiles (like Jesus' own mission). That calling, which Paul fulfilled so brilliantly, consisted of four main goals:

1. To open their eyes to God's light coming into their darkness
2. To deliver them from the power of Satan to the power of God
3. To enable them to receive forgiveness for their sins
4. To give them a place among the saints who are made holy by Jesus

vv. 19–23—Paul restates his theme. In all of his preaching, including his calling Jew and Gentile to repentance of mind and deed, he was only fulfilling what Moses and the prophets had predicted about the Messiah. The Lord's Christ would suffer (Isa. 53:4–9), be the first to rise from the dead (Ps. 16:10), and proclaim light to Jews and Gentiles (Isa. 9:2).

v. 24—What caused Festus' surprising interruption? Blaiklock suggests:

> Paul was heard without impatience while he confined his argument to the abstract consideration of theological dogma. It was when he spoke specifically of a historic Christ, raised from the dead within living memory, that the audience grew restless. Something like the same situation had developed in Athens. Festus, thoroughly irritated, broke in with a rudeness at variance with the correct bearing which had so far done him credit. (Blaiklock, *The Acts of the Apostles*, 185)

The preaching of the cross and resurrection is foolishness to those who are perishing (1 Cor. 1:18, 15:14–19).

vv. 25–27—Paul handles Festus' outburst graciously but truthfully. What he says is both true and reasonable. Furthermore, his intended audience, King Agrippa, has the background to understand what Paul is saying. Since he believes the prophets, he should be open to their fulfillment.

vv. 28–29—Paul's direct question brings the matter too close to home for Agrippa. He sees clearly what Paul had been trying to do—to persuade him to accept Christ. Paul doesn't apologize for trying to convert Agrippa with his speech. Whether it takes a short time or a long time, Paul's earnest desire, expressed throughout all of his ministry, was that everyone might be a follower of Christ as he was. He graciously adds, "except for these chains."

vv. 30–32—Though Paul's defense does not convert Agrippa, it is successful in persuading the king that Paul was sensible and not a criminal. He could have been freed if he had not appealed to Caesar, but it appears that God's plan included Paul traveling to Rome as a prisoner.

APPLY

vv. 10–11—Even though Paul remembered the terrible things he had done, he knew that he was forgiven. Have you completely accepted God's forgiveness for the terrible things you've done?

v. 14—Do you see that disobedience to Christ always ends up hurting you?

MEMORIZE

Acts 26:29

This is a goal for your ministry to your friends.

PRAY

A: Praise the Light of the World.

C: Confess any disobedience to the vision God has given you.

T: Thank God for forgiveness and new life.

S: Intercede for someone walking in darkness.

TELL

How might you tell a Jewish friend that Jesus fulfills the prophecies about the Messiah, using this passage?

JUNE 11

A DIFFICULT VOYAGE TO ROME

Pray for the ability to see God's hand in even the difficult journeys.

READ

Acts 27:1–26

OBSERVE

The final "we" section in Acts is from 27:1–28:16.

vv. 1–12—Paul's final journey (at least in the book of Acts) begins. Again, it is a centurion who treats him kindly. Julius was a member of the Imperial Regiment, "a special corps who acted as liaison officers between the Emperor and the provinces" (Barclay, Commentaries, 199). Adramyttium was situated on the northeast shore of the Aegean Sea, just south of Troas. Ramsay suggests that the only way Luke and Aristarchus were able to accompany Paul is that "they must have gone as slaves" (Ramsay, St. Paul, 316). It's also possible that Aristarchus was under arrest, or that he later volunteered to be arrested to stay with Paul, for in Colossians 4:10, Paul refers to him as "my fellow prisoner."

The first stop was Sidon, sister city to Tyre, where Julius allowed Paul opportunity for Christian fellowship and refreshment. They passed "to the lee of Cyprus," which meant to the north of it, and landed at Myra in south-central Asia Minor (modern Turkey, where almost 400 years later, St. Nicholas would be named bishop). The ship from Alexandria was carrying a cargo of corn and would not have been a sleek sailing vessel. Crete is a large island southeast of Macedonia (Greece), and Fair Havens was a harbor there. The Egyptians and Romans turned up their noses at wintering in a lower-class location (despite the name) and decided to press on to a better location in Crete, Phoenix (or Phoenice, in some translations). They would soon come to regret their disregard of Paul's advice. Sailing after the Fast (the Day of Atonement), which usually occurred in October, was very problematic, and Paul was by now a veteran seaman, after his three missionary journeys.

It's clear that Luke kept a daily log of their progress. Thomas Walker writes, "There is no such detailed record of the working of an ancient ship in the whole of classical literature" (Walker, 543). Though Luke was not a sailor, entire books have been written based on his descriptions.

vv. 13–20—Initially, the decision by the Egyptians and Romans seemed like a good one, but the gentle south wind turned into a violent northeaster, and it was impossible to land in Phoenix. They were blown out to sea and had to resort to drastic measures. Passing ropes under the ship to shore it up and throwing the cargo and tackle overboard were all acts of desperation. The sandbars of Syrtis were the Bermuda triangle of the Mediterranean, where many ships had been wrecked and many crews lost their lives. Fortunately, the ship avoided that graveyard.

vv. 21–26—Paul was realistic yet optimistic. The reality was that they should have listened to him. That would have preserved the ship. Since they didn't, the ship would be lost, but the men would be saved. God graciously gave Paul a vision that he shared with his fellow passengers and the crew. It took faith for them to believe someone who was not a professional sailor, but like the disciples with Jesus and the sailors with Jonah, they didn't have much choice.

APPLY

v. 11—Can you think of any mistakes you've made because you refused to listen to sound advice? How will you go about seeking wise counsel in the future?

vv. 21–25—Are you a mixture of realism and optimism? That's the only appropriate outlook for Christians who know that the ultimate victory belongs to Christ, though the interim will be full of trouble.

PRAY

A: Praise the God of land and sea.

C: Confess the times you have stubbornly gone alone and disregarded advice.

T: Thank God for good advisors.

S: Ask God to provide wise counselors.

TELL

Approach someone to be your advisor in a particular area. Look for someone "full of the Holy Spirit and wisdom" (Acts 6:3) who has expertise in the area you need.

JUNE 12

SHIPWRECK

PRAY

Pray that when a crisis occurs, you might have a cool head like Paul.

READ

Acts 27:27–44

OBSERVE

vv. 27–32—After fourteen nights of storm-tossed seas, even the saltiest of sailors would be exhausted. From their experience, they knew that if the ship hit rocks at even a depth of thirty feet, there was a good chance that very few of those on board would make it to land. It's clear that they didn't fully believe Paul's prophecy. In a sneaky move, the crew tried to quietly let down the lifeboat while pretending to drop additional anchors. They didn't fool Paul. He believed that God's promise of protection for everyone only applied if everyone stayed with the boat. Julius, who was probably upset when Paul told him of the plot, had his soldiers cut the leads to the lifeboat and set it adrift.

vv. 33–38—Paul's third intervention during this storm was to encourage everyone to eat. Paul knew that they must keep up their strength. Even though we have God's promises, we still need to use our sanctified common sense to cooperate with his Spirit. Paul's breaking of the bread seems almost sacramental. Whenever we eat, we are thanking God for his eucharist (good gift of grace). This is especially true when we're in a desperate situation.

vv. 39–44—The sailors' fears were realized. When the ship struck a sandbar, it was dashed to pieces by the surf. However, yet another surreptitious plan was brewing.

The soldiers, who were probably concerned about the penalty for those who let prisoners escape, had planned to kill the prisoners. It is unclear how Julius discovered their plot and how Luke heard about it. But the good centurion prevented the plot from succeeding. All 276 people on board made it to shore safely, some by swimming and some by simply floating. The traditional site of the shipwreck, on the northeast coast of Malta, is now called St. Paul's Bay.

APPLY

vv. 31–33—God has promised protection for his people (see Ps. 46:1–5). He also expects us to be careful and not foolish. On the other hand, fear and paranoia about safety may reflect a lack of faith. Where do you find the balance between prudence and paranoia, faith and foolishness?

PRAY

A: Praise God, our fortress and strength.

C: Confess your foolishness and/or paranoia.

T: Thank God for preserving your life.

S: Intercede for those whose work involves facing danger.

TELL

Discuss with a friend or your small group how much safety-consciousness is healthy.

JUNE 13

FROM SNAKEBITE TO SAFETY

PRAY

Pray for a renewed appreciation for God's faithfulness and providence.

READ

Acts 28:1–16

OBSERVE

v. 1—The island of Malta is south of the "big toe" of Italy, below the much larger island of Sicily.

vv. 2–6—The word translated as "islanders" in the NIV is *barbaroi*, but it doesn't necessarily mean "barbarians." The Greeks used that word for all foreigners who spoke their own native language instead of Greek. Bruce writes, "The natives of Malta were largely of Phoenician extraction, and their language was a Phoenician dialect" (Bruce, *Acts*, 521). The fact that they showed the shipwrecked foreigners unusual kindness by building a fire (the Mediterranean Sea in early November would have been very cold) and welcoming them shows that they were the opposite of barbarians. Paul, who had shown himself to be a great practical help on board, continued his usefulness on land. A poisonous snake, which probably looked like a stick as it hid among the wood for warmth, crawled out of the fire and sank its fangs into Paul. The NIV translation does not capture the true sense of the natives' words. "Justice" is the translation of the Greek *Dike*, the goddess of justice and revenge (Nemesis in Roman mythology). This crowd was the opposite of the people of Lystra, who first declared Paul and Silas to be gods then stoned them (Acts 14:11–19). The people of Malta first thought that Paul was a murderer, then declared him to be a god.

vv. 7–10—The father of Publius probably suffered from what Dr. Richard Long-necker identifies as "Malta fever." The microorganism that causes it was identified in 1887 and traced to the milk of Maltese goats. The primary symptoms are fever and diarrhea, which can last anywhere from four months to two years (Longnecker, *Acts*, 565). Not only was the father of the chief official healed instantly, so were the rest of the sick people on the island. Luke uses a different verb from other New Testament writers to describe the healings, *therapeuo*. It was the word used for medical treatment, but there is no suggestion that the treatment consisted of anything other than Paul's touch and prayer.

vv. 11–16—The shipwrecked men spent from mid-November until mid-February on Malta. At that time, navigation was safe again, and they boarded their third ship to complete the journey. The twin gods, Castor and Pollux, were the sons of Jupiter (Zeus in Roman mythology). They were the gods of navigation and the patrons of seafarers. Syracuse is the capital of the island of Sicily. Rhegium is on the "toe" of Italy, and Puteoli is on the Gulf of Naples. Only a few miles outside of Puteoli, they would have come to the famous Appian Way, which led straight to Rome, "the oldest, straightest and most perfectly made of all the Roman roads" (Longnecker, 568). The Forum of Appius was forty miles from Rome and the Three Taverns thirty miles from the great city. In Rome, Paul was under *custodia militaris*, or what we would call house arrest. Rather than a bracelet around his ankle, he was chained to a Roman soldier by his right wrist twenty-four hours a day. That may be one reason he had to dictate the letters he wrote from Rome.

APPLY

v. 2—Is it your regular practice to show kindness to strangers? Hebrews 13:2 says, *"for by so doing some people have entertained angels without knowing it."*

v. 4—Be wary of suggesting that someone's misfortune is God's punishment.

v. 15—Are you willing to go out of your way to honor a brother or sister in Christ? Those acts of sacrificial love can be tremendously encouraging.

PRAY

A: Praise the God who heals.

C: Confess your failure to go out of your way to honor others.

T: Thank God for those who have done so for you.

S: Ask God for the opportunity to show honor to at least one person this week.

TELL

It is good to honor others by telling them how much they mean to you. A letter is sometimes more effective than an email or a verbal message.

JUNE 14

THE GOSPEL IS UNFETTERED IN ROME

Pray for the same concern for those in your life and their salvation as Paul had.

Acts 28:17–31

Lloyd Ogilvie calls this last section of Acts "The End of the Beginning," a fitting title. Most scholars believe Paul was taken to Rome around 60–62 AD and released in 61–63 AD. He then had a period of relative freedom in which he traveled and ministered. He was later arrested again and returned to Rome, where he wrote the Prison Epistles (including 2 Timothy, his last letter). He was executed there around 65–67 AD. This passage gives a snapshot of what happened when he was first under house arrest in the early 60s in the imperial city of Italy.

vv. 17–22—Paul never stopped loving and caring. He wanted his Jewish brothers and sisters in Rome to know that he was not trying to tear down their faith but to share with them about Jesus. The Jewish leaders in Judea probably did not send letters to Rome because they felt that it was futile. If they couldn't influence a judicial proceeding in their own backyard, they surely wouldn't have any influence in Rome. They were probably happy to be rid of Paul and to have him in prison far away. Little did they know that his pen was more dangerous in a prison cell in Rome than his person was in a synagogue in Jerusalem.

vv. 23–28—The real reason Paul called the Jews to meet him wasn't to present a defense for his case, but to present a defense for his faith. He was supremely eloquent in arguing from the Hebrew Scriptures that Jesus is the Messiah. As usual, some believed, but some would not. This had to be frustrating to Paul. He quotes Isaiah 6:9–10 (as Jesus did in Matthew 13:13–15) not to condemn the unbelieving Jews, but to warn them. Though they would not listen, salvation would be offered to those who would, the Gentiles. The most reliable manuscripts of Acts don't include verse 29, which seems to be a reiteration of verse 25.

vv. 30–31—The last two verses of Acts picture Paul in a glorious situation. Jewish and Gentile Christians came to see him, and he likely continued to minister to many of the same people while he was there. There was no hindrance to his preaching and teaching. It is likely that Julius had something to do with that. Out of his gratitude for what Paul did on the voyage, the centurion may have used his influence to make sure that Paul was not put in a typical Roman prison. We know from Philippians that many members of the Praetorian Guard who were assigned to him became believers; all of them heard the Gospel from Paul's lips. Though one hand was chained, the Gospel was not fettered, and the message of the kingdom continued to be proclaimed by the greatest missionary in history. The book of Acts ends as it began, with the Gospel of the kingdom of God and the Lord Jesus Christ being proclaimed boldly.

APPLY

vv. 25–28—Have you ever shared the Gospel with someone so thoroughly that you have placed the onus of responsibility on them?

vv. 30–31—Many people would see imprisonment, even in a minimum security situation, as the pits and complain about it endlessly. Paul made the best of every situation. How do you respond to difficult situations?

MEMORIZE

Acts 28:31

This should encourage all believers to proclaim the Gospel.

PRAY

A: Praise God, who works all things together for good.

C: Confess the ways you have complained about your circumstances.

T: Thank God that you have the ability to proclaim the Gospel.

S: Ask God to open doors for you to share Christ and to give you the courage to boldly charge through those doors.

TELL

Discuss with your small group how Paul can be a model for your ministry together.

JUNE 15

THE BOOK THAT MOST CHANGED HISTORY

Pray that God would truly speak to you through this book that has changed so many lives throughout history.

READ

Romans 1:1–17

OBSERVE

Take off your shoes—you are about to tread on holy ground. Paul's letter to the Romans is one of the peaks of Scripture. God has used this letter in many people's lives.

1. A verse from Romans (13:14) was instrumental in St. Augustine's conversion. The change was so dramatic that later, when he was walking down the street, he saw a woman he had lived with. He walked past her and she said, "Augustine, don't you remember? It's me!" His answer was, "Yes, but it's no longer me." Augustine's commentary on Romans is still a definitive work.

2. Romans 1:17 pierced the heart of Martin Luther, a German monk. He was so caught up in works-righteousness that he confessed his confessions. Justification by faith alone transformed him, and with him all of history. *Sola fides* (by faith alone) became one of the rallying cries of the Reformation, the event that influenced modern history more than any other. Luther called Romans "the clearest gospel of all."

3. Luther's commentary on Romans was used by God to convert John Wesley,

the great eighteenth-century evangelist who founded the Methodist church and was an instrumental social reformer. Wesley's heart was "strangely warmed" when he heard Luther's commentary read at a Moravian prayer meeting.

4. In America, the preaching of Romans 4:5 by the great Puritan Jonathan Edwards initiated the Great Awakening, the revival many historians believe led to the American Revolution.

5. In the twentieth century, Karl Barth's commentary on Romans in 1919 led to a revival in theological interest and helped to stem the tide of liberalism, at least for a while. While it's dangerous to mention Barth's neo-orthodox theology in the same breath as Augustine, Luther, Wesley, and Edwards, his rediscovery of Romans did change lives. If you don't want to know Christ deeply, don't read Romans. God is prone to use this book to change people's minds and hearts. J. I. Packer writes, "When the message of Romans gets into a man's heart, there is no telling what may happen" (Packer, *Knowing God*, 230).

There is a general consensus among scholars that Paul wrote Romans during a three-month stay in Corinth (Acts 20:2–3). The church at Rome was already a well-established Christian community. It was probably begun by some of the very first Christians who had been converted through Peter's sermon at Pentecost. Paul desired to visit Rome, not to begin a ministry there, but to enjoy the fellowship and mutual edification of the Romans as he pressed on to Spain, his final missionary destination (which he probably never reached, see Rom. 15:24).

Romans is Paul's major work. The letter is written with precision. It isn't an occasional epistle (like the Corinthian letters, which respond to questions and problems) but the crystallization of Paul's thinking. The structure is a beautifully unified progression—what he writes in one section can't be isolated from the rest. Calvin wrote, "If we understand this epistle, we have a passage opened up to us to the understanding of the whole of Scripture" (Calvin, *The Epistles of Paul the Apostle to the Romans and to the Thessalonians*, 2). Let's begin the journey.

vv. 1–7—The salutation is similar to those in other New Testament letters, but it is longer and more complex. "In verses 2–4 there appears a statement about the Gospel of God which may be described as a creedal formula, a statement of faith" (Palmer, *Salvation by Surprise: A Commentary on the Book of Romans*, 17). This may have been a version of a well-known creed of the early church, for what Paul says here corresponds closely with Peter's *kerygma* (announcement) of the Gospel. The common features are these:

1. The prophets witness to the Christ (Acts 2:17–21).
2. Jesus Christ is the true center of the Gospel (Acts 2:22–24).
3. He is the Son of God and the heir of David (Acts 2:25–29).
4. His deity is confirmed by his resurrection (Acts 2:30–56).
5. He calls all men to belong to him (Acts 2:37–39).

The mention of David indicates that Paul was rehearsing the *kerygma*. The apostle is much more prone to stress Christ's relationship to Abraham rather than to

David. The introduction to Romans looks back to the first announcement of the Gospel and stresses the centrality of Jesus Christ, fully God and fully man. "Paul teaches us that the whole Gospel is contained in Christ. To move even a step from Christ means to withdraw oneself from the Gospel" (Calvin, *The Epistles of Paul the Apostle to the Romans and to the Thessalonians*, 15).

vv. 8–15—In Paul's letters, the greeting is almost always (with the exception of Galatians) followed by a prayer of thanksgiving. He has tremendous gratitude to God for the church at Rome, even though he had nothing to do with its growth. What a testimony to the effectiveness of a church—the faith of its members is proclaimed throughout the world. "Paul knows nothing of a faith which is so concealed that none of it is visible" (Bruner, *The Christbook*, 15). Because of their faith, Paul desires to have fellowship, a mutual exchange, with the Romans. Just as he writes in 1 Corinthians 9, Paul sees himself owing a tremendous debt to the whole world, by virtue of his calling as an apostle. "The preaching of the Gospel is in his blood, and he cannot refrain from it; he is never 'off duty' but must constantly be at it" (Bruce, *Paul: Apostle of the Heart Set Free*, 75–76). To get an idea of the importance of Rome in ancient times, think of London, Paris, Tokyo, New York, and Beijing rolled into one.

vv. 16–17—Here is the great statement of the theme of Romans. Let's consider these verses individually.

1. How could Paul say in verse 16, *"I am not ashamed of the gospel, because it is the power of God"*? Here was the story of an obscure Jew who had been wiped out by the left hand of Rome, and Paul had the nerve to talk about power. The Romans knew power and how to wield it. As for the Greeks (the literal word Paul uses that the NIV translated "Gentiles"), they sought salvation in knowledge (1 Cor. 1:22). The simple Gospel held little appeal for them. Herein lies the paradox, the scandal of the cross and the empty tomb. In them, the greatest power in the universe is displayed. "The Gospel is not a truth among other truths. Rather it sets a question mark against all truths" (Barth, *Epistle to the Romans*, 35).
2. In verse 17, Paul introduces a new concept of righteousness, a righteousness that sets people free. Read what a dramatic effect this verse had on the pioneer of the Reformation. Luther writes:

> I greatly longed to understand Paul's Epistle to the Romans, and nothing stood in the way but that one expression, "the righteousness of God," because I took it to mean that righteousness whereby God is righteous and deals righteously in punishing the unrighteous... Night and day I pondered until... I grasped the truth that the righteousness of God is that righteousness whereby, through grace and sheer mercy, he justifies us by faith. Thereupon I felt myself to be reborn and to have gone through open doors into paradise. The whole of Scripture took on a new meaning, and whereas before "the righteousness of God" had filled me with hate, now it became to me inexpressibly sweet in greater love. This passage of Paul became to me a gateway to heaven. (Luther, *Luther's Works*, 179)

"Alien righteousness," justification by faith alone, and the power of God for salvation will become major themes as we get further into Romans.

APPLY

v. 8—If Paul were writing about your church, could he say that your faith is proclaimed in all the world? How about your whole city, school, place of business, or neighborhood?

vv. 11–12—When you meet with other Christians, does true fellowship with mutual exchange take place, or does a small group give while others receive? How can you change that?

v. 16—Do you see the Gospel as the most powerful force in the universe? What evidence is there in your life of that belief?

MEMORIZE

Romans 1:16–17

This is the theme of Romans, which is crucial to the New Testament.

PRAY

A: Praise the righteousness of God.

C: Confess the ways that you have been ashamed of the Gospel.

T: Thank God for your church.

S: Ask God to change your life through the study of Romans.

TELL

Look for the opportunity to share the good news of Christ with someone in a natural way. Don't be ashamed of the Gospel.

JUNE 16

THE GENTILES: GUILTY

PRAY

Pray for a realistic, unsentimental, yet hopeful view of man as you study this passage.

READ

Romans 1:18–32

OBSERVE

Before he elaborates on the righteousness that comes by faith, Paul must show why it is urgent for mankind to become right with God. Bruce comments, "As things are, men are 'in the wrong' with God and his wrath is revealed against them" (Bruce, *Romans*, 81). Palmer explains:

> The book's first major section begins as if the author were an Amos or John the Baptist, pacing back and forth within a great universal courtroom. In 1:18-3:20, Paul the prosecutor is speaking and the case against the accused is carefully established line upon line. (Palmer, *Salvation by Surprise: A Commentary on the Book of Romans*, 36)

vv. 18–32—Humanism is the dominant philosophy of both ancient Greece and modern people. It says mankind is continually improving through education. Rather than a progression, Paul indicates a retrogression. From the beginning of time, people knew that God is one, eternal, and powerful. His creation is a witness to all people of his goodness and power. However, we attempted to repress the truth. The result is a series of exchanges that break down man's vital relationships.

1. Relationship with God: They worship the creature rather than the Creator. Verse 23 graphically illustrated the religion of ancient Egypt. Pharaoh Ikhnaton was a monotheist, but his revelation was rejected. The Egyptians then worshiped a series of gods—first the Pharaoh (mortal man); then the mythical Phoenix, which rose to life from its own ashes (birds); then the cat and the cow (mammals); and finally, the cobra (reptiles). Humans are "incurably religious" since they were created with a "God-sized vacuum" (Pascal). When they reject their loving Creator, they must worship something. Ultimately they worship the object of their fear (the snake). They attempt to "make a pact with the devil" to placate the powers around them, which all seem hostile when they are out of relationship with divine providence.
2. Relationship with fellow human beings: Sexual relationships become perverted (vv. 24, 26–27), and people seek to destroy one another. Note that all of the sins mentioned in vv. 29–31 are against other people except God-hate, which is the root of all the others.
3. Relationship with self: Our self-understanding becomes blurred when the truth of God is exchanged for a lie.

A key phrase repeated three times is, "God gave them up." This doesn't mean that God turns his back on mankind, but that He allows them to experience the results of their sin (separation from God) through the effects of sins (actions that stem from that broken relationship). Sins are cumulative in their effects. From the beginning of the passage to the end, the situation becomes worse and worse. The bottom of the vicious cycle is reached in verse 32. Not only does the man in sin know that what he is doing leads to death, he approves of others who do the same thing. It's bad enough to do evil yourself, but wanting others to follow your example is evidence of a hard heart. The cycle has gone even one step further than Paul imagined. Not only do people do sinful things and approve of others who do them, they demand that everyone else approve of their sinful behavior. Calvin used this passage to support his doctrine of "total depravity"—that man apart from God is afflicted by sin in his entire being. But Paul (and Calvin) do not present man as a hopeless worm. Palmer writes:

> In the intensity of his prosecution, Paul never loses sight of the importance and value of man himself. Though men and women are guilty of sin, in deep trouble with God, each other and the earth, nevertheless, the human being never becomes an object of contempt. In fact, the *freedom* of man, which the Apostle insists upon, becomes a principal ingredient in the crisis. (Palmer, *Salvation by Surprise: A Commentary on the Book of Romans*, 37)

Calvin shows us clearly the purpose of Paul's prosecution. The word of judgment must be related to the word of hope in the rest of Romans. Calvin puts it this way:

> His object is to instruct us where salvation is to be sought. He has stated that we can obtain it only by the Gospel, but because the flesh will not willingly humble itself to the point of ascribing the praise of salvation to the grace of God alone, Paul shows

that the whole world is guilty of eternal death. (Calvin, *The Epistles of Paul the Apostle to the Romans and to the Thessalonians*, 30)

APPLY

v. 18—Do you have trouble accepting the concept of the wrath of God? Can a God who is not just in punishing sin be truly merciful?

v. 20—Though general revelation in nature is enough to show us that there is a God, it is not enough to show us how to be saved. We must have special revelation in Jesus Christ.

v. 30—How is disobedience to parents a result of an improper relationship with God?

MEMORIZE

Romans 1:18

PRAY

A: Praise the God of justice.

C: Confess any of the sins you have committed from the list in verses 29–31.

T: Thank God for his grace. One of the marks of a dark heart is a failure to give thanks (v. 21).

S: Ask God to help you be faithful in the three relationships this passage deals with.

TELL

Are people basically evil? Discuss this in your small group, giving evidence for your position.

JUNE 17

THE PERSON WHO JUDGES OTHERS: GUILTY

PRAY

As Paul develops his prosecution of all mankind, ask God to help you keep in mind the whole message of Romans—that this radical disease needs a radical cure. Rejoice that the cure has been provided, but don't be afraid to look closely at the illness.

READ

Romans 2:1–16

OBSERVE

Although Romans 1:18–32 described the vast majority of people in the ancient world (and the modern world), there was another side to Paul's society. It was represented primarily by the Jews and the pagan moral philosophers who would have condemned vulgar idolatry, homosexuality, and sins against one's neighbor as strongly as Paul did. This section is addressed to them (it actually continues through 3:8).

v. 1—Luther has a profound analysis of this key verse. Paul is saying several things in a few words. Luther writes:

> This mistake (of condemning others when one is guilty himself) is committed by all who are outside of Christ; for while the righteous (true believers) make it a point to accuse themselves in thought, word, and deed, the unrighteous make it a point always to accuse and judge others, at least in their hearts. (Luther, *Luther's Works*, 36)

Even though moralists might not commit the obvious gross transgressions, they are in the same class as those who do (sinners). As an illustration, Luther writes, "Misers usually accuse and condemn adulterers while they forget their own sins. Adulterers again may treat misers the same way. Just so, the haughty may charge others with their faults" (Luther, *Luther's Works*, 36). A classic example was Seneca, the Stoic philosopher and poet who practiced and taught daily self-examination, ridiculed idolatry, and was a moral guide to the Romans. But he was the tutor of Nero, one of the most depraved men in history, and he plotted with the emperor to kill Nero's mother. Luther reminds us, "Therefore, it is impossible for such wicked to be guiltless, unless they become justified through Christ" (Luther, *Luther's Works*, 37).

vv. 2–11—Paul articulates important principles of judgment here. God's judgment is always just (v. 2), and none of the guilty will escape it (v. 3). God's judgment of infant Israel was immediate. They needed graphic examples of how God hates sin. In the New Covenant (New Testament), judgment is usually postponed until death. Those who reject Christ are "storing up wrath" for the day of judgment. If God's immediate judgment was awesome to behold, what will his stored-up wrath look like? Although verses 6–9 seem to suggest that God's judgment is based on works, we must understand that Paul is dealing in 1:18–3:20 with the works of humanity, the deeds that show they are all lost in sin. In the last analysis, only the person who is in Christ can do anything good (God's will, performed by God's Spirit). All others, those who do not obey the truth, will do evil. A key principle in judgment is God's impartiality. He is no respecter of nationality, money, social status, or anything else humans value so highly.

vv. 12–16—Some interpreters have read a great deal out of this passage. Some go so far as to suggest that it teaches universal salvation on the basis of works. Some use it to deny the validity of Christian missions to the heathen, since they can be saved on their own. The passage does present a possible hope for the man who is ignorant of the Bible (the "Gentile" in the NIV, Greek *barbaroi*), but the hope is faint. *"All who sin apart from the law"* includes all Gentiles, as the apostle points out in 3:23. All societies in history, whether they have had few laws or many, are known by the fact that their members have not kept even the minimal laws they have set. It is not by works that they will be made right with God. The law requires righteousness—a right relationship with God. It's possible that a pagan who has responded in faith to the revelation of God that he has seen (1:19–23) will respond to Christ when he appears before his judgment seat. This was true of the Old Testament saints, who had only a partial revelation of the triune God. Jesus said, *"Abraham rejoiced that he was to see my day; he saw it and was glad"* (John 8:56). C. S. Lewis deals with this difficult question in the final book of his *Chronicles of Narnia* series, *The Last Battle*. In the story, Emeth the Calormene, who had worshiped the evil god Tash, comes into the presence of Aslan (the Christ figure) after Emeth's death. In relating his meeting with Aslan, Emeth says:

> Then I fell at his feet and thought, "Surely this is the hour of death, for the Lion (who is worthy of all honor) will know that I have served Tash all my days and not him." But the Glorious One bent down his golden head and touched my forehead with his tongue and said, "Son, thou art welcome." But I said, "Alas, Lord, I am no son of

Thine, but the servant of Tash." He answered, "Child, all the service thou hast done to Tash I account as service done to me. No service which is vile can be done to me, and none which is not vile can be done to him." (Lewis, *The Last Battle*, 164–165)

Keep in mind that this is C. S. Lewis and not Scripture, but it is an interesting attempt to apply this passage. The slim possibility that the heathen can be saved by keeping a clear conscience should not discourage us from being as aggressive in missions as Paul was and as Jesus commanded us to be. God knows the secrets of people's hearts through and through. It is good news that he is the judge.

APPLY

v. 1—Is Luther's statement true of you? Are you more conscious of your own sin than judgmental toward the sins of others?

v. 11—Are you guilty of partiality—paying more attention to people you like or people who can do something for you?

v. 16—How would you answer the question, "What happens to the person who has never heard about Christ?"

MEMORIZE

Romans 2:11

PRAY

A: Praise God, who is impartial.

C: Confess times you've passed judgment on someone else for something you've done.

T: Thank God for his patience.

S: Intercede for someone who is judgmental.

TELL

Discuss Romans 2:12–16 with your small group. Be careful not to go beyond what the Scripture actually says.

JUNE 18

THE JEWS: GUILTY

Ask God to continue to speak positively to you even in the midst of a portion of Scripture that emphasizes bad news.

READ

Romans 2:17–3:8

OBSERVE

Chapters 9–11 amplify Paul's theology of the Jews. Here, we will concentrate on their guilt before God rather than on God's plan for them.

vv. 17–24—The previous section on judging others certainly applied to the Jews, who were the epitome of morality in the ancient world. But here Paul turns the spotlight on the Jews. Bruce paraphrases this passage, "You approve the more excellent way, for you have learned it from the law; but why not take an honest look at yourself: Have you no defects?" (Bruce, *Romans*, 91). In the list of sins (vv. 21–24), Paul speaks in generalities, but he may have specific events in mind. *"Do you rob temples?"* might refer to a notorious scandal that took place in Rome in 49 AD, when four Jews persuaded a noble Roman lady to contribute to the temple in Jerusalem but used the money for themselves. When the matter was discovered, Tiberius expelled all Jews from Rome. Incidents like this gave the God of the Jews a bad name (v. 24).

vv. 25–29—The key verses here are 28 and 29. The Jews put their confidence in outward appearances, including the bodily evidence that they were the covenant people, circumcision. It was of value if a person kept the whole law. But to break any part of it was to be guilty as a lawbreaker (Gal. 5:3). God views the heart as well as the action. Jesus made this distinction powerfully in the Sermon on the Mount and elsewhere. The ending of verse 29 is a play on words. The word "Jew" means "praise." The true Jew receives his praise not from men but from God.

vv. 3:1–8—From what he wrote in chapter 2, we might expect that Paul would deny any advantage from belonging to the Jewish nation. But he doesn't dismiss his heritage. The Jews were given the Word of God—the revelation of his person and purpose in history. Of all peoples, they should have accepted the Messiah when he came. But many proved to be unfaithful. That doesn't mean that God is unfaithful or unfair to condemn unbelieving Jews (this theme will be taken up in chapters 9–11). Paul is so sure of God's holiness, justice, and righteousness that it's hard for him to write, even hypothetically, that God could be "unjust in bringing his wrath." He has to qualify that statement immediately. Paul will pick up this argument again in 6:1. The Jew who rejects God's grace and clings to the law is justly condemned.

APPLY

v. 29—Are you a Jew according to this definition?

v. 3:5—Do you truly believe that you are deserving of God's wrath apart from his mercy?

MEMORIZE

Romans 3:4a

Let God be true and every human being a liar.

PRAY

A: Praise God from the heart.

C: Confess any hypocrisy (vv. 21–24).

T: Thank God for telling us the truth.

S: Ask God to help you to praise him inwardly and outwardly today.

TELL

Be careful that you don't base your testimony on what you do, but on what God has done for you.

JUNE 19

THE WORLD: GUILTY

Pray to have a similar concern for the lost world as the Father does.

Romans 3:9–20

The prosecutor delivers a stunning summation of his case using the words of the law against any who would dare to think that they are justified by the law. These words have universal significance as well.

vv. 9–18—The argument has come full circle. The heathen (Gentile), the pagan moralist (Greek), and the man who relies upon the law (Jew) are all condemned. Paul strings together six Old Testament quotes (Ps. 141:1–2; 53:1–2; 5:9; 140:3; 36:1; and Isa. 59:7–8) to show that Jews and Greeks share in the same problem. Look carefully at the evidence he piles up here.

1. *"There is no one righteous, not even one."* There is no person who is, in and of himself or herself, properly related to God.
2. *"There is no one who seeks God."* The natural person doesn't even want to know God. People don't seek God for the same reason a criminal doesn't seek a policeman. He's too threatening. He cramps our style, so we run away from him, content to be his enemies.
3. *"There is no one who does good."* Even the things that appear to be good are

done for selfish reasons when God doesn't motivate them. Luther called them "bad good works."

4. *"Their throats are open graves; their tongues practice deceit."* Many things that the man in rebellion says are designed to deceive, hurt, and blaspheme.

5. *"Their feet are swift to shed blood."* If words aren't destructive enough, violent actions are used against fellow men. Contrast this with the feet of the man of God in Isaiah 52:7.

6. *"There is no fear of God before their eyes."* Like Romans 1:32, this verse describes the ultimate kind of sin. The rebel mocks God and symbolically shakes his fist in the face of his Maker.

vv. 19–20—God has the last word. The law convinces and convicts people of their sin. Palmer writes, "What the law succeeds in doing, it does well; namely, in compounding guilt, or rightly portraying the extent of men's brokenness" (Palmer, *Salvation by Surprise: A Commentary on the Book of Romans*, 50). The powerful conclusion is that "every mouth may be silenced" as its owner stands before the bench of the judge of all people. The law can only make us aware of our sin, it has no power to do away with sin. Mankind is totally and irretrievably lost. Nothing—not ethics, philosophy, religion, sacrifice, or transcendental experience—can solve the crisis. We require "total help for total need" (Barth, *Epistle to the Romans*, 72).

APPLY

vv. 9–18—Some theologians say that the doctrine of original sin was created by Augustine. Based on this passage, do you agree?

v. 11—Arminian theology believes that people are "sick" but not "dead" in sin. Does this verse support that position?

vv. 19–20—Do you really believe these verses? What do they say about your friends who are counting on their good deeds to get to heaven?

MEMORIZE

Romans 3:20

Remember that no one will get to heaven by doing good.

PRAY

A: Praise God for being the righteous judge.

C: Confess your flawed view of people, if you have one.

T: Thank God for telling you the truth.

S: Intercede for someone who is trusting his or her good works for eternal life.

TELL

Share the message of this passage with that person.

JUNE 20

JUSTIFICATION BY GRACE ALONE THROUGH FAITH ALONE

PRAY

Pray that this key passage of Scripture might be indelibly impressed on your heart and mind.

READ

Romans 3:21–31

OBSERVE

v. 21—*"But now"*—these two words mark the great transition in Romans (and all of history). The prosecutor of all people strides across the courtroom and becomes the attorney for the defense. The righteousness of God is a key concept in Romans (1:17, 3:10, 6:19). As an attribute of God, righteousness describes his holiness and purity, his faithfulness to his promises, and his aversion to sin. As an attribute of people, righteousness means a right relationship with God, which brings us into conformity with his will and moral standards. Since no one is righteous in and of himself or herself, reconciliation with God must come from outside. Luther called this "alien righteousness," the amazing process whereby the believer's guilt is laid on Christ and Christ's merit (righteousness) is laid on believers. We will study the classical statement of this crucial doctrine when we come to 2 Corinthians 5:21.

vv. 22–23—Two commentators, one from the sixteenth and one from the twentieth century, shed light on these two verses. Luther deals with the rebellious objector who says:

We believe therefore that we must be justified by God, but this we desire to achieve by our prayers, repentance, and confessions. We do not want Christ, for God can give us his righteousness even without Christ. To this the Apostle replies, "Such a wicked demand God neither will nor can fulfill (since he is faithful to his nature), for Christ is God; righteousness for justification is given us only through faith in Jesus Christ." So God has willed it, and so God is pleased to do, and this he will never change. (Luther, *Luther's Works*, 61)

Commentator Earl Palmer relates verses 22 and 23 in this way: "The central fact of history is the event of Jesus Christ, and it is the law and prophets which receive their meaning and purpose from him ... in that they attest to the primacy of Jesus Christ" (Palmer, *Salvation by Surprise: A Commentary on the Book of Romans*, 52). All have sinned, and the righteousness of God is limited to all who believe.

vv. 24–26—The theme of salvation is so powerful that Paul musters the wealth of his experience and knowledge to describe it. Palmer writes, "The richness of the salvation vocabulary within the Book of Romans by its very complexity points up the wholesale nature of the redemption event" (Palmer, *Salvation by Surprise: A Commentary on the Book of Romans*, 53). Let's look at some of this vocabulary more closely.

1. "Justified" was a term used in the Roman legal system to describe an acquittal. It is more than a pardon, it also means that the demands of the law are fully satisfied.
2. The classic definition of "grace" is unmerited favor; we receive the gift of forgiveness and eternal life when we deserve punishment. In Greek culture, grace (*charis*) was "that which causes joy (*chara*)." The Greeks longed for a gracious life that would provide a sense of fulfillment. Christians find it in the grace of God.
3. "Redemption" was the word used in the slave market for the act of buying back (ransoming) a slave. The word would evoke a strong image for Jews, causing them to think immediately of God's redemption of Israel from Egypt. Every Christian must be redeemed from slavery to Satan and sin. The price of redemption was thirty pieces of silver, exactly what Judas was paid to betray Jesus.
4. "A sacrifice of atonement" is literally "the covering" in Greek. The word is used for the mercy seat (Heb. 9:5), the place within the Ark of the Covenant where it was believed that God resided in power. On the holiest of holy days, the Day of Atonement, the priest sprinkled blood on the mercy seat. It was the only time of the year that the Holy of Holies could be entered. Christ is the perfect covering. His blood was shed once and for all, and his sacrifice never needs to be repeated. The mercy seat provides expiation (our sin is covered) as well as propitiation (God's wrath is satisfied).
5. Paul says that God "had left the sins committed beforehand unpunished." (Some translations instead use the phrase "passed over" in verse 25.) Paul is referring to the supreme act of God's mercy (kindness that withholds punishment) in the Old Testament, when he passed over the Jewish homes

that had blood covering the doorposts (Exod. 12). In verse 26, Paul stresses that all of these benefits come to believers through faith. Faith is the means by which God's righteousness is imputed to mankind.

vv. 27–31—The entire thrust of these verses is to say two important things:

1. We can add nothing to the finished work of Christ. The cross, the supreme display of God's love, happened apart from anything we could do.
2. It is only by faith that the message becomes personal. Luther felt this so strongly that he added the word "alone" after "faith" in his German translation of verse 28. Although he was wrong to add to Scripture, he was right in his interpretation of the sense of the passage. Faith alone makes it possible to say, "Jesus died for me."

APPLY

vv. 24–26—Which of these descriptions are most helpful to your understanding of the cross? Why does Paul often say, "Grace *and* mercy?"

vv. 27–31—If we can do nothing to earn our salvation, is there anything we can do to lose it?

MEMORIZE

Romans 3:23

This verse is key to understanding the total need the New Testament presents.

PRAY

A: Praise the God of grace.

C: Confess your total inability to do anything to contribute to your salvation.

T: Thank God that he did everything.

S: Ask God to deepen your appreciation of the cross.

TELL

Tell one person today what a joy it is to be a Christian.

JUNE 21

ABRAHAM, A GREAT EXAMPLE OF FAITH

PRAY

Pray to be strengthened, apply this passage to your life, and live by faith today.

READ

Romans 4:1–25

OBSERVE

In Romans 3:21, Paul asserts that the righteousness of God was shown in the law and the prophets (Old Testament). Chapter 4 illustrates that truth from the life of Abraham, with a brief glance at the experience of David.

vv. 1–5—The doctrine of justification by faith is not just a New Testament idea. It appears as early as Genesis 15:6, which is the passage Paul quotes. The experience of Abraham illustrates that it has always been trust in God that mattered. Imagine the faith necessary to leave your homeland for an unknown destination promised by a God whom your parents didn't even know—or the trust necessary to believe that your ninety-year-old wife would bear a son. It's not that Abraham's trust was perfect. In the case of his heir, his faith weakened, and he had a child through Sarah's handmaid, Hagar. But God continued to be faithful to his promise. This is the key: God's faithfulness, God's initiative, and God's gift. It is God who accounts (reckons) even weak faith as the perfect righteousness of God.

vv. 6–8—There is a strong link between Abraham, the father of the Jewish nation, and David, the father of the Messiah (1:3). Though obvious sinners, both were primarily men of faith (1 Kings 15:3). The link between Genesis 15:6 and Psalm 32:2 is the common verb "count." Bruce explains:

The link is not merely a formal one: the non-imputation of sin, in which the Psalmist rejoices, amounts to the positive imputation of righteousness or pronouncement of acquittal, for there can be no verdict of "not proven" in God's law court. (Bruce, *Romans*, 115–116)

vv. 9–12—The Jews and Judaizers made a big deal of circumcision. To them, it was necessary to be circumcised before one could become righteous. Paul counters with the fact that Abraham's circumcision was only a sign or seal of what had already happened fourteen years before—God's declaration of Abraham's righteousness. His faith is the key ingredient, not his circumcision. Therefore, Abraham is truly the forefather of all who have faith in Christ (Jew and Gentile alike), not those who merely have the physical sign of circumcision (Jews).

vv. 13–25—This is the crucial application of Abraham's faith to us. Abraham had to trust God for his heir, even to the extent of being willing to lose the long-awaited son (Gen. 22). We have to believe ("trust," "have faith") that God raised Christ from the dead and that he died for us. In verses 24–25, Paul connects the cross to the crucial event of the resurrection. Good Friday must be tied to Easter. It is only through Jesus' resurrection that his triumph over sin and death is clearly seen. Barth calls it the verdict of God on the finished work of Christ. Just as Abraham's faith made him the father of all nations, Christ's death and resurrection is not limited to first-century Christians. He was put to death for *our* sins and raised for *our* justification. We can never read Romans as merely a theological treatise. It has to be God's Word to us, which is ever new and personal.

APPLY

v. 18—Where do you need to trust God for a difficult situation today?

vv. 23–25—Meditate on the cross. Do you see how seriously God takes sin? Do you see how much God loves you? Do you see the resurrection in a new light—that it brought new life not only for Jesus but for you?

MEMORIZE

Romans 4:3

PRAY

A: Praise the God of Abraham.

C: Confess your lack of faith.

T: Thank God that Christ's righteousness is counted to you.

S: Ask God to help you show more grace and love toward others.

TELL

Share with someone who questions whether God can use him or her that if he used obvious sinners like Abraham and David in spectacular ways, he can use anyone.

JUNE 22

THE RESULTS OF JUSTIFICATION

PRAY

Pray that this revolutionary passage might touch you in the same way it affected Martin Luther.

READ

Romans 5:1–11

OBSERVE

This passage begins the third major section of Romans (chapters 5–8), which presents a tremendous description of the results of justification by faith—what it means to live the Christian life in the power of the Holy Spirit. No part of Romans is unimportant, but this section is one of the most important parts of Scripture.

vv. 1–5—The first result of justification by faith is that we have peace with God. Both the Hebrew *shalom* and the Greek *eirene* describe harmony through right relationships. In addition to this peace, Paul stresses our access to the Father, the source of grace. We former rebels can stand firm in his presence because we are represented by our mediator, Jesus Christ (1 Tim. 2:5). Verses 2–5 have a progression that is common to Paul. He lists five gifts that help us to rejoice:

1. Suffering: The Christian can rejoice in persecution and hardship, knowing that the effect in our lives will be beneficial.
2. Endurance: Luther points out that tribulation and suffering act as a refining fire. He writes: "If someone is carnal, weak, blind, wicked, irascible, haughty and so forth, tribulation will make him more carnal,

weak, blind, wicked and irritable. On the other hand, if one is spiritual, strong, wise, pious, gentle and humble, he will become more spiritual, powerful, wise, pious, gentle and humble. As the Psalmist says in Psalm 4:1, 'Thou hast enlarged me when I was in distress'" (Luther, *Luther's Works*, 74–75).

3. Character: When we've stood the test, we have the internal proof that Christ is in us. Someone once defined character as "what you do when no one else is looking."

4. Hope: This is not wishful thinking, but the eager expectation of Christ's action on behalf of our need, both now and eternally. Barth comments, "Death is deprived of its power. When we recognize that in suffering and brokenness it is God whom we encounter, that we have been cast up against Him and bound to Him...faith discovers God to be the Originator of all things, and awaits all from Him" (Barth, *Epistle to the Romans*, 157).

5. Love: What a graphic description the apostle gives here—love has been poured into our hearts through the gift of the Holy Spirit. He is God in us, and we can only know God's love as a result of the Spirit abiding in us and we in him. Bruce notes, "In this passage, we have described the 'twin blessings of the Gospel,' peace and joy. As one preacher put it, 'peace is joy resting; joy is peace dancing'" (Bruce, *Romans*, 120).

vv. 6–11—A classic statement of *agape* love is found in verse 8. God's love is independent of the worthiness or the response of the one who is loved. He loves because he is God and chooses to do so. Verse 9 is a powerful verse of assurance for the Christian. We have nothing to fear in the judgment of God because the blood of Christ has cleansed us so that we are no longer sinners (in a broken relationship) in the sight of God, though we continue to sin. We are reconciled to God through the death of Christ, and now our living Lord continually intercedes for us before the Father. He sends us the Holy Spirit and his gifts, which enable us to grow. We have two beautiful descriptions of the cross: the objective—*"At the right time ... Christ died for the ungodly"*—and the subjective—*"We also boast in God through our Lord Jesus Christ."* The Christian life must contain both a knowledge of the Gospel truth and an experience of the power of the Gospel in our lives.

APPLY

v. 3—Do you truly rejoice in your sufferings and see them as opportunities for growth?

v. 8—Christ loved the ungodly to the extent of dying for us. Are you willing to make a special effort to love a "difficult" person in your life?

MEMORIZE

Romans 5:8

Remember what Christ's love is all about.

PRAY

A: Praise the God of peace.

C: Confess your resentment of suffering.

T: Thank God for your access to him through prayer.

S: Ask God for peace and joy today.

TELL

Tell that difficult person that you love him or her.

JUNE 23

THE TWO ADAMS

PRAY

Pray that you might come face to face with both the hopelessness of those who live in union with the first Adam and the hope of those who live in union with the last Adam.

READ

Romans 5:12–21

OBSERVE

One of the most important features of Paul's christology is his portrayal of Jesus as the last Adam, in contrast to the first Adam.

vv. 12–14—This is one of the clearest statements in the Bible of the doctrine of original sin, or as it's sometimes known, "sin passed from Adam." Some have misunderstood this doctrine, thinking that we are unfairly punished for someone else's sin. This is hardly the case, for as verse 12 affirms, we have said "yes" to sin (as Adam did) over and over again. Original sin means that all human beings have a sinful nature and that it is both individual and corporate. As Isaiah said, *"I am ruined! For I am a man of unclean lips, and I live among a people of unclean lips"* (Isa. 6:5). Earl Palmer gives an excellent illustration of this doctrine:

> It is like three ship passengers who happen to get washed overboard in mid-Atlantic. The reasons for slipping off the deck vary from individual to individual (vv. 12–14). Each individual retains his own distinctiveness in the water as on the deck (v. 12). But as each one discovers his own plight and finds his companions also in the same cold

water, it is meaningless to discuss or debate degrees of fault, status, or privileges (one is first class, the other economy), individual swimming skill (those with skill in the law and tradition versus those without). The point is that the realization of the immensity of the crisis has established new priorities and has created a new solidarity in that each of the three now knows the meaning of *total* need for which the *only* help is *total* help. (Palmer, *Salvation by Surprise: A Commentary on the Book of Romans*, 63)

vv. 15–17—Total help could only be provided by one who did not share in the total need because his original nature was divine, not human. Although "he had to be made like them, fully human in every way" (Heb. 2:17) and he "has been tempted in every way, just as we are" (Heb. 4:15), the important distinction is his perfection—"yet without sin." There is no question in Paul's mind as to which Adam is more powerful; it is not a battle of two equals. Barth writes:

> The two factors are not of equal importance; nor is there a strict balance between them. Life in Adam and life in Christ are not an ever-recurring cycle of sin and righteousness, death and life.... Christ is contrasted with Adam as the goal and purpose of the movement.... As the goal, Christ does not merely expose a distinction. He forces a decision between the two factors. By doing this, He is not merely second, but the *last* Adam (1 Corinthians 15:45). The life which springs from death is wholly pre-eminent over the life which engenders death and is enclosed by it. There is a death which is the death of death and this is the theme of the Gospel (1:1, 16). (Barth, *Epistle to the Romans*, 165–166)

vv. 18–21—These verses conclude and summarize the argument. The only point that needs to be clarified is the use of the word "all" in verse 18. It is clear from the context of the surrounding verses that in verse 18, "all" means without distinction, not without exception. In other words, there will be no distinction between Jew or Greek, rich or poor, slave or free, male or female (Gal. 3:28). Every class or category of humanity can come to Christ, but not every individual will come. This is the usual way Paul's use of the word "all" should be interpreted.

APPLY

v. 14—Do you believe that in order for the analogy in this passage to be valid, the Adam of Genesis had to be a real individual rather than a mythical representative of mankind?

vv. 16–17—How can you, one who has received the abundance of grace and who reigns in new life through Christ, continue to look down on yourself?

MEMORIZE

Romans 5:19

This verse captures the two-Adams analogy.

PRAY

A: Praise the last Adam.

C: Confess your trespasses.

T: Thank God for your redeemed status. Give him thanks.

S: Intercede for someone lost in sin.

TELL

Share Earl Palmer's "man overboard" analogy with someone.

JUNE 24

DEAD TO SIN AND ALIVE TO GOD

PRAY

Pray for convinction of how important it is to "walk your talk" as a Christian.

READ

Romans 6:1–23

OBSERVE

In Romans 3:21–5:21, Paul has dealt with justification, or becoming a Christian. In chapter 6, he begins his theological treatise on sanctification, or being a Christian.

vv. 1–2—The first five words of chapter 6 form a question that it takes the rest of Romans to answer: *"What shall we say then?"* This question picks up the idea of reigning in righteousness from 5:21. Some people had perverted the doctrine of justification by grace alone through faith alone and introduced antinomianism (meaning "against law"), a system which teaches that Christians have no need to follow God's law. Russian monk Rasputin exemplified antinomianism. He tried to sin all that he could so that he could experience more of God's grace. Gnosticism, the heresy which plagued the Church at the end of the first century, was also antinomian. The church father Iranaeus described the ethics of Gnosticism like this:

> For as gold cast into the dirt does not lose its beauty, but maintains its own nature … so they suffer no harm and do not lose their spiritual nature by any acts at all which they do. Therefore, even the most perfect among them do, without fear, everything

that is forbidden. (as quoted in Palmer, *Salvation by Surprise: A Commentary on the Book of Romans*, 75)

Paul's response is a fervent exclamation that is difficult to translate. The NIV reads, *"By no means!"* Others translate it, *"God forbid!"*

vv. 3–14—Part of Paul's argument against antinomianism is taken from the sacrament of adult baptism. Though there is a difference of opinion about whether the Church practiced infant baptism, there is no dispute that the majority of those baptized in the early Church were adults. It stands to reason that this would be the case for a brand new church. There is also no question that the early church practiced baptism by immersion. The symbolism of the rite was this: when the convert was taken under the water, it was symbolic of his death to sin. When he was lifted out of the water, it symbolized resurrection into new life in Christ. It is clear from baptism that sin is no longer to reign over our bodies. Christ is in control.

vv. 15–23—The other analogy is taken from slavery. We are the slave of whomever we obey. The non-Christian has no choice but to be the slave of sin. We shouldn't be surprised by anything done by the person who doesn't know Christ. The Christian, on the other hand, is the slave of Christ, obedient to his teachings. There is no other possibility; you are either the slave of one or the other. The wages (resulting payment) of slavery to sin is spiritual death, but the wages of slavery to God is freedom, the freedom of eternal life. It is both a free gift and a freeing gift.

APPLY

vv. 1–2—Augustine wrote, "Love God and do whatever you will," yet he was not an antinomian. What was the crucial understanding behind his words?

vv. 3–14—Do you sometimes presume upon the grace of God and think, "It doesn't matter what I do, God will forgive me anyway?"

vv. 15–23—Whose slave are you—the world's or God's? Are you obeying the world too much in what you watch, what you wear, or what you say?

MEMORIZE

Romans 6:23

PRAY

A: Praise the glory of the father.

C: Confess any slavery to the world.

T: Thank God for freedom in Christ to do good.

S: Ask God to show you any antinomian attitudes you might have.

TELL

Discuss with your small group how Christians are to be in the world but not slaves to it.

JUNE 25

THE CHRISTIAN STRUGGLE

PRAY

Pray for the honesty to identify Paul's struggle as your own and to embrace his solution.

READ

Romans 7:1–25

OBSERVE

Romans 7 is the great autobiographical description of Paul's struggle between the flesh and the Spirit. Those who accuse the apostle of self-righteousness and spiritual pride have never taken this chapter seriously. It is an immense help to the rest of us who continually struggle to obey the law of God. Some argue that Paul is writing this chapter to describe his experience before his conversion, but the use of the present tense and his cry in verse 25 argue strongly against that idea. Since he is describing his experience as a Christian, Romans 7 is a powerful argument against those who believe the doctrine of perfectionism—that Christians can achieve a state in which they no longer sin. If one of the greatest Christians in history struggled with sin, so will we.

vv. 1–6—Once again, we can't study this chapter in isolation. Chapter 6 ended on the note of freedom—we have been freed *from* sin and freed *for* obedience. As soon as Paul talks of obedience, the question of standards comes up. Earl Palmer states the issue with clarity:

Paul's use of "law" is indeed complicated but may be understood when we keep in mind that he is using the word in a twofold sense. First he refers to the law as the plumb line of God by which we have always been judged. He also intends a second interpretation of law as that way of life that was never able to create newness, produce hope, reconciliation or life. In other words, Paul interprets law in this second sense, in terms of its crucial shortcomings. Although the law has been held over against the warped and crooked foundations of man and his civilizations for centuries, it cannot of itself heal or mend or straighten; it only mocks the inadequacies of man and their children. Paul then goes on to make an obvious point in 7:6: God is the master builder who Himself establishes the righteous foundation so that the work upon the whole house may get underway. In this sense the building is set free from work stoppages caused by endless appeals to the law for measurement and evaluation. (Palmer, *Salvation by Surprise: A Commentary on the Book of Romans*, 80)

Palmer adds the builder analogy to Paul's marriage analogy. Marriage vows are binding as long as one's mate is alive. In the same way, the standard of the law is binding only to one who is "alive" to the law. When we become Christians, as Paul argues in chapter 6, we are dead to sin, which is measured by the law. We have new life in the Spirit, a theme Paul develops beautifully in chapter 8.

vv. 7–25—Having introduced the concept of life in the Spirit, Paul must deal with the flesh and the evil that is continually with him. His argument here is profound and complex, but let's try to summarize it.

1. The law is not sin; it is good since it comes from God.
2. The law makes us aware of sin—without God's commandments we wouldn't know what is sin and what isn't.
3. When we know what is sin and still do it, we become spiritually dead.
4. All Christians are in that situation—we want to do good, but in our flesh, we are powerless to do so. Luther described the Christian as *simul justus et peccator*, at the same time justified and a sinner.
5. Are we, then, without hope and wretched? No! For through Jesus Christ our Lord we can be delivered. This is the great theme of chapter 8. But we can't fully appreciate the power of the Holy Spirit until we've wrestled with the flesh and lost the battle.

APPLY

vv. 12–15—Briefly rewrite and paraphrase these verses, putting yourself and your experience in the place of the Apostle Paul.

vv. 16–23—In light of your own struggles with sin, how does reading about Paul's conflict make you feel? How is this a model for a healthy, realistic self-image?

vv. 24–25—When have you sensed Jesus rescuing you from sin or situations that were too big for you to handle? How does Jesus help you now?

MEMORIZE

Romans 7:15

Remember the dilemma of the flesh and the will apart from the enabling power of the Holy Spirit.

PRAY

A: Praise God and his law.

C: Confess the recent works of your flesh.

T: Thank God for his total forgiveness.

S: Ask God to enable you to live in the Spirit and not in the flesh today.

TELL

Share your paraphrase with someone close to you.

JUNE 26

LIFE IN THE SPIRIT

PRAY

Pray that you may not rely on your own abilities to live like Christ, but that you might rely on the Spirit who dwells within you.

READ

Romans 8:1–17

OBSERVE

Romans 8 is the climax of this great work. Some have considered this chapter the "Mt. Everest of Scripture." This section answers the key question, "How is it possible to live the Christian life, given the claims of a holy God and the inherent weakness of the disciple?"

vv. 1–4—This section restates 5:1–5 in different language. Romans 8:1 is a great verse that no Christian should ever forget. We have peace with God. We are not his enemies but his friends; therefore, we have nothing to fear. Bruce writes:

> The word translated "condemnation" means "punishment following sentence." There is no reason why those who are 'in Christ Jesus' should go on doing penal servitude as though they had never been pardoned and never been liberated from the prison-house of sin. (Bruce, *Romans*, 159)

The Christian obeys a higher law (which doesn't mean that he disobeys the lower law), and that is the law of the Spirit of life. The "righteous requirement of the law" (v. 4) is summarized in Romans 13:9 as, *"You shall love your neighbor as yourself."* Bruce continues his helpful analysis:

> Christian holiness is not a matter of painstaking conformity to the precepts of an external law-code, it is rather a question of the Holy Spirit's producing His fruit in the life, reproducing those graces which were seen in perfection in the life of Christ. (Bruce, *Romans*, 162)

vv. 5–8—Paul stresses the importance of the mind. The area of our thought life is the real battleground for all sin (Matt. 15:18–19) and all righteousness. The word Paul uses for repentance means literally "a change (or renewal) of the mind."

vv. 9–11—Look at the rich mixture of words used to describe the Holy Spirit: *"The Spirit of God," "The Spirit of Christ," "Christ … in you," "The Spirit of him who raised Jesus from the dead," "His Spirit who lives in you."* The Holy Spirit is the source of the Christian life because he is God's very nature within us. Paul provides crucial teaching on the Holy Spirit and his ministry in this passage. 1) All Christians have the Spirit of God. We need no second "baptism in the Holy Spirit" to receive him. He is in us from the moment of conversion (Eph. 1:13–14). Those who suggest that we don't fully possess the Holy Spirit at conversion are saying, according to verse 9, that we don't fully belong to Christ.

2) The Spirit who dwells within us gives life to our spirits and to our bodies. John Murray writes:

> Since this refers to the resurrection from the dead we might have expected the Apostle to say "dead bodies" rather than "mortal bodies" (v. 10). But the language is significant. The term "mortal" describes the bodies of believers from the aspect of the mortality that belongs to them in this life prior to the event of death. And, although it is as dead bodies they will be made alive at the resurrection, yet the identification of them as "mortal bodies" shows that it is the same bodies which believers now possess that will be made alive at the resurrection (cf. 1 Cor. 15:35–54). (Murray, *The Epistle to the Romans*, 291–292)

vv. 12–17—How do we know that we are in Christ? Palmer writes:

> The assurance that proves to the Christian that he is in fact "making it" as a Christian is not a dossier of his own successes with the law, his checklist in outdoing the Pharisees when it comes to righteousness, or a log of mystic breakthroughs. The assurance that really sets him free is the inner witness of God's Spirit with his own spirit that he is a child of God. (Palmer, *Salvation by Surprise: A Commentary on the Book of Romans*, 96–97)

The Spirit leads us. He gives us the Spirit of sonship, so that we can call the Father "Daddy." Verse 17 points forward to verses 18–25 and our inheritance, the glorification promised to us in eternity. Suffering is an important part of the sanctification process (2 Cor. 4:16); we are involved with Christ in sorrow as well as in joy. The child of God is part of God's family "in plenty and in want, in joy and in sorrow, in sickness and in health" until death brings us to perfect union.

APPLY

v. 1—Remember Romans 8:1 when you feel guilty or depressed.

vv. 5–8—Are you letting your flesh control you, or are you controlling your flesh in the power of the Holy Spirit? How does that apply to what you read, what you watch, and your conversations? Are you meditating on God's Word and other things that are designed to renew your mind?

v. 17—Do you welcome only the crown of the Christian life, while you resent the cross?

MEMORIZE

Romans 8:1

PRAY

A: Praise God the Holy Spirit.

C: Confess any sins that might be grieving him.

T: Thank God that he is your Daddy.

S: Ask God for sensitivity to the Spirit's presence leading you today.

TELL

Discuss the importance of the battleground of the mind with your small group.

JUNE 27

OUR SURE SALVATION

Pray that you might be eager and open to being moved by this mountaintop passage.

READ

Romans 8:18–39

OBSERVE

The great theme of Romans is the power of God for salvation. Salvation consists of three parts: forgiveness for the past in justification (Rom. 3:21–5:21); strength for the present in sanctification (Rom. 6:1–8:17); and hope for the future in glorification (Rom. 8:18–39). This passage speaks with exalted poetry of our certain future hope. We will see this in three sections: verses 18–25 reveal a sure hope; verses 26–30 reveal a sure help; and verses 31–39 reveal a sure salvation.

vv. 18–25—About hope in suffering, Bruce writes:

> It is not merely that the glory is a compensation for the suffering; it actually grows out of the suffering. There is an organized relation between the two for the believer as surely as there was for his Lord. (Bruce, *Romans*, 168)

The important point to remember when we suffer for Christ is that any sacrifice we make will be so pale as to be forgotten when we compare it to the vivid joys of heaven. Verses 19–22 teach that this glorification is on a cosmic and universal scale. Just as nature was cursed in the Fall (Gen. 3:17–19) and has been "groaning as in the pains of childbirth," it will also be glorified at the coming of Christ. As we've noted before, Christian hope is not wishful thinking but eager expectation. Paul adds that patience is an important corollary to the hope that we have in Christ.

vv. 26–30—The key to living the Christian life is to allow the Holy Spirit to work through us. We are unable even to pray in a way that is effective and pleasing to God. But the Spirit prays for us! The Spirit's prayer is always effective because he searches both our hearts and God's (1 Cor. 2:10–11). Romans 8:28 is one of the greatest but most misunderstood verses in the Bible. It does not mean that everything that happens is good, but that whatever happens to a Christian, even if it is evil in itself, God will work together for good. The promise is only to those who love God, those whom he has elected (called according to his purpose) for salvation. The New English Bible has an attractive translation of this verse that carries over the subject of "working together" from the previous verse: *"He pleads for God's own people in God's own way; and in everything, as we know, he cooperates for good with those who love God."* We'll deal more fully with the subject of election when we study chapter 9, but note one thing in verse 29—the Christian is conformed by God to the image of his Son. People were created in God's image (Gen. 1:26), but that image was marred by the Fall. In Christ, the image is restored.

vv. 31–39—What can be said about this incredible passage? Palmer writes:

> Paul's spare use of words, the sweep of thoughts that each short phrase brings to the mind of the reader, makes this text a classic in the Greek language. The text is prose of superb style and inner force. (Palmer, *Salvation by Surprise: A Commentary on the Book of Romans*, 111)

Let's take a brief look at some of Paul's profound thoughts:

1. *"God is for us."* We can "sweep aside every threat that may undo us in view of the greater power that is in our favor. Only four words, a sentence that may be spoken with four distinct emphases. *God* is for us. God *is* for us. God is *for* us. God is for *us*" (Palmer, *Salvation by Surprise: A Commentary on the Book of Romans*, 112).
2. *"Who then is the one who condemns?"* The only one with any right to condemn us would be a perfect person, and he died to save us from condemnation (John 3:17). This is so simple and self-evident, yet we often feel that Christ is condemning us in our weakness, rather than praying for strength for us. He is *for* us. This recalls the beginning of the chapter and ties it all together.
3. *"We are more than conquerors through him who loved us."* We need not fear Satan or his kingdom; he fears us when we are living in the power of the Spirit. As Luther's great hymn, "A Mighty Fortress Is Our God," says, "The prince of darkness grim, We tremble not for him; His rage we can endure, For lo! His doom is sure; One little word shall fell him."
4. *"Nor anything else in all creation will be able to separate us from the love of God that is in Christ Jesus our Lord."* Hallelujah! This is heaven.

APPLY

v. 18—When you're going through hard times, understand them in the context of eternity. It helps to remember that they are not worth comparing to the glory that will be revealed in us.

vv. 26–34—Have you ever sensed the Spirit and the Son praying for you? They are!

v. 28—What is an example of something God has "worked for good" in your past? Is there something you're struggling with in the present? How can your past inform your present?

v. 29—What does it mean to be created in God's image and to have that image restored in Christ?

v. 37—Keep in mind that you are more than a conqueror through him who loves you.

MEMORIZE

Romans 8:28

PRAY

A: Praise the God of glory.

C: Confess your failure to trust in his help.

T: Thank God for his help in times past.

S: Spend some time meditating on this passage, and let the Spirit pray for you.

TELL

Encourage a Christian brother or sister with verse 31.

JUNE 28

PAUL'S SORROW

PRAY

Pray that you might appreciate the way God works in history, just as Paul does in this passage.

READ

Romans 9:1–33

OBSERVE

Chapters 9–11 are parenthetical in Paul's argument. He could have moved very naturally from 8:39 to 12:1, but when he said that nothing can separate us from the love of God in Christ Jesus, a nagging problem came to his mind. What about his Jewish kinsmen?

vv. 1–5—These verses are full of emotion. To grasp the significance of verse 3, think for a moment about how precious Paul's salvation was to him (look at statements like Rom. 8:18, Gal. 2:20, and Phil. 1:21). Yet he would be willing to be cursed and lose his salvation if only his fellow Jews could have the scales removed from their eyes as he had. (Of course, that decision was not Paul's to make, as the chapter confirms.) The Jews had experienced every advantage possible to prepare them for the Messiah, including:

1. Adoption: They were collectively called the sons of God (Hosea 11:1).
2. Divine glory: They saw the *Shekinah* of the Tabernacle (Exod. 40:34) and the temple (1 Kings 8:10).

3. Covenants: God established covenants with Abraham (Gen. 12:1–3), Moses (Exod. 24:8), Joshua (Josh. 8:30), and David (2 Sam. 23:5).
4. Receiving of the law: God gave them his perfect moral law (Exod. 20:1) as well as civil and ceremonial law.
5. Temple worship: The regulations for temple worship were spelled out in Leviticus.
6. Promises: The Old Testament is full of God's promises (Isa. 59:20–21).
7. Patriarchs: God spoke to and through Abraham, Isaac, Jacob, and Jacob's twelve sons.
8. Christ: The Messianic promises of the Old Testament are fulfilled in Jesus of Nazareth. *"He came to that which was His own, but His own did not receive Him"* (John 1:11).

vv. 6–33—This passage, along with 8:29–30, is the section of Scripture most often used to support the doctrine of election. Predestination is the larger concept, the idea that God foreordained all that comes to pass. Election deals with the specific aspect of God's predestination concerning salvation. This doctrine is frequently grossly misunderstood or ignored. Let's examine it as simply as possible from these two passages and a few others:

1. God is sovereign over all things, including salvation (Rom. 8:30).
2. People are helpless to save themselves; we are dead in trespasses and sins (Rom. 9:6, Eph. 2:1).
3. God calls (elects) certain people to be saved and gives them the Holy Spirit so that they can receive Christ (Rom. 9:11, 18, 27).
4. God does not reveal the principles on which he makes his choices (Rom. 9:15, 20).
5. Nobody deserves salvation. Therefore, the fact that God chooses some is a reflection of his mercy (Rom. 8:14–15). Bruce writes, "If he were compelled to be merciful by some cause outside himself, not only would His mercy be so much the less mercy, but he would be so much the less God" (Bruce, *Romans*, 188).
6. God has the right to have mercy on whom he will have mercy and to harden the heart of those he chooses to harden (Rom. 9:14–18).
7. We have no right to question his decisions (Rom. 9:19–26).

Some people attempt to make a distinction between foreknowledge and election. They believe that even though God knows who will respond, that doesn't mean that he makes them respond or not respond. This is a misunderstanding of the word "foreknew" in 8:29, which really means "loved beforehand." God doesn't just know who will be saved beforehand. This passage makes it clear (as do many others) that he decides who will be saved beforehand. One reason a lot of Americans have difficulty with the doctrine of election is that it doesn't fit neatly into our concept of American democracy. The kingdom of God is not a democracy. Paul's purpose in dealing with this difficult doctrine is to explain why the Gentiles now have become God's people. It is God's sovereign will.

APPLY

v. 3—Is there anyone who is not a Christian for whom you have this much love? Paul spent most of his missionary career reaching out to Jews. What are you doing to bring that person to Christ?

vv. 6–9—Do you believe that Christians are the new Israel of faith? This passage can help you explain how the idea of God's "chosen people" has been applied to the Gentiles.

vv. 10–33—What do you believe concerning election? Can you defend your position biblically? In these verses, Paul addresses several of the objections people have.

MEMORIZE

Romans 9:16

This is Paul's position on election in a few words.

PRAY

A: Praise God's sovereign choices.

C: Confess any lack of love for "your people."

T: Thank God that someone loved you enough to share the Gospel with you.

S: Intercede for a Jewish person's conversion.

TELL

If you have a friendly small group, discuss the doctrine of election.

JUNE 29

MISPLACED ZEAL

Pray for Paul's compassion and truthfulness as you study this key passage.

Romans 10:1–21

vv. 1–4—The key problem with the Jews is the same problem with every person who rejects Christ—self-righteousness. Even Paul relied on his works for salvation (Phil. 3:4–6) until he realized that it was only through the grace of Christ (Phil. 3:7–11) that true righteousness is obtained. The greatest obstacle to knowing Christ is a vision problem—are my eyes focused on him or myself? Christ—not what I can do—is the goal of the law. Zeal is generally a good thing, but misplaced zeal (like the Jews') can actually stand in the way of humbly coming to Christ.

vv. 5–13—Many scholars believe that verses 9 and 10 were a creedal formula of the early church. Notice that the focus isn't on what we do, but on what we believe. Confessing with our lips doesn't bring salvation. The words are simply an outpouring of the inward grace that is received through faith.

Most people today are like the Jews, trusting in a false formula for salvation: faith + works = salvation. They express it in a variety of ways: "I've never deliberately hurt anyone;" "I've tried to live a good life;" or "If God grades on the curve, I'll at least pass." The problem, as Paul argued so eloquently in chapters 1–3, is that no one is good enough.

The correct formula is: faith = salvation (+ works). It may seem that the distinction between the formulas is subtle, but it is all-important. Paul will show in Romans 12–16 that saving faith is accompanied by good works enabled by the Holy Spirit. These works don't earn salvation, they are a byproduct of it. The heart of the Reformation conflict was over the difference in these formulas. Luther insisted that Scripture teaches justification by faith alone. The Roman Catholic Church, especially at the Council of Trent, rejected that doctrine as *anathema* (cursed). There are many who try to minimize the difference, but it is a crucial distinction.

vv. 14–21—This passage and Matthew 28:18–20 are two eloquent statements of the great missionary mandate of the church. It is God's will that every nation hears the good news in a way they can understand, and we must never forget it. Israel couldn't claim ignorance. The Gospel was preached and lived powerfully in the midst of Israel. There is a graphic metaphor in verse 21. From Isaiah 65, Paul shows that God has symbolically held out his hand in friendship to Israel, but in their disobedience and rebellion, they ignored his offer and slapped his hand away. Chapters 9 and 10 show a paradox. Even though it was God's will to cut off the Jews (chapter 9), they are still guilty and responsible for their sinful disobedience in ignoring the gift of Christ (chapter 10). It is much the same as the situation with Judas. It was God's sovereign will, prophesied hundreds of years before, that the Messiah would be betrayed. But Judas was still a responsible moral agent who was guilty of the betrayal.

APPLY

vv. 1–4—When you consider your relationship with God, do you emphasize works, or do you focus on God's grace and indwelling power?

vv. 14–17—What is your responsibility in this great mandate? What are you doing to help spread the Word throughout the world?

MEMORIZE

Romans 10:9–10

PRAY

A: Praise the Lord of all.

C: Confess your lack of zeal for world evangelism.

T: Thank God for missionaries.

S: Intercede for a particular Gospel-proclaiming family in a tough situation.

TELL

Remind someone who has "a zeal that is not based on knowledge" that we rely on God's grace rather than our works.

JUNE 30

ISRAEL'S REJECTION IS NOT FINAL

PRAY

Thank God for what you understand of his will and for what you don't understand yet.

READ

Romans 11:1–36

OBSERVE

vv. 1–10—At this juncture, Paul is careful to point out that not all of the Israelites have rejected God. Just as in the time of Elijah (1 Kings 19), there is always a remnant of faithful believers, of whom Paul is an example. The earliest church, of course, was composed totally of Jews who accepted Jesus as the Messiah. But their standing was on the basis of grace, not works.

vv. 11–24—The dominant image in this chapter is the olive tree. We've mentioned before that this picture would be familiar to students of the Old Testament as a symbol for Israel itself. Paul describes the natural branches (Jews) being broken off from the tree. Wild shoots (Gentiles) were grafted onto the tree in their place. To appreciate this analogy, we need something of Paul's knowledge of gardening. The grafting of wild olive branches onto a cultivated tree produced new vitality and increased the flow of oil (which is a symbol of the Holy Spirit). The key is faith.

vv. 25–31—A phrase Paul has used repeatedly is, "how much more." The natural branches were cut off for a reason, but when God sees fit to graft them back on, there will be much rejoicing in heaven. Verse 29 reinforces the fact that God's covenant with Abraham still stands. Jews today are still discovering Jesus as their

Messiah. Jews from every tribe and nation will be saved, though not every individual, just as not every individual Jew was lost. Some people apply verse 29 to spiritual gifts—once you've received a gift it can never be taken away. But Solomon lost his wisdom due to idolatry, and Samson lost his strength due to lust. Paul is referring here to the gifts and calling God gave to Israel, which will be restored in time.

vv. 33–36—This beautiful doxology ("words of glory") concludes chapters 9–11 in a fitting way. God's wisdom and judgment are beyond our scope, but we can praise his goodness even when we don't understand all of the particulars.

APPLY

v. 4—Keep this verse in mind when you feel like you're alone spiritually at work, school or home.

vv. 18–21—Don't become proud in your faith.

vv. 33–36—Do you feel that you have to have everything figured out before you can praise God? Praise him that he is beyond our limited understanding.

MEMORIZE

Romans 11:36

This is a wonderful statement of praise.

PRAY

A: Praise our wise God.

C: Confess your lack of wisdom.

T: Thank God that he is greater and wiser than you.

S: Intercede for groups like Jews for Jesus.

TELL

Spend time in your next small group in doxology, praising and thanking God.

WORKS CITED

Publisher's Note:

This works cited list is meant to be a helpful resource for the reader. Dorst compiled this book over many years, and some of his resources are no longer available in the same format, or the original source cannot be located. Thus, we have worked to provide a citation in general, but the page number may not correspond to the work we have listed. In many cases, the reader might be able to google search the passage and find a source that will work.

Myron S. Augsburger, *Matthew*, (Thomas Nelson, 2003).

William Barclay, *The Gospel of Mark*, (Westminster John Knox Press, 2017)

Karl Barth, *The Epistle to the Ephesians*, (Baker, 2017).

George Raymond Beasley-Murray, *John*, (1987).

E. M. Blaiklock, *The Acts of the Apostles: an Historical Commentary*, (Eerdmans, 1979).

F. F. Bruce, *The Book of Acts*, (Eerdmans, 1988).

F. F. Bruce, *Paul, Apostle of the Heart Set Free*, (Eerdmans, 2000).

F. F. Bruce, *The Epistle of Paul to the Romans: an Introduction and Commentary*, (Martino Publishing, 2011).

Frederick Dale Bruner, *Matthew: The Christbook, Matthew 1-12*, (Eerdmans, 2004).

Jean Calvin, David Wishart Torrance, Thomas Forsyth Torrance, *A Harmony of the Gospels Matthew, Mark and Luke*, (Eerdmans, 1994).

Jean Calvin, John Calvin, *Acts 1-13*, (Eerdmans, 1995).

Jean Calvin, John Calvin, *The Epistles of Paul the Apostle to the Romans and to the Thessalonians*, (Eerdmans, 1995).

R. Alan Cole, *The Gospel According to Mark*, (Eerdmans, 1989).

Frederic William Farrar, *The Life and Work of St. Paul*, (1909).

Roger Fredrikson, *John* (Thomas Nelson, 2003).

Joseph Garlington, "The Pruning Process," *New Wine Magazine*, May 1980.

Norval Geldenhuys, Frederick Fyvie Bruce, *Commentary on the Gospel of Luke*, (1977).

Michael Green, *Matthew for Today*, (W Publishing Group, 1989).

Donald A. Hagner, *Matthew 14-28, Volume 33B*, (Zondervan Academic, 2018).

G. Hanson, *The Resurrection and the Life*, (1911).

Horace, *The Epistles of Horace*, (Farrar, Straus and Giroux, 2015).

Stanley Horton, *The Book of Acts: A Commentary*, (2001).

C. S. Lewis, *The Last Battle*, (HarperCollins Children's Books, 2014).

Richard Longnecker, *Can We Reproduce the Exegesis of the New Testament?*, (1969).

Martin Luther, *Sermon on the Mount and the Magnificat*.

Martin Luther, Jaroslav Jan Pelikan, *Luther's Works*, (1955).

Kirk MacGregor, *A Historical and Theological Investigation of John's Gospel*, (Palgrave Macmillan, 2020).

Leon Morris, *The Gospel According to Luke: an Introduction and Commentary*, (Eerdmans, 2002).

Leon Morris, *The Gospel According to John*, (Eerdmans, 1971).

Robert H. Mounce, *Matthew*, (Paternoster, 1991).

John Murray, *The Epistle to the Romans*, (Eerdmans, 1997).

Lloyd J. Ogilvie, *The Preacher's Commentary Series, Volume 28: Acts*, (Thomas Nelson, 2010).

J. I. Packer, *Knowing God*, (InterVarsity Press).

Earl Palmer, *Salvation by Surprise: A Commentary on the Book of Romans*, (1999).

John Piper, *Desiring God*, (Multnomah, 1996).

W. M. Ramsay, *St. Paul*, (Kregel Academic, 2001).

J. A. T. Robinson, *The Priority of John*, (Wipf and Stock Publishers, 2011).

Arthur Rendle Short, *Modern Discovery and the Bible*, (1957).

R. C. Sproul and J. I. Packer, *Knowing Scripture*, (IVP Books, 2016).

John Stott, *The Cross of Christ*, (InterVarsity Press, 2012).

John Stott, *The Spirit, the Church, and the World*, (InterVarsity Press, 1990).

Thomas James Thorburn, *The Resurrection Narratives and Modern Criticism*, (Trieste Publishing, 2017).

David J. Williams, *Acts (Understanding the Bible Commentary Series*, (Baker Books, 2011).

ABOUT WHITE BLACKBIRD BOOKS

White blackbirds are extremely rare, but they are real. They are blackbirds that have turned white over the years as their feathers have come in and out over and over again. They are a redemptive picture of something you would never expect to see but that has slowly come into existence over time.

There is plenty of hurt and brokenness in the world. There is the hopelessness that comes in the midst of lost jobs, lost health, lost homes, lost marriages, lost children, lost parents, lost dreams, loss.

But there also are many white blackbirds. There are healed marriages, children who come home, friends who are reconciled. There are hurts healed, children fostered and adopted, communities restored. Some would call these events entirely natural, but really they are unexpected miracles.

The books in this series are not commentaries, nor are they meant to be the final word. Rather, they are a collage of biblical truth applied to current times and places. The authors share their poverty and trust the Lord to use their words to strengthen and encourage his people. Consider these books as entries into the discussion.

May this series help you in your quest to know Christ as he is found in the Gospel through the Scriptures. May you look for and even expect the rare white blackbirds of God's redemption through Christ in your midst. May you be thankful when you look down and see your feathers have turned. May you also rejoice when you see that others have been unexpectedly transformed by Jesus.

ALSO BY WHITE BLACKBIRD BOOKS

All Are Welcome: Toward a Multi-Everything Church

The Almost Dancer

Birth of Joy: Philippians

Choosing a Church: A Biblical and Practical Guide

Christ in the Time of Corona: Stories of Faith, Hope, and Love

Co-Laborers, Co-Heirs: A Family Conversation

Doing God's Work

Driven by Desire

EmbRACE: A Biblical Study on Justice and Race

Ever Light and Dark: Telling Secrets, Telling the Truth

Everything Is Meaningless? Ecclesiastes

Faithful Doubt: Habakkuk

Firstfruits of a New Creation

Heal Us Emmanuel: A Call for Racial Reconciliation, Representation, and Unity in the Church

Hear Us, Emmanuel: Another Call for Racial Reconciliation, Representation, and Unity in the Church

Insufficient: Pursuing Grace-Based Pastoral Competence

The Organized Pastor: Systems to Care for People Well

Questions of the Heart: Leaning In, Listening For, and Loving Well Toward True Identity in Christ

Rooted: The Apostles' Creed

A Sometimes Stumbling Life

To You I Lift Up My Soul: Confessions and Prayers

Urban Hinterlands: Planting the Gospel in Uncool Places

Follow whiteblackbirdbooks.pub for titles and releases.

Made in the USA
Columbia, SC
23 June 2021